# The History of Africa

There is a paradox about Africa: it remains a subject that attracts considerable attention yet rarely is there a full appreciation of its complexity. African historiography has typically consisted of writing Africa for Europe – instead of writing Africa for itself, as itself, from its own perspectives. *The History of Africa* redresses this by letting the perspectives of Africans themselves take center stage.

Authoritative and comprehensive, this book provides a wide-ranging history of Africa from earliest prehistory to the present day – using the cultural, social, political, and economic lenses of Africa as instruments to illuminate the ordinary lives of Africans. The result is a fresh new survey that includes a wealth of indigenous ideas, African concepts, and traditional outlooks that have escaped the writing of African history in the West.

This straightforward, illustrated, and factual text allows the reader to access the major developments, personalities, and events on the African continent. Written by a world expert, this groundbreaking survey is an indispensable guide to African history.

**Molefi Kete Asante** is Professor in the Department of African American Studies at Temple University in Philadelphia. He is the founding editor of the *Journal of Black Studies* and has published 63 books including *100 Greatest African Americans* (2002) and the high school text *African American History* (second edition 2001).

# The History of Africa

## The quest for eternal harmony

**Molefi Kete Asante**

Routledge
Taylor & Francis Group

NEW YORK AND LONDON

First published 2007
by Routledge
270 Madison Ave, New York, NY 10016

Simultaneously published in the USA and Canada
by Routledge
2 Park Square, Milton Park, Abingdon, Oxon OX14 4RN

*Routledge is an imprint of the Taylor & Francis Group, an informa
business*

Typeset in Sabon by Saxon Graphics Ltd, Derby
Printed and bound in Great Britain by The Cromwell Press,
Trowbridge, Wiltshire

*Library of Congress Cataloging in Publication Data*
Asante, Molefi, 1942–
    The history of Africa : the quest for harmony / Molefi Kete Asante.
      p. cm.
    Simultaneously published in the USA and Canada.
    Includes bibliographical references and index
    1. Africa—History. 2. Africa—Civilization. I. Title.
    DT20.A83 2007
    960—dc22
                                                        2006021528


*British Library Cataloguing in Publication Data*
A catalogue record for this book is available from the British Library

ISBN-10: 0–415–77138–2 (hbk)
ISBN-10: 0–415–77139–0 (pbk)

ISBN-13: 978–0–415–77138–2 (hbk)
ISBN-13: 978–0–415–77139–9 (pbk)

**DEDICATED TO THE FATHERS OF AFRICAN HISTORY**

CHEIKH ANTA DIOP

JOSEPH KI-ZERBO

KENNETH O. DIKE

J. F. ADE-AJAYI

BONIFACE I. OBICHERE

ALBERT A. ADU-BOAHEN

DJIBRIL T. NIANE

ALI MAZRUI

# Contents

# Illustrations

# Acknowledgments

Writing any book that involves as many sources and resources as a continental history demands that the writer interacts with lots of colleagues. I owe many people thanks for their encouragement, suggestions, debates, and general good will. I would like to thank Dr. Maulana Karenga, Dr. Kwame Botwe-Asamoah, Professor Kofi Opoku Asare, Dr. Ama Mazama, Dr. Wade Nobles, Dr. Asa Hilliard, Dr. Theophile Obenga, Dr. Katherine Bankole, Dr. Catherine Godboldte, Dr. Miriam Maat Ka Re Monges, Dr. George Sefa Dei, Dr. Minmin Wang, Dr. Mark Christian, Dr. Daryl Zizwe Poe, Dr. Garvey Lundy, Dr. Christel Temple, Dr. Yoshitaka Miiki, and Dr. Xing Lu for their intellectual support. My gratitude to the librarians at Temple University, the Schomburg Center for Black Research, and the Amistad Center for Black Research at Tulane University. Renee Arnold, my research assistant, has been invaluable in her prodigious search for sources and information. I am grateful to her for the assistance she gave me on this project. I thank Ana Monteiro for help with the index.

I have benefited from the works of all of the African historians who have gone before me. But I am most indebted to the insights, creativity, provocative questions, and keen interpretations of African historians such as W. E. B. DuBois, Anna Julia Cooper, Carter G. Woodson, Iba der Thiam, Joseph Ki-Zerbo, Yosef ben-Jochannon, Charshee McIntyre, John Henrik Clarke, John Jackson, William Leo Hansberry, Joseph Harris, and Chancellor Williams. They were, in many ways, intellectual pioneers cutting down giant myths about Africa as they traveled along their way undaunted by the challenges of traditional interpretations about Africa. To my friends at the University of Ghana, Legon, the University of Venda in South Africa, the University of Nigeria, Nsukka, Université de Cheikh Anta Diop in Senegal, and the Kenyatta University, I owe a great deal of gratitude for the use of their collections. I have also benefited from the archives of Lincoln University in Pennsylvania and my own home institution, Temple University.

Although my thanks and best wishes to my wife, Ana Yenenga, come last, she has been the most important influence on my work, my work habits, and my expectations. As an editor and technical writer, she has taught me many things about the art of writing. I count her as my best friend, critic, and nurturer and dedicate this volume to her and the African people of Central and South America who are finding their own direction to the history of the African continent.

# Preface

Standing on the banks of the mighty Congo River several years ago I reflected on the vastness of the African continent. This was just one of the great rivers of Africa, although a magnificent one in its own right; the Congo impacted me with its size and volume and suggestion of the massiveness of Africa.

By the time I had determined that this book must be written, I had climbed the pyramids of Khufu and Khafre, entered the tombs of the dead in the Valley of the Kings, walked across stretches of the hot Sahara, surveyed Great Zimbabwe from the hilltop, and slept in the rainforest while the earth poured out its soul in massive pans of rain. But there on the green fertile banks of the Congo, I could feel the years of power, sense the immensity of the continent from this particular angle. I think it was then that I decided to write a narrative history of Africa.

I was born in southern Georgia, the great, great grandson of enslaved Africans, according to mitochondrial and Y-chromosome DNA tests, of Nubian and Yoruba ancestry, amidst the tall pine trees of the coastal plains, a very long way from the African continent physically, but very close to the questing spirit and the collective psychology of Africa. As if a magnet is pulling me, I have been drawn to the continent more than 75 times, living and working in Zimbabwe, serving as an external examiner in Kenya and Nigeria, being made a king (Nana Okru Asante Peasah, Kyidomhene of Tafo) in Ghana, consulting with presidents in South Africa, Zimbabwe, and Senegal, and relaxing on the beaches of Senegal, Ghana, and Tanzania. However, my interest in the continent was more than casual or social; it was academic and intellectual. I realized that most of the people I knew in colleges and in the general community understood very little about Africa; I felt the need to write this book for those people.

My earliest intellectual interest in the African continent was provoked by several outstanding professors at the University of California, Los Angeles, where I trained for a doctorate in communication with a cognate field in history. My professors were Gary B. Nash, Ronald Takaki, Terence Ranger, and, perhaps most influential, Boniface Obichere. I also had the opportunity to listen to the lectures of Robert Farris Thompson, Masisi Kunene, and Janheinz Jahn. What characterized these scholars was a common excitement about either African or African American history. I inherited much of their love for the careful study of history. While none of my professors was an Afrocentrist, they were all committed to discovering as much as possible the meaning of African history in the light of what they had been taught. Each of them went on to contribute to scholarship about the experiences of Africans in the Diaspora or on the African continent.

Scholars in African American studies, African studies, and history have continued to write books and articles exploring certain aspects of the vast history of Africa. Of course, this has meant that there have been many eager students of African history seeking to establish for themselves and others a place in the pantheon of writers on this subject. Therefore, we have scores of books, many volumes of interpretations, and numerous videos and other documents explaining in detail every aspect of the continent. There is a paradox about Africa; it remains a subject that attracts considerable attention although there has never been a full appreciation of its complexity.

The purpose of *The History of Africa*, given the many books that have been written about Africa, is to provide a straightforward, illustrated, and factual text told from the standpoint of Africans themselves. It is a book that allows African agency to dominate the interpretations and explanations of the facts on the ground. In this way *The History of Africa* will give the readers a chronological and critical examination of the extensive history of Africa. The objective of my endeavor was to use the cultural, social, political, and economic lenses of Africa as instruments to explicate the ordinary lives of Africans within the context of their own experiences.

This is not a book about Europeans in Africa, nor is it a book about how Europeans interpret Africa. Rather it is the story of Africa as Africans tell it themselves and as they see the grand movements and personalities that constitute the panoply of heroes who have traversed that history. While the work draws upon the very extensive research that has been done by European and American historians, I have tried to place the works of African historians in the center of this narrative, thus rewriting and reorienting African history from the standpoint of Africans as subjects.

We should not obfuscate the central tendencies of the African people in regards to their vision of their own nations and leaders. What Africa sees or has said it sees is a much more interesting subject for this book since it is clear to me that the overwhelming emphasis in the literature and orature of the continent has been the subject of harmony, balance, and order. These represent the calling cards of the eternal quest in African history.

In one sense the aims of this book are modest: to present in the most challenging manner a simple, basic book that will allow the student and lay reader access to the major developments, personalities, and events on the African continent. To do this I began with man's earliest origins, spent some time discussing the prehistory of Africa, and then entered the fascinating world of African development through the origin of human civilization. What grabbed my attention in my research was the wealth of indigenous ideas, African concepts, and traditional outlooks that have escaped the writing of African history in the West. Too much of African historiography has been about writing Africa for Europe without writing Africa for itself, as itself, from its own perspectives. To truly know a continent, one must study, travel, allow the aromas, rhythms, dances, and visual sights to dominate one's being; only then, it seems to me, can one really ask the proper questions, seek the best answers, and arrive at the most knowledgeable and creative interpretations based on Africa's own authentic voice. I have tried to present to readers a book that expands our view and vision of the continent from the staid old notions of Africa as helpless, stagnant, or crippled in its potential.

In the West the ignorance of Africa is palpable, like a monster that invades our brains with disbelief, deception, and disinterest, yet is everywhere around us. We are victims of probably the most uninformed educated people in the world on the subject of Africa. Owing to the colonial experiences of Europe, the Europeans tend to engage the African continent in ways that have not been done by Americans. Nevertheless, what I desire of this book is a wide readership in the United States, Europe, Africa, and Asia with particular emphasis on those readers in schools and colleges, as well as among ordinary people, in order that they may have a unifying view of the vast continent. The reader should come away from the book with a fresh attitude about the continent and about its people. The intent in this work is to make no easy commentaries for which there is no plausibility and to argue only those lines that are rich enough to produce vast amounts of data about the history of the continent that is ancestral home to more than forty million citizens of the United States, nearly seventy million Brazilians, another fifty million South Americans, five to seven million who live in Europe and the Pacific, and about forty million people of the Caribbean, as well as the nearly one billion Africans who live on the continent.

All books are written with debts. I owe a great debt to numerous mentors, collaborators, and friends who, knowing of my interest in the subject, have encouraged me to do what I had outlined on African history several years ago but had not found the right moment to start. My reading in the field has been extensive and I have written and researched Africa for many years in English, French, and German, but I am also familiar with Akan, Yoruba, KiSwahili, Arabic, and Mdw Ntr. Yet this is the first time that I have embarked on such a comprehensive treatment of the African continent. It has been a thrilling process; Africa has revealed yet more secrets to me in the writing of this book. Thus, to write a history of Africa is to write a major part of the history of the world, since Africa's contributions to humanity are fundamental and expansive. I offer this book as my contribution to human understanding.

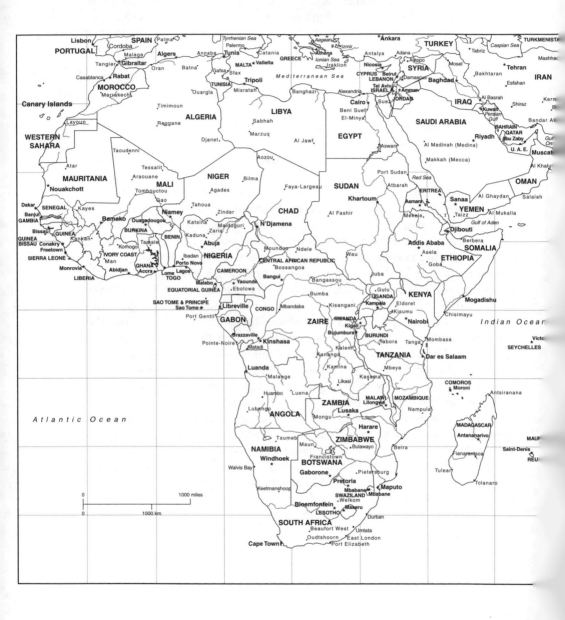

## The Great Rift Valley

The Great Rift Valley is an immense natural geological rift stretching 3000 miles from Mozambique in Southeast Africa to Syria in Southwest Asia. What is called the valley, the main geographical and geological feature, is from 16 to 40 miles in width and a few hundred to several thousand feet deep. Created through the separation of the African and Arabian tectonic plates starting around 35 million years ago in the north, and by the ongoing separation of East Africa from the rest of Africa along the East African Rift, which began about 15 million years ago, the Great Rift Valley is one of Africa's most prominent physical features. It is a giant fault that eventually splits the older Ethiopian region into halves.

One half of the valley is called the Western Rift, with some of the tallest peaks in Africa, including the Virunga, Mitumba, and Ruwenzori or Mountains of the Moon, and some of the deepest lakes in the world, including the 4700 feet deep Lake Tanganyika. There are other lakes, some among the largest freshwater bodies in the world, in the Rift Valley. There is the Eastern Rift that is on the side of the Red Sea and the Indian Ocean. Since the lakes in the Eastern Rift have no outlet to the sea, they tend to be shallower and have a high mineral content as the evaporation of water leaves the salts in the lake bed. For example, Lake Magadi is actually sodium carbonate, while Lake Elmenteita, Lake Baringo, Lake Bogoria, and Lake Nakuru are alkaline. Lake Naivasha is supplied by springs to support its vast biological diversity.

So incredible is the Great Rift Valley that its formation, driven by geothermal activity, has caused the lithosphere to thin from a typical continental thickness of 40 km to 20 km. This means that in a few million years there might be a split and the eastern part of Africa could be separated from the mainland. This is because of the shifting tectonic plates. Many unique situations are found in this part of Africa. This is a densely volcanic area with mountains such as Mount Karisimbi, Mount Kenya, Kilimanjaro, Mount Meru, Nyiragongo, and the Crater Highlands in Tanzania. It is believed that Ol Doinyo Lengai Volcano remains the only natrocarbonatite volcano on earth making it an unusual hotspot.

The Rift Valley has been a rich area for finding the ancestors of modern humans. That is why I have called it one of the engines of the African civilization. As an area that has given us various anthropological discoveries, it is a valley of hominids and *Homo sapiens*. The rapidly eroding highlands have filled the valley with massive amounts of sediment that have led to an almost perfect laboratory for the preservation of fossils for anthropological research. The bones of many human ancestors have been found in the area. Thus, alongside the Sahara Generator and the Rainforest Home, the Great Rift Valley has also played a major role in the peopling and protecting of the people of Africa.

## The iron factor

It is clearly logical to see three loci of African civilization: the Sahara, the rainforest and the Great Rift Valley. They are all critical to understanding

Africa's quest for eternal harmony, as humans gained an understanding of living in either the desert, the forest, or the great savannas. With the appearance of iron, first in East Africa and then in West Africa, Africans began, long before Europeans, to gain authority over the land. This was so because with iron humans had the ability to make tools that lasted longer. Gradually from about 1200 BCE the knowledge of iron-smelting spread to other regions of Africa and the world. The rise of Meroe, an iron-making society, in the Nile Valley would spark a critical turn in Africa's history. There would be a transformation in warfare that would have wider impact on the future of the continent.

## Periodization

Every historian since the time of Ibn Khaldun has wrestled with periodization. How does one divide the broad stretches of time that constitute the period of human activity? What is the best method for slicing up the events and experiences of humans? These questions and numerous corollaries have dogged each step of the professional historian; they have been equally important in this volume. Clearly I could not write a history of Africa with a periodization coming from outside the continent; this has to be a history of Africa with African periods. I also determined that the best way to handle the massive store of information about Africa was to use the simplest method of historical writing, which is chronological, albeit I must admit that the challenges of the material at times meant that I had to use mixed methods to ferret out a particular theme. Nevertheless, the overall impression that the reader should get is of a volume that moves forward in time, covering seven specific swathes of African history: the Time of Awakening, the Age of Literacy, the Moment of Realization, the Age of Construction, the Time of Chaos, the Age of Reconstruction, and the Time for Consolidation.

# Part I

# The time of awakening

"At the dawn of the universe, Maat was the food of the gods"

# 1   Africa and the origin of humanity

In the 1950s and 1960s the Senegalese genius Cheikh Anta Diop, scientist, linguist, and historian, proposed the important thesis that Africa was not only the cradle of humanity but also the cradle of civilization (Diop 1993). He was not the first to make such a suggestion but he was the first African scholar to defend the thesis in several provocative books including *The African Origin of Civilization* (1974) and the major anthropological work *Civilization or Barbarism* (1991). Diop's work challenged the very heart of the doctrines of racism and the negative arguments that had been made against Africa by many European and American authors. It was Diop's contention in his doctoral dissertation at the Sorbonne in France not only that Africa was the home of humanity and civilization but that Europe had "stolen" or "distorted" much of the African record. This charge created a wave of intellectual resistance that would follow Diop for most of his life because he had challenged the idea of European superiority. Diop's arguments gained in respectability as the wall of ignorance established by decades of racist science came tumbling down. Indeed, a host of other scientists in fields as dissimilar as archaeology and linguistics wrote books and articles that illuminated the findings of Cheikh Anta Diop. Authors such as Martin Bernal, Theophile Obenga, and Basil Davidson have shown the truth of Diop's initial thesis. Indeed, Africa is the home of all living humans. Furthermore, it is source of many of the technological innovations that laid the foundation for modern industrial and informational societies.

## Documentation of the Origins

Africa stands at the very beginning of the origin of humanity. In no other continent have scientists found such extensive evidence of our origins as in Africa. If that were its only distinction it would be enough to engage our attention. The early evolution of humans has been so detailed on this continent that one could not write a complete history of humanity without delving into the prehistory of Africa. The word *prehistory* is used to refer to the time before writing was available. There is enough evidence from fossilized bones and stone tools to allow scientists to recover information that will generate plausible arguments for African origin.

Animal or plants which die and whose remains are captured by the geological formation of rocks are turned into fossils. Later when a human being digs up the rock, breaks open the stone, or by chance stumbles upon a broken rock and discovers the fossilized matter that may have been left inside the rock for millions of years we have evidence of what life was like during the time of that animal or plant. Modern science can date these fossils with highly developed techniques such as Carbon-14 to approximate their age.

Carbon-14 may be called an atomic clock that can be used for dating purposes because it is based on the radioactive decay of the isotope carbon-14, which has a half-life of 5730 years. Since Carbon-14 is produced continuously in the Earth's upper atmosphere by the bombardment of nitrogen by neutrons from cosmic rays scientists have a fairly good idea about its existence and character. We know this much from science: the newly formed radiocarbon becomes mixed with the nonradioactive carbon in the carbon dioxide in the air, and it gets into all living plants and animals. Actually, all carbon in living organisms contains a constant proportion of radiocarbon to nonradioactive carbon. Thus, after the organism dies, the amount of radiocarbon gradually decreases as it reverts to nitrogen-14 by radioactive decay. By measuring the amount of radioactivity remaining in organic materials, the amount of carbon-14 can be calculated and the time of death can be determined. Therefore, if carbon from a plant sample is found to contain only half as much carbon-14 as that from a living plant, the estimated age of the plant sample would be 5730 years.

This method is good for recent prehistory, meaning less than 50,000 years. For example, if you were interested in establishing the time period of King Tutankhamen, you could use samples of materials, leather, and cloth, taken from his burial coffin. You could use charcoal, the organic remains of burnt plants, to discover the age of ancient trees. One could use the samples collected from strata in Olduvai Gorge, East Africa, which enveloped the fossil remains of *Zinjanthropus* and *Homo habilis*, thought to be precursors to humans, to discover their age.

Animals or plants which die and whose remains are captured by the geological formation of rocks are turned into fossils. Later when a human being digs up the rock, breaks open the stone, or by chance stumbles upon a broken rock and discovers the matter that may have been left inside the rock for millions of years we have evidence of what life was like during the time of that animal or plant. Modern science can date the organic materials in rocks with highly developed techniques such as carbon-14 dating to approximate the age of organic materials.

Carbon-14 may be called an atomic clock which can be used for dating purposes because it displays the decay of the radioactive isotope carbon-14, which has a half-life of 5730 years. Since carbon-14 is produced continuously in the Earth's upper atmosphere by the bombardment of nitrogen by neutrons from cosmic rays scientists have a fairly good idea about its existence and character. It works like this: the newly formed radiocarbon becomes mixed with the nonradioactive carbon in the carbon dioxide of the air, and it gets into all living plants and animals. Actually, all carbon in living organisms contains a constant proportion of radiocarbon to non radioactive carbon. Thus, after the organism dies, the amount of radiocarbon gradually decreases as it reverts to nitrogen-14 by radioactive decay. By measuring the amount of radioactivity remaining, the amount of carbon-14 in the materials can be calculated and the time of death can be determined. Therefore, if carbon from a preserved plant sample is found to contain only half as much carbon-14 as a living plant, the estimated age of the old plant sample would be 5730 years.

This method is good for recent prehistory, that is, less than 50,000 years. For example, if you were interested in the cloth wrappings of a mummified bull buried in a pyramid, you could use samples from the cloth. You could use charcoal, the remains of burnt plants, and discover the age of ancient trees. One could use the samples collected from strata in Olduvai Gorge, East Africa, which enveloped the fossil remains of *Zinjanthropus* and *Homo habilis*, thought to be precursors to humans.

## Toward the hominids and beyond

Modern humans belong to what scientists have referred to as the primate family of hominids, a biological term meaning human or human-like creatures who walk upright on two legs and have enlarged brains. According to science we are the only remaining hominid although at an earlier stage of human evolution there were many different hominid species. The evidence suggests that millions of years ago other primates such as the chimpanzee, the ape, and the gorilla, called pongids (modern apes and gibbons and their ancestors), separated from the group that became hominids. Recent scientists have demonstrated through DNA that we share 99 percent of the same DNA as chimpanzees.

It is clear that humans know only a small fraction of what happened in the evolving of hominids, but we know enough to say that between 10 million and 4 million years ago hominids moved from the forest to the savannas of East Africa. We know from the fossil remains that they were standing upright, walking on two legs (bipedal) and stretching their arms over their heads.

There are many theories about why and how hominids did what they did. One theory is that to survive in the open plains and savannas they needed to stand upright, so that they could see long distances and spot predators who hunted them for food. Thus, the first hominids to stand upright did so on the African continent. Indeed, hominids could not have stood upright anywhere else since these were the earliest.

Since the 1920s scholars and scientists have been investigating the various links in the chain of human evolution, looking at the archaeological record as well as the biological record. In 1925 a South African named Raymond Dart made the first find and would make many subsequent finds in South Africa (Jackson 1998, pp. 42–4; Walker 1957). In a limestone cave in Taung, South Africa, he discovered the buried skull of a six-year-old creature. It was ape-like in appearance but had certain human characteristics such as the shape of the back of the skull, which gave some indication of how the neck muscles would have been attached. Indeed, Dart assumed from this structure that the creature walked upright on two legs and probably had a forward stoop. Dart named the creature he had discovered in the cave *Australopithecus* (Southern Ape). Many other finds were made and added to the category *Australopithecine*. These came from other caves in South Africa. It did not take long for other scientists to find Australopithecines in East Africa, particularly in Olduvai Gorge in northern Tanzania, the Great Rift Valley of central Kenya and the Lake Turkana area of Kenya, and the Omo River valley in Ethiopia.

The 1970s was a very fruitful period for discovery in East Africa. In 1972 Richard Leakey, the son of the famous scientist Louis Leakey, found skull 1470 near East Turkana in Kenya, which looked quite human. This find was to be topped by the remarkable discovery in 1975 of the remains of an Australopithecine group of thirteen adults and children near Hadar in Ethiopia. Then in 1976 human footprints were discovered close to an extinct volcano near Olduvai. They were set in what would have been volcanic ash from 3¼ million years ago when an eruption of the volcano must have killed the creatures who made them.

Recent information from many sources has extended our understanding but has also placed the origin of Australopithecines farther back than we had ever realized was possible. Indeed, some scientists say that we have to look to the Fayum Depression in Egypt for the earliest known ancestors of both hominids and pongids. Here, west of the Nile, several species of primates have been found and one possible candidate for the earliest ancestor of hominids and pongids is called *Aegyptopithecus* and dates to 30 million years ago. Paleontologists, those who study fossilized life forms, now believe that the separation of hominids from pongids may have occurred around 8 million years ago.

New candidates have appeared on the scene every year as scientists have been investigating furiously the evidence on the African continent. *Sahelanthropus tchadensis* was found in 2002 in the country of Chad and represents the oldest known fossil of a hominid. It has been dated to 7 million years. The fossil shows signs of modernity in that its teeth are relatively small and its face is flat and does not jut out like that of a chimpanzee. More and more hominids have to be incorporated into the family as scientists discover more examples. Indeed, prior to the finding of *Sahelanthropus tchadensis* in Chad, scientists had thought that Ethiopia and Kenya would yield the most interesting results since they are the places where *Ardipithecus ramidus* was discovered in the Awash area of Ethiopia, dating to 4.5 million years. Prior to this, *Australopithecus anamensis* was discovered near Lake Turkana in Kenya. Perhaps the most heralded of all these finds was that of *Dinqnesh*, called *Lucy* by Americans. Found in the Hadar region of Ethiopia by Maurice Taieb and Donald Johanson in 1974, *Dinqnesh* was an upright biped belonging to the species *Australopithecus afarensis,* and dated to 3 million years ago.

Quite recently anthropologists have noted that there were other hominids around. *Australopithecus afarensis* has been found in Ethiopia but also in Chad. There was some mobility in the way this species got around the continent. However, the famous Taung child studied by Raymond Dart belonged to the *Australopithecus africanus* branch of the hominid family and was the oldest example. Yet there were other hominids such as *Australopithecus aethiopicus, Australopithecus Boisei,* and *Australopithecus robustus.* It is believed that they were vegetarians. The latest species of hominids to be discovered was *Australopithecus garhi* (garhi means surprise in the Ethiopian language of the region where the fossils were found). This group dates from around 3 million years ago. They appear to have been meat and vegetable eaters as well as a tool makers.

The most widely accepted classification of early hominids categorizes them in two separate genera. The earliest, as discussed above, is *Australopithecus.* The second is *Homo,* and among the more familiar are *Homo habilis, Homo erectus,* and *H. sapiens.*

In 2006, Sileshi Semaw, director of the Gona Paleoanthropological Research Project in Ethiopia, and his colleagues discovered the skull of a small human ancestor in an area near Gawis, Ethiopia, that could be another part of the puzzle of modern humans. The scientists found parts of an early human cranium believed to be between 500,000 and 250,000 years old.

## Modern humans

The next step in the hominid line is called "*Homo*" meaning man. The first was named *Homo habilis,* that is a "handy human." This form dates from 2 to 3 million years ago. *Homo habilis* has many characteristics that distinguish it from *Australopithecus.* In the first place, the skull is rounder and higher and the cranial capacity is nearly 700 cc (compared with 1450 cc for modern humans and 400 cc for *Australopithecus*). *Homo habilis* is associated with making tools although the species seems to have retained the ability to climb trees. Deposits of stone tools have been found in Gona and Hadar in Ethiopia as well as Senga in the Congo. These Oldowan tools as they are called could have been used to cut meat, that is, the meat of game, as well as to fight predators.

After *Homo habilis* came *Homo erectus,* or "upright man." This species appeared about 2.3 million years ago and it is thought to have survived in Asia as late as 53,000 years ago. If you saw *Homo erectus* and just looked at him or her from the neck downward the creature would look just like a modern human. It was in the size of the brain that difference still occurred with modern humans. The brain size of *Homo erectus* was about 1000 cc, which is about 450 cc less than the cranial capacity of modern humans.

Now enter the modern humans. There is still debate, although science has just about put an end to it, about whether there was a monogenetic or a polygenetic origin of humans (Cavalli-Sforza 1991, pp. 72–8). The polygenetic model suggests that humans emerged in different parts of the world or developed directly from *Homo erectus* in different regions of the world.

The monogenetic model argues that the evolution of humans was a single event that occurred in Africa and that *H. sapiens* (modern human) expanded outward, driven by the Sahara pump during the Weichsel/Wisconsin/Wurm Ice Age (which ended about 10,000 years ago), when populations were displaced.

Most scholars now believe that the type *Homo neanderthalensis* was an evolutionary dead-end. This is a type found only in Europe but which is not shown, from either archaeological or biological sources, to have direct descendants in modern humans.

## Part II

# The age of literacy

"At the Egyptian city of Naucratis, there was a famous old god, whose name was Thoth. He was the inventor of many arts, such as arithmetic and calculation and geometry and astronomy and draughts and dice. But his great discovery was the use of letters." (Socrates, as recorded by Plato)

# 2 Africa and the beginning of civilization

## In the beginning

John Henrik Clarke, once called the Dean of African American historians, said that "Civilization emerged first on the African continent and all other continents are the inheritors of those first humans who occupied the African land mass" (Jackson 2001, p. 3). Clarke's words only echo the views of scores of scholars, those who specifically study Africa, and established a baseline for a discussion of Africa and the beginning of civilization. Clarke also contended that "Most Western historians have not been willing to admit that there is an African history to be written about, and that this history predates the emergence of Europe by thousands of years" (Jackson 2001, p. 3). Since we know that humans first appeared on the African continent according to the archaeological and biological records, we know also that the first humans to be able to manage their affairs in the physical environment in which they lived were Africans.

What did it take for the first Africans to confront their living environment? What kinds of things did they have to learn? What experiences would these first humans have to deal with given the fact that they were approaching this environment as *neophytes*, that is, new ones? We can surmise from the data that humans retained knowledge that had accumulated during the age of the hominids. They learned what was dangerous and what was not. They knew that you could fall off a cliff and die. They knew that certain foods were poisonous and would kill you.

Early hominids lived in the savannas and hunted in both the savannas and the rainforests. They used the hand-axe, which had evolved from the earlier use of stone choppers as tools. It took many centuries for early humans in East Africa to arrive at the point where the hand-axe with its characteristic two cutting edges meeting at a fine point overtook the use of the single jagged-edge chopper. Nevertheless, it did not take as long for these early Africans to develop scrapers and hammers. Although these tools have been found earlier in Africa than anywhere else, they were originally named by European archaeologists as Acheulian, after the European type site in France where they were first found. I have preferred to use the term Kamoa hand-axe after the earlier site in Congo where such stone implements were discovered. Indeed, the majority of such sites exist on the continent of Africa and not in Europe or Asia. Some of these sites may date as far back as 1½ million years ago.

## Necessity and invention

The appearance of *H. sapiens* nearly 250,000 years ago meant that modern humans would be able, with their larger brain, to advance their living conditions, better protect their young, engage in more skilled ways of capturing prey, and develop familial emotions that would cause them to act in concert in the face of danger on the African plains.

Let us assume that a child is born to a woman and man. What are the basic requirements of this group? They need food to eat. They need shelter to protect themselves from the weather. They need something to cover their bodies in order to keep warm if the temperature gets too low. They need tools and weapons to defend their lives from predatory animals. At the fundamental level they will need these things, hence we say *food, shelter, clothes,* and *tools.*

The infant will need to be cared for while the mother and father gather food. How will the child be tended during the time that the mother is working? There are some options, choices. One could either leave the child alone, with one of the parents, with friends, or carry the child to work. What we see in African history is that the mother practiced carrying the baby with her, most often wrapped tightly to her back (Dove 1998).

Who is the child anyway? How do you distinguish one child from another? What must be done to make it clear that a particular child is being called or asked for when the parent has more than one child? There has to be a way to make this distinction. Humans conceived of the naming process as a way to deal with distinctions.

There are many different approaches to naming. However, before names can appear certain other explanations and descriptions must be made. For example, in contemporary Ghana children are often named after the days of the week. Of course, a society must have developed a way to call days before people in that society could use day-names. Most likely the early humans in Africa named their children after the expression they had given for an ancestor. Here again the ancestor must be called by some name. Many people named their children according to natural phenomena, that is, a storm, an earthquake, the movement of the trees. Some gave their children names that reflected the type of person the parents wanted the child to become. None of this could have happened without language.

All systems of naming have had to be developed. Africans were the first to deal with this problem. Just as you could not name people after the days of the week until you had established a calendar, a system of days, weeks, months, and years, you could not name your children after the ancestors until the ancestors themselves had been identified as worthwhile. Everything was process, time, development.

Although naming is not one of the four basic necessities in order for humans to survive, it is important for civilization. Alongside food, shelter, clothes, and tools, naming constitutes a response to a situation. This is the beginning of any civilization. How you respond to situations is at the core of how you build your civilization. Naming was a step in the process of gaining control over a limited part of human destiny. Even if one could not prevent death, one could name people and the processes that existed between birth and death. Language allowed one to talk about things, feelings, family, life, death, and birth.

There were two ways that Africans approached food. It was *gathered* from existing trees, bushes, and fields, and very early in human development Africans developed ways to catch fish and so fishing became an important part of the food-gathering process. It is easy to see how gathering, fishing, and hunting became the earliest forms of food collection.

Later Africans were to add *farming*, that is, the idea that one could plant today and harvest tomorrow. This process came about through learned behavior. Early humans saw the cycle of the food-bearing bushes and trees and their experiences taught them the importance of planning for the next year. Africans learned how to grow their own food crops, tame their own animals, build their own shelter, and make their own tools in response to the environment. Scholars believe that by 12,000 years ago Africans had perfected the techniques of hunting, fishing, and gathering. They were at the dawn of farming (Krzyzaniak 1991, p. 518; see also Schoenbrun 1993, pp. 1–31).

Evidence of *microlithic* culture has been found widespread throughout the savanna grasslands of Central Africa, particularly in Zambia. Indeed, in the excavation of Gwisho Springs in the Kafue valley of Zambia archaeologists have found one of the world's largest caches of microlith technology. An incredible range of vegetable matter as well as tools of stone and bone have been discovered alongside 30 human skeletons. This is a rather recent site, dating only to 2000 BCE. Obviously this is not an isolated site and scientists are now discovering all over this region examples of early human settlements. Some evidence such as the cave paintings pushes the organization of settlements and establishment of group life back to nearly 50,000 years ago. Large areas of Africa have rock paintings; by 1965 more than 100,000 had been found in the continent. It is estimated by scientists that there are more than 500,000 such paintings in caves and under ledges of mountains, constituting a veritable treasure house of the art of antiquity. Southern Algeria alone has yielded more than 25,000 paintings.

Prehistoric rock paintings are found in every area of the continent. Indeed, huge areas of South Africa, Zimbabwe, Tanzania, Ethiopia, Libya, and Algeria contain these markings of ancient Africans. What do they show? They tell of a people who believed in communication and had some idea about how to record their thoughts, ideas, and activities. In fact the Blombos Cave, a site in South Africa, reveals decorated ochre blocks and polished spear heads that have been dated to 40,000 BP (Before the Present).

Having the ability to communicate and think meant that early Africans could conceive of the future, observe the maturation process of children, learn from the pregnancy of women and the time that it took for an infant to be born, and expect certain rewards based upon current actions. In fact, maternity was probably the first real scientific laboratory for early humans. They watched the transformation of the woman and the birth of an infant with awe.

Africa did not experience the Wurm/Wisconsin glaciation between 50,000 and 15,000 BP. It was however affected by the changes in Europe and the Northern Hemisphere because the Sahara, that great generator, was wetter and cooler in its eastern part, while the western part was drier and cooler.

## Racializing African history

Modern historians have often racialized African history, creating a historical profile based in ideas of racial superiority. This is seen in the work of the popular historian J. D. Fage, who wrote (1978, pp. 5–6) that "Race is a contentious, indeed emotive, theme" and then went on to say that blackness as a mark of Africans created problems when discussing African history. Indeed, Fage claimed inaccurately that the people of North Africa belonged to the Neanderthal group, while those south of the Sahara belonged to the Rhodesioid group. This was a specious argument, relying on false concepts and ideology, but it remained an argument that had currency, however worthless, among many historians because Fage was such an important writer. However, science has proved that Neanderthals, named for the area in Germany where the fossils were first discovered, were a dead-end line in hominid evolution. There never was a biological or cultural group that could be called Rhodesioid, although Cecil John Rhodes and his followers would have liked to follow up the naming of the territory that became Zimbabwe "Rhodesia" with a Rhodesian hominid. One sees the callousness of this type of history when it is known that the name Fage assigned to Africans "south of the Sahara" was based on the name of a white man, Cecil John Rhodes, one of the key British imperialists in Africa. Although Fage criticized the racist historian C. G. Seligman's *Races of Africa*, in which Seligman went so far as to speak of northern Africans as "Europeans," his own work lacks sensitivity to the African reality as well. While Fage noted that Seligman used this description because he believed that "white" was superior to "black," his own discussion of race and Africa is not without difficulty. For him the question of the northern Africans is also problematic because "there is no satisfactory general name in modern use for the men of Caucasoid stock who do not live in Asia or Europe, as most Caucasoids do, but who are native to Africa in that they have been resident there for many thousands of years" (Fage 1978, p. 6).

Prior to 2000 BCE all of the people of northern Africa were black in color. Furthermore, before the seventh century CE, North Africa was peopled mainly by black people and people who migrated from Europe in the ninth century BCE. There were no large populations of Arabs in North Africa before the rise of Islam and the religious movement that gave rise to the fervor for making converts of other people. Actually the Amazighs (so-called Berber) people have been in Africa much longer than the Arabs, but certainly not as long as the indigenous Africans. The Amazighs are culturally Africans and have not been interested in the racial politics of Europeans who claim that the Amazighs, because of skin color, are Europeans. The question of race in Africa is not the same question as in America or in Europe. A person whose ancestors have been in Africa for several thousands years is clearly African in behavior, attitude, and response to environment. Blackness is a color but it is also an experience, that is, a cultural and historical experience related to social practice, language, and cultural expressions.

In the early twenty-first century there are about 3 million Amazighs, which is not a large population out of approximately a billion people on the continent of Africa, yet a distinct enough population to view themselves as of different origin than Arabs, who came to Africa in large numbers in the seventh century CE. Amazighs claim to have been in the continent for at least 1500 years before the Arab invasions. Historians who have concentrated on this population, which lives in Algeria, Morocco, Libya, and Mauritania have often missed the point of this African group's African claim. They want to be identified as Africans. Their closest neighbors are the Hausa, Peul, Mossi, and Tamaschek ethnic groups. Intermarriage between these groups over the years has meant that many people called Amazigh are so culturally and geographically African, wearing amulets and believing in djinn (spirits), eating the same foods as their neighbors, and singing and dancing in the same way, that it is nonsense to speak of them in any other way. Like many indigenous Africans they are nominal believers in the Qur'an but maintain strong cultural connections to their ancestors. A proper reading of African history must always begin with Africa as the source and the inspiration for deeds done on the continent. One does not have to look outside of Africa to explain African creations, phenomena, or activities. No aliens from Mars will be found responsible for building Great Zimbabwe or the Great Pyramids. Thus, whatever cultural expressions one finds among the Amazighs must be seen as African expressions. They are neither European, as we understand Europe, nor Asian, but African.

Africa has been denied its own agency for too long because of racialized readings of the records. Many historians view Africa as the recipient of everything, the creator of nothing. This not only is untrue but has distorted the African record so badly that it takes critical analysis to remove the piles of intellectual trash about Africa. New articles and books have suggested in no uncertain terms that Africa was far more involved in its own creation than it has been given credit for heretofore because of racist readings (see Butzer 1976, pp. 76–92; Hassan 1993, p. 560; O'Connor 1972, ch. 4).

## Predynastic cultures of the Nile Valley

The predynastic cultures of the ancient Nile Valley appear to have three distinct periods in Upper Egypt, where they were most prominent: the Gerzean, Badarian, and Naqada cultures. These are named for villages or areas where certain prehistoric tools and materials were discovered. The Gerzean period is the earliest, arising around 8000 BCE. The Badarian culture is so named because certain tools and material evidence were discovered at el-Badari near Asyut. The products of the Badarian culture extend to 5000 BCE and are more complex than those found in sites in the Fayum and the Delta region of the Nile Valley. Grave sites of the Badarians show the dead buried with the head pointed toward the south and the face toward the west. Archaeologists have discovered blue-glazed steatite beads, anklets, bracelets, and necklaces. We also know from the burial sites that the Badarians used cosmetic materials for eye paint from substances such as malachite. There does not seem to be a break between the Badarian and Naqada cultures in Upper Egypt.

Naqada is located on the west side of the Nile about 50 miles north of the modern city of Luxor. The early stage of this culture was about 4000 BCE. One can see that the burial customs of the Badarians, with the dead being buried with some of their material objects, continues among the Naqada people. However, there is a distinct type of pottery, a black-topped ware, vessels with a black rim around the neck and a red body. There are also palettes designed like antelopes, hippopotami, fish, and turtles. From the energy of the Badarian and Naqada cultures the people of the Nile Valley were primed to influence human history in Africa for ever. An inheritance that included farming, fishing, and hunting in a very fertile and productive part of the earth was enough to propel the civilization to greater heights.

## Farming in the Nile Valley

In the Nile Valley there was a concentration of heavy-yielding grasses called *cereals*. These were barley and wheat in northeastern Africa and sorghum and millet in the tropical regions to the south. Here on the fertile banks of the Nile, human beings began the intensive protection of wild plants where they grew and then began the practice of hoeing and ploughing to encourage the special crops while discouraging the grasses that were not useful for food. Perhaps farming may be said to have come into being when plant selection occurred. This would have been when a woman or man chose to keep the seeds of strong plants while rejecting the seeds of the weaker ones. Agriculture had taken a great leap in the valley. With the development of farming, which originated in crop cultivation and grain gathering and selection along the banks of the Nile, we see an increase in the food supply.

An increase in the food supply brought about larger families, more permanent houses, and more complex societal organization. Women could bear more children and keep them at home without having to carry them with them during hunting and gathering campaigns. They could farm right around their own houses. Thus, settled communities arose and these communities needed people to specialize in certain activities. There were people who became expert in fishing, others became especially skilled in repairing tools and equipment of farmers and fishers, and still others were knowledgeable as guides and expedition leaders. These latter experts became extraordinarily important in determining the best farm lands and the best fishing areas. A good family with members operating in different capacities could extend its range quite easily. Indeed, with surplus food there was no need for everyone to be involved in food production. This meant that the equality of the communal arrangements under the old hunter-gatherer form was broken down because now some people could simply control the surplus by keeping it in store houses while other people kept producing. Those who were non-producing usually got rich in the sense that they held more food than those who produced it. If you did not have food for some reason, you could always get it by exchange from those who held it in storage.

## Pastoralism in the valley

The keeping and herding of domestic animals such as sheep, goats, and cattle also led to advantages in community building. Since animals were a great source of protein for children and adults and milk for infants it meant that the families could sustain themselves on their herds as well as their farms. Of course, they would need to move in search of new pastures as one place became overgrazed. This did not seem to be an obstacle for these early dwellers along the banks of the river inasmuch as there were many pastures that had never been grazed by domesticated animals. Using the animals, goats, sheep, and cattle as transportation they could move quite far over land. The search for seasonal pastures became so ordinary, so regular and customary that after a while the pastoralists came to expect to move. Here we have the beginnings of the nomadic way of life for some families, who simply packed all of their mats, poles, water bottles, and tools and moved to another place. On the other hand, those who were sedentary, that is, non-pastoralists, had settled into their routine of waiting for the next planting season. And so it was along the Nile Valley and its environs that human beings started to develop the patterns that would result in the complex societies that we now know.

# 3   The rise of Kemet/Egypt

The first major civilization of Africa, indeed in the world, to make a definitive impact on the direction of human culture was that of the united country called Kemet by Africans and much later called Egypt by the Greeks. Kemet means the "land of the blacks" or "the black country." It was the favorite name for the land that the Greeks later called "Aeguptos," after the Egyptian word "hikuptah" meaning colloquially the "houses of Ptah."

Kemet stands in a special place in relationship to other ancient civilizations. It is the first instance of human beings organizing themselves into a *nation* comprised of many different ethnic and social communities. This is therefore the first nation on earth, created and developed out of values of the African environment. There had been communities of people, settlers of various farming lands, pastoral groups moving from one place to another, but for the first time in human history with the establishment of Egypt a nation was born with many towns and villages brought under the control of a central government. The millennia-old patterns of life, customs that had been transmitted from generation to generation, and the beliefs in the supernatural with all attendant names and designations for deities became more than a family or clan achievement; those aspects of life were now national. Christopher Ehret sees the development of an Egyptian culture as directly related to beliefs, customs, traditions, and patterns that had "sub-Saharan roots" (Ehret 2002, p. 93). According to Ehret, people arriving in the Nile Valley before 10,000 BCE probably introduced the idea of using wild grasses as food, new religion, and clan deities (2002, p. 93).

## Unification

The unification of Kemet under the rule of Narmer, the *Per-aa*, meaning "Great House" (Hebrew *pharaoh*) in 3400 BCE was one of the most historic moments in history. Narmer, who was also called Menes, a king of the south, conquered the other kings of the Nile Valley, uniting much of the Nile Valley under the White Crown of Upper Kemet. When he had subdued the northern part of the valley, called Lower Kemet, he wore the Red Crown of that region, thus combining the White and the Red Crowns of Kemet as the supreme, reigning symbol of god on earth, Per-aa. Since the Nile runs down to the north from the African highlands the north is called Lower Kemet and the South is

*Figure 3.1* Egyptian boy at Edfu, near the temple of Heru
© Molefi Kete Asante

Upper Kemet. The Nile flows from Uganda and Ethiopia down toward the Mediterranean. Narmer united 42 *nomes*, each one ruled by a *nomarch*, and often identified as 42 different ethnic groups or administrative kingships, under his rule. There were 22 nomes in Upper Egypt (southern) and 20 nomes in Lower Eygpt (northern). By bringing all of these nomes under one para-mount king, the Per-aa, the Egyptians created a multidimensional nation, while most societies were still insisting on single ethnic identities.

## The Per-aa

The Per-aa was a divine king, a pattern found throughout Africa. This meant that the king was an incarnation of god. Since this was an original African idea probably deriving from the south the Kemetic king was follow-ing an ancient tradition where the earlier leaders had been religious leaders, those capable of providing food for the people and explaining the various natural events occurring in the lives of the people. Direct descent from god assured the leaders of legitimacy. No one was above the Per-aa and no one dared to challenge him directly because it would be challenging the very presence of god. No king could serve the people if he did not have the direct link to the supreme deity.

All priesthoods recognized the Per-aa as the son of god. In fact, one of the names of the Per-aa was "*sa Ra,*" meaning the "son of god." This reinforced in the minds of the people that the Per-aa was divine. In the maintenance of the national spirit and stability it was essential that the king be viewed as infallible. There was nothing that could save a king who had been found less than divine. Indeed, the first order of business for a newly installed king was to establish his patrimony. He had to demonstrate that he was a descendant of Ausar (Greek, *Osiris*), with the Heru (Horus) personality, the one who could keep the people free because he had inherited the mark of divinity.

## The dynasties

The kings of Kemet are traditionally grouped into thirty families, called dynasties. Each dynasty represents a family of kings. As long as there are descendant of the first king of the line the dynasty is alive, but when the last descendant dies a new dynasty is formed and reigns until its last heir dies. Kemet begins with a first dynasty, and from the time of its first dynasty until the last one is the longest period of any government on the face of the earth. No kingdom, nation, or government has existed as long as the nation of Kemet. It lasted 3000 years! Compare that with the fact that in 2006 the United States had existed for 215 years, while Nigeria was a mere 46 years old as a nation.

Like many other nations Kemet had its problems, periods of instability, squabbles over leadership, attempted coups d'états, and internal intrigue, yet the presence of the person who was considered Per-aa had a lot to do with the unity of the nation. His presence, overpowering in its religious and social significance, stamped him as divine.

The balance between humanity and divinity was affirmed by rituals. In most cases, the priests who officiated at the national ceremonies did so in the name of the divine king but served as representatives of both the divine and the human. They were sacred in their own right, but not divine. They were human, but channels for the divine. When they sang the opening of the mouths of the gods in the morning they were singing for eternity, and when they closed the gates of the temples at night they were protecting all that was important from the possibility of human chaos. The divine Per-aa held in his or her person this precarious balance between nature and the spirit, between harmony and disharmony, between today and tomorrow. So rich were the experiences and so long the condition of those experiences that Kemet is the first civilization for which we have a complete chronology going back several thousand years. It is from Manetho, the historian asked by Ptolemy to write a history, that we have a general idea of the time periods of Kemet. There are some disputes, because there are a few fragmented accounts of chronology that differ from Manetho's account, yet scholars have maintained Manetho's records for the general outline of Kemetic history (Asante 1990, pp. 68–72).

Most scholars recognize these important phases of Kemetic history:

Archaic Period (3400–2600 BCE)

Old Kingdom (2685–2000 BCE)

First Intermediate Period (2200–200 BCE)

Middle Kingdom (2040–1785 BCE)

Second Intermediate Period (1800–1600 BCE)

New Kingdom (1570–1085 BCE)

Resurgent Kingdom (750–590 BCE)

## The natural order of the state

Two elements, the River Nile and the eternal sun, are at the core of ancient Kemet and its history. It is impossible to speak of Kemet without speaking of the ever-present sun and the eternal flowing of the Nile. Both are written in the very heart of the ancient country. In fact, the constancy of the sun was a phenomenon that had a lot to do with the ancient people's response to the natural and the supernatural. In its earliest manifestations as religious the sun was identified with the divine. In much the same way the Nile was called by the divine name *Hapy*. Thus the sun in its manifestations of Ra, Ptah, Atum, or Amen was a sun deity and could not be knocked off its eternal perch. Every Kemetic person related everything in his or her life to the ordered flowing of the Nile and the regularity of the sun.

Rainfall is almost unheard of in Kemet. All water is derived from the Nile and yet because of the sun and the heat the desert has encroached upon the banks of the river. It is easy to speak of Kemet as a ribbon of water through a desert because the green areas of vegetation are very narrow and hug the river's banks. The ever-growing Sahara has squeezed the green land ever more tightly to make a narrow green velvet strip along the banks of the river.

The life-giving Nile is fed by two initial streams, the *White Nile*, rising out of the mountains of Uganda, and the *Blue Nile*, called the *Abay* by the Ethiopians. Once the waters are joined in Sudan they are then urged along by the *Atbara* River, which enters the Nile stream and pushes it down toward the sea at a quickened pace. Like the deep dark waters of the Nile coming from the south, civilization riding on the shoulders of the Africans who brought to the northern lands their concepts of the divine, social organization, and ancestral devotion flowed endlessly into the rich land of Kemet. This was "Ta Mery," the Beloved Land.

When the conquering southern king Narmer, also called Menes or Aha, united the nomes as the *Two Lands*, a political development of historic proportion occurred because never in history had a king undertaken such a huge bureaucratic task. How do you keep such a nation together? What would it take to support such a massive political structure? How would the king protect all of the people in the new nation? These were questions that it would take years to work out in the new nation, but Menes had the experience of his own kingship in the south and that of his many predecessors. Kemet was not without experience. Humans had been living in the Nile Valley for thousands of years before the appearance of the conqueror.

Kemet was mainly a country of peasants, farmers making a subsistence living off the food they grew for their families and the little bit they were able to barter for other items they needed. Civil servants, who were mainly scribes and tax collectors, served the political bureaucracy to the point of trying to determine how much people owed the government in grain or other products. These officers of the Per-aa supervised the building of boats and the construction of irrigation canals, and recorded the rise and fall of the Nile. Indeed, it was their recording of the Nile that gave them the information they needed for taxation. Using the *Nilometer*, a special well created to measure the depth of the river, these civil servants made certain that every bit of the Beloved Land was recorded for administrative purposes. Overseeing the many public building projects, including the digging of canals, the draining of marshes, and the building of pyramids and palaces, were skilled scribes and priests dedicated to the maintenance of the kingdom.

Other officials kept time. They were important officials who saw to it that the people were prepared for the inundation of the Nile and also for the harvest. Watching the heavens and the Nile as they did, they perfected, as much as was possible without digital instrumentation, the regularizing of time. These African priests were the first astronomers and the first inventors of a calendar. They would climb to the top of temples and watch the sky all night long. In Kemet this was easy because there were hardly any clouds in the night-time sky. They soon discovered that the appearance of a star they named Sepdet (which is now called Sirius) was associated with the beginning of the Nile flood.

These priests understood that one could create a calendar if there was a regular event that was predictable. Nothing was more regular, it seemed to them, than the fact that the Nile flooded and then subsided. About the time of our June the waters would rise, and the flood period (Akhet) would last until October, covering the entire valley with thick black silt from Uganda, Ethiopia, and Sudan. The earth would thus be prepared for the sowing and growing period (Peret). By the end of February the harvest time (Shemu) would start, and it ended with the new inundation (Table 1). This cycle defined the predictable agricultural year. One could have a pretty good idea about the agricultural year, but there was a problem of exactness because the floods could be late, or could be early, and therefore one did not have exact timing. This variability in terms of range of days from one year to the next created perplexing problems.

*Table 1* The agricultural year

| Season | Month |
| --- | --- |
| Akhet<br>"inundation" | Tehuti<br>Phaophi<br>Aithir<br>Choiak |
| Peret<br>"emergence" | Tobi<br>Mechir<br>Phamenoth<br>Pharmuthi |
| Shemu<br>"planting" | Pakhonsu<br>Payni<br>Epiphi<br>Mesore |

However, the priests, students of history and ancient records as well as of the stars and the earth, saw a connection between Sepdet's appearance and the beginning of the Nile flood. It was thought that the floods were caused by the tears shed by Mother Auset (Isis) after the killing of her husband Ausar (Osiris) by his brother Seth. Sepdet, therefore, was the cosmic return of Auset.

Sepdet, also called Sothis and Sirius, had its heliacal rising in early July 3000 years ago, but because of the wobble of the earth on its axis it is now a few weeks later. It was a solid predictor of the recurring flood and defined the exact length of the trip of the earth around the sun. The first new moon following the reappearance of Sirius after it disappeared below the horizon for 70 days was established as the first day of the new year, called by the ancient Africans of the Nile Valley *wepet senet*, and of the Akhet (flood) period, even if the Nile had not yet begun to flood (Finch 1991).

The work of the priests was not done simply because they had established the time of the new year. They wanted to know how to divide the time between the wepet senets. They observed that there were four moon periods that fitted into each of the three seasons, or better yet they fitted them into the three seasons because they were not exact. The lunar month has 29½ days, resulting in "short" or "long" years of 12 or 13 new moons. They did not bother with this little problem, because with the appearance of Sepdet and the new year the calendar went back to baseline. The calendar was still not accurate enough and created problems when trying to give someone a date when their taxes were due. If there is one thing a government wants to do on time, it is to collect taxes. Thus, during the Old Kingdom, there was a priestly agreement to have a standard calendar with twelve months of thirty days. Each month had decades equal to thirty days. The work was not yet complete, because this agreed-upon public calendar was short and did not coordinate well with the agricultural and lunar calendar. Five extra days called the *heriu renpet* were added at the end of the year and were celebrated with religious festivities. By making this type of reform the ancient Africans in Egypt missed the true length of the solar year by only a quarter of a day! This was spectacular science based on trial, error, correction, prediction. Nevertheless, as brilliant a construction as this was, the lunar calendar and the public calendar increased by one day every four years. So, in 1461 years the calendar slipped through a whole year, meaning that, according to one calendar, it could be the time of harvest, although in reality the flood was just receding!

Years were identified with the Per-aa. For example, one actual date (from the so-called Ebers Calendar) appears as "Year 9 under the Majesty of the King of Upper and Lower Kemet, Djeserkare. The Feast of the Opening of the Year III Shemu 9. The going forth of Sepdet." Djeserkare is one of the names of Amenhotep I; thus we can state this date as "in year 9 of the reign of Amenhotep I, the heliacal rising of Sirius came on the 3rd month of Shemu, day 9."

## The creation of the universe

The political ideology of Kemet was made durable by the intense preoccupation of the people with religious and moral ideas. Indeed, one can say that the basis for the longevity of the nation was probably its commitment to the ideologies that were formed by the priesthoods at On (Heliopolis), Hermopolis, and Men-nefer.

In Kemet the people usually honored gods in triads, such that in Waset the triad consisted of Amen, Mut, and Khonsu and at Men-nefer it was Ptah, Sekhmet, and Nefertem. This was the idea of the father, mother, and child modeled after the original triad of Ausar, Auset, and Heru. But there was always a single supreme deity worshipped as the almighty god by the people of Kemet. This single deity was most often the male father figure. For example, at Waset the figure was Amen and at Men-nefer he was Ptah.

There was no supreme deity older than Ra, Atum or Ra-Atum, the deity of the university city of On, called by the Greeks Heliopolis, the City of the Sun. Ra was a sky god depicted in human form who was said to have created himself. He came forth out of the Nun, the primordial waters. The eight parts of his body which he brought into existence were grouped into four pairs of deities, two male and two female. They were Shu, the god of air, and Tefnut the goddess of moisture, the earth god Geb and the sky goddess Nut, Set and Nebhet, and Ausar and Auset. This was called the *Doctrine of Heliopolis.*

At Hermopolis, Tehuti, called variously Thoth and Hermes, brought into existence a set of gods by calling out their names. They laid the egg from which the sun was formed. These primeval gods were four male frogs and four female snakes. They were called the Eight, or Ogdoad. Tehuti, the Greek Hermes, was identified with an ibis and was usually depicted with a writing quill in his hand. According to the Kemetic tradition he was the father of writing, mathematics, languages, keeping of accounts, magic, the legal system, and the game of draughts. His wife was the divine librarian Seshat, who inscribed the record of every person's life on the Tree of Heaven. In essence, this was a different doctrine than that taught at Heliopolis and it has been called the *Doctrine of Hermopolis.*

A third doctrine emerged at Men-nefer itself. It was founded on the belief that Ptah, the chief god of the area, was coeval with the waters of Nun from which the god Atum arose. Therefore, Ptah was older than Atum. It was asserted that Ptah created Ra-Atum by thought: thus Ptah was Universal Mind, self-conceived, and self-existent. All other gods were seen as his projection so that Tehuti was thought to be his tongue and Heru was said to be his heart. This was called the *Doctrine of Men-nefer.*

# 4 The elements of early African civilization

## Writing

Writing occurred in Kemet about the same time as the first dynasty. It is believed that writing was invented around 3400 BCE in Kemet, about 300 years before we see a cuneiform system of writing on clay tablets in Mesopotamia, today's Iraq. In Kemet writing was done on almost any type of surface, but the favorite was papyrus, a reed that grew in the Nile, now found far south of Egypt in Sudan. Immediately writing served three purposes:

1. recording of historical events;
2. communication between the king, priests, and scribes;
3. literary and instructional writings.

The mythical traditions of Kemet say that Tehuti was the father of writing. This was repeated so many times in ancient Kemet that it became an accepted explanation for the origin of writing.

Recent scholarship by German archaeologist Günter Dreyer seems to substantiate the position that has been taken by Afrocentrist scholars since the 1950s that writing is an African, not a southwest Asian, creation. Dreyer, director of the German Institute of Archaeology in Cairo, found writing on a group of small bone or ivory labels dating from 3300 to 3200 BCE. Since we understand writing to mean a symbolic representation of language, not pictures representing concrete objects, then we have the first indication of writing anywhere in the world right in Africa. What Dreyer found were labels attached to bags of linen and oil in the tomb of King Scorpion I in Egypt. The labels seemed to indicate the origin of the commodities. Like the symbolic systems of pictographs that preceded writing, the inscriptions contained symbols, but they were more than pictographs. Pictographs cannot be called true writing, but rather are drawings that represent specific words or objects. Thus a pictograph of a leg might stand for a leg, and that of a toe for a toe. Dreyer maintains that the labels he discovered and studied carry inscriptions with phonetic significance. That would make them a symbolic representation of language or true writing. Dreyer claims that studying the labels helped him to deciper even earlier inscriptions on pottery found in the same cemetery. These inscriptions, dating from 3400 to

3300, put ancient Egyptian writing at a date much earlier than anything anyone has found in Mesopotamia (Dreyer 1999).

Of course there are now scholars who believe that it is necessary to consider pictographs as systems that contained all the possibilities of information storage and therefore the ultimate origin of writing. In this case again, the idea of using markings to store information occurred on the continent of Africa before it happened anywhere else. The interesting work done by Ayele Bekerie (1997) in his award-winning work on Ethiopic has revealed that the discussion of writing in Africa is even more complex than has been intimated in the work of various scholars.

The ancient people of Kemet attributed writing to the god Tehuti, who was the scribe and historian of the gods as well as the keeper of the calendar and the inventor of mathematics, art, and science. It was this deity who was also said to be responsible for the creation of speech and who had the power to transform speech into material objects. In some ways this may relate to the African belief, first observed in Kemet, that in order to achieve immortality one's name must be spoken or preserved for ever.

## Architecture

The earliest form of architecture was developed in Kemet, where the first masonry construction was the Saqqara Pyramid built by Imhotep for Per-aa Zoser in the Third Dynasty. The Saqqara site was not simply the step pyramid structure that was used as a burial chamber but was also a huge complex of temples, including a funerary temple that still stands today.

*Figure 4.1* User-maat-re, Setep-n-Re, the Heru name of Ramses II, Eighteenth Dynasty
© Molefi Kete Asante

The Sphinx is said by some to have been carved nearly 15,000 years ago. Others dispute this, saying that the stone sculpture dates from the time of the Per-aa Khafre. We know, of course, that it was not called "sphinx" by the ancient Kemetic people. The name sphinx derives from the Greek word "sphingo," to strangle, based on the Greek sphinx's habit of strangling its victims. The name was subsequently applied to Egyptian sculptures by Greek travelers. They called this the Great Sphinx, although the construction of the "Great Sphinx" predates any in Greece. The people of Kemet called it Heru-em-akt – meaning Heru (Horus in Greek) of the Horizon; sometimes it was referred to as the Bw-Heru (Place of Heru) and also as Ra-Horakhty (Ra of Two Horizons).

The African people were the greatest builders of "sphinxes," so much so that European scholars have categorized them by type: androsphinx (lion body with human head), ovisosphinx (lion body with ram head), and hierocosphinx (lion body with hawk head). One can think of these sculptures, when they appear in front of temples like the great Karnak or Luxor temples, as protectors and guardians. Since the finding of the Great Sphinx by Napoleon's army in 1798, hundreds of sphinxes have been dug out of the sands. The prodigious nature of the ancient Egyptian artists and artisans seemed unsurpassed by human hands.

One cannot overemphasize the grandeur of the architectural treasures of Kemet because nowhere in the world is there such a collection of ancient buildings. All of ancient Greece and Rome do not amount to the architectural inheritance of Kemet. Organizing a bureaucracy with the purpose of constructing large temples, tombs, and public buildings became one of the strengths of the Kemetic society. Temples like the massive Karnak temple at Waset and the tombs of the kings and queens in the Valley of the Kings and the Valley of the Queens took enormous capabilities and the Kemetic people mastered all of the required skills to produce the most perfect buildings of their day.

The Kemetic people were great stone builders. They built on a large scale, in relationship to gods, it seemed, and not in relation to humans. During the Third and Fourth Dynasties we see the construction of the giant pyramids, including the three principal pyramids at the Giza plateau: for Khufu, Khafre, and Menkaure.

It is the pyramid (mr) built by Khufu of the Fourth Dynasty around the year 2560 BCE that we call the Great Pyramid, one of the Seven Wonders of the World. The tradition of pyramid building started in ancient Kemet as a replacement for the *mastaba* or "platform" type of royal tomb. When several stacked mastabas were used it was possible to create a step pyramid.

Khufu's pyramid took about twenty years to build. First, the site was prepared; blocks of stone were transported down the Nile and placed at the site. An outer casing (which cannot be seen now) was then used to smooth the surface. Although it is not known definitely how the blocks were put in place, many theories have been advanced. For example, one theory involves the construction of a straight or spiral ramp that was raised as the construction proceeded. This ramp, coated with mud and

*Figure 4.2*  Avenue of Sphinxes, Luxor
© Molefi Kete Asante

water, eased the displacement of the blocks, which were pushed (or pulled) into place. A second theory suggests that the blocks were placed using long levers with a short angled foot. Both of these theories are practical and could have worked. Of course, there are wilder theories such as "aliens from Mars," and levitation of stones by music.

Certainly, humans have wondered about the pyramids of Giza. They were referred to as "the Granaries of Joseph" and "the Mountains of Pharaoh." When Napoleon invaded Egypt in 1798, he was overwhelmed with pride when he made his famous quote: "Soldats! Du haut de ces Pyramides, 40 siècles nous contemplent" (Soldiers! From the top of these Pyramids, 40 centuries are looking at us.)

## Philosophy

Several factors led to the Kemetic origin of philosophy. In the first place it was necessary to explain the challenges of the physical universe in terms that agreed with the spiritual ideas of the people. Second, it was important that the Per-aa received good solid information that was the result of reflection, not someone just providing an opinion. The Per-aa appreciated the priest, scribe, vizier, philosopher who had given thought to the questions put before him. There were numerous philosophers, wisdom seekers and teachers, in ancient Kemet.

It is impossible to mention all of the Kemetic philosophers but it is necessary to provide you with several of the most important ones.

*Imhotep* was the first philosopher to deal with the question of volume, time, the nature of illness, physical and mental disease, and immortality. He was the first philosopher in human history. He lived around 2700 BCE. As the first human being to be deified, that is, made a deity by his society, he stands at the very top of African and world philosophy so great were his deeds. Imhotep, like the Greek Socrates who lived nearly 2200 years later, is known basically by what others said about him because his own writings are not extant.

*Ptahhotep* wrote around 2414 BCE and was known as the philosopher who wrote the first book on what it means to grow old. His treatise on aging was a deep reflection on the meaning of youth and age. He is considered the father of ethical doctrines.

*Merikare* wrote around 1990 BCE, on the value of speaking well and using common sense in human relationships.

*Sehotipibre* wrote around 1991 BCE. His concern was with allegiance to the king. He might be called a nationalist philosopher because he argued that loyalty to the king was the most important function of the citizen.

*Amenemhat* wrote around 1991 BCE and was called the first cynical philosopher because he warned his readers to be wary of those who called themselves friends.

*Amenhotep, son of Hapu*, was priest, vizier, and philosopher during the Eighteenth Dynasty and was active around 1400 BCE. He was deified, becoming the second living human being in Africa to be made a deity, by his community after his death. His wisdom was extraordinary and he was thought to have mastered all of the knowledge of the ancients.

*Duauf* was the philosopher who wrote about the love of books. He was the educational philosopher, one who cherished the idea of learning, and wrote around 1340 BCE that the young must learn to appreciate books.

*Akhenaton* was a religious philosopher, believing that the god Aton was the only God, the sole God. He changed the religious doctrine of Kemet and moved the capital city in order to practice his newly declared religion of the only God. He lived around 1300 BCE.

All of these Kemetic philosophers lived hundreds of years before the first Greek philosopher. Indeed, the first Greek philosopher was Thales of Miletus, who studied in Kemet. He lived around 600 BCE.

## The emergence of mathematics

The first books of mathematics are Kemetic books. No books on mathematical propositions existed in the world before the African books produced in the Nile Valley and now called the *Rhind Papyrus*. Like the Ebers Papyrus in medicine, the Rhind Papyrus is a document that introduces to the world Kemetic mathematics and science. At a time before the emergence of any civilization with a scientific bent outside of Africa, this society, the Kemetic culture, gave the world mathematics and also geometry. To a large extent this was necessary because of the annual flooding of the Nile, which wiped out the boundaries between farmers; some system had to be devised to make it possible to establish or reestablish whose land ended where when the floods had receded. The Egyptians claimed, as reported by Herodotus, that Tehuti was responsible for creating geometry, but that was probably because it was such an ancient science that no one remembered when it was created.

## The abundance of deities

Kemet was full of deities. In some senses, it was the prototypical African society with divinities appearing in every aspect of human life. In fact, everything was either a deity, related to a deity, or had the potential of being a deity. A deity is something that is or has been made into a god. Even *Nun*, chaos, the primordial waste of water in which all life was immanent, was a deity. Nun was guarded by four frog- and serpent-headed deities. It was from this watery substance that Atum, the god of creation, arose. He was represented as a bearded old man, sometimes with the head of a frog, a beetle, or a serpent. He was often called "the complete one."

Atum, Ra, Ptah, and Amen were all names of the creator deity. It is said that Atum as the creator brought into existence Shu, air, and Tefnut, moisture. In time Shu and Tefnut had children, who were Geb, the earth, and Nut, the sky. In turn, Geb and Nut brought into being Ausar, Auset, Seth, and Nebhet, two brothers and two sisters. The first four beings might be called celestial beings, or sky beings, and the last four, terrestrial or earth beings:

| Celestial | Terrestrial |
|-----------|-------------|
| Shu | Ausar |
| Tefnut | Auset |
| Geb | Seth |
| Nut | Nebhet |

## The legend of Ausar (Osiris)

The Kemetic people had maintained the legend of Ausar in their oral traditions and there are a few fragments of the story in papyri. However, the best-recorded version of this legend is that from the early first-century Greek writer Plutarch. The story is told that Seth and Ausar were entrusted with the rule of Kemet. During their care for the land, the part that was under Ausar prospered while that under Seth declined and it was like waste land. This angered Seth, and because he was so enraged he decided to murder his brother. He tricked Ausar into climbing into a casket, which was then sealed and thrown into the Nile.

Ausar was mourned by Auset, his sister, who loved him. After a long search she found his body and brought him back to Kemet. Then assuming the form of a kite she magically gave birth to her son, *Heru*, called Horus by the Greeks. However, all the time that Auset was protecting the corpse of Ausar, Seth was out looking for it. When he discovered the corpse he hacked the body into fourteen parts and scattered them around Kemet.

Now Auset had to search again for the body of Auset, she loved him so. She left her son, Heru, with her sister Nebhet and went out looking for Ausar. Indeed, she found the body in pieces. Where she collected a piece of his body she erected a shrine to his honor. Locate on a map of Egypt some of these sites: *Abydos, Biga Island, Philae.* Here were some of the sites where Auset found Ausar's body parts.

Ausar was restored to earthly life and appointed Lord of the Underworld and judge of the dead as well as the symbol of the resurrected life. Actually he came to represent the practice of *mummification* and with his green or black coloring he represented the regeneration of the earth. Ausar is restored on the earth; Seth is ultimately defeated by Heru, who inherits the throne of his father Ausar. The authority inherited by Heru meant that he had to avenge his father, symbolic of the eternal struggle between good and evil, between order and chaos. Thus, every king was the reincarnation of Heru in life and Ausar in death. Theophile Obenga, writing in *Pour une nouvelle histoire*, says "Le mythe osirien est peut-être le plus ancient mythe agraire de l'humanité" (Obenga 1980, p. 45). Agriculture was an ancient practice in Egypt and the cycle of life and death was familiar to every person.

## The eternal mummification

Mummification was derived from knowing about the natural desiccation of corpses in pit burials in the dry desert sands. After cleaning and evisceration, that is, the removal of the organs, the corpse was then dried with natron, a naturally occurring form of sodium carbonate. The organs were treated separately and preserved in special vessels known as canopic jars.

The process of mummification lasted for seventy days because there was a complex ritual that went along with it. The people did not just meet and wrap the body and then place it in a tomb. Certain ceremonies were necessary in order that the person should have eternal life. Just prior to burying the corpse there was a massive funeral ceremony with dignitaries carefully scrutinizing the priestly activities surrounding the ritual of mummification. Then they had a special ritual called "Opening the Mouth." This involved touching the mouth and head of the corpse with special instruments to restore the senses.

Finally inside the burial chamber all types of food and drink were placed near the deceased so that he or she might have all that was needed in the afterlife. They would even have change of clothes and other essentials for someone going on a long journey. In case someone should destroy the food and the clothing, they were repeated by artists on the sides of the walls. Outside of the chamber a stele was erected to tell who the person was and his station in life, and to pronounce his good deeds.

The Kemetic society lasted a long time, more than 3000 years, and during that time burials changed. In the beginning it was only the king who received a grand ritual burial, as seen in the Old Kingdom pyramid burials. By the New Kingdom, royalty and nobles were given elaborate burials; this still remained out of reach of the majority of the people.

Of course, recent research has shown that many of the commoners in Kemet were also buried in their own tombs. The idea was that as the sun set in the world of the living it was rising in the underworld. Everybody who died was really going to a place where he or she would continue to live. This was a democratizing of the rituals of death.

Since the afterlife was possible for any pure soul so long as they could provide the proper equipment and instruments for navigating the perilous realm of the underworld, anyone could declare himself a pure soul. However, the soul would have to survive the treacherous journey of the underworld to the judgment where Ausar presided. The heart was weighed against the feather of Maat to verify its lightness and purity. One could look forward to a peaceful afterlife in the Fields of Iaru, that is, the Elysian Fields.

There was nothing more important to the ancient Kemetic person than the afterlife. Some people say that these Africans were concerned with death. In fact, it was just the opposite. They were not concerned with death so much as they were deeply involved in the afterlife. Their obsession with life was for its infinite prolongation.

This was no easy task. It required the people to do lots of things to prepare the body for continuation of life after death.

A person was made up of some important parts according to the Kemetic people. They included the body, the name, the spirit double, and the soul. Now mummification was the process that was used to prolong life.

## The idea of Maat

Maulana Karenga states that the starting point for any real discussion of the ethical ideals of ancient Egypt must be Maat (Karenga 2003, p. 5). In the minds of the ancient Kemetic people, Maat was the idea that it was necessary to possess order, balance, harmony, justice, truth, righteousness, and reciprocity as minima for holding back chaos in every aspect of life. How do you hold back chaos if it is not by advancing the idea of Maat? During every major period of Kemet's history the idea was to establish a relationship with Maat. If the people maintained Maat they would be strong. If they lost Maat, they would be weak. This was a dictum that Africans understood.

D. T. Niane, the scholar who popularly introduced the world to the Epic of Sundiata, explained the Maatic concept when discussing the religious and political aspects of African culture faced with diversity by saying that "the traditional religion was able to remain a living force, pervading even the institutions and rituals of power at Koumbi as at Niani, and in Yatenga, Kanem and Mwenemutapa. But tolerance was the rule, enabling Mali and Ethiopia to mix a variety of peoples belonging to different religions" (Niane 1988, p. 262). It was this ability to accept diversity and difference that underscored the African society's desire for mutuality and communality from the dawn of human civilization.

# 5 Governance and the political stability of Kemet

The government of ancient Kemet was highly centralized and the Per-aa was the principal link between the people and the deities. He was able to control this large population because as divine king he was given respect and reverence, plus he had a huge official bureaucracy that assisted him in keeping control of the land. Kemet extended about 620 miles from Aswan (Syene) to the Mediterranean Sea. In order to effectively govern such a large territory, as you have seen above, the king had to use other people to run the day to day business of the country. These were usually well-educated civil servants, mainly scribes and tax collectors. The role of these officers remained permanent even when the country changed kings. Actually kings and dynasties came and went but the overall pattern of the country changed little in thousands of years.

### The first dynastic kings

Manetho, who lived during the Ptolemaic (Greek) reign in Kemet, is responsible for providing the broad outline of Kemetic history by writing the kings list for the dynasties. According to him the first king of the First Dynasty was Aha. It is from Manetho that we learn that the first two dynasties were Thinite, that is, the capital city was a town called This, located near Abydos. All of the tombs of the First Dynasty kings and some of the Second Dynasty kings have been discovered at Abydos.

The Thinite Period is given variously as 3400–2700 BCE or 3150–2700 BCE. Afrocentrist scholars prefer the earlier date because it places the origin of the dynasties closer to the origin of writing. Others believe that Manetho's dates may lead more closely to the later date. Whatever the case, we know that the name of the first king (Aha, Narmer, Menes) represents the founder of the city of Men-nefer, the initiator of the priesthood to Sobek, the crocodile god. He would have been the one to create the Apis-bull priesthood at Men-nefer and the one responsible for creating the unified nation. His wife was Neithhotep. Aha (Menes or Narmer) set in motion the long history of the Kemetic dynasties. He participated in his *Sed* festival, that is, the Jubilee festival, celebrated Sokar, the mummified falcon deity, and initiated a series of wars against the Nubians and Libyans.

According to the records of the *Turin Canon*, Aha was succeeded by Menes, who was in turn succeeded by Ity. The next king after Ity was Djer.

King Djer kept up wars with Nubia, Libya, and Sinai. He was buried with the rest of his court. It is not known if they were obliged to die with him to accompany him into the afterlife or if they were buried successively in the same tomb.

A text from the reign of Djer has raised the question of what type of calendar was being used. It is on an ivory tablet that seems to show a representation of the dog-star Sirius in the form of the goddess Sothis, depicted in the guise of a seated cow holding between her horns a plant that symbolized the year (Vandier 1952, pp. 842–3; Drioton and Vandier 1962, p. 161; Grimal, 1992, p. 51). This sign seems to indicate that from the time of Djer onwards Kemetic society had linked the heliacal rising and the beginning of the year, that is, they had invented the solar calendar.

Let's face it. They created the calendar on the basis of what was most readily available to them as a symbol of regularity, the flooding of the Nile. The year was divided up into three seasons of our thirty-day months. The seasons themselves were determined by the character of the Nile. For example, the first season was the inundation itself (Akhet), the second season was the planting season (Peret), and the third was the time of harvest (Shemmu).

Now it happened that the first flooding of the Nile which was chosen as the beginning of the new year was observed at the latitude of Men-nefer, the center of the universe, at the same time as the heliacal rising of Sirius. Actually this phenomenon is thought to have taken place on July 19 of the Julian calendar (or about a month earlier on the Gregorian calendar), but not on every July 19 because the real solar year is actually 365 days, five hours, 48 minutes and 45.51 seconds. Also the fact that the discrepancy of a quarter of a day per year lengthened the gap between the two phenomena meant that an adjustment should be made. The discrepancy could only be adjusted after a complete cycle of 1460 years, the Sothic period. The synchronization of the first day of the solar year and the rising of Sirius was recorded at least once in Kemetic history, in 139 CE.

We know something precise about Kemetic history because the people recorded various points in time within these Sothic periods. Thus, the terminal points that can be dated are 1317, 2773, and 4323 BCE, working off the fact that the phenomena were observed in 139 CE. It is unlikely that the solar calendar existed before 4323 BCE because the civilization would not have been sufficiently developed at that time.

By the end of the Thinite Period, King Khasekhemwy, who was married to princess Nimaatapis, the mother of King Djoser, had consolidated the territorial gains of his predecessors and built a prosperous foundation for the kings to follow.

## The Old Kingdom

When the Old Kingdom started, with the Third Dynasty, the country had already succeeded in forming the titulature for the Per-aa. The king had three names: the Heru name (which expressed his role as divine heir to the throne), the name of King of Upper and Lower Kemet *(nsw-bity)*, and a *nebty* name (reflecting the crown prince's career before coronation).

Djoser, whose Heru name was Netjerykhet, is famous because he inaugurated stone-built architecture with the assistance of the genius of Imhotep. The relationship between the Per-aa and Imhotep established a pattern for king and advisor for succeeding dynasties. Imhotep was not a politician, but an excellent physician and architect. The positions he is known to have held are lector-priest, high priest, physician, and architect. Legend has it that he was also the vizier of the king.

Additional literature about Imhotep describes him in striking ways. He is seen as patron of the arts and sciences and the personification of wisdom. It is a fact that we know more about him because of his intellect rather than his literary production. The evidence of his abilities is in the recognition accorded him by his peers. They referred to him as a wise counselor, like the attributes of Ptah, the creator god of Men-nefer. Indeed, Imhotep was called the "son of Ptah" in the Turin Canon. He was later deified with his own priesthood and called upon to help those who had difficulties in daily life. The Greeks, many years later, knew him as Imouthes and thought of him as their own god of medicine by the name of Asclepius.

Imhotep's immortality lasted for centuries inasmuch as he, unlike his ruler Djoser, was deified. Djoser could only manage a pyramid built at Saqqara by his wise counselor Imhotep and often called the Step Pyramid; it was the first such architectural monument in history.

In the Fourth Dynasty Kemet saw another conquering king in the person of Sneferu. The Palermo Stone suggests that he was fond of military campaigns and led an expedition against the Nubians to crush a revolt in the Dodekaschoenus region. He captured 7000 soldiers. Despite his martial expeditions he is said to have been a king of a genial personality, so much so that he was deified during the Middle Kingdom. There are many references to his reign, meaning that succeeding generations found him to be an enduring personality. His interactions with Nubia were important for Kemet because the southern country provided ivory, gold, incense, ebony, ostrich eggs, panther skins, and giraffes and monkeys.

## The pyramids of Giza

The Fourth Dynasty is dominated by the building projects at Giza. Khufu's pyramid transformed him into one of the most important figures in Kemetic history. Khufu's builder was Hemiunu, who was also the king's vizier. So highly was he thought of by the king that he was allowed to choose his own site in Giza and build his own tomb with a statue of himself inside.

During the Fourth Dynasty two other kings stand out for their contributions: Khafre, and his son Menkaure. The first of these kings ruled for twenty-five years and restored the power of the royal family. He was responsible for ordering the building of the Great Sphinx. He wanted the statue of a man with a lion's body cut out of a colossal block of stone. It is said that Khafre wanted his own image with a *nemes*-wig carved into the stone. This was the *shesep ankh*, living image. His pyramid stands on the same plateau as that of his father Khufu and his son Menkaure who succeeded him.

Menkaure lost one son, and his second son, Shepseskaf, came to power and completed Menkaure's mortuary temple and probably his pyramid, which was the third and smallest of the kings' pyramids at Giza.

## The Middle Kingdom

The main elements of the country had been established at the dawn of its history and all subsequent kings and queens ruled the country according to the old principles. When Narmer (Menes) established the country he set in motion a system that lasted about a thousand years until it was abruptly disturbed by a collapse of the central government in 2200 BCE. A number of factors may have contributed to this collapse of central authority. In the first place, the Sahara Desert was rapidly drying up and the arable land was getting to be less and less. Large populations of people from the deserts came into the Nile Valley and crowded the small land areas adjacent to the river. For a little over 200 years, taxes were not paid, the rule of law declined, and people were essentially on their own.

This period, called the First Intermediate Period (2200–2040 BCE), did not come to an end until the establishment of the Eleventh Dynasty, which brought unity again in the country and set about reasserting the central authority. During the Middle Kingdom (2040–1785 BCE), as it was called, the country prospered and the Per-aa assumed full control over the land. Taxes were collected, wrongdoers were punished, the shrines were restored, and the important task of irrigation was brought more under the authority of the king. Kemet also conquered Nubia during this time in one of the see-saw battles between those countries. The Fayum Depression was the site of a major irrigation project to improve the lives of the people who lived in that region of the country.

Mentuhotep II, the Great Unifier, came to power after Intef III in about 2061 BCE. Like many of his successors he came from the south, from the powerful town of Waset (often called Thebes or Luxor), and reestablished authority over the territory in the north, which had been under the rule of some princes of a northern town.

When Mentuhotep had completed his conquest he was given a new name, "Nebhotepre, the son of Ra." Back in those days when one said "son of Ra" it was the same as saying "son of God." Mentuhotep also declared his southern origins by giving himself a name that meant "Divine is the White Crown." The White Crown represented the south of Kemet and the Red Crown represented the north. Mentuhotep is shown in his sculptures to be a man of a wise presence with large eyes, dark skin, and full lips. He was a wise Per-aa. He reinstated the local rulers in some of the provinces, put in governors who would be loyal to him, and moved the capital to the city of Waset. It had been in several cities, including Men-nefer and This. Three of the prime ministers who worked for Mentuhotep were called Dagi, Bebi, and Ipy.

Mentuhotep ruled so effectively, building so many shrines and temples in all parts of the country, reunifying the country, that he was able to take a new name in his thirty-ninth year, "Sematawy, He who unifies the Two Lands."

Like other conquering kings, Mentuhotep felt the need to lead an expedition into Libya to fight the Tjemehu and the Tjehenu. He also turned his army against the Mentjiu nomads of the Sinai Peninsula. In this way he protected the country from the Asiatics, whom he forced back across the Litani River. To the south he sent expeditions on several occasions to pacify Nubia, which remained independent although the chancellor Khety had occupied areas of Nubia on behalf of the king.

During the Middle Kingdom subsequent kings built upon the work of Mentuhotep II. In fact, the son of Mentuhotep II, Mentuhotep III, came to power and consolidated the rule of Kemet over the eastern Delta, and built fortresses to protect against the incursions of the Asiatics. The delta defenses were the creation of Mentuhotep II but they were restored and reinforced by Mentuhotep III. One of the great trading expeditions that Mentuhotep III is known for is the trade with Punt. This trade had gone on for centuries but had been interrupted and now it was reestablished under his rule.

When the Eleventh Dynasty ended, three men contended for the kingship. One was Amenemope from Elephantine, another was Intef in Waset, and the other was Segerseni from Nubia. Amenemope won the office and thus began the Twelfth Dynasty. In many ways when we see three Africans vying for the same office it is like some contemporary politics when three individuals seek the same job.

Amenemope proved to be a good administrator. He kept governors in place who had supported him for the kingship and kept up the defense of the borders. He moved the capital city from Waset, the area where Intef had been strong, to a city near el-Lisht. His son, Senurset, called by the Greeks Sesostris, was a great general. One day when Senurset was returning from a battle with the Libyans and some enemies of his father, he heard that his father had been assassinated. This was about the middle of February 1962 BCE. It turned out that there had been a conspiracy in his harem. When Senurset arrived he had to subdue certain elements in the capital who had assumed control. Two books were written on the conspiracy to control the information and to subdue the hearsay. In the New Kingdom there would be another book, *Prophecies of Neferti*, that would serve as a school text about the situation. It would become one of the most read books in Kemet.

However, the first book was about a young man named Sinuhe, in Senurset's entourage, who overheard the conversation about the death of Senurset's father. He got scared and ran away because he believed he had heard something he should not have heard. He got as far away as Syria, having passed through the Delta and into the Suez isthmus. In Syria, one of the Bedouins recently under the control of Egypt took him in and adopted him. He was given honor and a big title as a chief, but he longed for Kemet. Sinuhe had great nostalgia for Kemet. He wrote to Senurset, who agreed to give him a royal pardon, and he returned to Kemet and lived there until his death.

The moral story of a repentant former official who was pardoned by his king made a big splash and must have been in the Top Ten of books for the year it was published. Several hundred copies of the *Story of Sinuhe* have survived. Another popular text from the Middle Kingdom is *Amenemope I*, a text that explained the legitimacy of the succession to the king after he was assassinated.

Senurset followed in the path of his father, Amenemope I, in foreign affairs. He established control over Nubia, and by the eighteenth year of his reign had put an outpost at Buhen in the Nubian country. Leaving a garrison in Nubia between the First and Second Cataracts he made incursions into the area of Kush which occupied the region between the Second and Third Cataracts. Senurset's name has been found on stones in the area of Dongola (much later the capital of the Makurra kingdom of Nubia, which defeated the Muslim army in 651 CE) and it is known that he traded with Kerma. Senurset felt at home in the area south of Kemet. It is known that he got enough stone blocks from this area to create sixty sphinxes and 150 statues.

Few kings had been any more active than Senurset, who exploited gold from Koptos and who quarried in Wadi Hammamat and sent expeditions to Hatnub in the twenty-third and thirty-first years of his reign. Commerce was continued with Syria and Palestine, and Kemet influenced the oases in the Libyan desert.

The kings who followed Senurset kept peace with their neighbors in the tradition of their ancestors. In fact, Amenemope II went so far as to have his own expedition to Punt, a favorite trading partner of the Middle Kingdom kings.

Something happened during the reign of Senurset II, who succeeded Amenemope II, that was to have a wide-ranging impact on the country. Khnemhotep, the governor of the Oryx nome in the northeast, received the Abisha "*Hyksos*" people and their tribute. These were people from Asia who moved into the northeastern part of Kemet to settle and farm. They would later prove to be more than settlers and more than a nuisance; they would exert their influence and authority over the people of Kemet in that part of the country. But at that time they were simply showing their allegiance to the Kemetic governor of the province. One could say that it was a political move but there is no way to verify this except to argue from history, and thus hindsight, that they did not mean to be under the authority of the Kemetic people for ever.

Two officials of the Middle Kingdom period, Mesehti and Djefaihapy, have become famous for the written contents of their coffins. Scholars call the writings that are found on funerary caskets coffin texts. Since Mesehti's career as an official spanned both the Eleventh and Twelfth Dynasties the information found in his tomb gives a record of that era. The coffin texts from his tomb are among the most important ever found. In the case of Djefaihapy, his coffin contained writing about the Egyptian legal system. There are ten funerary contracts surrounding his tomb that show the thinking of the legal minds of Kemet.

It is good to remember that the Middle Kingdom was the time when Kemetic literature reached its highest level of form and content. Actually when modern students of Egypt study the ancient language they study it from the period of the Middle Kingdom because of its perfection.

Several forms of writing appear during this time, though some had existed previously. For example, there was instructional writing called *sebayet*. The Kemetic word for "wisdom" or "wise" was "*seba*." The *sebayet* were usually written in the form of instructions to a younger person. Among the more popular ones that have been preserved are *Instructions of Kagemni, Maxims of Djedefhor, Admonitions, Instructions for Merikare*, and *Maxims of Ptahhotep*. These works and many others are really philosophical works though they have been called by non-Africans simply "wisdom literature." Also composed during the Middle Kingdom was perhaps the most commonly referred to *sebayet*, called *Kemyt*, the excellent "sum" of all instructions.

There is certainly a similarity with the ancient name of the country, Kemet, in this *sebayet*. Indeed, the book *Kemyt* was the exact image of the country Kemet, whose meaning is the "black nation," the most perfect model of the universe.

The ancient people of Kemet were the most prolific writers in the world during the Middle Kingdom. The book *Satire of Trades* has survived in over one hundred manuscripts, obviously mass produced by the scribes who were kept busy by the creative and philosophical writers as well as by the ordinary officials who employed them. *Satire of Trades* was written by Khety, the son of Duauf.

Political books such as *Instructions to the Vizier, Prophecy of Neferti, Loyalist Instruction, Instructions of a Man to his Son, Instructions of Amenemope I* and others sought to provide the people with ways to maintain balance and harmony in the society. These were the books that the leading officials referred to for direction and guidance.

It should not be thought that the Middle Kingdom was only the time of high art and literature; it was also the time of drama and mythology. Writers were eager to demonstrate their creative abilities by writing epics and narratives of rituals such as the *Drama of the Coronation*, the *Memphite Drama*, the *Tale of Isis and Ra*, the *Tale of Horus and Seth*, and the *Destruction of Humanity*.

Other writings of importance are the *Dispute of a Man with his Ba*, the *Teachings of Khakheperreseneb* and numerous royal hymns. This era of Kemetic history produced more written documents such as letters, administrative texts, autobiographical accounts, historical notes, medical and mathematical treatises, veterinary fragments, poetry, and priestly rituals. In addition, scholars have found the earliest known example of *onomastica* in the world in Kemet: a catalogue of words listing different entities and items in society such as birds, occupations, animals, plants, and toponyms. This type of book, which was to be found in other societies in years to come, was used to train the best scribes and orators. Eloquence, an element in the total training of the scribe, had to be taught and the *onomastica* was an easy way to provide the student with a store of arguments and lists. The Greeks would later discover aspects of the *onomastica* and use it to train students in rhetoric.

Given the extent of the writing and the quality of the literature one can see why the Middle Kingdom period has been referred to as the Classical Period of Kemetic history. To say "classical" is to mean that it is worthy of emulation and has demonstrated an impact on other periods and times.

## The Second Intermediate Period

The Hyksos gained control over the Thirteenth Dynasty in about 1633 BCE. The founder of the first Hyksos dynasty was Salitis. He asked the Nubians to ally themselves with the Hyksos in order to contain Kemet. Who were these Hyksos? Their name, *Hyksos*, is a Greek version of the Kemetic term *Hekaw-Khasut* (the chiefs of foreign lands). We do not know what race they were from this description. However, it seems that these were the Asiatics with whom the Kemetic people had fought: Setjetiu, Aamu, and Mentjiu of Asia or Retjenu.

Their rise to power was through infiltration at first and then violence at the end. It is believed that they introduced the harnessed horse into Kemet, even though it is clear that the horse was already known in the Nile Valley region.

## The New Kingdom

### The Eighteenth Dynasty

The princes of Waset rose against the Hyksos under Kamose and completed the crushing of the Hyksos forces under Ahmose. When Ahmose came to power around 1570 BCE he was about ten years old. He ruled for twenty-five years, dying at 35 years of age. By the time he was 21 he had already begun to engage the Nubians and the Hyksos in battle. In three military campaigns all the way up to the Second Cataract Ahmose defeated Nubia and brought it once more under the control of the Wasetian government. This deprived the Hyksos of one of their most reliable allies. He then turned his eyes toward Men-nefer, the capital that had been taken over by the Hyksos. Regaining the capital, he continued his conquest of the Hyksos in lower Kemet, ridding the Delta region of the Hyksos power. The Kemetic army under Ahmose also captured Avaris, and then went into Asia to capture the fortified town of Sharuhen in southwestern Palestine. In Palestine he annexed the wealthy ports of Phoenicia. Every time he defeated an enemy he would return to Waset for a parade and celebration. The final stage of the reconquest took place in the sixteenth year of Ahmose's reign. As a young man of 26 years of age, Ahmose had transformed the power base in Kemet from one where the Hyksos held insolent power to one where the people had reassumed their liberty, which of course was always in opposition to the foreign power. Thus, at an early age Ahmose had shown that force, not opinion, was the key to expelling the enemies of society.

There has never been a dynasty of kings as great as those of the powerful Eighteenth Dynasty of ancient Egypt. This was the first unified dynasty after the Hyksos defeat. Many years later Manetho, the historian who recorded the invasion of the Hyksos, said that "Amen was displeased with us and there came up unexpectedly from the East men ignoble of race who had the audacity to invade our land." The Kemetic people believed that the conquest by the Hyksos was a bitter humiliation. After all they were not Assyrians or Persians, considered reasonable opponents, but only a group of southwest Asian nomads with no particular civilization to their credit.

Table 2 The kings of the Eighteenth Dynasty

| | |
|---|---|
| Ahmose | Tuthmoses IV |
| Amenhotep I | Amenhotep III |
| Tuthmoses I | Amenhotep IV/Akhenaten |
| Tuthmoses II | Tutankhamen |
| Hatshepsut | Ay |
| Tuthmoses III | Horemhab |
| Amenhotep II | |

However, it took not disdain but actual fighting to rid the country of the conquering Shepherd Kings, another name by which they were known.

Ahmose is thought to have been a person of commanding presence once he reached the age of 21, probably standing more than six feet tall, with broad shoulders, and a well-built frame. His skin color tended toward ebony, like the kings who would follow him on the southern seat at Waset. At the height of his career he was favorably compared with the earlier conquering kings of Kemet, Narmer, Senurset I, and Mentuhotep. In the future other kings and some queens would be compared with him. But for this moment in history, Ahmose was truly the man. He would set Kemet on a path of imperial ambition, seeking to ensure that its enemies would never again create havoc by invading the holy land. Under the kings of the Eighteenth Dynasty, Kemet became the leader of the world and huge amounts of wealth poured into its cities from abroad. J. E. Manchip White called this Egypt's "glittering, flamboyant moment of fulfillment" (White 1970, p. 164).

Ahmose married Nefertari, whose name meant "the most beautiful one of them all," not to be confused with Ramses II's wife Nefertari, or with Nefertiti, the wife of Amenhotep IV, called also Akhenaten. Nefertari was a common name of the Eighteenth Dynasty, probably becoming so because it was the name of the favorite wife of the first king of that family. She became an important part of the dynasty; indeed her shrine and priesthood lasted for many centuries after her death. The Eighteenth Dynasty was known for strong women who were important in their own right, or as wives of the Per-aas.

A son, Amenhotep I, was born to Ahmose and Nefertari. He carried out the policies of his father toward the Asiatics as well as in Nubia, Kemet's neighbor and rival on its southern borders. At his death he was succeeded by Tuthmoses I, who rose to the throne declaring that the northeastern border of Kemet would be the River Euphrates. He sent expeditions as far south as the Third (actually the fourth counting down the river) Cataract. This was one of the first imperial declarations by a Kemetic Per-aa, though others had operated as if they believed that Kemet should exercise absolute control over the entire area of southwest Asia, including the lands of the Bedouins, now known as Arabia.

Amenhotep I's son Amenemhat died prematurely. Tuthmoses I was the son of Amenhotep I by a concubine. This fact meant that he was not completely of the royal lineage; therefore a marriage with his half-sister Ahmes, the daughter of Amenhotep I by the legitimate queen, had to be arranged. He effectively shut off any discussion of his legitimacy to be king by assuring that his divine lineage would be protected. From the union of Tuthmoses I and Ahmes came two children, a daughter Hatshepsut, and Amenemope, a son. Amenemope did not reach the throne; however, Hatshepsut would.

Tuthmoses I died knowing that he had secured the outer boundaries of Kemet as his father and grandfather had done. But he left an inconclusive situation in the succession. Hatshepsut married her half-brother by her father and a concubine named Mutnofret. Her husband eventually became king under the name Tuthmoses II. When Tuthmoses II ascended to power the country was rich, powerful, exuberant, and imperial. Although he had to quell rebellions in Syria and Nubia, the two most worrisome states, Tuthmoses II can be said to have managed the affairs of state quite well. What he did not do, however, was manage the affairs of the succession. Like his father and grandfather, he left a seriously complicated situation when it came to the succession to power. Who would be king after Tuthmoses II? Would it be Tuthmoses' sister-wife, Hatshepsut, the child of Tuthmoses I by his queen, Ahmes?

The royal offspring of Tuthmoses II and Hatshepsut consisted of a daughter, Neferure. So when Tuthmoses II died Hatshepsut married her daughter Neferure to her stepson, Tuthmoses III, who was the child of Tuthmoses II by a concubine named Ausar.

The young boy was only six years old at the death of his father. Hatshepsut became the regent for the young king, ruling in his stead because of his youth. Evidence of the regency is found on a stele in the rock tomb of Inene of Amun on the west bank of the Nile at Waset. It reads:

> The King went up to heaven and was united with the gods. His son took his place as King of the Two Lands and he was the sovereign on the throne of his father. His sister, the God's Wife Hatshepsut, dealt with the affairs of the state: the Two Lands were under her government and taxes were paid to her.
>
> (Urk. IV 59, 13–60, 3)

Hatshepsut soon abandoned the pretext and had herself crowned as king. She had bestowed upon her the complete titulature of a Kemetic Per-aa. She was "Maatkare," meaning "Maat is the Ka of Ra." In addition, she was called "Khnemet Amen Hatshepsut," that is, "She who embraces Amen, foremost among women." Once Hatshepsut had usurped the crown, the young Tuthmoses III, who was about nine years old at the time, was no longer the co-regent. Hatshepsut ignored the young boy and acted as if Tuthmoses II, her half-brother to whom she was married, had never existed, and set about establishing a co-regency with her dead father Tuthmoses I.

Hatshepsut was as gifted as any man in Kemetic history at assuming the controls of government. She was not to be treated lightly because she did not tread lightly over the land. Indeed, her scribes incorporated her fabrication into the official documents of the country in such a way as to declare her "sa Ra," "the son of God."

During her reign she governed with the support of a strong inner circle that showed complete loyalty to her. One such person was Senemut. He had been born in humble circumstances in Armant and came to the attention of Hatshepsut as a mature individual. He was gifted as an architect, eloquent of speech, a master of political in-fighting with knowledge enough to protect the queen who was serving as king, and perhaps a very close personal friend. The gossip of the day was that he had an intimate relationship with the queen. One theory is that Senemut was responsible for educating Hatshepsut's only daughter Neferure. One of Senemut's brothers, Senimen, was the tutor, steward, and nurse for Neferure. Beyond this family connection many statues in Kemet associate Senemut with the queen. One might say that he was her male companion. As a cultured and educated man he was also able to understand the role she had to play when she donned the beard of a man as king on certain ceremonial occasions. A person who was both steward of the royal family and superintendent of the buildings of the god Amen had to be someone for whom the queen had high admiration. It is likely that Hatshepsut ensured her rule by choosing the wisest person she knew to be her closest counsel. In Senemut's tomb at Deir el-Bahri there are indications that he was an astronomer because of the astronomical drawings in the ceiling of the tomb. Also in the tomb at Qurna there are two drawings of the tomb, plans of the tomb itself, and copies of religious and literary texts including the *Satire of the Trades*, *The Tale of Sinuhe*, and *The Instruction of Amenemope I* (Hayes 1942). Indeed Senemut was the one responsible for transporting and erecting the *tekken* (obelisks) so famous during Hatshepsut's reign. Senemut planned the construction of Hatshepsut's mortuary temple at Deir el-Bahri and also planned a second tomb for himself in front of her temple. He already had a tomb for himself at Sheikh Abd el-Qurna. About the nineteenth year of Hatshepsut's rule Senemut disappears from the record. This was about three or four years before the queen herself died. It is not known whether the forces allied with Tuthmoses III, who was a young adult by this time, organized against Hatshepsut and her clique causing Senemut to choose sides, or whether he was dismissed by the queen, which is hard to believe, or died. What is clear is that Senemut had lost power and presence before the end of Hatshepsut's reign.

However, the royal entourage was not completely vanquished. There was still an important man by the name of Hapuseneb, whose mother Ahhotep was related to the royal family, who was a member of Hatshepsut's inner circle. He was responsible for carrying out the construction of the temple at Deir el-Bahri and was then made high priest of Amen. He was in such a high position that he was able to make his son the Scribe of the Treasury of Amen.

Hatshepsut had not been solely dependent upon Senemut, though it is true that he was a dominant figure in the court during his lifetime; there were others, including Nehesi, the chancellor, who had influence on the throne. In the ninth year of Hatshepsut's reign Nehesi had led an expedition to Punt (Somalia) in something of a revival of the Middle Kingdom tradition of sending expeditions to Punt for trade. It is credible to suggest that Punt also sent trading missions to Kemet although we do not have such records at the time. However, absence of evidence is not the same as evidence of absence. The expedition of Nehesi on behalf of Hatshepsut is recounted with great detail on the walls of a mortuary temple which is dedicated to the goddess Hat-heru (Hathor). Hatshepsut was also well served by the Chief Steward Amenhotep, who erected the two *tekken* at Karnak, and by Useramen, who was her vizier from the fifth year of her reign.

The achievements of Maatkare are not small. She remains the most dominant woman in antiquity in terms of her political and diplomatic achievements for her nation. As a woman serving as absolute ruler of a great country in antiquity she has no equal. She revived the foreign policy portfolio of the country, erected the most beautiful and powerful *tekken*, appointed a new Viceroy of Kush called Inebni to replace Seni, who had held the post since the time of Tuthmoses II, and defended the borders of the country.

A group of texts at the mortuary temple at the foot of the Deir el-Bahri cliffs, next to the mortuary temple of the great Eleventh Dynasty king Nebhepetre Mentuhotep II, contain representations of her as king. The text "Of the Youth of Hatshepsut" was both a political statement and a historical narrative. This text actually was reproduced by Tuthmoses III at Waset and in one scene it shows:

> Hatshepsut is enthroned by Atum and receives the crowns and royal titles. After being proclaimed king by the gods, she must still be crowned by mankind. Her human father, Tuthmoses I, introduces her to the royal court, nominates her and has her acclaimed as heir. As soon as her titulature has been announced she undergoes a further rite of purification.
>
> (*Urk.* IV 216, 1–265–5)

*Figure* 5.1 Temple of Hatshepsut, funerary buildings, Valley of the Queens
© Molefi Kete Asante

Hatshepsut reigned until 1458 BCE, which was the twenty-second year of the reign of Tuthmoses III. At that time he finally regained the throne. He would reign thirty-three more years. It is to be noted that although it was customary for succeeding kings to have their own names engraved over the names of their predecessors or to erase their predecessors' names altogether, never had the activity of erasing the memory of a predecessor been so furiously carried out as under Tuthmoses III.

Tuthmoses III became the greatest conquering king of the ancient world. He was the "Lion of Africa" so to speak, the king of all the kings, the master of the universe, and no king stood next to him as his equal.

It was as if he had been preparing all of his life to be king. The difficulties he had with Hatshepsut were experiences that would assist him in his dealings with foreign kings and internal political forces. The fact that he had watched from the sidelines, learned from the stories other members of the royal courts told of their travels and involvements with international affairs, gave him a vision that had rarely existed in Kemet. Tuthmoses III would exert the military might and mastery of Kemet in so deadly a fashion that the enemies of the nation would beg for mercy.

The first challenge to the new king was a revolt by the main Asiatic people united under the prince of Kadesh, who had the support of Mitanni. This was a powerful union threatening the hegemony of Kemet in southwest Asia, a land that had been subdued by Kemet since the time of Ahmose. Tuthmoses III immediately began a campaign to bring the wayward nations back under Kemetic authority. He had to make seventeen military campaigns into Asia in order to succeed. He finally pacified Kadesh. Mitanni is also call Hurrian and that civilization was contemporary with one called Kassite in Babylon. These were the remnant people when the Babylonian kingdom of King Hammurapi disintegrated after reaching its peak around the fifteenth century BCE.

Mitanni seems to have been the main instigator of conflict with Kemet. It was the chief power in the area but always kept Kemet embroiled in local disputes between the various Syrian city-states. Tuthmoses III had inscribed in the *Annals* in the Temple of Amen at Waset the stages of the conflict between Kemet and Mitanni. He launched a campaign to regain Retjenu. Accordingly he set out from the eastern Delta and went via Gaza to the plains of Megiddo by a narrow passage. He laid siege to the town for seven months until it finally fell into the hands of his soldiers. Heading toward Tyre he captured Yanoam, Nuhasse, and Herenkeru. He seized the wheat harvest of the plains of Megiddo and had it transported to Kemet. Each year he made an inspection tour of southwest Asia to ensure that they were paying their tribute and honoring his authority. He had a botanical wall painted at Karnak, a sort of sequel to the wall at the mortuary temple of Hatshepsut, where the flora and fauna of Punt were recorded.

About four years after he started his campaigns into southwest Asia he had to undertake a more extensive series of conquests. He conquered Djahy, the coastal plains of Palestine, the city of Kadesh again, Ullaza, and Ardata, destroying the wheat and orchards in the process.

The very next year the Kemetic army under the leadership of their war-king Tuthmoses III struck at Syria from the sea. They devastated the area, marching to Ardata to reconquer that city. It seemed to Tuthmoses III that the campaign in southwest Asia would have to be an annual affair since it had happened five times before. He resorted to a policy of taking the captive princes to Kemet for indoctrination. This was to be a policy used by many other African nations in warfare. In this the sixth campaign Tuthmoses III brought back thirty-six sons of kings. They were kept as hostages before being sent back to succeed to their fathers' thrones.

Even this practice did not pacify the lands. Several other campaigns had to be fought. He completely destroyed the city of Ullaza and occupied the ports of Phoenicia. He returned home and received an ambassador, according to the records, from an unidentified Asian country who came to pay homage.

As Per-aa Tuthmoses III probably believed that Hatshepsut had not paid much attention to the enemies gathering to compete with Kemet. This is why he felt a need to eventually confront Mitanni directly. His engineers found a reliable way to cross the Euphrates. They first hauled specially made boats across the desert, reached Mishrife (ancient Qatna) on the east side of the Orontes River, then headed to the Euphrates. He pillaged the area, defeated towns south of Carchemish, passed back over to the west and headed north on the Orontes to Niy, which would be the northern boundary of Kemet's influence from then on. Before returning to Kemet Tuthmoses III hunted elephants at Niy, as Tuthmoses I had done before him. He assured himself that the kings of Mitanni, Assur, and the Hittites would pay their tribute to Kemet.

Several more campaigns were launched against Mitanni. Perhaps the most important one was the sixteenth campaign, coming in the forty-second year of Tuthmoses III's reign. He seized the port of Arqata near Tripoli, destroyed the city of Tunip, took three cities around Kadesh, and wiped out a massive Mitannian army. After this battle there was a twelve-year gap in the war between Kemet and Mitanni. So great was the victory for Kemet, however, that Tuthmoses III received tribute from cities that had not even fought his army.

Tuthmoses III launched only one campaign southward into Nubia and this came near the end of his reign, in his fiftieth year (counting the years of Hatshepsut) as king. The aim of the campaign into Nubia was to reinforce Kemet's influence as far as the Fourth (Third) Cataract. Already the relationship between the Nubians and Kemetic people had been one of integration, assimilation, confederation, separation, conquest, and appeasement. It was like the history of the modern nations of Africa or Europe that have had border disputes going on for scores of years. The oldest known text from the massive Nubian temple complex of Gebel Barkal dates from the forty-seventh year of Tuthmoses III.

While it is true that Tuthmoses III was the greatest military leader in history at this point he was not only a mighty soldier who led his armies in battle; he was also a remarkable builder. During his last years Kemet was at peace with most of its neighbors and the king devoted much time to pursuing the projects that his predecessors had started. When Tuthmoses I reigned he had his architect Inenem initiate a reconstruction of the Temple of Amen at Waset. Tuthmoses III took up this work, adding to the Temple of Amen and erasing as much as he could of the image and name of Hatshepsut in the massive temple complex. To condemn her to oblivion seemed to be his intention, by keeping the monuments that she had built but hammering out her name so that one could not tell who was responsible for an edifice. No fate, not even death, is worse than this for a Kemetic person.

Of course, since she was a prolific builder Tuthmoses III was not able to destroy all references to her. For example, her name is found at Armant in the Temple of Montu as well as in Beni Hassan, where she had dedicated a rock temple to the goddess Pakhet, whom the Greeks called Artemis (their goddess of hunting). At the temple to Pakhet, Hatshepsut had listed the names of the buildings which she dedicated to the gods, the temples at Cusae, Antinoe, and Hermopolis, a chapel dedicated to Hat-heru at Faras, a temple at Buhen, a temple of Satis and Khnum at Elephantine. Tuthmoses III was just as prolific, building in Kemet and Nubia with a flurry of activity in honor of the gods.

Tuthmoses III wanted to avoid all disputes of succession and so appointed as his successor his son Amenhotep II, by his second wife Hatshepsut II Merire.

Tuthmoses III soon became legendary. He had already been large but in death he became even larger, a person for whom myths were made; a man whose deeds and monuments would have ensured immortality gained even more from his creativity, love of botany, literary ability, and love of knowledge. His intellectual gifts were more durable than buildings. He was well educated, read the ancient texts, revived the tradition of piety for the ancestors. He compiled a list of his ancestors at Karnak and his care of their monuments suggests the piety of a man who knows his place in history and sees himself as being counted among the ancestors also. Indeed, Tuthmoses III's vizier, Rekhmire, is considered one of Kemet's most honored intellectuals. His tomb has both literature and the decorative arts, fitting accoutrements for a man who served such a giant figure.

Yet, of course, Tuthmoses III's military feats are awesome. His crossing of the Euphrates became a legend among Kemetic military officers. They were fascinated by his ability to make the proper boats to cross the river and to do it without the Mitanni king knowing that they would drag them across Syria. This was a backdrop for the story of the taking of Joppa by the famous general Djehuty which appears in Papyrus Harris 500. It describes how Djehuty killed the prince of Joppa (modern Jaffa), who had come on a diplomatic mission, and then captured the city of Joppa by slipping 200 soldiers inside the city hidden in baskets. Elements of this African story were to appear in subsequent legendary exploits of Darius and the taking of Babylon, Homer's tale of the Trojan horse in the *Iliad*, and Ali Baba and the Forty Thieves in the *Arabian Nights*. The fact that Djehuty is less remembered has more to do with the writing of history than with the great distance between us and his exploits.

Aakheperure Amenhotep II, who had served with his father as co-regent for the last days of his life, was a young man of a strong physique. It is said that no soldier could bend his bow. He was not shy about his physical strength, demonstrating on every possible occasion how fit he was to be Per-aa of Kemet. Unlike his father he was no intellectual; he was a sportsman, an athlete with the ability to please the crowds because of his control of his body. He made sports a major part of the decoration of tombs that came after him. Other kings would have paintings of themselves shooting birds, fishing, or running. Nevertheless he quickly established his prowess by leading a campaign against the Syrians in his third year. He personally captured and later killed seven princes of Kadesh in front of the Temple of Amen-Ra in Waset, and had some of their bodies displayed on the walls of the two most important military cities in his empire, Waset and Napata, the latter city located in Nubia. Rarely had Kemet seen such utter brutality on the part of its Per-aa.

Amenhotep II soon learned that he would have to test his strength again against the Syrians. In two further campaigns he sought to destroy the resistance to the Kemetic empire in Syria. The battles took place on the heights of Niy in the seventh and ninth regnal years as a result of a revolt in Syria started by the town of Carchemish. In the end Kemet lost the region between the Orontes and Euphrates rivers, although the texts describe the abundant booty that was gained from the adventures. Indeed among the prisoners of war were 3600 Apiru, an ethnic group distinct from the Shosu Bedouin, who were enumerated in the text separately. Apiru appear in Cappadocia in the nineteenth century BCE and in Mari and Alalakh in the eighteenth century BCE. Nicolas Grimal (1992, p. 219) says:

> They [Apiru] are synonymous with the Hebrews mentioned in the Amarna correspondence; by Amenophis [Amenhotep] II's time they seem to have become integrated into the societies to which they had emigrated, playing marginal roles as mercenaries or servants, as in the events described in The Taking of Joppa. In Egypt they appear during the reign of Tuthmosis III as wine-makers in the Theban tombs of the Second Prophet of Amun Puymre and the herald Intef.

After Amenhotep II's disastrous showing against Mitanni, Kemet reached an accord with the Mitannites, who were now threatened from the Hittite empire under Tudhaliyas II. Kemet kept parts of the Palestinian coast and Mitanni kept the northern part of Syria. Amenhotep II took the hand of the daughter of the king of Mitanni in marriage, sealing the union between the two states.

At the death of Amenhotep II the crown passed to Tuthmoses IV because of the premature death of his elder brother, who would have been the real heir. Tuthmoses IV had a stele made at the Great Sphinx (Harmachis) to commemorate an unusual act of piety when he was a youth. He loved to hunt and one day he was hunting near the Great Sphinx, which was buried under the sand. He lay down to sleep and when he awoke he saw the outlines of the Sphinx under the sand. According to the text:

> He discovered the majesty of this venerable god who spoke to him as a father speaks to his son: "Look at me, gaze upon me, Tuthmoses my son.

It is I, your father Harmachis-Khepri-Ra-Atum. I will give you my kingdom on earth at the head of all that live; you will wear the white crown and the red crown on the throne of Geb as heir; the country will belong to you in its length and breadth, as well as everything that is lit by the eye of the universe ...See, my condition is that of a sick man, for my body is totally ravaged. The desert sand on which I stand is engulfing me."

(Zivie 1976, pp. 130–1)

Tuthmoses IV reverently removed the sand from the Great Sphinx and in return he became the king of Kemet, rising to the throne that he had not expected. His reign lasted for only nine years, for he died at the age of 30. However, one interesting fact is that Tuthmoses IV was active in the area of Men-nefer and not so much in Waset, the central region of Eighteenth Dynasty activities. After all, the chief nobles and intellectuals were buried in Waset and had their activities in that region. The vizier Amenemope and his brother Sennefer, the Mayor of Waset, Kenamun, the Steward of the Royal Palace at Men-nefer, his brother Kaemheryibsen, the Third Prophet of Amen, the Chief Priests of Amen, Meri and Amenemhat, the Chief of the Granaries, Menkheperraseneb, and the Royal Scribe Userhat all had their tombs and monuments in Waset. However, the young king constructed a temple in the vicinity of the Sphinx and left a deposit containing a *shenu* (cartouche) in the temple of Ptah at Men-nefer.

The death of Tuthmoses IV brought to the kingship Amenhotep III, one of the most refined of all Per-aas. Kemet reached its zenith in terms of culture and refinement, receiving once again imports of ideas, concepts, and products from its southern neighbor Nubia. Amenhotep III was the son of Tuthmoses IV by a concubine named Mutemwia. When he reached the throne as king he was only 12 years old and his mother served as his regent. In the second year of his reign, when he was 14, he married a woman of non-royal blood, Tiye, who was to exert more power and influence than any woman in the history of Kemet, with maybe the exception of Hatshepsut, who was herself a king. Tiye was the daughter of a man of some distinction named Yuya and his wife Tuya. They would also become a significant part of Kemetic history. Like other examples in early African history we already see the relationship between men and women as cooperative rather than as dominating. This is not seen at this time in any other civilization. Yuya and Tuya assisted one of their sons, Ay, in becoming king after Tutankhamen. However, in all of the activities of the court, Queen Tiye played a steadying role in securing power. She bore six children for Amenhotep III. The first, probably called Tuthmoses, died in youth; then came the future Amenhotep IV as well as four daughters, two of whom (Satamen and Ausar) were given the title of queen. In the end, Queen Tiye would be the wife of a king, the mother of a king, the grandmother of a king, the sister of a king, and the mother of two queens. Never in history had a woman stood in such a powerful position in the halls of power. In some respects Queen Tiye was a tremendous influence on the Eighteenth Dynasty because of her character, her strong personality, and her intimate knowledge of the royal court, but she was also influential because she lived a long time and was able to maintain her influence over the royal house despite the fact that Amenhotep III brought many concubines from Asia. Queen Tiye was the first person to really exploit the role of the royal wife (the King's Great Wife: *ḥmt nsw wrt*), which superseded the term 'queen mother' (*mwt nsw*) as the traditional indication of matriarchy.

Amenhotep III was at peace with the world, having only to make one campaign to put down a revolt. Kemet was appreciated all over the world and the name of Amenhotep III has been found in texts and on monuments in Crete, Mycenae, Anatolia (Turkey), Aetolia, Yemen, Babylon, and Assur. The king was the greatest builder the country had ever seen until this time. He covered Kemet and Nubia with monuments, including a temple with a colonnade dedicated to Tuthmoses III at Elephantine, and built a temple to Amen "Lord of the Ways" at Wadi es-Sebua and the temple of Heru at Aniba. Many other temples were established by Amenhotep III in Men-nefer; at Saqqara he started the Serapeum to the sacred Apis bulls; he raised colossal statues of baboons at Abydos, ordered the building of the Luxor temple as the southern harem of Amen-Ra, and established at the temple of Mut of Asheru to the south of the Karnak temple a garden of 600 statues of the goddess Sekhmet. Many of these statues are on display at Luxor Museum, the British Museum, and the Louvre. I have personally seen the one located in the shrine to Sekhmet at Karnak and have imagined the awe that must have come over the people when they saw all 600!

The only substantial remains of Amenhotep III's mortuary temple are the two colossal statues called the Colossi of Memnon that originally stood in front of the pylon to the temple. It is not known exactly why the Greeks many years later chose to call these statues Colossi of Memnon when in fact they were colossi of the great king Amenhotep III himself. Some have claimed that it was because when the Kemetic people said that the name of the statues was "Nebmaatre," the visiting Greeks heard it as "Mimmuria" and they related it to the name of the hero Memnon, Ethiopian, who was son of Aurora (the dawn) and commander of the Ethiopian troops in the Trojan War who was killed by Achilles. Who else could it have been for the Greeks? They were in Africa, the people they saw looked just like other Africans, and for them these had to be images of an Ethiopian. Memnon was an African and so here in Kemet the Greeks mistook the statues of Amenhotep III for Memnon. Since that time these great colossi of the majestic king have been called the Colossi of Memnon. In 27 BCE an earthquake created a fissure in the blocks which caused a whizzing sound every morning as the moisture that had built up in the fissure during the night was evaporated by the sun. Years later the Roman emperor Septimus Severus as an act of respect tried to repair the fissure. Since that time the colossi have not spoken; it could be said that he sealed the tongue of the whistling colossi.

Amenhotep III's fascination with imports from Asia, whether concubines or religious ideas, may have laid the foundation for the waywardness of his son Amenhotep IV. A preoccupation with Heliopolitan (Onian) theology by Amenhotep III may have been the instigator for the new emphasis on Aten.

Since the priests of Heliopolis had wavered in their own convictions in order to please the king, the gods of the East, particularly Ishtar, Mithra, Varuna, and Indra, were received with tolerance on the part of the religious leaders of that powerful center. It may have been a political move on their part, since the strength of the priesthood of Amen-Ra at Waset was unquestioned and held political sway over the country by virtue of its close relationship with the kings of the Eighteenth Dynasty. The only way that Heliopolis could reassert itself was through pleasing the fantasies, avocations, interests, and curiosities of the king.

It is reported that one of the greatest pleasures of Amenhotep III was sailing with Queen Tiye in his boat, *The Splendor of Aten*, on the artificial lake in his palace grounds. So the name of the deity Aten appears in the reign of Amenhotep III years before Aten would be elevated by the king's son as the sole god. The father obviously had opened a door that he would not be able to shut before his death. His death would leave the door ajar and his son, Amenhotep IV, carrying out his own agenda, would enter the door of no return.

The rise of Amenhotep IV (1370–1352 BCE) to the seat of power as the wealthiest and most feared of all kings was to precipitate a downward spiral leading to disaster for the royal family and confusion for the Kemetic people. His coronation name was Neferkheperura, meaning the "transformations of Ra are beautiful," and he added to this title the epithet *wa-n-ra*, meaning the "unique one of Ra." Thus, the young king came to his position with promise and enthusiasm but was immediately confronted with political and theological decisions that would have a lasting impact on history. Already in Men-nefer and Waset there were rumblings among the priesthoods concerned about Asiatic gods in Heliopolis, money being spent on the restoration of sanctuaries and shrines at Heliopolis, and the construction of the Serapeum, intended to contain the remains of the Apis bulls, at Saqqara. The royal centers of Waset and Men-nefer seemed destined to be ignored by Amenhotep IV as they had been under his father, Amenhotep III. But the priests, particularly the priests of Waset, were not without considerable power of their own.

In his second year Amenhotep IV changed his religion and his name. While Amenhotep signifies "Amen is satisfied," the king changed his name to *Akhenaten*, which means "Glory to Aten." He had unleashed a heresy at the door of heaven. In a thousand years or maybe two thousand years no Kemetic king had ever challenged the ruling theocracy so frontally. Furthermore, he married his cousin Nefertiti, the daughter of Ay and Tiye II, the granddaughter of Yuya and Tuya. Some have suggested that she was really Tadukhipa, the young woman sent by the Mitannian king to marry Amenhotep III, but he died before the nuptials could be celebrated and she changed her name and was wedded to Amenhotep IV. There is no evidence to support this often repeated suggestion. Nefertiti went with him to many religious ceremonies depicted by the artists in intimate family settings on the walls of the temples and in tombs of what is called the Amarna (Akhetaten) period. Of course, in the Great Hymn to Aten we see the king alone, knowing the sole god Aten.

Here I give an extract from the "Great Hymn to the Aten", which is found on the west wall of Ay's tomb in el-Amarna. Some have compared it to Psalm 104, but of course it was written long before the Psalms.

When you set in western lightland,
Earth is in darkness as if in death;
One sleeps in rooms, head covered,
One eye does not see another.
If they were robbed of their goods,
That are under their heads,
People would not remark on it.
Every lion comes from its den,
All serpents bite;
Darkness hovers, earth remains silent,
As their maker rests in lightland.
Earth brightens when you dawn in lightland,
When you shine as Aten of daytime;
As you banish the darkness,
As you send your rays,
The Two Lands are in festivity.
Awaken they stand on their feet,
You have roused them;
Bodies cleansed, dressed,
Their arms adore your appearance.
The entire land sets out to work,
All beasts graze on their herbs;
Trees, herbs are sprouting,
Birds fly from their nests,
Their wings greeting your ka.
All flocks alight on their feet,
All that fly and alight,
They live when you dawn for them.
Ships sail north, sail south as well,
Roads lie open when you rise;
The fish in the river dart before you,
Your rays are in the midst of the sea.
Who makes seed grow in women,
Who creates people from sperm;
Who feeds the son in his mother's womb,
Who soothes him to still his tears.
Nurse in the womb,
Giver of breath,
To nourish all that he made,
When he comes from the womb to breathe,
On the day of his birth,
You open wide his mouth,
You supply his needs.

When the chick in the egg speaks in the shell,
You give him breath within to sustain him;
When you have made him complete,
To break out from the egg,
He comes out from the egg,
To announce his completion,
Walking on his own legs.

(Asante and Abarry 1996, pp. 76–7, trans. M. K. Asante)

Akhenaten was almost reckless in the way that he built temples in honor of Aten at Karnak. They were subsequently torn down by the people in an act of religious fervor and bitterness against the intrusions of the priests of Aten. Evidence of these small sandstone blocks used by an unskilled work-force appears in the discovery of *talatat* (Arabic for the decorated blocks). They were crudely decorated in a lively style. Although the king was himself the chief architect, his chief sculptor was named Bek. Akhenaten carried out his plans in spite of warnings, expressions of concern, and actual apprehension on the part of his royal court. There was a reason for the worry.

The High Priests of Waset, Her and Suti, were the most powerful officials in the land. They held in their stores much of the wealth of the empire. They were the keepers of the people's dreams, memories, secrets, and wishes for eternal life. Nothing could be more shattering to Her and Suti than a Per-aa who refused to honor Amen-Ra. What could have been in the mind of the young king, since it was Amen-Ra who had made the Eighteenth Dynasty great and had been the god of Ahmose and all of his descendants? Why would not the king serve and honor He who had made all things possible? Indeed, Amenhotep III, his father, when he could not find relief from his illness from the Heliopolitan priests and the gods of Asia, went to the priests at Karnak and proposed to enlarge the temples and add to the shrines in honor of Amen-Ra. The Mitannian king, Tushratta, had sent him a stone image of Ishtar to assist in his health. He had sought to enlist divine power in the battle against his illness since his first *sed* festival in the thirty-fourth year of his reign. The scenes on the walls of the temple at Soleb and those in the Wasetian tomb of Kheruef, Steward of the King's Great Wife, show Amenhotep III as weak and feeble. In fact, Amenhotep III ruled in his last years with his son as co-regent. Amenhotep IV did not really become king in his own right until around 1378 BCE.

But if the father had shown trust in the priests of Amen-Ra, why would the son be so opposed? Could it be that the son believed that the priests of Waset failed his father in his time of greatest need? Was it possible that the king resented the political and economic influence that Her and Suti had over the royal court? We will never know for certain but one thing we do know, because of the records, is that Akhenaten sailed downstream from Waset with his royal entourage and established a new city for the Per-aa: *Akhetaten*, meaning "Horizon of Aten." It was built in a rather inhospitable spot in Middle Kemet. The king had his builders erect temples to Aten, whom he worshipped in opposition to the powerful Wasetian deity, Amen-Ra.

The fact that Akhenaten celebrated and worshipped Aten to the exclusion of other gods has won for him the accolade "the father of monotheism." But this is a misunderstanding of the nature of Kemetic religion. Actually it would be better to suggest that Aten was the individual deity selected by Akhenaten as his sole god. It was not that the Kemetic people believed in several supreme gods, because they did not. The names of the supreme were many, but the idea was one god. So what did Akhenaten add to this idea of religion? He made Aten as the sun the actual deity. This was not the first sun deity in the religion of Kemet. In fact, Ra and Atum were much older as sun gods, but they were different aspects of the same force. However, the Kemetic people did not see the sun as an actual deity; they saw the sun as representing the supreme deity. This is the difference between Aten and Ra. One was the actual sun disk and its rays and the latter was the conceptual idea of the sun as the mighty giver of life, health, and prosperity. So for Akhenaten the Aten as the sun was to supplant Amen-Ra.

Akhenaten spared no vigor in attacking Amen-Ra. He had the name of the god chiseled out of every monument where it was written; even where the name of Amen occurred with the old name, Amenhotep, it was erased. The fury with which he assaulted the name of the mighty Amen-Ra, who had been the principal deity of Kemet, was exceptional and difficult to explain except in political terms. He wanted to break the ironclad hold that Her and Suti had on the country. They dictated how much wealth they needed to carry out their roles of dispensing food and materials to the masses and they wanted a king who cajoled them, honored their work, and respected their role as the keepers of the traditions.

In Waset, although as Per-aa he was chief priest, he would have to depend upon the high priests for information, political support, and spiritual advice; but here in Akhetaten, near the modern village of el-Amarna, he was the major priest and prophet of the new deity. Yet it became increasingly clear that this fanatical heresy initiated by Akhenaten and supported vigorously by his wife, Nefertiti, would create an equal resistance in the priesthood of Amen-Ra.

Queen Tiye, a woman of considerable political acumen, tried to mediate between her son and the priests of Waset. After all, life in the desert was much different from that in Waset or Men-nefer. The idea of her son going against the traditions of his ancestors did not sit well with her, but even more he was without the support of the elites of Waset in the case of war with Kemet's enemies. The schism brought so much acrimony and so many he-said-she-said accusations that Queen Tiye, who held a moderate and practical view of the Atenist controversy, probably believing that it was all right for Akhenaten to explore it himself but that he should not have attacked Amen-Ra, kept up her efforts to bridge the theological gulf.

In time the king was made to relent by the economic pressures brought upon him and his entourage located in the desert. With his wealth running out, the priests of Amen-Ra controlling the gold supply, and his health unstable, Akhenaten was eventually forced to abandon his pipe dreams. At Waset, Her and Suti maintained the daily religious functions of the great *ipet-sut* (Karnak) temple complex and waited for the acquiescence of the king. How could Akhenaten hope to prevail against the implacable belief of the high priests that their position was supported by two thousand years of theological and philosophical doctrine? Indeed, the heresy attacked the very soul of the cultural and political foundation upon which the Kemetic civilization rested. Where was the trinity of gods in the Atenist's construction? At least the ancient texts and the oral narratives underscored the importance of maintaining Maat: order, balance, harmony, justice, righteousness, truth, and reciprocity. To unsettle the spirit of Maat was to strike at the very heart of the nation.

According to the record, Akhenaten, his body exhausted by the heat of the desert and the greater heat of growing resentment and resistance from inside the royal family, sent his son-in-law Smenkhara to Waset to discuss the terms of capitulation (White 1970, p. 172). Compounding the tragedy that had been set in motion by Akhenaten's decision, his wife Nefertiti, along with their son Tutankhaten, moved to the outskirts of Akhetaten to a place called the "Fortress of Aten" and soon disappeared from the historical record. One of her daughters, Meritaten, took her place alongside the king in depictions of ceremonies. All the while Kemet was losing its Asian empire as kings revolted with no resistance from the Kemetic palace, and other political activities unfolded outside of the ear and eye of the pious Akhenaten, such as when the prince of Kadesh captured most of Syria, the prince of Amurru captured Phoenicia, and the Palestinians took on Megiddo and Jerusalem. Bit by bit Kemet lost its eastern buffer zone while its king, sedated by religion, wrote poetry to Aten.

Scholars have discovered a cache of letters called the *Amarna Letters* that show that neither Akhenaten nor his father Amenhotep III understood much about foreign policy. Amenhotep had inherited an empire at its height but did nothing to sustain it and passed it on to his son, who opted out of the political sphere to the extent that he alienated his leading citizens and refused to engage with the international crises that developed during his tenure as king. Furthermore, a state of near famine existed near the end of Akhenaten's rule and it might be said that he paid limited attention to the infrastructure of the country, the irrigation canals, the Nilometers, the dams, and the building projects outside of Akhetaten. He would be reviled by some of the Kemetic people as "the great criminal of Akhetaten." It is ironic that some historians have seen him in better light than the people who lived during his time.

Akhenaten and Nefertiti had six daughters. It is not clear whether Smenkhara and Tutankhaten were actually their sons, nephews or only sons-in-law. The record is inconclusive on this point; however, we believe that it is possible that they were the direct descendants of Akhenaten and Nefertiti. Akhenaten sent Smenkhara to Waset to search for a way back to the capital city. From wall paintings in the tomb of Merire at el-Amarna where the king is face to face with Smenkhara in his twelfth regnal year one could assume that there was a co-regency at this point. We do know that both Smenkhara and Tutankhaten married daughters of Akhenaten, making them sons-in-law.

This would mean that they married their own sisters, which was not so rare among the royal family as to be considered outrageous.

Smenkhara became king upon the death of Akhenaten and served only two years, probably only a few months as the sole king. He was 20 years old when he died. Like his father he was buried in Akhetaten, although once there was harmony between the royal family and Waset Smenkhara's body was reburied in the Valley of the Kings.

Tutankhaten was nine years old when he gained the regency. Queen Tiye was influential in getting him married to Ankhesenpaaten. Soon thereafter the royal family transferred to the royal residence at Men-nefer. In addition, he established temporary residence in Waset at the palace of Malkata. Akhetaten was abandoned by the king and remained in existence only to house and keep those older members of Akhenaten's entourage who would not have been welcomed in Waset or Men-nefer. The whole heretical plan, from the drawings of the city plans to the abandonment, was less than thirty years.

When the young king Tutankhaten (the living image of Aten) was brought before the priests of Amen at Waset his name was changed to Tutankhamen, "the living image of Amen." Guided by the Divine Father Ay the young king prostrated himself before the god Amen and then issued an edict restoring the worship of Amen for the royal family. His repentance for his father was extensive and seen in his works. He built a tomb for himself near his grandfather Amenhotep III, erected two lions of Amenhotep III at Soleb, added buildings to the temple of Amen at Karnak, and began work on his mortuary temple at Medinet Habu. After a reign of only nine years, the young king died, the last descendant of Ahmose.

Ay, the trusted vizier of Tutankhamen, became king and served for four years before he died.

At this juncture in the history of Kemet it was a military man, Horemhab, who stepped forward. He had been the chief of the Joint Chiefs of Staff, so to speak, under Tutankhamen. Having become knowledgeable of the world in his post he had also been a spokesman for the government of Ay. He had made a diplomatic mission to Nubia that resulted in the prince of Miam (Aniba) coming to see King Tutankhamen at his court. He had also been by the side of King Tutankhamen when he undertook a "show-the-flag" tour of Palestine. So Horemhab, although not a royal himself, had associated enough with the royal family to be next in line for the rulership of the country.

As the restorer of established order Horemhab sought to live up to his royal titulature. His Heru name was "Powerful bull with wise decisions." His Golden Heru name was "He who is satisfied with Truth and who causes the Two Lands to increase." His Two Ladies name was "With countless miracles in *ipet sut*."

Horemhab built at Medinet Habu, dedicated a rock temple to Amen and Djehuty at Gebel el-Silsila, erected buildings in Men-nefer and at Heliopolis, and devoted enormous energy to reasserting the importance of *ipet sut* (Karnak). For him it was truly the "most sacred of places." He then moved to decentralize government. He issued a decree that was engraved on a stele at Karnak to restore order to the nation. He corrected injustices, appointed judges and regional tribunes, and restored the local religious leaders to their places of importance. Legal authority was equally shared between Waset and Men-nefer. He reinstituted the national army in two parts, one in the south and one in the north, as had been done before the Amarna disaster. His tomb is in the Valley of the Kings. Since he had no male survivors the kingship went to another general, an elderly man from the Delta named Ramses. He had served with Horemhab and would begin a new dynasty, the Nineteenth.

## The Nineteenth or Ramessid Dynasty

Ramses I served as king for two years only. During this time he sent his son Seti I (1318–1298 BCE) on a mission to Nubia, continuing the policies of outward vigilance begun by his predecessor. With the death of his father Seti I ascended the throne of the Two Lands.

Seti I proved to be a forceful and brilliant leader. He dealt firmly with revolting nations in Asia and opened the trade routes for Kemetic traders and merchants. In one of the most creative campaigns of any army in antiquity he moved on the Amorites, Arameans, and Hamathians by dividing his army into three sections: the Army of Ra, the Army of Seth, and the Army of Amen. As his enemies were moving rapidly to join and form one powerful army, Seti I's forces severally met the enemy and defeated them. He reasserted Kemet's control over the Syrian plains and Palestine. His major architectural contribution was the temple of Ausar at Abydos although he also did work on the massive hypostyle hall at Karnak, continuing the work done by his father, Ramses I.

Ramses II, the Great (1298–1232 BCE), was probably the greatest Per-aa in history. He was magnificent as a builder and a commander-in-chief, bringing glory to Kemet far beyond its borders and beyond his lifetime. To understand Ramses II it is important to know that he ruled for a very long time, perhaps the second longest reign of any Per-aa. This gave him the opportunity to choose what he wanted to do, how he would do it, and how it would be explained in history. If it were necessary to rewrite history, Ramses II would rewrite it. He was a prodigious father with more than 50 daughters and 100 sons. Indeed, he executed everything on a large scale. He was the first man to build a temple for a woman who was not a god. He built a temple at Abu Simbel for his favorite wife, the Nubian beauty Nefertari ("The most beautiful one among them all"), besides his own temple to Amen, Ptah, Atum, and himself. One writer says this about Ramses: "He was a lavish usurper of the buildings of his forerunners and an untiring fabricator of obelisks and colossal statues" (White 1970, p. 177). His prenomen was "*usermaatra-setep-n-ra*," meaning "Maat is the strength of Ra, chosen by Ra."

Everywhere in Kemet the evidence of Ramses II is before your eyes. Some historians speak of his self-glorification because of the size of his contributions and his obviously forward way of promoting his deeds. But all monuments of kings reflect their self-glorification. It is likely a fact that since Ramses II lived longer than most he had more time to write inscriptions, to erase some of his predecessors' writings, and to have many scribes willing to do his bidding.

*Figure 5.2* Temple at Abu Simbel
© Molefi Kete Asante

Just four years after he came to power he led a mighty force into Palestine to break the stalemate that existed between the Hittite and Kemetic powers. It had gone on for a decade. Muwattalish had organized a "coalition of the willing" made up of twenty nations. Ramses II marched in front of his army with great confidence as he set out to teach them a lesson. Taking a page from his father, Seti I, Ramses II dispatched his army in four corps. Ramses II himself headed the column of the Army of Amen. He was followed at a distance of 5–10 miles by the Army of Ra, and this corps was followed at a distance by the Army of Ptah, and then it in turn was followed at a distance of some miles by the Army of Seth, bringing up the rearguard.

Ramses II took the Army of Amen across the Orontes River and encamped just outside Kadesh. The Hittites, observing the scattered Kemetic forces, stole around between them in the middle of the night. When the Army of Amen forded the river the next morning they met a brutal reception from the Hittites. Many of the soldiers broke and ran for Kadesh. Ramses II found himself confronting a superior enemy with only a part of his army. The Army of Ra could add only a little to the morale of Ramses' forces. Of course, the Armies of Ptah and Seth were hopelessly too far back and on the wrong side of the river to add anything to the battle.

Realizing the situation, Ramses II regained his composure, ordered his troops to positions with coolness, demonstrated his own courage in battle, and managed to make an excellent fight of the situation. Neither side gained a decisive advantage although the Kemetic forces did maintain their positions. Ramses was hardened by this battle. He led a massive army through

Canaan and marched north into Naharina, an area that the Kemetic army knew well because they had fought well there during the Eighteenth Dynasty.

Ramses II had re-created the boundaries established by Tuthmoses III, heretofore the greatest conquering king of Kemet. This made Ramses II feel that he had finally made a place in history for himself, one similar to what Tuthmoses III had achieved. There would be other battles but the continuing struggle with Asia would occupy the mind of the king for many years. In fact, both the Hittites and the Kemetic people had to look warily at the Assyrians, who were gathering strength. Actually when the first great warrior king of Ashur, Shalmaneser I, overran Mitanni and reached the Euphrates, Ramses and the king of Hatti, Hattushilish III, united against the common enemy.

In one of the first treaties of alliance in military history, the Hittite king sent a silver tablet to Ramses in 1277 BCE offering to swear to eternal peace, to trade prisoners, and to come to each other's assistance in the case of foreign aggression. The terms of the treaty were inscribed on the walls of Karnak and at the Ramesseum. For fifty years the treaty between the two great powers held up and kept peace in southwest Asia. It only came apart when the two old kings were too weak to check the unbridled swashbuckling of new immigrants coming across the plains from the Black Sea region.

When the great king died his thirteenth son, Merenptah, came to the throne. However, the Nineteenth Dynasty came to a pathetic end with about five coups d'état or usurpations of the crown. In the end, the Ramessid Dynasty, so much dominated by the powerful Ramses II, had spent its energy in maintaining the image of power but disintegration was already at the gates. It would take a massive reconstruction of buildings, irrigation canals, and sacred shrines as well as a military campaign against the various rebellious regions of the country to keep it from total disorder.

## The Resurgent Kingdom

### *The Twenty-fifth or Southern Dynasty*

Piankhy, the Mighty, descended upon Kemet from his base in Nubia to restore order and balance, to meet the challenges of rebellion, and to reassert the power of Amen in Kemet. He initiated the Resurgent Kingdom and established the famous Twenty-fifth Dynasty of kings coming from Nubia up around the Third Cataract (the Fourth by European historians) along the River Nile. His main city was Napata, located in Nubia. From this city he ruled over Nubia and Kemet. In the twenty-first year of his reign he would confront the final challenge to his authority over the land. A king in the north of Kemet would seek to exercise his own dominance over the Nile Valley. When Tefnakht, lord of Sais in the Delta, started a campaign to gain control over his neighbors in the north as a way of exerting influence in the Nile Valley to prevent Piankhy's advance, he courted great danger. Thus, in 730 BCE, when he had annexed Tanis and Bubastis, fortified towns of the eastern Delta, gained the allegiance of the rulers of Hermopolis and Herakleopolis and turned toward Upper Kemet, he was to meet Piankhy's generals. Defeated and disenchanted, the forces of Tefnakht ran for refuge to

Hermopolis, which was besieged by the Nubian army. Tefnakht himself escaped and fled northward.

Piankhy decided to take things into his own capable hands. In passing through Waset he celebrated the great Festival of the New Year and the Festival of Opet at Karnak and asked for the support of Amen, Mut, and Khonsu as he made his way north. Piankhy, one of the best strategists and most gifted warrior kings in Kemet's history, met Tefnakht's allies and lieutenants at Hermopolis and they surrendered. There was no method so effective to secure acceptance of power as the string of victories Piankhy brought with him. Peftjauawybastet of Herakleopolis, without waiting for battle, surrendered his town to the Nubian-Kemetic king and conceded with a speech that made history. He said in effect:

> Hail to you, Heru, mighty king,
> Bull attacking bulls!
> The netherworld seized me,
> I foundered in darkness,
> But it was you who gave me the rays of his face!
> I could find no friend on the day of distress,
> Who would stand up on battle day,
> Except you, oh mighty king,
> You drove the darkness from me!
> I shall serve with my property,
> My life is because of your dwelling;
> You are Horakhty above the immortal stars!
> As he is king so are you,
> As he is immortal you are immortal,
> King of Upper and Lower Egypt, Piankhy ever living!
> (Lichtheim 1980, p. 73)

It was not unusual for the Nubians to be praised for their brilliant archery and horsemanship. The name of Kush, their specific country, was often called Ta-Seti (The Land of the Bow) because of the military skills of the Nubians. The generalship of Piankhy himself was unquestioned. It may be that there were some people who were deceived by the accoutrements of power presented by Piankhy when he marched triumphantly into the various towns, but there was no intent to deceive them about the nature of his love for the Nile Valley civilizations. He had come to relieve the burdens which his brothers and sisters had been unable to remove with all of their efforts. He had come as a monarch seeking to raise the people from any form of servility. His speeches given to the elites of the towns, the priests and scribes of the courts and temples, were short and to the point, often flying like darts, shooting out toward the enemies of Egypt. But over all, Piankhy was less of a speaker than a doer.

In the next few weeks Piankhy marched further north, receiving surrender after surrender, until he arrived at Men-nefer, where Tefnakht had reassembled a few forces. The great king besieged the city with siege towers, and when the city fell the coalition that supported Tefnakht surrendered and fell on their faces before the mighty conquering king. Piankhy, grateful for his victory over the coalition, turned to Heliopolis, where he celebrated the ritual in honor of Ra as a reenactment of his own coronation. The text says:

> His Majesty went to the camp on the west of Iti. His purification was done: he was cleansed in the pool of Kebeh; his face was bathed in the river of Nun, in which Ra bathes his face. He proceeded to the High Sand in Heliopolis. A great oblation was made on the High Sand in Heliopolis before the face of Ra at his rising, consisting of white oxen, milk, myrrh, incense, and all kinds of sweet-smelling plants.
>
> Going in procession to the temple of Ra. Entering the temple with adorations. The chief lector-priest's praising god and repulsing the rebels from the king. Performing the ritual of the robing room; putting on the *sedeb* garment; cleansing him with incense and cold water; presenting him the garlands of the Pyramidion House; bringing him the amulets.
>
> Mounting the stairs to the great window to view Ra in the Pyramidion House. The king stood by himself alone. Breaking the seals of the bolts, opening the doors; viewing his father Ra in the holy Pyramidion House; adorning the morning bark of Ra and the evening bark of Atum. Closing the doors, applying the clay, sealing with the king's own seal, and instructing the priests: "I have inspected the seal. No other king who may arise shall enter here." They placed themselves on their bellies before his majesty, saying: "Abide forever without end, Horus beloved of Heliopolis!"
>
> Entering the temple of Atum. Worshipping the image of this father Atum-Khepri, Great One of Heliopolis.
>
> (Victory Stele 101–6, trans. Lichtheim 1980, p. 77)

When the jubilee was over and the ceremony concluded, various rulers and religious officials came to pay tribute to Piankhy. Osorkon IV of Tanis came, and so did Prince Pediese of Athribis, who carried with him all his earthly possessions as tribute to the Per-aa. All came but Tefnakht, who had once again escaped from Men-nefer. He did send a message to Piankhy hoping for negotiations. This is what the renegade leader of the north wrote to the great king:

> "Is Your Majesty's heart not cooled by the things you did to me? While I am under a just reproach, you did not smite me in accordance with my crime. Weigh in the balance, count by weight, and multiply it against me threefold! But leave the seed, that you may gather it in time. Do not cut down the grove to its roots! Have mercy! Dread of you is in my body: fear of you is in my bones!
>
> I sit not at the beer feast; the harp is not brought for me. I eat the bread of the hungry; I drink the water of the thirsty, since the day you heard my name! Illness is in my bones, my head is bald, my clothes are rags, till Neith is appeased toward me! Long is the course you led against me, and your face is against me yet! It is a year that has purged my *ka* and cleansed

your servant of his fault! Let my goods be received into the treasury: gold and all precious stones, the best of the horses, and payment of every kind. Send me a messenger quickly, to drive the fear from my heart! Let me go to the temple in his presence, to cleanse myself by a divine oath!"

His Majesty sent the chief lector-priest Pediamen-nest-tawy and the commander Purem. Tefnakht presented him with silver and gold, clothing and all precious stones. He went to the temple; he praised god; he cleansed himself by a divine oath, saying: I will not disobey the King's command. I will not thrust aside His Majesty's words. I will not do wrong to a count without your knowledge. I will only do what the King said. I will not disobey what he has commanded. Then His Majesty's heart was satisfied with it.

(Victory Stele 101–6, trans. Lichtheim 1980, p. 77)

Few Per-aas received as many gifts as Piankhy from his defeated enemies. While it is true that some of the statements of conceding may have been his foes' way of protecting their own heads, Piankhy was revered and honored by many people in the Nile Valley. In a show of magnanimity Piankhy reappointed four of the chiefs as governors but chose to deal only with Nimlot because he was circumcised and clean. This is the way the text reads:

At dawn of the next day there came the two rulers of Upper Egypt and the two chiefs of Lower Egypt, the uraeus wearers, to kiss the ground to the might of His Majesty. Now the kings and counts of Lower Egypt who came to see His Majesty's beauty, their legs were the legs of women. They could not enter the palace because they were uncircumcised and were eaters of fish, which is an abomination to the palace. But King Nimlot entered the palace because he was clean and did not eat fish. The three stood there while the one entered the palace.

Then the ships were loaded with silver, gold, copper and clothing; everything of Lower Egypt, every product of Syria, and all plants of god's land, Punt. His Majesty sailed south, his heart joyful, and all those near him shouting. West and East took up the announcement, shouting around his majesty, this was their song of jubilation:

> "Oh mighty ruler, oh mighty ruler,
> Piankhy, mighty ruler!
> You return having taken Lower Kemet,
> You made bulls into women!
> Joyful is the woman who bore you,
> The man who begot you!
> The valley dwellers worship your mother,
> She is like the cow that bore the bull!
> You are eternal,
> Your might abides forever,
> Oh ruler, loved of Waset!"

(Victory Stele 147–59, found in Lichtheim 1980, p. 80,<br>retranslated by M. K. Asante)

His victory over Tefnakht is described on a stele (found by Said Pasha in 1862) established at Gebel Barkal at the temple of Amen. The text was a confirmation of Piankhy's power over Upper and Lower Kemet. A description of the Per-aa's conquest is quite eloquent and sounds like a royal recitation in the classical sense where the phrases are reminiscent of the ancient literary texts which were in the library at the temple of Amen at Gebel Barkal. The king had copies of this text placed at Waset in the sacred chambers of Karnak and at Men-nefer, but only the Gebel Barkal text has survived the ravages of time.

> His Majesty wrote to the counts and generals who were in Egypt, the commander Purem, and the commander Lemersekny, and every commander of His Majesty who was in Egypt: "Enter combat, engage in battle; surround it, lay siege to it, capture its people, its cattle, its ships on the river! Let not the farmers go to the field, let not the ploughmen plough. Beset the Hare nome; fight against it daily!" Then they did so.
>
> Then His Majesty sent an army to Egypt and charged them strictly: "Do not attack by night in the manner of draughts-playing; fight when one can see. Challenge him to battle from afar. If he proposes to await the infantry and chariotry of another town, then sit still until his troops come. Fight when he proposes. Also if he has allies in another town, let them be awaited. The counts whom he brings to help him, and any trusted Libyan troops, let them be challenged to battle in advance, saying 'You whose name we do not know, who musters the troops! Harness the best steeds of your stable, form your battle line, and know that Amen is the god who sent us!'
>
> When you have reached Thebes [Waset] at Iput-isut, go into the water. Cleanse yourself in the river; wear the best linen. Rest the bow; loosen the arrow. Boast not to the lord of might, for the brave has no might without him. He makes the weak-armed strong-armed, so that the many flee before the few, and a single one conquers a thousand men! Sprinkle yourself with water of his altars; kiss the earth before his face. Say to him: 'Give us the way. May we fight in the shade of your arm! The troop you sent, when it charges, may the many tremble before it!'"
>
> (Victory Stele 8–14, trans. Lichtheim 1980, p. 69)

There was a long tradition of piety for Amen among the Nubians. In fact, it is believed that the earliest recognition of Amen was in Nubia. Certainly we know that the first elements of the monarchy were found in Nubia long before we have this evidence in Kemet proper. So Piankhy was clearly concerned about the lax manner in which his Kemetic neighbors were practicing the religion devoted to the Hidden One. The temple of Amen at Gebel Barkal was one of the largest temples in the Nile Valley. It was as distinguished in Nubia as Karnak was in Kemet. A succession of kings had ruled from Napata under the watchful eye of Amen. The royal priests of Amen in Gebel Barkal had been influenced by the traditions left by Tuthmoses III, to be sure, but they were also originators and initiators of their own rituals and ceremonies based upon the history of their people.

Piankhy did not materialize out of thin air to be king. The first named king of this region of Nubia, often referred to as Kush, was Alara. History records at least six kings, who are not named, before him in Napata. One could conceivably date the Napata Dynasty back to the tenth century BCE if one estimates each reign to be about twenty years. Some kings ruled more and some ruled less. Alara himself ascended the throne in 780 BCE. We know more about his brother, Kashta, who came to power in 760 BCE.

Kashta was a conquering king, extending the rule of Kush at least to the modern town of Aswan at the Sixth Cataract (First by Europeans), and maybe even to Waset. There is definitely a stele dedicated by him to Khnum at Elephantine. We also know that when Kashta became Per-aa he took the coronation name Maatre.

Kashta had several children. Two of his sons, Piankhy and Shabaka, ascended to the throne. Piankhy married the daughter of Alara and came to power in 747 BCE. His immediate goal was to extend the power of Kush throughout the entire Nile Valley down to the Mediterranean Sea.

In his ten years as Per-aa over the combined kingdom, Piankhy changed the landscape of the politics of Nubia-Kemet, the combined empire. He had set out from Napata, with the blessings of the priests of Amen at Gebel Barkal, with the fervor of a campaigner, the inheritor of the Waset spiritual tradition, to institute a rearmament program for Amen. To do this he would need to recall the advice of the high priests of Amen at Gebel Barkal to "go with Amen." Kemet and its customs were not unfamiliar to Piankhy; after all, his father Kashta and uncle Alara had both visited upon Upper Kemet the wrath of Kush.

Piankhy overran Waset, defeated Iuput I, and took the city under his protection and named his daughter Amenirdis I the Divine Adoratrice of Ipet Isut under the direction of Shepenwepet I. In this action he took control over the temple complex, giving the Nubians direct authority in matters of religion.

Preferring to rule from the cosmopolitan city of the south, Napata, Piankhy returned to his capital city in Kush and ruled from there as the paramount king, the king of kings, the lord of lords, the mighty Per-aa over Nubia and Kemet. Speculation has been made that Piankhy would have felt out of place in Men-nefer or Waset, but nothing could be farther from the truth. At this moment in the Nile Valley history the food of the two people was the same, the dress was virtually the same, the religion was the same, the script was the same, the relatedness to the continent of Africa was the same, and the people were more alike than not in their appearance, countenance, rituals, music, and dance. In fact, the similarities between the two African neighbors were as close as those between modern Germany and France. Indeed, perhaps closer if you take into consideration that most Germans are Protestants and most French are Catholics. Both Nubia and Kemet, at this time in history, were under the powerful influence of the priests of Amen. Given this situation it was not unusual or strange for the great king to want to rule from the familiar surroundings of his beautiful city in Nubia. Politically it might have been a mistake, because even with his garrisons and the army fortresses manned in the Delta the distance to the Delta from the south was very great for communication.

Soon the irrepressible chief Tefnakht, as wily as ever, was back in the business of building his power base. With Piankhy safely ensconced in his capital city of Napata, working with remnants of the Libyan dynasty that ruled in Kemet Tefnakht became the undisputed heavyweight king of the Delta. His son Bocchoris succeeded him (some claim this as the Twenty-fourth Dynasty). Briefly between Piankhy and his son Shabaka there existed the rule of Tefnakht and Bocchoris, but this interjection was not to last. When Shabaka learned that Bocchoris was moving toward Middle Kemet from his fortifications in the Delta he captured the northern king and then, to make an example of him, burned him alive, indicating that he would not be as lenient as his father Piankhy had been with those who challenged Nubian power.

Establishing his capital city at Waset, Shabaka began the restoration of the temple buildings, adding to them, improving the grounds of Ipet Isut, and demonstrating his own piety and solemnity. Shabaka's rule was distinguished by nationwide renovations of temples and putting down the occasional rebellions in the Delta. When he died he was succeeded by his son Shabataka, who ruled for ten years, but it was his nephew Taharka, a son of Piankhy's, who was the real power behind the scene. The young prince Taharka marched into Palestine to meet Sennacherib's Ashur army, a growing challenge to Kemet. The defeat of Ashur was overwhelming although some have claimed that Sennacherib's forces were decimated by a pestilence. This may be true, but it is nevertheless also true that the mighty machines of war brought into Palestine to meet the army of Ashur were awesome and the Nubian-Kemetic army under the generalship of one of the most skillful military leaders of ancient Kemet showed bravery and courage in conquering a dangerous enemy. Sennacherib's sons murdered their father in 690 BCE. This was the year that Taharka came to power as Per-aa in Kemet. It is believed that Taharka had Shabataka assassinated, believing that the he was ill-prepared to defend the country and unable to marshal the forces necessary for the defense of the homeland.

When Taharka (690–664 BCE) assumed the reins of government as the Per-aa, he set out to remake the empire as it had been under Mentuhotep, Tuthmoses III, and Ramses II. It would once again be the nation that all others feared and respected. This was not some mad fantasy of the king but a concrete plan since he knew from experience that it was possible to extend the northeastern boundaries to the Orontes River and the southern boundaries to the junction of the Blue and White Niles.

Taharka's coronation as king shows his proud attitude. He arranged for his mother to travel almost 1200 miles (1930 kilometers) from Napata to Men-nefer in the north of Egypt for his coronation. This is about as far as from New York to Chicago. She made the long trip to the ancient capital of northern Egypt and saw her son on the throne of Egypt. According to historical inscription, "She rejoiced exceedingly after beholding the beauty of His Majesty Taharka ... Crowned upon the throne of Upper and Lower Egypt."

To protect the Delta and the eastern regions of the country, Taharka established a capital city at Tanis as well as preserving his right to Men-nefer, Waset, and Napata. He kept up supplies to his allies in Palestine against the interests of Esarhaddon, the new king of Ashur. In Waset, the seat of real spiritual and religious power, he appointed Mentuemhat as governor and insured that he also had an appointment as a priest of Amen. The priests of Amen were not supposed to be involved in civil matters, but the fact that Mentuemhat was both a civil and a religious figure meant he could participate in both. Taharka put governors at Men-nefer and Napata as well. Soon the kingdom of Kemet had reasserted its authority and influence over a wide area of Africa and Asia. North Africa and southwest Asia were both under the authority of the Nubian Per-aa, who was the mightiest king on earth when he ruled the Nile Valley.

The Assyrians were on the rise in the east, sacking town after town, while Taharka was encouraging his allies in Palestine to bolster their defenses. In 671 BCE, Esarhaddon decided to invade Kemet directly. Instead of stopping at the fortified capital of Tanis the Assyrian army attacked the historic city of Men-nefer, captured Taharka's family, and escaped back to Asia. Meanwhile Taharka was able to take most of his troops to the south, moving all the way up to Napata to avoid the Assyrians. The Assyrians forced many of the Delta princes to take Assyrian names and to rename their towns with Assyrian names. Neko, the chief of Sais, one of Bocchoris' sons, had to perform this ignoble act.

It did not take the military genius Taharka long to plot his return to Men-nefer. He swooped down on the city, his troops going overland and down the river in multicolored boats flying the colors of the mighty gods of Amen, Ra, and Atum, and defeated the Assyrians, routing them from their hold on the town. When Esarhaddon heard the news that Taharka had reasserted his control over the town he sent reinforcements to Kemet. The king himself was leading the charge until he was struck down with some mysterious illness and died *en route* to battle.

Taharka also revived literature and poetry. One source gives information about Taharka's personal style and temperament. According to the source, Taharka once had his soldiers race through the desert at night for a distance of 30 miles; this race was longer than the Greek marathon, which is 26 miles. Taharka's race took five hours. He rode alongside the runners on horseback. Then, at the end of the race, he rewarded both winners and losers!

When Taharka's tomb was excavated, researchers found more than a thousand small statues called *shawabtis*, funerary statuettes, which are suppose to serve a dead person in the afterlife. A huge pyramid marks Taharka's burial place at Nuri.

One of Taharka's great-grandsons was a king named Aspelta. He ruled from 600 BCE to 580 BCE, after Nubia and Egypt had been defeated by the Assyrians. Aspelta's brother Anlamani ruled before him, from 620 to 600 BCE, but Anlamani could not control the incursions, or small-scale invasions, of other nations into the land. Aspelta had long disputed his brother's accession to the throne and seemed eager to take the throne for himself instead. Although there is not much historical evidence to tell us about Aspelta and Anlamani, it seems that Aspelta was the greater king. One indication that Aspelta was a great king is his tomb at Nuri, which contained many luxury items. Unlike many of the graves at the Nuri cemetery,

Aspelta's was not completely robbed. Many works of art, precious metals, vases, and alabaster boxes were still in his tomb when it was found. Aspelta seems to have been a powerful and wealthy king, but like his brother Anlamani, his armies were eventually defeated. Nubia was no longer a major factor in the political equation in the Mediterranean world.

By 666 BCE Ashurbanipal, the king of Assyria, led an army as far south as Waset. He pillaged towns and cities, took the wealth of temples, over-turned statues and stelae, and occupied the major cities of the country. Mentuemhat was able to diplomatically save Waset from the sword. But two years later, upon the death of Taharka, the Assyrians came again into the country as Ashurbanipal sought to put down any rebellions against his authority. Tanutamen led the armies of Nubia and Kemet against the Assyrians on this occasion. A third invasion by Ashurbanipal destroyed the remnants of the Twenty-fifth Dynasty and Kemet's Fourth Golden Age, after the Old Kingdom's Pyramid Age of the Third and Fourth Dynasties, the Middle Kingdom's Golden Age of the Twelfth Dynasty, and the New Kingdom's Restoration Age of the Eighteenth and Nineteenth Dynasties had come to an end. The Resurgent Kingdom's light, which shined so brightly on the world, was finally snuffed out.

The succeeding dynasties were little more than rehearsals for the final end of one of the greatest civilizations of antiquity. Increasingly Kemet faced enor-mous pressure from outside its borders and the rebellious territories it once controlled were now empires in their own right. Other more distant nations saw Kemet as the prize fatted calf to be captured and used for royal banquets. With its wealth, history, literature, culture, and stores of exotic goods and products, Kemet remained even in its waning days a nation that others envied.

So it was that the country under the princes of Sais, so-called Saites, lost prestige and power in the ancient world. Psammetichus I and his son Neko (609–594 BCE) had pursued a policy of extending the boundaries of Kemet into Asia again, only to find that it was not as easy as it had been in the days of Tuthmoses III and Ramses II. In fact, the armies of Kemet fought on the side of the Assyrians under their last emperor Ashuruballit II against the Babylonians under Nabopolassar and the Medes under Cyaxares. The Kemetic army fell upon King Josias of Judah, who was an ally of Babylon, killing him and wiping out his forces. They installed Joachim in Josias' place and moved on to subdue Syria. Neko must have felt that he was the reincarnation of Tuthmoses III for a while, but only too brief a while because the forces of Kemet met the army of the young heir to the throne of Babylon, Nebuchadnezzar, in 605 BCE, at Carchemish and were destroyed by the young Babylonian.

Neko retired to the Delta region and concentrated the rest of his reign on the affairs of Kemet. He dispatched a group of enterprising Phoenicians in his service on a mission to explore trade routes around the coast of Africa. J. E. Manchip White writes, "The mariners appear to have accomplished the periplus or circumnavigation of the entire African continent, an enter-prise which took them three years" (White 1970, p. 199). He constructed an overland route between the Mediterranean and the Red Sea.

Psammetichus II came to power after Neko and ruled for six years from 594 to 588 BCE. His reign was not remarkable for any major achievement. Since the seat of power was now in the Delta Psammetichus II sent an ill-fated expedition, under Amasis, a future Per-aa, to Upper Kemet and Nubia to subdue the population.

The next king was Apries, who ruled from 588–568 BCE. Almost immediately he sent ships and troops to blockade Tyre and Sidon in Phoenicia. It was during this time that the Jews were led off to captivity in Babylon. Some escaped to Kemet and were settled as far south as Elephantine.

Apries lost his kingship to Amasis because of a military intervention in a dispute between some Greek colonists of Cyrene and Libya. The expeditionary force was defeated and Kemet was enraged at the Per-aa. After political wrangling for two years, Amasis was chosen to be the Per-aa. His reign was prosperous and he had pretty good relations with the growing Greek colony in the north. The presence of the Greeks in the north would eventually come to haunt the country but during this period Amasis saw the Greeks as necessary supports for the trade missions across the Mediterranean Sea.

Amasis was confronted with a new power, Persia. He aligned Kemet with Nabonidus of Babylon and Croesus of Lydia to stop the advance of Persia and Mede. In the Peloponnesus, Sparta and Samos, the eastern Greek island, joined in league with smaller city-states to oppose the Persian-Medean juggernaut. None of this could stop the advance of Cyrus and his Persian army. He had turned against his Mede overlord Astyages and now controlled both aggressive military machines. Cyrus defeated Nabonidus and Croesus and left Kemet without any credible allies. It could only await its fate. Cyrus would be followed to the throne of Persia by Cambyses.

Persia invaded Kemet in 525 BCE, becoming the third force, after the Hyksos and the Assyrians, to invade the Nile Valley from outside. At the time of the attack Psammetichus III had been Per-aa for only about a year. It was an unfortunate time for him because the Persians annihilated the Kemetic forces on sea and land. On the sea the Kemetic commander of the fleet betrayed the defense preparation of the Per-aa and delivered up ships to the enemy. When Men-nefer fell to the conquerors, Psammetichus III committed suicide rather than be ruled by the Persians.

Cambyses initiated a new dynasty, the Twenty-seventh Dynasty, and Persians sat on the seat of Heru. Following all of the rites and ceremonies, Cambyses adopted many Kemetic traditions and customs. He made a special pilgrimage to Ipet Isut at Waset and went as far upstream as Elephantine. He tried to go to Napata but was prevented by the armies of Nubia; Cambyses then left the Nile Valley. Darius I came to Kemet in 518 BCE to put down some unrest that the Persian governor in charge could not handle or had handled ineptly. Darius ordered a temple to be built in honor of Amen-Ra at el-Kharga Oasis in the desert. He imitated the Per-aas and completed Neko's canal between the Mediterranean and the Red Sea.

Kemet proved difficult to govern from abroad and a succession of Persian kings had to come to the Nile Valley to quell disturbances. Darius was defeated at Marathon around 491 BCE and Xerxes arrived in Kemet to wave the big stick of Persian might for all of those who seemed to dislike the rule of the outsiders.

The last native Kemetic dynasty was the Thirtieth Dynasty (378–341 BCE). It was led by Nectanebo (378–361 BCE), who regarded himself as an inheritor of the virtues of the goddess Neith. He would be succeeded by Teos (361–359 BCE). Both would try to lessen the dependence on Greek mercenary soldiers although by this time there was a strong reliance upon these mercenaries since the Delta princes had found it increasingly difficult to count on the southerners coming to defend them. Nectanebo almost lost the kingdom when Syria marched on Kemet just as he was trying to rid the country of the Greeks. Teos wanted to use the Greek mercenaries but he wanted them to be in subordinate positions in the army. He took 80,000 Kemetic troops, 10,000 Greek troops, and a thousand or so Spartan troops to take Syria. On the battlefield, Teos' brother deserted him and went back to Kemet, where he proclaimed himself Nectanebo II.

On a persistent downward spiral now, Kemet was headed for disaster. Nectanebo II held the Persians at bay for nine years and finally in 341 BCE, after being deserted by his Greek mercenaries, was defeated by the Persians. The last Kemetic king had passed from history.

The succeeding years would see brutality on a massive scale against the Kemetic people. Artaxerxes III Okhos (341–338 BCE) was probably a maniac; at least, he operated as if nothing and no one mattered except his own personal desire to see everyone who did not bow to him killed. He organized an army of 300,000, which he sent into the Nile Valley to destroy, rape, pillage, and steal. During the rule of Artaxerxes III and his son, Oarses (338–335 BCE), Kemet was subjected to the harshest rule the people had ever seen. Such terror, looting, and wanton brutality had never been witnessed in the Nile Valley, a valley well acquainted with conquerors. At length, a eunuch named Bogoas poisoned both Artaxerxes and Oarses. He then offered the throne to Darius III Codoman (335–332 BCE), who accepted and quickly rewarded Bogoas by forcing him to swallow poison that he had made himself.

It would now be Alexander the Macedonian who would enter the picture in Kemet after having destroyed Darius at Persepolis and eliminating the Persian hegemony. He would turn his full attention to Kemet. Bringing an end to Persian rule in Kemet, Alexander appointed his general, Ptolemy, as the leader of the country. Alexander himself would worship the god Amen and ask the Oracle to make him the "son of Ra," which is the same thing as the son of God. He would become, like all Per-aas, a divine ruler as the son of Ra and the incarnation of Heru.

Alexander would leave Kemet and die at Babylon of typhoid fever. Alexandria, a city erected around the ancient town of Rhacostas, would be dedicated to him. In time writers would claim that the Greeks built Alexandria, when in fact it had been a famous trading and temple center long before the expansion that was called Alexandria.

Ptolemy, son of Lagus, who called himself "Soter I," that is, "savior," became the founder of the Greek Dynasty in Kemet. Ptolemy II Philadelphos (285–247 BCE) may be singled out as one of the important rulers of the dynasty because he was the builder of the Pharos in Alexandria and a patron of the library. Ptolemy III Euergetes (247–222 BCE) led a couple of military campaigns but his reign is most famous because of the terrible famine that occurred in Kemet while he sat on the throne. Another Greek Per-aa, Ptolemy V Epiphanes (209–182 BCE), was responsible for trying to restore some of the ancient temples, hoping to reclaim the glory and the magic of a Kemet long before his time. More than a hundred years later, in 51 BCE, Ptolemy XIV ascended to the throne with his sister and wife Cleopatra VII Philopates (glory to her father). They were the children of Ptolemy XII Nothos, who himself was the son of Ptolemy XI by a concubine. Ptolemy XII married Cleopatra V, his sister. Cleopatra V died of complications of childbirth soon after the birth of Cleopatra VII.

Increasingly Rome was asserting its authority throughout the region. Thus, the team of Ptolemy and Cleopatra served essentially as puppets under the protection of the Roman Senate. Pompey, the great Roman general, was appointed as overlord. At length, Ptolemy quarreled with Cleopatra and had her banished from power. Pompey, defeated in battle at Pharsalia, escaped to Egypt and was murdered by Ptolemy XIII. Soon Julius Caesar brought a massive army to Egypt to reassert Rome's power and to avenge the death of the brilliant general, Pompey. Ptolemy XIII for his part was drowned fleeing from Caesar. Cleopatra was restored to power and Caesar appointed Ptolemy XIV, who was only eleven years old at the time, as her co-regent. Caesar was 52 and without an heir when he met the young queen, and from their union a child was born by "Caesarian" section and named Ptolemy XV Caesarion. Then in 45 BCE Cleopatra had Ptolemy XIV poisoned and her own son, Ptolemy XV, by Caesar elected to the co-regency. She lived openly with Caesar in Rome and her statue stood in the Temple of Venus in Rome. When Caesar was killed on the Ides of March, Cleopatra fled Rome and headed to Egypt. Two years later she found Mark Antony charming and took him as her lover. He left his first wife Fulvia in Rome and had three children by Cleopatra. They were called Alexander Helios and Cleopatra Selene, twins, and Ptolemy Philadelphos. Mark Antony married Octavia, the sister of his rival Octavian, just as Cleopatra was giving birth to their third child in 36 BCE. It should be pointed out that Cleopatra Selene went on to become Queen of Armenia, Media, and Parthia. She married Juba, the King of Numidia, a gifted ruler, and was named Queen of Mauritania.

The story of Cleopatra's death is one of myth and legend. It was first recorded by Plutarch, who was born 75 years after the death of Cleopatra. In his account, Plutarch lays down the story that was to become standard after Shakespeare's theatrical version. The account says that when Mark Antony had been defeated by Octavian, Cleopatra sent the conqueror, the future Emperor Augustus, a sealed letter which he opened immediately. She asked him to allow her to be buried with Antony. Interpreting this as a suicide note, Octavian sent his guards to Cleopatra's chamber, where she was under house arrest, and they discovered Cleopatra, lying on a golden couch in her royal robes, and her two maids, Eiras and Charmion, dead or dying from the bites of a snake that had been smuggled into her chamber in a basket of figs. It is quite possible that this story from Plutarch and the words of Octavian are mythical. In fact, it is inconceivable that a single snake could have killed all three women within the time frame that was given by Octavian and his men. Supposedly the guards immediately rushed to the chamber once the suicide note was received, only to find the women dying. Normally if one is bitten by a cobra, the snake represented by the uraeus symbol of Egypt, it would take about two hours to die. Also the snake would not necessarily be able to produce three successive attacks where enough venom is produced to kill someone. It is possible but not probable. So what is the truth of this situation? It appears that Octavian was the only one who had a vested interest in the death of the queen. It is likely that he had her killed and then staged the story of her suicide pact with Mark Antony. Soon after Cleopatra's murder, Octavian had her son Caesarion put to death.

Mark Antony lost the battle of Actium in 30 BCE; he was dead and so was Cleopatra and her heir, so Octavian could claim the title "Emperor Augustus" and bring Egypt, which had long been under the influence of Rome, into the empire as a province. One group of interlopers in Africa, the Greeks, had been replaced by another group of interlopers, and the masses of African people suffered under the repression and oppression of Rome as they had under the power of the Ptolemies.

## Part III

# The moment of realization

"The river crosses the path. The path crosses the river. Which is older? The river is from long ago." (Okomfo Anokye)

# 6 The emergence of the great river kingdoms

Nothing so accurately describes African geography or topography as the term "awesome." As the Sahara is the largest desert in the world and the rainforest the second largest in the world, the rivers of Africa are enormous and powerful as they drain and replenish the continent. Africa is as much a river reality as it is a desert or savanna reality, in the sense that rivers provide food, homes, and transportation for millions of people on the continent. Africa can boast of two of the ten longest rivers in the world, with the Nile being the longest.

There are hundreds of rivers crisscrossing the continent. Some are long, others are short, but all are rivers with history surrounding them. One can speak, for example, of the River Tano in Ghana with all of its symbolism for the Akan people. Among them it is a historic and sacred river. The River Pra, where Osei Tutu I met his death at the hands of the Akyem, is also a river sanctified by ritual and myth. There is the Limpopo River, known for the many wars fought on its banks as the twentieth-century African revolutionaries crossed into South Africa from Zimbabwe to fight against apartheid. The Senegal River is infamous as the first river the Portuguese crossed in their quest for enslaved Africans. In every country in the tropical region of Africa there are numerous rivers used for transportation and fishing. Many African people are known as river dwellers. In fact, there is an ethnic group that is referred to as Ijaw, sometimes called "Rivers" people. In Benin, there are people who build their houses on stilts on the small streams that drain into the Atlantic Ocean. The streams and rivers have always served as transportation routes. In fact, Gloria Chuku says in her book *Igbo Women and Economic Transformation in Southeastern Nigeria, 1900–1960* that "traders were able to move around, far and wide, with their merchandise mostly by canoes on the waterways (Chuku 2005, p. 45).

Africa has five great rivers: *Congo*, *Niger*, *Nile*, *Orange*, and *Zambezi*. The largest rivers rise in the highlands and plateaus of central Africa and flow hundreds of miles to the sea. These rivers and their tributaries comprise a massive drainage of the continent and are navigable on the plateaus and in the coastal lowlands. I will discuss each river in alphabetical order.

## The Congo

The Congo River flows northward across the equator and then heads southwest, crossing the equator a second time before emptying heavily into the Atlantic Ocean. From its origins in the highlands of southeast Congo to its outlet into the sea the river is 2720 miles long. Actually this is the eighth longest river in the world, the second longest in Africa, second only to the incredibly long Nile.

The flow of the Congo is principally through the Democratic Republic of Congo, although it also flows through the Central African Republic, Zambia, Angola, Cameroon, and Tanzania. It is a powerful river, ranging in width from 0.5 to 10 miles depending on when and where you see it. I once stood on its broad banks outside of Kinshasa and could not see the other bank. The river looked like a magnificent lake but it was moving like a river!

Some geographers suggest that the Congo starts at the Chambeshi River. If one takes that as the origin then the river would be 2900 miles long. However, most writers have accepted the idea that the river forms at the juncture of the Lualaba and Luvua Rivers. The Congo flows northward towards Malebo Falls, called by the Belgian colonial government "Stanley Falls" after a white explorer.

The river runs past Kisangani and then takes on a counter-clockwise course toward the Atlantic Ocean. It feeds a river basin that covers over 1.6 million square miles. The Congo can dispose of 1.2 million cubic feet of water per second. The river and its tributaries flow through the second largest rainforest in the world; only the Amazon rainforest is larger. The river also has the second largest flow and the second largest watershed of any river.

Imagine a river with 4000 islands! The great Congo also has fifty islands that are at least 10 miles long. About 250 miles of the Congo are not navigable because of the presence of the numerous islands and some cataracts such as the Livingstone Falls. These beautiful waterfalls are named for the Scottish missionary David Livingstone. Of course, they had a name before Livingstone. These deep canyons create a powerful energy that causes the river to rush rapidly down past the cities of Matadi and Boma and into the ocean at Muanda. When European sailors first saw the drainage of the Congo as they sailed down the west coast of Africa they were startled by its great and massive thrust into the ocean.

Many of the massive rivers of the world are fed by tributaries. This is true in the case of the Congo, into which numerous rivers pour their water along its hundreds of miles journey. This means that the river has become the most important transportation source in the central part of Africa. For thousands of years people have been able to travel the Congo for nearly 2500 miles and then other tributaries for thousands of miles more. The Ubangi River, a huge river itself, is the major tributary but it is also joined by the Lomami, the Aruwimi, and the Kasai. Taken together, that is, the Congo and its tributaries, the transportation system accounts for 10,000 miles of navigable routes throughout Central Africa connecting people to far distant populations and ideas. Stretched out, these miles would represent a distance three times as long as the distance between Anchorage,

Alaska, and New York city. What an incredible natural gift to the African continent, whose people have used these waters from the earliest times!

The Portuguese sailor Diogo Cão visited the mouth of the Congo in 1482, the same year that the Portuguese began to build their fortress at Elmina in what is today called Ghana. Indeed, other Europeans followed Cão years later. The English sent an expedition up the river as far as Isangila in 1816. The American Henry Morton Stanley was the first European to navigate the river to its source and to discover that the Lualaba was not the source of the Nile as had been thought by some Europeans.

Despite the fact that the Congo is such a heavily used river, it remains one of the purest of the world's major rivers. There are two main reasons for this situation. In the first place, the river remains relatively unpolluted because there are no massive industrial or chemical sites along its length feeding it with industrial waste and sewage. Second, the river is not polluted by agricultural irrigation because it is unnecessary in this region of the world.

It is not clear how the political officials of the two Congo nations will view the river in the future, but the idea of a clean river, one not degraded by industrial or human pollution, is one that should be encouraged. Although it is pristine by the standards of other rivers, the Congo will remain a major source of transportation for the foreseeable future for much of the trade of the region, including sugar, coffee, cotton, copper, palm oil, and various and numerous fruits and vegetables.

Humans have occupied the region of the Congo River for thousands of years. However, it was with the rise of the Congo kingdom from those who had settled along the banks of the rivers that we get the first real empire in the region. The Congo Kingdom lasted for nearly one thousand years, perfecting its system of governance and creating uniquely beautiful art out of its own cosmology. It was not until the arrival of the Portuguese in 1483 that the Congo experienced a contest for its land and authority in the central region of Africa. Its dominance as a power, both ideologically and militarily, had been neither questioned nor challenged by any other power until the Portuguese opened up the slave trade. Within two hundred years of dealings with the Portuguese, the Congo Kingdom was a weakened, ruined empire, only a shell of its former self. It broke into warring factions in 1665 following battles with European forces that had managed to challenge the authority of the king, infiltrate agents into the royal house, and create internal turmoil among the subjects of the kingdom.

This was the river of the Congo Kingdom.

## The Niger

The mighty Niger, the most storied river of West Africa, drains five nations. More than twenty different ethnic groups depend upon this river for food, water, and transportation. It is the principal river of the western part of the continent, running for over 2500 miles, challenging the Congo in length. It is the third longest river in Africa, exceeded only by the Nile and the Congo. The Niger River runs through Guinea, Mali, Niger, Benin, and Nigeria in a huge arc from the highlands of Guinea until it finally discharges into the

Gulf of Guinea at the massive delta known as the Oil Rivers, a mere 1000 miles from its origin. The main tributary feeding the Niger is the Benue River, itself a major source of food and transportation.

The Niger River starts just 150 miles from the coast of the Atlantic but runs away from the coast to the northwest and into the Sahara Desert, passing Bamoko and Timbuktu, only to make a giant turn to the southeast in its dash to the Gulf of Guinea. The course of the river has been known by traders and fishermen for hundreds of years but Europeans entering West Africa were baffled by the river that ran to the desert. Ancient Romans believed that the river was a part of the Nile, a sort of western branch of that river. Some other Europeans were sure that it flowed to the west to join the Senegal River and pour out into the Atlantic Ocean on the western side of Africa.

It is believed by scientists that the Niger River was originally two rivers. The upper Niger, from the source in the Guinea highlands to the bend at Timbuktu, is one river and the river from Timbuktu to the delta, the lower Niger, is a second river. The scientists say that the upper Niger once flowed into a lake near Timbuktu which has now disappeared. The second part of the current river is said to have started from the lake and rushed southeast toward the sea. As the Sahara dried up around 6000–1000 BCE the two rivers altered their courses and joined each other.

No river bend has ever been as significant as the Niger River Bend. It was the focus of the great civilizations of Mali, Gao, and Songhay and many lesser civilizations. Since it is the closest water source to the Sahara Desert the Niger River Bend became the main focal point for many cultures, the meeting of east and west, north and south, and the central market area for regional businesses. Thus, the Niger River Bend was and remains a key trading area for the lucrative business along the Niger.

The word *Niger* is thought to originate with the Tuareg (Tamaschek) language *gher n gherem* with the meaning of "river of rivers." For a long time some writers have thought that the word came from the Latin word for "black." It is now accepted that the name of the river had a more indigenous origin.

The ancestors of many Africans say, "Where there is a river, there is abundance." While this may be an overstretched proverb, it is definitely the case with the Niger. River traffic carried timber, rubber, palm products, and imported goods from one town to the next. The Niger has remained a lifeline for the people of the region. During the rainy season the heavy rains in the highlands of Guinea feed the river and it swells until it reaches the flat expanses of the Malian savanna. Here there are often floods and the waters spread out into numerous connected streams forming many lagoons. Africans speak of this as the "inland delta" because of the freshwater marshlands that cover a huge area nearly 20 by 300 miles in area. This is one of the greatest areas for African rice farming and the marshlands yield bountiful crops of this staple. There is also millet and sorghum, both plants being generously watered by the floodwaters of the Niger. Sometimes it becomes necessary for the people living outside of the flood region to irrigate their farms by carrying water in skin bottles to their areas.

Down through the centuries African fishermen have depended upon the annual floods to create spawning grounds for the Nile perch. Indeed during the period December to March the waters recede and the fattened fish are left to flounder around in the shallow water, making them easy catches for the fishermen.

This winding ribbon of water replenishes the land and makes it possible for the villages, towns, and cities along its way, and some a great distance from it, to survive off its bountiful food supply. Oil has been found in its delta, further making the Niger a river of abundance. And the raffia from this area is so strong and resilient that it makes good material for building houses and for floor mats. Some people also make and sell excellent raffia brooms.

The Mali, Gao, and Songhay empires were built on the back of this river.

## The Nile

No river in the world has the stature in our imagination occupied by the Nile. It is the longest river in the world. From its sources in the highlands of East Central Africa to the delta at the Mediterranean Sea the river travels 4184 miles. There are two main sources of the river, each with distinctive features. The White Nile, as it is called because of the many waterfalls, rapids and cataracts, rises in the mountainous countries of Burundi and Uganda and flows north until it is met by the Blue Nile, as it is called because of its depth (although in Ethiopia the people refer to it as the Abay River), and continues its flow northward receiving still more energy and water from the Atbara River as it makes its way through Sudan and Egypt.

It should be noted that the origin of the Nile has long been disputed. At one time some adventurers thought that the Congo was the source of the Nile. At other times writers have contended that you could not name one source for the White Nile because there are so many candidates. For example, some argue that the river really starts with the remote headstream called Runvyironza, an upper stream of the Kagera River in Burundi. But one could just as easily contend that the river starts with the Kyoga in Burundi or with Lake Nyanza (often called Lake Victoria) or with the lake variously named Lake Albert or Lake Mobutu Sese Seko, after the discredited leader of Zaire.

The Nile and its tributaries flow through nine African countries: Uganda, Sudan, Egypt, Ethiopia, Congo, Kenya, Tanzania, Rwanda, and Burundi. Finally as it makes its way north down toward the sea the great river forms a delta more than 120 miles wide with important branches such as the Rosetta (Rashid) and the Damietta (Dumyat). This is the widest habitable area of the Nile and it even has several lakes such as Edku, Burullus, and Manzala.

Numerous names have existed for the Nile. As you can probably guess, it was not called "Nile" until the Greeks named it after the word "Nelios", meaning "River Valley." What was the name given to the river by the people of Kemet? They called their river *Iteru* and related it to the deity *Hapi*, associated with fertility and regeneration. Thus, the river was either Iteru or Hapi for most of its historic life, not Nile.

Now more than 140 million people live along the route of the Nile. Since the river has been the source of culture and civilization for more than 5000 years, with cities and towns such as Behdet (Edfu), Elephantine, Waset (Luxor), and Syene (Aswan) developing around the great waterway, it has become the most fabled river in history. More monuments of antiquity appear near this river than for any other in the world. More than half of the world's great monuments of antiquity are located within 40 miles of its banks.

The empires of Kemet (Egypt) and Nubia found their strength and power in their ability to use this river for transportation, military maneuvers, large fleets of merchant ships, and ordinary daily life of fishing and recreation. It remains the lifeblood of the modern country of Egypt as it was the liquid that gave birth and life to the ancient country.

## The Orange River

The Orange River in southern Africa is one of the longest rivers in the world south of the Tropic of Capricorn. It rises in Lesotho's Maluti Mountains, less than 125 miles from the Indian Ocean, and then flows westward to the Atlantic Ocean for a distance of some 1300 miles. The river traverses the broad plains of the South African heartland and meanders its way northwest and west through a beautiful landscape. Its chief tributary is the Vaal River. As the Orange River flows through the southern part of the Kalahari and Namib deserts it faces high evaporation rates as the water is consumed by the heat and dryness. Actually in very dry years the Orange River dries up before it reaches the Atlantic Ocean.

Of course, inasmuch as humans have discovered that at the mouth of the river there are rich alluvial deposits of diamonds there have been many recreational travelers seeking their pot of diamonds. In the time prior to the coming of the Europeans the river was used for fishing, transportation as far as it would go, and religious purposes. The Africans believed that the river represented one of the great spirits of the continent and treated the river with special care. This was not unusual or extraordinary because in other parts of the continent Africans have responded the same way to rivers, and sometimes to trees, mountains, and other natural phenomena. The idea is that these phenomena represent spirit, energy, and should therefore be treated with respect. In a way it reminds me of the new call for environmentalism. Respect the trees, respect the rivers, and respect all of the creatures on the earth. Well, Africans who lived along the Orange River believed this dictum long before there was an organized environmental movement.

The Orange River basin drains about 400,000 square miles and covers portions of Botswana, Namibia, South Africa, and Lesotho, a country landlocked and surrounded by South Africa. The river forms the natural border between Namibia and South Africa before pouring into the Atlantic Ocean. The Sotho people of Lesotho call the river the *Senqu*. Before the whites came to the southern part of Africa this was the original name of the river, the Senqu.

The river is long and in its journey from its origin to the sea it passes through several climatological regions. The average annual rainfall for the river at its origin is about 1800 mm but this decreases to a mere 25 mm by the time it reaches its western limit.

Along with the Limpopo, the Orange River is the most important river in South Africa and one of the principal rivers sustaining the most populated economic areas. While it is true that the water resources of the Orange River are extensively exploited for irrigation, energy, and domestic use, it remains one of the least-known rivers in Africa. Yet ancient civilizations such as the Mapungubwe kingdom found resources from this river. It provided means of transportation as well as fish to the numerous people who lived near its shores.

## The Zambezi River

The incredible Zambezi starts in northwestern Zambia as an insignificant spring bubbling up between the roots of a tree and flows through Angola, Botswana, Zimbabwe, and finally Mozambique, emptying into the Indian Ocean 1653 miles from its headwaters. The great Zambezi is Africa's fourth largest river system after the Nile, Congo, and Niger rivers. The Bundu people of Zambia believe the river is Nyami Nyami, "the spirit of life," because it brings food, fish, and provides water to grow crops. It is a river that is widely used by humans and wildlife. The river and its environs are rich with crocodiles, elephants, hippopotami, baboons, hyenas, and lions.

Perhaps no river in Africa is as alive with life as the Zambezi. It is no wonder that the Bundu people named it Nyami Nyami. Indeed, humans find the river useful for transportation, ritual, irrigation, recreation, fishing, and hydropower. Nevertheless, it remains less developed for human settlement than the other rivers and has considerable areas reserved and protected for wildlife.

Along the route of the river is one of the most tropical areas in Africa. But there are also areas of near drought. The rainy season lasts from October to April. After April the land experiences the dry season, when the grasses turn brown and the river undergoes evaporation. One might say that the seasons and the course of the river conspire to make it one of the most dramatic rivers in Africa. It transforms itself from a placid, peaceful river flowing through sandy plains to a tumbling, boisterous one moving rapidly over rapids and falls until it reaches the most spectacular of all points in its flow: the marvelous Musi wa Tunya, "The Smoke that Thunders," called by David Livingstone "Victoria Falls." These falls are twice the size of Niagara Falls, at 350 feet high and 5500 feet wide. One gazes upon this sight with awe rarely experienced by humans. A waterfall one mile wide with a blanket of water twice as high as the Niagara Falls is phenomenal.

As one of the great rivers of Africa, the Zambezi like several of the others is the result of plate tectonics. The river, for example, starts near the boundaries of Angola, Congo, and Zambia and heads toward the Okavango Swamp in

Botswana. But it soon turns towards the northeast and then east until it ends in the Indian Ocean. Millions of years ago, when Africa was in the middle of the supercontinent called Pangea, long before humans occupied the earth, there were large inland seas, one of which was in present-day Botswana. It was into this inland sea that the ancient Zambezi flowed. However, when the supercontinent broke apart these inland seas drained and the new route of the Zambezi was created.

Every massive river in Africa has strong tributaries. The Zambezi flows from its headwaters until it is joined by the Kabompo River, originating in Zambia and then is joined by the Lungue-Gungo River coming from Angola. After flowing out of a swampy area in the north of Borotseland for nearly 400 miles, the river goes for 200 miles in a southward direction and then turns abruptly east to flow for 1000 miles to the sea. After Musi wa Tunya it flows through the narrow Batoka Gorge and then flattens out at the broad Gwembe Valley. Subsequently, two mighty tributaries enter it from the north. The Kafue River joins the the Zambezi 60 miles downstream from Lake Kariba, one of the sacred lakes of Central Africa, having originated in the Lukunga Swamp. To most Zambians the Kafue is the key river for their food supply since most of their fish comes directly from this river. The second major tributary is the Shire River, joining the Zambezi just 100 miles from its mouth at the Mozambique coast. The Shire starts in Lake Malawi, one of the picturesque lakes of the Great Rift Valley, and feeds the Zambezi with abundant water during the rainy season. Pumped by its tributaries and assisted by the deep drops in the gorges, the waters of the Zambezi rush through the zig-zag pathway cut by the river's power over millennia.

Before we leave the Zambezi it is useful to remember that although the river is thinly populated by pastoralists, farmers, and fishermen in its upper part, it provides humanity with the dramatic Ku-omboka Ceremony, where thousands of inhabitants around the river move annually to higher ground in a ritual of respect as the Zambezi floods the low-lying plains. This beautiful festival is Lozi in origin. The Lozi king has two estates, one at Lealui and the other at Limulunga. The latter one is on high ground and thus serves as the capital during the rainy season. The annual move from Lealui to Limulunga is a celebrated event in Zambia's festival year. Africa is replete with fascinating rituals of movement and the archetype of such rituals can be seen in the ancient Kemetic rites where the priests at Ipet Sut, the great temple of Karnak, gathered the image of the god Amen and moved in a procession to the temple of Luxor where the goddess Mut made her abode, and then placed the image of Amen in the temple of Luxor to consort with the goddess for several days before bringing him back to Ipet Sut in a parade of priests and high-ranking royals. Like that ancient ceremony, this one in Zambia restored the people's faith in their traditions and reminded them of the greatness of their divinities.

The wide floodplain of western Zambia is the homeland of the mighty Lozi kingdom. Here the Lozi have created their communities, collected their tales of valor, and lived their heroic lives remembering their own times of conquest and empire.

*Figure 6.1* Temple at Luxor
© Molefi Kete Asante

# Part IV

# The age of construction

"Something new is always coming out of Africa"

# 7 The spread of classical empires and kingdoms

Africa is home to a multiplicity of ethnic groups and diverse nationalities. It also has some of the oldest empires and kingdoms in the world. Kemet was not the only classical kingdom of Africa. No continent has ever had as many viable kingdoms and empires for as long a time as the continent of Africa. The last reigning monarch of Ethiopia, Haile Selassie, lost power in 1974 but even his demise did not end the role of traditional royalty on the continent. Traditional kings and queens abound all over the continent even at this present day. It is possible to get some idea of the past by encountering the present. What we see in many traditional kingdoms within the modern nation-state are the customs and practices that were ancient before foreign elements corrupted African traditions or values. Thus, when one considers the ancient kingdoms of Nubia, Axum, Carthage, Ghana, Mali, Songhay, and others one confronts the grandeur of African history.

## Nubia: the corridor of classical culture

Nubia is the name given to a region of Africa that included two important historical kingdoms: Kush and Meroe. The kingdom of Kush, which flourished much earlier than Meroe, was located between the Fourth Cataract (traditional Third) and the Sixth Cataract (traditional First). Kush rose around the fourth millennium BCE. It became a leading trading kingdom and reached its height between 1700 and 600 BCE. During this time it was the rival to Kemet in the Nile Valley. There were times that Kemet controlled Kush and other times that Kush controlled Kemet. The interactions between the peoples were much more like those between modern France and Germany or the United States and Canada. Influence went back and forth between the two nations but the Kushites believed that the Egyptians (Kemites) descended from them. This has not been the popular line taken by many European scholars, who have been anxious to see "civilization" go from the Mediterranean area into the "heart of darkest Africa." Unfortunately for those who take this line, obviously influenced by the belief that civilization could not "go down the Nile" as it did from the interior of Africa to the Mediterranean, the Egyptians themselves as well as others believed that the Egyptians were colonists sent by the Nubians.

The similarities between Kemet and Kush cannot simply be credited to the influence of Kemet on Kush. In fact, many of the innovations found in Kemet probably came down the river from Kush. The kingship itself reflected many attributes of Kushitic origin. Actually, long before the dynastic period in Kemet, the evidence of high civilization existed in Nubia. Between 3800 and 3100 BCE one finds the oldest tombs of a pharaonic type in Qustul in Nubia. There are thirty-three tombs of what is called the A-group type that appear in Cemetery L at Qustul, a small cemetery containing unusually large graves of this type. In one of these graves, "L-24," an incense burner was found. It had figures etched into the clay. It showed three ships sailing in procession to the royal palace. One of the ships carried a lion, perhaps a deity, maybe even Apedemak, the lion-headed deity of the Nubians. It showed also elements of royalty, a long robe, a flail, and the White Crown, all within the façade of a palace. This was discovered to be much older than the first dynasties in Kemet, and it was evidence of the world's first monarchy. Now it is possible to say with certainty that the Nubian culture in Kush developed before the Kemetic dynasties. An incense burner reflected the religious, philosophical, and artistic quality of the people.

Scientists believe that there were several groups of Africans living in the Nile Valley south of Kemet identified by the type of pottery they produced. Of course, this is speculative but it has become a part of the general understanding of Nubia. These scientists have given the designations A-group and C-group to these peoples. The A-group were those who lived in lower Nubia, closer to Kemet, and produced delicate pottery that was of a nomadic character. It did not seem that these people were sedentary. The C-group pottery was produced by those living in upper Nubia. Both groups coexisted. They also persisted in this type of pottery until around 1000 BCE.

The king was elected from the royal family and descent was reckoned from the mother's line. It may be because of this model that Africa, indeed the people of Nubia, both Kush and Meroe, have given the world the largest number of queens in history.

The ancient historians never considered Egypt anything but a part of Africa. Even more, Diodorus Siculus says that Kemet (Egypt) was populated from the interior by Ethiopians. Herodotus spoke of these Ethiopians as blameless. In fact, Herodotus describes how he was able to go south up the Nile as far as Elephantine around 450 BCE. He was unable to go farther for some unknown reason. Perhaps he could not find the proper guides or maybe he had run out of resources for the journey. He contented himself with the information that was given to him by the wise men of Elephantine. They told him about Meroe, which lay 600 miles farther south up the Nile. This is a part of Herodotus' report:

> I went as far as Elephantine to see what I could with my own eyes, but for the country still further south I had to be content with what I was told in answer to my questions. The most I could learn was that beyond Elephantine the county rises steeply; and in that part of the river boats have to be hauled along by ropes, one rope on each side, much as one

drags an ox. If the rope parts, the boat is gone in a moment, carried away by the force of the stream. These conditions last over a four days' journey, the river all the time winding greatly, like the Maeander, and the distance to be covered amounting to twelve *schoeni*. After this one reaches a level plain, where the river is divided by an island named Tachompso.

South of Elephantine the country is inhabited by Ethiopians [that is, Nubians and Kushites at this time] who also possess half of Tachompso, the other half being occupied by Egyptians. Beyond the island is a great lake, and round its shores live nomadic tribes of Ethiopians. After crossing the lake one comes again to the stream of the Nile, which flows into it. At this point one must land and travel along the bank of the river for forty days, because sharp rocks, some showing above the water and many just awash, make the river impracticable for boats. After the forty days' journey on land one takes another boat and in twelve days reaches a big city named Meroe, said to be the capital city of the Ethiopians. The inhabitants worship Zeus and Dionysus alone of the Gods, holding them in great honor. There is an oracle of Zeus there, and they make war according to its pronouncements, taking from it both the occasion and the object of their various expeditions.

(Herodotus, *The Histories*, Book II)

The word "Ethiopian" was applied by the Greeks to all people in Africa south of Egypt. Other Africans would have been called Libyans. The Greeks however recognized, as Aristotle did in *Physiognomonica*, two principal groups of Africans, the Ethiopians and the Egyptians. This was not a distinction in race but a distinction in nationality. Modern-day Ethiopia was not the ancient Ethiopia; actually, as we shall discuss, it was called Axum. In the ancient world, Ethiopia was located south of Kemet in the region that we call Nubia. This region is located today in the top third of the country of Sudan.

Kush had conquered all of Nubia by 1000 BCE. It was a country that believed its superior weapons used by expert archers could defeat any foe. The people of Kemet saw them as among the fiercest of fighters and had employed them in their own overseas armies in Asia. The capital city was first Kerma, a major port for goods moving north from the interior of Africa or goods moving south from the north. To protect their country and its wealth from the Kemetic nation the elites of Kush decided to move the capital city farther up the Nile to Napata, which became one of the greatest cities along the River Nile. It would be from this beautiful city that Piankhy would take his army down the Nile for conquest of Kemet.

Therefore, the glory of Napata was during the Twenty-fifth Dynasty of ancient Kemet, when the kings of Kush from Napata united the Nile Valley behind the power of the descendants of Piankhy. When the Kushite kings had returned to their capital city, the Kushites experienced growth and development problems in the narrow valley. Although they had done a lot to improve the lot of their people they found that the arable land was not enough to sustain an increasing population. This precipitated the Iron

Age for the Nile Valley, where Africans started to use the iron ore available to them. With a cosmopolitan population, highly literate, quite pious, and much traveled, having served as overlords of Kemet for a hundred years while maintaining their own cultural traditions and interacting with southern neighbors as well as trading with Mediterranean peoples, Kush exercised wide religious authority and controlled iron culture economics in the Upper Nile. They were able to supply traders with iron.

It was at Meroe that the Nubians expressed their cultural prowess in construction and agriculture by use of iron. The discovery and use of iron was a distinct achievement since the region was rich in iron ore. It would make the kingdom extremely strong from a nascent industrial sense where artisans would put the iron ore to use in many capacities, but especially for warfare and agriculture. Knowledge of iron-making meant that the Meroitic people could fabricate tools and weapons that would help to sustain their society. The iron farming implements were a necessity; the use of the iron sword and spear helped to make the kingdom of Meroe invincible. But it was not only iron that made Meroe a strong kingdom; it was also agriculturally self-sufficient, finding within its own borders enough food to feed its population and to allow the people leisure time to create art, to explore other areas of Africa, and to build huge buildings in honor of their religion.

The ruins of the ancient capital city tell us something about the life of the people. It is marked by royal pyramids, ancestral shrines, the Temple of the Sun and the remains of smelters' ovens used in iron-making.

There are 223 pyramids in Nubia, around Meroe and Napata. This is twice as many as found in Kemet. When the Kushite kings moved south to the Sudanese savanna and built a new capital at Meroe, they shifted their trade interest to the south and began extensive commerce with the nations that lay to the east and south of them. There had already been relationships between these peoples because of the River Nile but increasingly the Nubians made forays into the area far beyond their borders.

Evidence of the power of Kush, particularly between the fourth century BCE and 350 CE, is overwhelming. Ruins of the Meroitic temple at Musawwarat es-Sufra are called "The Great Enclosure." It is a massive area that lies south of Meroe near the First Cataract (Sixth Cataract in traditional terms). It was a pilgrimage site for believers in Amen who traveled many miles to find solace within its walls. Like other ruins along the Nile, this one tells us that the Nubian people were quite active in constructing buildings out of devotion to their beliefs. These were neither indolent nor ignorant people; they were the masters of their own destiny and believed that their craftsmen could meet any local need. They explored and traded along the fabled route that ran between Lake Chad in the west and the Red Sea port towns on the east. It is believed by many scholars that this route connected with the major center of iron production in West Africa, Jenne-Jeno. Excavations have shown this to be one of the richest archaeological fields in Africa. Located on the River Niger in the region of ancient Mali, the site of Jenne-Jeno was occupied from 400 BCE to 1400 CE and played an important role in the trans-Saharan trade (McIntosh 1995). Roderick and Susan

McIntosh excavated at Jenne-Jeno in 1977 and 1981. They returned to the site in 1994 for coring and more survey. They got money from several organizations in the United States to fund their work, including the National Science Foundation of the United States, the American Association of University Women, and the National Geographic Society (1994). Of course, as is the case in most research projects in Africa, the foreign researchers collaborated with African researchers whose names are rarely mentioned in the literature. In a sense it is much like the European scholars who claimed that Mungo Park "discovered" the River Niger though he was carried there by Africans, or that David Livingstone "found" the great waterfall of the River Zambezi although he was directed to it by Africans.

Jenne-Jeno, the original site of Jenne, was located about 2 miles from the present Jenne in a region that had known crop cultivation and animal husbandry from the first millennium BCE (Shaw 1977, pp. 69–125). We have some evidence that *Pennisetum americanum* and *Brachiaria deflexa* (Guinea millet) were grown at Karkarichinkat in Mali during the second millennium BCE. Furthermore, there is evidence at Tichitt, in Mauritania, that *Pennisetum* sp. (bullrush millet) was present in the first millennium BCE. According to Connah, "There is direct evidence for the cultivation of *Oryza glaberrima* (African rice), *Pennisetum* and sorghum at Jenne from the third century BCE onwards and of the cultivation of *Sorghum bicolor* at Daima and Niani from late in the first millennium CE" (Connah 2001, p. 111). Thus, given the fertility of the soil around the Niger, and the intensity of the agricultural activity, particularly during the recession of the floodwaters, one could surmise that the people of Jenne along the Sahelian routes traded with those coming from Nubian areas. Aboubacry Moussa Lam has shown the possibility of this kind of interaction between the eastern and western parts of the Sahelian region with his vast researches into the origin of the Peul (Lam 2003–4). Using data collected from African traditions and Egyptology, the author demonstrates the Nile origin of the Peul. His book *De l'origine égyptienne des Peuls* established him as the leader in this field as early as the 1990s. Works such as those by Lam serve to show that the continent was much more interactive than originally thought by the European historians who first encountered African people. As people of other continents have migrated to places other than where they were born, so have Africans. One cannot, therefore, say that the Kushites had no knowledge of the people of Jenne or vice versa. The Saharan Generator was as vigorous during the period of the Nubian kingdoms as it was to become in later years; it was filled with interactions, commercial and trade networks, and human migrations.

At the Great Enclosure of the Gebel Barkal temple, archaeologists have found a huge elephant statue. Unquestionably the people of Kush knew the elephant, as most Africans did, and probably had a very good idea of the strength of the animal. It may be that they sought to domesticate the elephant, something that was difficult to do with the African elephant, which was unlike the Indian elephant. The African elephant was much larger and much more temperamental than the smaller Indian elephant. Yet it is believed because of the numbers of elephant statues that appear in the ruins at

Musawwarat es-Sufra and other towns along the Nile that the Nubians had learned to use the elephants for some limited tasks. We know, of course, that Hannibal would employ African elephants in his battles with Rome.

Another powerful piece of surviving evidence attesting to the genius of the Nubian people is the south wall of the funerary chapel of pyramid N.11 at Meroe. There is an inscription which dates to the time of Queen Shanadakete (160 BCE), perhaps the first significant female ruler in world history who ruled as a woman. Hatshepsut of the Eighteenth Dynasty ruled as king, not as queen. Shanadakete was a powerful builder of temples, pyramids, and shrines to the gods. In the wall painting her husband is shown seated behind her, indicating that she is indeed the ruler and not the man. So pervasive was the Candace system of governance in Kush and Meroe that the queen was the central political and religious figure. The queens (see Table 3) ruled alone or were co-equal with their husbands as rulers. On this south wall at the funerary chapel one sees also the goddess Auset standing with protective, outstretched wings. Alongside the image of people coming to pay homage is a representation of Shanadakete's judgment before the god Ausar.

*Table 3*    Names and dates of some Nubian queens

| | |
|---|---|
| Bartare | 284–275 BCE |
| Shanadakete | 177–155 BCE |
| Amanirenas | 99–84 BCE |
| Amanishakete | 26–20 BCE |
| Amanitore | 25–41 CE |
| Amanikhatashan | 83–115 CE |

One queen, Amanirenas, early first century BCE, fought Julius Caesar's army to a standstill, wringing from him an agreement to keep the status quo between their two countries, meaning that the Romans would stay out of Nubia and the Nubians would not interfere with the Romans' control of Kemet. A stele inscribed with Meroitic cursive erected near Meroe by Queen Amanirenas has not been fully translated. Demotic script, a form of Egyptian writing for the masses, was used by the government of Kush at Napata. By the time the government had moved south to Meroe the ruling elite had developed their own script for communication, which is referred to as Meroitic. It is this script that has not been fully translated.

There is a relief at the Wad Ban Naga temple that shows another queen, Amanitore with her co-ruler and probably husband, Natakamani. The inscription is in the Kemetic and Meroitic hieroglyphics. It has been important in deciphering the Meroitic script. Anyone who writes that Natakamani was the principal ruler is probably privileging the texts of the Western world, especially the Roman texts. Clearly Natakamani is important but it is hard to see how he could have been any more significant than his co-ruler, Queen Amanitore. Both of their names reflect their relationship to the god Amen. In fact, "Amani" in both names is the Meroitic way of writing Amen. At the Lion Temple at Naga, south of Meroe, there is a relief of King Natakamani standing before the lion god Apedemek, Heru, and Amen. With his sash draped over his right shoulder, the king cuts an imposing figure. At the same temple there is a relief at the entrance pylons showing the queen and king striking their enemies.

One cannot overemphasize the fact that the kingdoms of Kush and Meroe in Nubia were independently created, richly developed in political and military terms, reflective of the religious temperament of the African people along the Nile, and prolific producers of red ware, burnished black ware and decorated cups with ankhs, animals, and stamped motifs as seen in the tombs of aristocrats at Faras.

Ominous developments were occurring on the borders of Meroe at the beginning of the current era. In fact, the Blemmyes, a strong, closely knit community of nomads, had put pressure on the northern frontier, frequently overrunning Napata, the religious center of the Meroitic kingdom. The River Nile, however, continued to give the region an outlet to the sea. Meroe was able to use the Nile with the permission of the Roman overlords. Meroe could also maintain its contact with Indian and Arab traders on the Red Sea coast. They traded with Hellenistic areas as well as with Hindu areas. But these communities saw the continuing weakness of the Meroitic kingdom; it no longer held the power it had during the golden age of Queen Shanadakete.

Thus, by the second century CE the country was occupied by the Nobatae, another African people much like the Blemmyes, who had developed a well-organized cavalry that often raced across the desert to attack villages and towns located on the river and then faded back into the desert from whence they had come. They terrorized the settled, agricultural population of Meroe. But it was neither the Blemmyes nor the Nobatae who would bring down the Meroitic kingdom but another neighbor farther to the east and south, Axum. By the fourth century CE the Axumite Empire had become the mightiest empire in eastern Africa. It probably rivaled Ghana in the west at this time. In 350 CE the precision archers and fast-moving cavalry of the Axumite Empire came upon Meroe like a plague and destroyed the city and the country of Meroe so utterly that it was never to rise again to the position it had held in history. Nobatia in the north with a capital at Faras, Muqurra with its capital at Dunqulah, and Alwa with its capital at Sawba would take over the old kingdom of Meroe.

## Axum: one of the four great empires

The Axumite Empire had been forming for a long time before its ultimate rise to power around 220 CE. By the time it conquered Meroe, the Empire of Axum was already one of the great kingdoms of the world. The Iranian prophet Mani, who lived from 216 to 276 CE and was the founder of Manicheism, a belief that all flesh was evil, wrote in a book called *Chapters* that there were four great empires in the world: Axum, Rome, Persia, and China.

The Axumite Empire grew up around the Tekezze River and expanded in every direction taking in the lands of neighboring people, conquering territories that had hitherto been independent, and controlling access to the Red Sea. One of the earliest centers of power was called Adulis. It was known for its physical beauty, the official residences, the public buildings, and the wealth of its citizens. The ancient city of Adulis was the commercial center of the Axumite Empire.

In the kingdom of Axum the city of Adulis was the brightest jewel of the realm. Indeed it was earlier in importance than the city of Axum itself. However, Adulis was not the only great city in the Axumite Empire although it was certainly the most significant in terms of commerce and military power because of its place on the sea coast. Cities such as Yeha and Kaskase may have been older than Adulis; they were definitely its rivals in terms of dynamism and energy in the various trades and professions that were to make Axum famous. While there are no specific dates on the origin of either of the cities we know that they had been inhabited more than 2000 years before the emergence of the Axumite Empire.

Axum was a kingdom rich with literate people. By the time of its greatest glory it was full of men and women who could read and speak Ge'ez, Latin, Greek, Arabic, Egyptian, Farsi, Meroitic, and other African languages. They wrote about their lives and their empire. They wrote dramas, history, and comedy. Indeed the ancient writings of the Axumite Empire tell their story in fascinating details. Stelae, that is, stone obelisks with writing on them, specifically erected to provide historical information, have been found throughout the area occupied by the empire. But everything was not history; they wrote about their feelings, their religion, and their interactions with other people. Borrowing a great deal, it seems, from the Nubians and Kemites, the people of Axum recorded their achievements for posterity. In addition to their writings we have many artifacts that reveal a very active civilization in commerce and artistic developments. The ancient Axumites created and erected monoliths, like the *tekken* of Kemet, that were massive in scale. These obelisks, as they are sometimes called, were meant to demonstrate the power and authority of the Axumite people. They built stelae, huge altars, throne bases, and other large stone structures. They also built houses for the nobles and elites that would be called mansions or palaces today. They were built mainly in Axum but also in Matara, where there are ruins of palaces and elaborate villas of the highest artistic quality. They reflect attention to detail and design representative of Axum's glory during the years of pre-eminence as an African empire. In design the house complex often seen in Axum was directly related to the concept of the African compound, where many structures serving different functions are connected by a common courtyard or walled-in walkway to show relationship. Thus, a family might use one small building for storage, another for sleeping, another for visitors, another for entertainment, and so forth. It is common in the West for people to have all functions under one roof.

Axumites, like Kemites and Kushites, used giant stones for historical markers, decrees, and boundaries. The use of pillars and columns of stone had, of course, long been an African practice, probably influenced by the large reeds found in the various rivers and streams in the northeast of the continent. However, in Axum the architects soon employed the huge stone culture on a monumental scale in the creation of Christian churches and tombs of kings.

Clearly a large part of the grandeur of these structures was religious. Like many cultures before them, the Axumites believed that it was necessary to demonstrate in their constructions their spiritual beliefs. By the time of the greatest glory of the empire, the kings and many of the nobles were Christian.

Many people in the outlying areas, away from the large cities, retained their beliefs in the traditional deities. Since Axum, a nation of several ethnic groups, was not comprised of just one group of people from the area, it had to juggle the faiths of many people in order to retain its control. This it did with great diplomacy.

It is hard to imagine an empire in antiquity with as much copper, precious stones, gold, pottery, glass, and ceramics as Axum. Even if we could imagine it, we would only have a pale copy of the robust original. Using these huge pieces of art for religious and ceremonial purposes meant that the empire had to constantly remind the subjects of the central authority and power of the Almighty. Iron was used to make utensils for worship. Gold vessels were regularly employed in the ceremonies and rituals. Yet it is the pottery that reveals for us the depth of the people's love for their civilization and belief in their king. We see how they were able to decorate the pottery with their history. It is true, "by their pottery, you shall know them."

Three periods are recognized in Axumite history: *dawning*, *glowing*, and *brilliant*. These represent the eras during which the Empire of Axum started, matured, and reached its zenith in power and majesty. The dawning stage ran from about 500 to 200 BCE; the glowing stage from 200 BCE to 99 CE; and the brilliant stage from 99 to 900 CE.

During the *dawning* stage Axum's architectural and cultural styles were being developed and the culture expressed itself in art and sculpture that has been found throughout the ancient land. It was during this stage that the people of Axum first became acquainted with the Arabic people of Yemen. They met, as one would think, first on the Red Sea and traded with each other across the sea. Soon the interactions were such that commerce brought them into conflict and they occasionally occupied each other's land. The Axumites influenced the culture of Yemen to the degree that one can still find remnants of the Axumite culture in some of the small towns of Yemen. The architecture of Yeha and Haoulti-Melazo in Axum can be found in Yemen. Undoubtedly the interactions went both ways as there are linguistic items that the two languages came to share because of the trade and political relationship. But in this early era there was already evidence of the growing military prowess of the Axumite people.

The *glowing* stage brings the Axumites into the Christian era. The interactions with the southern Arabians became weaker because of Axum's concentration on its own internal problems, rebellions against the central power, internal squabbles over the kingship, and the growing threats from other African nations. At the same time the country was producing majestic art with beautiful pottery and vases. Its key centers of influence had increased from the powerful Axum and the dynamic Adulis to the following cities:

| | |
|---|---|
| Yeha | Trade and commerce center |
| Li'Lay-Addi | Textile and perfume center |
| Gobo-Fench | Timber center |
| Haoulti | Iron and hunting center |
| Matara | Iron-smelting and bronze-casting |
| Fekya | Religious and art center |

These towns were the most vigorous in the empire and may have been among the most important centers of commerce, trade, and gossip in the whole of Africa during the glowing period of Axumite history. In addition, the chief port city, Adulis, the Red Sea center of activity, was Axum's main gateway to the world. It contained residences for important persons, a bustling trade in ship building, the outfitting of vessels, fishing, and trade with the world. Scholars have found more than 60 different inscriptions on the most ancient buildings of Adulis. These suggest that Axum was actively engaged in communication with other nations and kingdoms and that the historical events recorded are evidence of the lively discourse in thought, ceremony, and ritual in the city. Developments in art and agriculture were equally sophisticated and Adulis was the foundation for an even more expansive opening to the world.

The *brilliant* stage was the time of the greatest influence and power of the Axumite Empire. Indeed the society reached its full glory. Axum rose to brilliance about the same time as Rome, but two important neighbors, Nubia in Africa and Saba in Arabia, were in decline. Nubia had controlled the Nile and Saba had controlled much of the Red Sea trade. With Axum's rise at the expense of both of those countries it had gained enormous wealth and status, changing the political equation both in Africa and in Arabia. This impacted the extensive outreach of Rome, which had from time to time depended upon Saba and Nubia for its extended trade routes. It was now evident that it would be to Axum that Rome would turn to protect its ships in the Red Sea against the constant problem of pirates. To further cement its friendship with Rome, Axum agreed to prevent the Beja from attacking Rome's southern flank in the south of Egypt. Rome had ruled Egypt since 30 BCE and the death of Cleopatra. As the mightiest nation in Africa in the fourth century CE Axum exercised power and authority over politics and commercial activities in the region.

In one inscription the king of the Adulis area wrote: "Having commanded the peoples closest to my kingdom to preserve the peace, I bravely waged war and subjugated in battles the following peoples..." There is a long list of defeated enemies including Sennar, a country that was located near the Abay River, which had become a major source of irritation to the Axumite Empire. Also there was a country that was described as a land of "high mountains, cold winds, and mist," which could have been some other part of the present country of Ethiopia or Kenya or Uganda. These areas are known for their mist and cold weather. The king of Axum had a monument erected for himself just in case the Adulis region thought that it did not have to pay allegiance. The conquering king, whose name does not appear on the stele, having been rubbed out, says that he defeated all of his neighbors in the surrounding territories. In fact, he did more than defeat all the people who lived on the border with Egypt. He "again made the road from Egypt to Axum a thoroughfare" (Asante 1993, p. 85).

Heliodorus, a Greek, wrote a historical novel called *Aethiopica* around 280–300 CE set in the period when Persia ruled over Egypt, which was considerably earlier than the writing of the novel. In the novel, Nubia is described as being at the height of its power. Also in the novel there are lots of triumphal celebrations with different nations that have been conquered walking past the Nubian king so that he could review his conquered subjects. The kings came by, some of them bowing, others kneeling, and still others falling completely to the ground before the conqueror. However, when the king of Axum passed by the Nubian king, the novelist writes, the Axum king was standing erect, paying no tribute, and appearing as the last king to come before the Nubian. The Nubian expressed friendship with the Axum king and treated him as an equal. It would not be long before the Axumites conquered the Nubians. So even Axum's neighbors were thought by fictional writers to respect its power. Around 290 CE the king of Axum invaded Nubia and added it to his empire. In fact, the last king of Meroe whose name we know, Teceridamani, does not even appear in historical records after 254 CE. There were six Meroitic kings after him. Yet these kings remain anonymous because their names were worn off the stone stelae.

The evidence of the Axumite Empire's glory is everywhere, in all fields, during this time. Axum was the most advanced civilization Africa had produced by this time. It had superseded both Kemet and the Nubian kingdoms of Kush and Meroe and was a center of philosophical thinking and writing. Some of the wisest people lived in the towns of Axum and Adulis and some of the most respected artists, writers, and religious figures impacted the world from the Axumite Empire. They were outstanding in architecture, writing, language, religion, statesmanship, government, and bureaucracy. With the assistance of a well-developed bureaucracy made so because of the emergence of the Ge'ez language and the Church, they practiced an international politics that was advanced during its time. The people knew Greek and Latin and many of them were familiar with other languages, such as Arabic and Hebrew, because of the cosmopolitan nature of the empire. This meant that the concepts of good governance and fair trade were internationally acceptable because of the disciplined state that was based on order, justice, and righteousness, elements of the older Kemetic idea of *maat*.

At this point in Axum's history the culture was distinctively different from Nubia's or Kemet's; it was no mere replay of the earlier civilizations. It had emerged essentially on its own in Africa, away from the mainstream of the Nile Valley civilizations. Eventually, Axum had more contact with the Red Sea kingdoms and nations, including Yemen and Punt (Somalia). But its locus of power and center of culture would always remain the African continent. This was its source of religious, philosophical, and aesthetic ideals.

Axum, the lodestone and magnet of the empire, sat high on the plateau beyond the mountains one had to cross from Adulis. It was an eight-day journey from Adulis to Axum. The city was the seat of government and power. From this town the king ruled over the entire empire, sending out edicts, imposing taxes, minting coins, and raising an army in time of war. Its public buildings were grand, much like those of Nubia and Kemet, built in a rectangular shape, but its style of architecture was different, with tiers or floors that alternated in projecting outward and recessing inward.

By the brilliant age Axum was a deeply Christian country, the new religion having completely replaced the traditional religion based on the ancient deities in the capital city by the third century BCE. Of course, there were outlying areas where Christianity had not reached and did not reach during the entire period of the Axumite Empire. Yet the grandeur of the structures in Axum may have been related to the religious beliefs because the huge, monolithic dimensions and spaces of the buildings reflected a transcendent idea. They used granite mostly and created the obelisks, stone monoliths, entirely out of granite much like the earlier cultures of the Nile Valley had used the stone for their massive monuments.

Kaleb's tomb at Axum and the giant stelae, both meant to be funerary monuments to the kings, represent significant achievements in memorial architecture. The huge structures are elaborately carved and show repetition of characteristically African aesthetic designs. Other important architectural sites included Kohaito, Aratou, Adua, Ham, Mekalli, Tokonda, and of course Adulis, the gateway.

Public writings seem to have flourished during this time as well. The public decrees by officials, either the king or his representatives, showed a civilization that took communication seriously. Almost every public building had a written inscription as was in keeping with the tradition established by the African kingdoms and empires of the Nile Valley. In its public form, writing appeared everywhere. Thus once again it is inaccurate to speak of African civilization as without writing. There was as much or more writing in African antiquity as in any other ancient civilization. As there were large areas of Europe, North America, South America, Asia, and Australia without writing, so it was on the continent of Africa. But we have seen in previous discussions how the continent that gave the world writing also produced items based on the skill of writing. It was not just a dead skill but a very positive and vital activity of the people.

By the third century CE the Axumites had begun to use natural resources for everyday purposes. Gold, silver, and bronze were used to make coins throughout the empire. Unlike the Kemetic and Nubian civilizations, which did not make much use of coins, the Axumites were the first Africans to mint their own coins and to use them in external trade.

For their internal trade they used bronze coins mostly, but they relied mainly on a system of bartering. Axumite potters began to make pottery in new shapes and colors that were both beautifully decorated and functional. Clearly international trade helped to influence the local artisans, but it is also equally clear that Axum was not just a receiver of ideas; it was also a place that impacted on others.

In the middle of the fourth century CE, according to a sixth-century historian named Rufinus who wrote an *Ecclesiastical History*, a Syrian Christian was on his way to India through the Red Sea when he became shipwrecked. His two sons, Aedesius and Frumentius, were adopted by King Ella Amida of Axum and raised in the palace. When King Amida died and his son Ezana became king the two young Syrians, Aedesius and Frumentius, were brought into the court as advisors regarding the Christian nations and peoples. Ezana I ruled over a large kingdom that included the Beja, Arabia, Saba, Abyssinia, and Meroe. Most of these people had their own religions and they believed in their own gods. However, with the influence of Aedesius and Frumentius, who may have been in their teen years at the time of the shipwreck, many people in the Axumite state turned away from the ancient Axumite deities of Mahrem, Beher, Meder, and Astar. The two Syrians became enamored with the Axumite culture and passionate about Christianity and began to study all forms of Christian theology, including Arianism, which was named for Arius, a priest who lived in Alexandria during the latter part of the third century CE. The Beja represented the most difficult nation to subdue for the Axumites. Ezana I succeeded in defeating them by sending his two brothers, She'azana and Hadefa, to head the Axumite army during the decisive battle with the Beja. These two generals had become the country's leading military strategists and Ezana I wanted them to plan the conquest of the Beja once and for all. This ancient people had harassed the Kemites and the Nubians and now Axum was prepared to end the irritation of their hostile raiding parties. When the battle was over the Beja recognized the supremacy of Axum. As an act of complete authority over their enemies She'azana and Hadefa made the Beja soldiers, led by six of their surviving kings, walk to the court of Ezana I. It took four long months because it involved the royal houses of Beja, wives, children, and animals.

When they arrived in Axum the Beja bowed to the Axumite king. Ezana I could have killed the kings before the people, as some conquering kings had done, but his mercy and generosity knew no bounds. He let the Beja keep their families together, their animals, and the use of their language. Such was his respect for the Beja that he did all he could to assist them. He ordered 25,000 long-horned cattle, clothing, and food be given to the Beja kings. There was great rejoicing among the Axumites and the Beja. The Axumite king understood clearly the ancient African wisdom that said "The sun will shine on those who stand before it shines on those who kneel." There was no need to further humiliate the ancient Beja people. In one way the moving of the Beja anticipated the twentieth-century removal of many Beja, Nuba, and Nubians during the construction of the Aswan High Dam. The Beja people remain a strong ethnic group in northeast Africa even into the twenty-first century.

The country was a magnet for ideas. People came to the land from afar to trade, to study, and to see the wonderful objects that had been created by the Axumites. Its growing intellectual class was made up increasingly of religious thinkers, philosophers, and debaters. In the sixth century Cosmas Indicopleutes, a Greek writer and visitor, wrote that he found "everywhere in Axum and Adulis churches of Christians, bishops, martyrs, monks, and recluses by whom the Gospel of Christ is proclaimed." It is more likely that Indicopleutes found those "willing to be martyrs" than the actual martyrs in Axum and Adulis, but nevertheless he was quite impressed with what he saw. About 300 years later al-Yaqubi wrote that there were "mighty cities of the Abyssinians visited by Arab merchants of Dahlak." Perhaps unbeknown to al-Yaqubi the Arabs had knowledge of the Axumite kingdom even earlier, because we know that in the seventh century the king of Ethiopia gave protection to Muslims who had fled Arabia.

A century earlier, in 528 CE, the Axumite Empire had invaded Arabia and it ruled the Yemenite area until 575 CE, when problems at home forced the large contingent of troops kept in Yemen to return to support the king in his contest with pretenders to his power. In fact, the power of the home base had to be preserved in order to continue the kingdom. So great was the military power of Axum in defending itself from attack that its neighbors, Sennar and Meroe, still paid taxes and gave gifts to the Axumite king well into the seventh century. Thus, Axum is said in the book *Periplus of the Erythraeans* to be a "place to which all the ivory is brought from the countries beyond the Nile."

Axum's importance had to do with the sophisticated nature of its political and economic relationships with the rest of the world. It traded with India, China, Sri Lanka, Rome, Punt, Greece, Zanzibar, Persia, Kemet, Arabia, and Nubia. Its history is rich with the stories of the Queen of Sheba's visit to King Solomon and with the Gabaza Axum being the place where the Jewish Ark of the Covenant was kept, having been moved by King Menelik I from Jerusalem through Elephantine to the mountain kingdom of Axum.

Axum has often been called Ethiopia, a word that was used as a general term for Africa by those in Europe and Asia. Ethiopia is a Greek word that means "burnt faces." The nation of Axum was a specific kingdom within the boundaries of today's Ethiopia but is not to be identified as the same country. The present country of Ethiopia incorporated the ancient Axum into its own territory.

In ancient times it was not unheard of for the Greeks to speak of Ethiopians and mean Africans who were not Egyptians. Aristotle wrote in his book *Physiognomonica* about Ethiopians and Egyptians. Other writers such as Homer, Herodotus, and Diodorus Siculus wrote about Ethiopians meaning essentially Nubians.

Although present-day Ethiopia, a country dominated by the Oromo people, has a long history with the involvement of the Amharic and Tigrean emperors and kings, it is a complex empire of ethnic identities that comprise a remarkably resilient modern nation. As the inheritor and protector of the rich heritage of Axum it remains one of the most important nations in Africa.

## Carthage: Africa's Mediterranean powerhouse

African history is like a giant game of mankala, a widely played African game that is sometimes called oware, ohoro, or ayo. Players place seeds into various cups on the board until all of the seeds have been deposited. When one cup of human activity is empty another one seems to be full. At times it appears in the game of mankala that there are several cups with the same number of seeds in them. And so it is with the movement of history on the template of the African continent.

Carthage, called in Latin *Carthago*, was originally a Phoenician outpost established for trade with Africa and Spain. It occupied an area on the Mediterranean Sea in the present-day country of Tunisia and was the principal city influenced by the Phoenicians from modern-day Lebanon. The Phoenicians had an ancient capital called Tyre, a city that had been attacked many times by the ancient Kemites. It was from Tyre that the Phoenicians came to this part of Africa. It should be noted that the land was not uninhabited and one should not think that the Phoenicians found a vacant territory and then plopped a city down on that space. Rather this was an area on the coast that would attract many invaders.

The Phoenicians, Romans, Vandals, Byzantines, Arabs, Ottomans, and French captured that particular part of Africa throughout history. The earliest people were adventurers and immigrants traveling from East Africa toward the northwest part of the continent, which was in those days covered with savanna grass and small trees. It looked rather like present-day Tanzania or Kenya. There is evidence that humans occupied the place long before the Phoenicians. Indeed, there is evidence at the southern oasis town of Kebili, that human activity there dates back about 200,000 years.

An aggressive trading people, the Phoenicians first settled in Carthage around the seventh century BCE, about the time that the Twenty-fifth Dynasty was dominating Kemet. Among the port cities that the Phoenicians laid out were Hadrumetum and Hippo Diarrhytus. However, it is Carthage, the arch enemy of Rome, that makes a dramatic entry into African history from the northwest. The city's regional dominance lasted until the Punic Wars between Rome and Carthage, which began in 263 and ended in 146 BCE with Carthage defeated and its leaders and many of its people sold into slavery in Europe.

Although some myths claim that the city was established by Dido of Tyre or a queen of Tyre, these stories exist without much proof. We do know that merchants and explorers established a network of trade and commerce that made the city wealthy. Carthage became one of the wealthiest cities of its day. It was governed by an aristocracy of nobles and wealthy men who elected two magistrates, or suffetes as they were called, to carry out the wishes of the oligarchy. This had not been the pattern or tradition of the original inhabitants of the area but was a system imported from southwest Asia.

It should be remembered that this was an important cosmopolitan city and in some senses may be said to rival Alexandria on the Mediterranean at the time. Since the Ptolemaic pharaohs had been forced to acquiesce to Rome in many activities the city of Alexandria was not as important as it had been earlier. It would continue to lose power and influence as Carthage loomed large. Eventually in 30 BCE Alexandria would limp to its demise at the hands of Rome. Carthage would find its fate sealed at a much earlier date but the demise would be much more dramatic.

The religion of Carthage was eclectic. Carthaginians taught the fear of the gods as well as the state. The names of the local deities were Tanit, Melkart, and Eshmoun. The Phoenicians brought with them Baal, Asherah, and Baal Hammon. The priesthoods around these deities would last long after Africa became a Roman province. In fact, they would not disappear until the arrival of Christianity. The emperors of Rome had to use their soldiers to tear down the main temple dedicated to the deity Tanit in 421 CE.

In the third and second centuries BCE the city of Carthage was the shining star in an ever-increasing commercial empire. But it would eventually have to deal with Rome, an empire of its own with ambitions that included the north coast of Africa. Carthaginians established themselves on Sardinia, Malta, and the Balearic Islands. Men and women of distinction lived in the city. Indeed, the navigator Hanno sailed down the African coast as far as modern-day Sierra Leone in the fifth century BCE. Hanno of Carthage left a bronze plaque in a temple to Baal as testimony to his voyage. His eighteen-line travelogue, or "Periplus," was translated into Greek, and then copied many times by Greek and, later, Byzantine scribes. Our earliest manuscripts date from the ninth (*Palatinus Graecus 398*) and fourteenth (*Vatopedinus 655*) centuries CE.

In the Greek translation, Hanno was called king, which means he was probably a high Carthaginian magistrate known as a suffete. He says he traveled with about 30,000 men and women in sixty ships with fifty oars each, although 500 people in each ship sounds like an exaggeration. Hanno then describes his various stops along the way and his interaction with Africans on the coast. He met men as fast as horses and these people gave him interpreters. He then encountered crocodiles and water horses (hippopotami). He says they quickly passed by a frightening, noisy island in what was called the "Western Horn." After passing this island, they discovered a large mountain called the Chariot of the Gods, which was probably a volcano. Three days later, they were in the "Southern Horn," where they encountered hairy people who were called gorillas by the interpreters. Hanno's men were unable to capture their stone-throwing men, but were able to capture three of the women. After capturing the gorilla women, the Carthaginians flayed them in order to bring back the skins for display. At that point, having run out of provisions, Hanno decided to return to Carthage.

Pliny says Hanno was under orders to circumnavigate Africa, and may have done so – or at least gone as far as south of the equator. Depending on what he meant by gorilla, he could have gone to Sierra Leone, where one finds chimpanzees today, or to the Congo, where there are gorillas. Hanno thought they were human, but he had seen a variety of humans living in Carthage and these animals were not like them. It is believed he saw actual gorillas.

There were other outstanding citizens. The statesman Mago of Carthage negotiated treaties with the Etruscans, the Romans, and some Greek cities. Such was the interest of the commercial traders, the fierce combatants of trade, that they would go anywhere they could to find a market or secure a deal. Carthage was in its glory.

It goes without saying that the island of Sicily, barely 100 miles away from the coast, would become a target of Carthage. Africans settled first in the western part of the island but the Carthaginian army, made of Africans and Phoenicians under the leadership of Hamilcar Barca, was met by the king of Syracuse, Gelon, and defeated in 480 BCE at the battle of Himera. Thus, the Greek city-states of Sicily were preserved, but Carthage would not go away. I find it quite remarkable that Carthage sat out the Peloponnesian War, not even getting involved when the Athenians attacked Syracuse (415–413), but this was probably due to the shock of the defeat at Himera. Actually the grandson of Hamilcar, Hannibal (a much used name in Carthage just as Hamilcar Barca was used often), came back and destroyed the city of Himera in 409 BCE. It took a year for Carthage to get a good-sized mercenary army together, so Hannibal had only 5800 men available when the ships were ready in 408 BCE. He took them anyway, defeated the city of Selinus on Sicily, driving the Selinites back to their home territory, and waited through the winter until the main army, which may have numbered 60,000, landed at Motya. The year 409 saw him take Selinus by frontal assault. The town of Segesta, which had called in Carthage for protection, joined the Carthaginians. Now Hannibal was ready to attack Himera. Unlike what happened at Selinus, Himera beat off the first Carthaginian assault. Then the city of Syracuse recalled twenty-five ships from the Aegean Sea, where they had been fighting in the Peloponnesian War, and sent them to assist at Himera. Their arrival gave the Greeks control of the sea, so Hannibal resorted to an old war strategy; he broke camp and marched directly to the city of Syracuse. The Syracusans could not defend an ally, Himera, if their own home was under direct attack, so they withdrew both their ships and their men from Himera. Then Hannibal doubled back, captured Himera, and destroyed it, burning it to the ground. The captured women and children were given as prizes to the soldiers, while Hannibal took 3000 male prisoners to the spot where Hamilcar had died, and used them as a sacrifice to the spirit of his grandfather. Humans do not seem to learn the lesson of history that no amount of brutality called by the name of sacrifice can bring back the dead.

Three years later in 406 BCE, his fellow general, Himilco, brought the same fate to Acragas, modern-day Agrigento. He had taken over the army after disaster had struck Hannibal, who was on a second campaign against the Greek states. A plague infected his army, and many soldiers died, including Hannibal himself. Some claimed that this was punishment for violating the cemeteries of the dead in the defeated cities. Others simply saw it as the price of war. Nevertheless, the army vowed not to desecrate any graves and to order prayers and human sacrifices to appease the gods. A younger relative of Hannibal named Himilco took charge of the army and led them into Acragas, where they captured the city full of loot. What should have been the best of times became the worst of times.

At home there was trouble because in addition to the plague there was an African revolt against the oligarchy, and the Carthaginians concluded that the gods must be angry with them, if they would cheat them of their best opportunity to conquer all of Sicily. During the war their soldiers had destroyed temples belonging to Demeter and Persephone, two of the most popular Greek goddesses. They were told by Greek residents that they could end their misfortune by building two new temples in Carthage. As for Himilco, he committed suicide, and Mago succeeded him.

Nearly a hundred years later, 310–307 BCE, the absolute lord of Syracuse called Agathocles, the tyrant, threatened Carthage and other towns on the shores of Africa. When Agathocles died, Carthage had complete control over the western Mediterranean. It would be the Romans who would finally rise to the challenge laid down by Carthage, the African powerhouse of the north. By the third century BCE, the character of Carthage had changed drastically. It was practically all African in terms of its military and bureaucracy, but the rich Phoenician oligarchy still dictated the terms of life for the people. They were outnumbered by the locals and many immigrants were coming from other places in Africa and from various Phoenician colonies, yet the original leadership, although blacker and less tied to Tyre than it had ever been, saw itself as the nobility. Rome challenged the power of Carthage and sought to wrest control of the western Mediterranean in the famous Punic Wars, called such because of the Latin name for the Phoenicians, that is Poeni. These two nations had seen a long period of relative peace, since the Carthaginians probably saw Rome as just one more Etruscan outpost. They had signed treaties in 510, 348, and 306 BCE. These agreements pledged cooperation against piracy on the high seas. Rome also promised not to trade in the Carthaginian Empire without Carthaginian supervision, and if Roman ships were blown by storm to any place in the empire besides Carthage and Sicily, they agreed that they should leave in five days. What caused the political change was the fact that the Greek-speaking countries between the two states were about to disappear. Indeed, Rome was also expanding its reach in the Mediterranean. War seemed inevitable and so it was.

The first of these wars (264–241) cost Carthage all its possessions in Sicily. Immediately after the First Punic War a great uprising of the African soldiers from the interior occurred in 240 BCE. Hanno the Great, a legendary politician and a friend of the nobility as well as a member of the Barcas clan, sought to make himself the overlord of Carthage, replacing the Carthaginian oligarchy with one-man rule. He tried to make himself popular by giving out free food, and then called upon the indigenous Africans and their local kings, particularly those from Morocco, to back him for leadership with their weapons. The uprising failed, Hanno was crucified, and most of his family members were executed. However, it was hard to wipe out a ruling family completely, and the Barcas made a comeback, ruling Carthage again at a later date.

A powerful leader, Hamilcar Barca, born in Africa and devoted to Carthage, was credited with putting down the revolt. He quickly diverted attention from the internal divisions by launching a military campaign in Spain to compensate for the loss of Sicilian possessions. This campaign was continued by Hasdrubal.

Carthage would continue to grow and develop even after the initial defeat. A second war with Rome would occur and be called the Second Punic War (218–201 BCE). This was one of the great wars of history. Although the Carthaginian general was the brilliant African general Hannibal the Great, Carthage was still defeated. Two reasons might be given for the defeat of Carthage during the Second Punic War. The first was the fighting ability and skill of Roman generals Quintus Fabius Maximus Rullianus and Scipio Africanus Major. The second reason was the political divisions in Carthage. The leaders could not get their act together and ended up denying Hannibal the supplies he needed to wage war. This meant that the handwriting was finally on the wall for the great commercial empire.

Nevertheless, the events that placed Hannibal's name in African history, alongside those of Senurset I, Mentuhotep, Ahmose, Thutmoses III, Ramses II, Piankhy, Taharka, Amanirensis, Ezana I, Shaka, Sundiata, Nzingha, and Yenenga, are as brilliant in terms of overcoming obstacles on the battlefield as any ever undertaken by any general. He was the greatest general of his age. Unquestionably he excelled all other military commanders in strategy and skill. His battles were mostly victories. All authorities and experts agree that if it were not for the divisions and confusion in his home base he would have taken Rome. He cherished the engagement with Rome and believed that it was his destiny to extend the African empire of Carthage into Europe. One might say that he had the spirit of a warrior even when his own country did not understand his commitment to victory over the Romans. So at 25 he became the commander-in-chief of the armies of Carthage and his name, Hannibal Barca, soon brought fear to the enemies of Carthage. He swore to his father that he would always hate the Romans.

Thus, the conflicts personal and political in Carthage notwithstanding, and the difficulties of establishing the proper lines of communication notwithstanding, Hannibal vowed to surmount all obstacles in his quest for victory. In 218 CE he crossed the Rhône, fought the Gauls, and continued his march up the left bank of the river. Scipio, the Roman general, arrived three days later at the place where Hannibal had crossed the river. Scipio sailed back to Italy with the intention of meeting Hannibal when he should descend from the Alps. Hannibal sent his brother Hasdrubal into Spain to engage Gnaeus, Scipio's brother. Hannibal continued his march up the Rhone till he came to the Isara. Marching along the river, he crossed the Alps with African elephants, descended into the valley of the Dora Baltea, and followed the course of the river till he arrived in the territories of the Insubrian Gauls.

The five months march cost Hannibal many men. The passage over the Alps was not an easy feat; it was something nearly unthinkable. According to a statement engraved by his order on a column at Lacinium, in the country of the Brutii, which Polybius saw, Hannibal's army was reduced to 12,000 Africans, 8000 Spaniards, and 6000 cavalry when he arrived in the territories of the Insubrian Gauls. He recruited Insubrians to his army since his forces were depleted by the long march. They turned southward and encountered Cornelius Scipio on the right bank of the River Ticinus.

In the battle which ensued the Romans were defeated, and Scipio, with the remainder of the army, retreated on the left bank of the Po, crossed the river before Hannibal could overtake him and encamped near Placentia. With the approach of Hannibal he retreated more to the south, and took a stand on the right bank of the Trebia, where he waited for the arrival of the army under the other consul, T. Sempronius. Sempronius had already crossed over into Sicily with the intention of sailing to Africa to engage Carthage when he was asked to return to help protect Rome. When the two armies joined, Sempronius decided, against the advice of Scipio, to risk another battle. The skill and bravery of Hannibal's African army again prevailed; the Romans were entirely defeated. Their troops ran for their lives, taking shelter wherever they could find it, mostly behind the walls of fortified cities. Because of these victories, the whole of Cisalpine Gaul fell into the hands of Hannibal; and the Gauls, who on his first arrival were prevented from joining him by the presence of Scipio's army in their country, began to assist Hannibal with both men and supplies with enthusiasm.

In the following year, 217 BCE, the Romans levied two new armies to oppose Hannibal. One army was posted at Arretium, under the command of the consul Flaminius, and the other at Ariminum, under the consul Servilius. Hannibal decided, after looking at the options and considering the military advantages, to attack Flaminius first. In his march southward through the swamps of the basin of the Arnus, his army suffered greatly, and he himself lost the sight of one eye. After resting his troops for a short time in the neighborhood of Faesulae, he marched past Arretium, searching the country for food as he went. He punished villages and towns that tried to defend themselves, hoping to draw Flaminius to a battle.

Flaminius, who appears to have been hot-tempered and of poor judgment, hastily followed Hannibal; and was trapped in the basin of Lake Trasimenus. He was completely defeated by the Carthaginians, whose troops came down from the mountains which encircle the valley. Three or four days afterwards, Hannibal cut off a detachment of Roman cavalry, about 4000 men, which had been sent by Servilius to assist his compatriot. Hannibal wanted to win over the affections of the other states and therefore he dismissed without ransom all the prisoners whom he took in battle and gave them an opportunity of joining his army as he marched slowly along the eastern side of the peninsula, through Umbria and Picenum, into Apulia. However, the cooperation was not as much as he had expected. Rome appointed Q. Fabius Maximus dictator after the defeat of Flaminius, and Maximus put in place a defensive system of warfare for the rest of the year. In the following year, 216 BCE, the Romans decided to meet Hannibal again in battle. An army of 80,000 foot soldiers and 6000 cavalry was raised, which was commanded by the consuls L. Aemilius Paulus and C. Terentius Varro. The Carthaginian army now amounted to 40,000 foot soldiers and 10,000 cavalry. Both armies were encamped in the neighborhood of Cannae in Apulia.

According to Polybius the carnage was quite incredible in the Roman defeat at Cannae. The loss is placed at 70,000 men destroyed, with the exception of 3000 men who escaped to the neighboring cities, and also all the cavalry, with the exception of 300 belonging to the allies and 70 that escaped with Varro. A detachment of 10,000 foot soldiers, which had been sent to surprise the Carthaginian camp, was obliged to surrender as prisoners. The consul L. Aemilius and the two consuls of the former year, Servilius and Attilius, were also among the slain. Hannibal lost only 4000 Gauls, 1500 Africans and Spaniards, and 200 horses. This victory placed the whole of lower Italy in the power of Hannibal, but it was not followed by the kind of capitulation that Hannibal had hoped for as some of the states continued to be devoted to Rome.

Hannibal was unable to make any new campaigns for the further conquest of Italy till he received new troops. Hasdrubal was accordingly ordered to march from Spain to Hannibal's assistance. Gnaeus Scipio, as already observed, had been left in Spain to oppose Hasdrubal. He was afterwards joined by P. Cornelius Scipio, and the war was carried on for several years until the Roman army was entirely defeated by Hasdrubal in 212 BCE. Both the Scipios fell in the battle.

Hasdrubal was now preparing to join his brother, but was prevented by the arrival of the young P. Cornelius Scipio in Spain in 210 BCE, who quickly recovered what the Romans had lost. In 210 BCE he took Carthago Nova; and it was not till 207 BCE, when the Carthaginians had lost almost all their dominions in Spain, that Hasdrubal set out to join his brother in Italy. He crossed the Alps without meeting any opposition from the Gauls and arrived at Placentia before the Romans were aware that he had entered Italy. After besieging this town without success, he continued his march southward; but before he could join forces with Hannibal, he was attacked by the consuls C. Claudius Nero and M. Livius on the banks of the Metaurus in Umbria. Hasdrubal's army, weakened from the long march, was cut to pieces, and the general himself fell in the battle. This misfortune obliged Hannibal to act on the defensive; and from this time till his departure from Italy in 203 BCE he was confined to Bruttium. Yet it is to the credit of his superior military skill that he was able to maintain his army in a hostile country without any assistance from his own government.

After he had conquered Spain from Carthage, in 204 BCE, Scipio crossed over into Africa to carry the war into Hannibal's country. He employed the assistance and support of Masinissa, a Numidian prince who wanted independence from the Carthaginians. Scipio gained two victories over the Carthaginians. The Carthaginians called their great commander home to defend the city. He returned to Carthage, landing at Septis, and advanced to Zama, five days to the west of Carthage. There he met Scipio's army and was entirely defeated. Nearly 20,000 Carthaginians lost their lives in the battle of Zama. About the same numbers were taken prisoner. The Carthaginians were obliged to sue for peace, and thus ended the Second Punic War, 201 BCE. After the conclusion of the war, Hannibal applied himself to clean up the government. He reduced the power of the perpetual judges and provided for the proper collection of the public revenue, which had been embezzled. He was supported by the people in these reforms; but he incurred the enmity of many powerful men, who told the Romans that he was endeavoring to persuade his countrymen to join Antiochus, king of Syria, in a war against them.

A Roman embassy was sent to Carthage to demand the punishment of Hannibal as a disturber of the public peace. On reflection, Hannibal, aware that he would not be able to resist his enemies, escaped from the city and sailed to Tyre. From there he went to Ephesus to join Antiochus in 196 BCE. One day, when he had fled to Syria, he had a meeting with King Antiochus of Syria, who had kept him out of the intimate discussions of war with the Romans, and after calling to mind his defeats of the Roman army and his hatred for the Romans, he gave this account:

> My father Hamilcar, when I was a small boy not more than nine years old, just as he was setting out from Carthage to Spain as commander-

in-chief, offered up victims to Jupiter, greatest and best of gods. While this ceremony was being performed, he asked me if I would like to go with him on the campaign. I eagerly accepted and began to beg him not to hesitate to take me with him. Thereupon he said, *I will do it, provided you will give me the pledge that I ask.* With that he led me to the altar on which he had begun his sacrifice, and having dismissed all the others, he bade me lay hold of the altar and swear that I would never be a friend to the Romans. For my part, up to my present time of life, I have kept the oath which I swore to my father so faithfully, that no one ought to doubt that in the future I shall be of the same mind. Therefore, if you have any kindly intentions with regard to the Roman people, you will be wise to hide them from me; but when you prepare war, you will go counter to your own interests if you do not make me the leader in that enterprise.

If Hannibal's advice as to the conduct of the war had been followed, the result of the contest might have been different; but he was only employed in a subordinate command, and the Syrians were defeated. Hannibal was obliged to seek refuge at the court of Prusias, king of Bithynia, where he remained about five years, and on one occasion obtained a victory over Eumenes, king of Pergamus. The Romans sent an embassy to the king of Bithynia demanding that Hannibal be given up. Instead of going with the Romans, where he knew he would be tortured, he drank poison and killed himself in Nicomedia in Bithynia, in 183 BCE, during the sixty-fifth year of his age.

No historian of Carthage ever told the story of Hannibal because with the decline of the country it would be left to the enemies of Hannibal to write the narrative of his life, yet even the reports of his enemies suggest that he was the greatest military strategist of his day. Polybius remarks:

How wonderful is it that in the course of sixteen years, during which he maintained the war in Italy, he should never once dismiss his army from the field, and yet be able, like a good governor, to keep in subjection so great a multitude, and to confine them within the bounds of their duty, so that they never mutinied against him nor quarrelled among themselves. Though his army was composed of people of various countries – including Africans from Mauritania and Morocco as well as Carthage, Spaniards, Gauls, Carthaginians, Italians, and Greeks – men who had different laws, different customs, and different languages, and, in a word, nothing among them that was common – yet, so dexterous was this African leader's management that, notwithstanding this great diversity, he forced all of them to acknowledge one authority, and to yield obedience to one command. And this, too, he accomplished in the midst of very varied fortune. How high as well as just an opinion must these things convey to us of his ability in war! It may be affirmed with confidence that if he had first tried his strength in the other parts of the world and had come last to attack the Romans, he could scarcely have failed in any part of his design.

(As quoted in Morris 1897)

Unable to recover enough to discover the kind of unity that was necessary for far-flung activities, the city of Carthage found itself in deep political trouble, with leaders creating their own factions and native Africans fighting against the nobles, who remained tied to Phoenicia though it was long gone from the scene as a major power. This gave Cato the Elder reason to launch another war, the Third Punic War, 149–146 BCE, which ended with the total destruction of Carthaginian power and the burning of the city by Scipio Africanus Minor. Romans later undertook to build a new city (Colonia Junonia) on the spot in 122 BCE, calling it the capital of Africa Proconsularis, but the project failed. A new city was founded in 44 BCE and under Augustus became an important center of Roman administration. Carthage was later (439–533 CE) the capital of the Vandals and was recovered (533) for the Byzantine Empire by Belisarius, which kept it for 150 years. Destroyed by the Arabs in 698, the city rose again as a populated place for a few centuries. Now it was strictly under the influence of the Arab Muslims. The Arabs had taken all of North Africa by the start of the eighth century, and, with Kairouan as its capital, the whole of North Africa became a fruitful province of the fast-expanding Islamic empire controlled by the caliphs in Damascus. Soon the Amazighs, who may have represented some elements of the Phoenicians and Vandals as well as earlier invading groups, adopted Islamic religious teachings, but they hated their harsh treatment by the Arabs. Their uprisings continued until 909, when a group of Amazigh Shiites, the Fatimids, pulled together disaffected Amazighs and Tuaregs and briefly retook North Africa back from the Arabs. Their capital was built on the coast at Mahdia, but the unity was to be short-lived because of religious differences. Some of the people returned to Sunni Islam and the unity was slowly destroyed. In the end, the great and mighty empire that was Carthage was reduced to a series of ruins, mainly of Roman construction, that today can tell the visitor little about the former might and power of this African nation. Like the history of Carthage, much of the history of West Africa came through the hands of non-African writers. Although there were indigenous sources as well as material evidence from excavations, cemeteries, pottery, and oral traditions, the major historians of the fourteenth to seventeenth centuries were the Arabic-speaking historians who traveled across Africa.

# 8 The Sudanic empires: historians and their narratives

Four historians who wrote in Arabic are responsible for much of what we know about the Sudanic empires of Ghana, Mali, and Songhay. They are Abd al-Rahman ibn Mohammad ibn Khaldun, Ibn Battuta, Chihab Addine Abul-Abbas Ahmad ben Fadhl al-Umari, and Leo Africanus.

## Ibn Khaldun (1332–1395 CE)

Ibn Khaldun's chief contribution may be his first volume aimed at an analysis of historical events. This volume, known as *Muqaddimah* or "Prolegomena," was based on Ibn Khaldun's unique approach and original contribution and became a masterpiece in literature on philosophy of history and sociology. The work sought to identify psychological, economic, and social facts that contribute to the advancement of human civilization. In this context, he tried to show how group feelings, *al-'Asabiyya*, give rise to the ascent of new civilizations. He identified an almost rhythmic repetition of rise and fall in human civilization, and analyzed factors contributing to it. In some senses, Ibn Khaldun's work either created or continued stereotypical comments about Africans. He writes of Africans:

> Their qualities of character, moreover, are close to those of dumb animals. It has even been reported that most of the blacks of the first [climatic] zone dwell in caves and thickets, eat herbs, live in savage isolation and do not congregate, and eat each other. The same applies to the Slavs. The reason for this is that their remoteness from being temperate produces in them a disposition and character similar to those of the dumb animals, and they become correspondingly remote from humanity.
>
> (Ibn Khaldun 1967, p. 59)

This is not just bad science, it is in poor taste considering the fact that several of the countries where he made his living had been dominated by Africans years earlier and the civilizations of Africa from whence came much of his inspiration, resources, and knowledge were those created by black people. Thus, I cannot accept the appraisal of Ibn Khaldun's work as "brilliant" in regard to Africa although I am able to see that *Muqaddimah* became an important independent book apart from the rest of Ibn Khaldun's historical work (Niane 1997, p. 4). Important to the history of Africa is the fact that Ibn Khaldun did set out the list of rulers of Mali until the year 1390 (Niane 1997, p. 4).

## Ibn Battuta (1304–1369 CE)

Abu Abdullah Muhammad ibn Battuta, also known as Shams ad-Din, was born at Tangier, Morocco, on 24 February 1304 CE. He left Tangier on Thursday, 14 June 1325, when he was 21 years of age. His travels lasted for about thirty years, after which he returned to Fez, Morocco, at the court of Sultan Abu 'Inan and dictated accounts of his journeys to Ibn Juzay. These are known as the Travels (*Rihala*) of Ibn Battuta. He died at Fez in 1369.

Ibn Battuta was the only medieval traveler who is known to have visited the lands of every Muslim ruler of his time. He also traveled across Africa, visiting Mali, Kanem Borno, and the Swahili coast. He also went to Sri Lanka, China, Byzantium (Turkey), and south Russia, visiting more than forty countries. Ibn Battuta was the greatest traveler of his era, covering over 75,000 miles, a figure not surpassed by any other medieval traveler (Dunn 2005).

## Chihab Addine Abul-Abbas Ahmad ben Fadhl al-Umari (1300–1384 CE)

Al-Umari provided essential information about the African continent while he served as secretary to the Mamluk court of Egypt between 1340 and 1348. There are two important pieces of information we get from his writings. One of them is the information about the *hajj* of the great Malian Mansa Kankan Musa. He recorded that the mansa dispensed so much gold that its value fell in Egypt and the value of gold did not recover for a decade, thus describing the wealth of the Mali Empire. Second, al-Umari also recorded his interviews with Mansa Kankan Musa about his brother, Abubakari II, the previous mansa. Mansa Kankan Musa told al-Umari that Abubakari had abdicated the throne to journey to a land across the ocean, leading contemporary writers, the American Leo Wiener, the Guyanese historian Ivan van Sertima, the Canadian Michael Bradley, and the Malian historian Gaoussou Diawara to theorize that Abubakari II reached the Americas before Columbus, who went to the Americas in 1492 (Wiener 1992; Sertima 1976; Bradley 1992; Diawara 1992).

## Leo Africanus (1485–1554 CE)

Leo Africanus' Arabic name was Al-Hasan ibn Muhammed el-Wazzan ez-Zayyat. He was born in Granada in Moorish Spain but was expelled along with his parents and thousands of other Moors by Ferdinand and Isabella in 1492. They settled in Fez, Morocco, and he traveled with his uncle on diplomatic missions as a teenager. Captured by Christian pirates, he was sold as a slave to Pope Leo X. During the time he worked for the Catholic

Church administration as a slave, the pope was impressed with his learning and freed him. He was baptized under the name "Johannis Leo de Medici," and the pope commissioned him to write in Italian the detailed survey of Africa. He also taught Arabic in Rome and wrote in Arabic a description of his journeys in Africa (issued in Italian in 1526), and this book became the only source known to the Europeans about the interior of Africa. An English translation (1600) was reissued by the Hakluyt Society as *The History and Description of Africa* (3 vols, 1896, reprinted in 1963). Timbuktu became the byword for remote cities, although Leo wrote of it as a center of trade, education, and learning. It is Leo Africanus' description of Timbuktu that has remained the most impressive account of that ancient city. He visited the region twice and was told many things about the cultures of the African people. In fact, Africanus' accounts were the only ones that the Europeans had for many years of the fabulous city of Timbuktu. When he died in 1554 in Tunis he had reconverted to Islam.

## The Ghana Empire: the emergence of an imperial society

Even with all we know about it the Ghana Empire still causes us to pause and reflect on the incredible will of a people to produce between the great forest and the great desert a mighty civilization that encompassed the best elements of both regions. There are three important sources of information about the ancient lands of West Africa: archaeological excavations, books by Africans and Arabs, and oral histories.

Around 300 BCE a group of people, probably Soninke, formed themselves into a formidable trading kingdom near the upper waters of the majestic Niger River. This state soon became an empire that impacted on all of its neighbors, was written about by travelers, and influenced the course of West African history. Its name became known as Ghana, a name that was really the title of paramount king. Just as the ancient Egyptians called their paramount king Pharaoh, and the Asante called their paramount king Asantehene, the Soninke state called its king Ghana, meaning war king. Succeeding kings were known by their own names preceded by the title "Ghana." The country was soon called by the title given to the king. Among the Soninke the kingdom was called Wagadu. The Soninke people spoke one of the languages of the Mande group, languages that are found throughout West Africa. They traded with the Amazighs in the north and with the Wolof to the south and west of them.

In 773 CE we find the first reference to the Ghana Empire, although it certainly existed before this time if one takes archaeological evidence. A tradition recorded in the famous *Tarikh as-Sudan*, a history written by Abderrahman es-Saadi in Timbuktu in 1650, says there were twenty-two kings of Ghana before the beginning of the Muslim era (622 CE). One could easily see how this number of kings, give or take a few, could push the earliest recorded king back to 300 CE. However, it is more than likely, based on evidence found of pottery and other materials, that the kingdom started at least 600 years earlier. It was not to reach its full bloom until much later but already in those early years the kingdom of the Soninke was becoming a powerful trading nation.

Because the kingdom had become so efficient at trading salt and gold the king was soon given a new title, Kaya Maghan, meaning the "master of the gold." Inasmuch as the king controlled and regulated the export of the precious metal he was indeed its lord and master. No neighboring king was allowed to approach the Ghana in majesty or power.

Kings came from the descent lines of the first ancestors. No one could be Ghana who did not trace his origins to the first ancestors, usually female. Most African societies prior to Islam and Christianity were matrilineal. In order to deal with the increased demands on the kingdom because of the vigorous trade with the Amazighs, the Wagadu Empire chose its leaders for their skill in trade, negotiation, and warfare. The king grew very wealthy. A king of Wagadu could command an army of many thousands, use the services of many servants and messengers, and employ many traders and interpreters to deal with the Amazighs, Wolof, Serer, and other people.

The capital city of Wagadu was called Kumbi Saleh. This town is about 200 miles north of present-day Bamako. Caravans regularly crossed the desert from here, going through Taghaza to Tripoli and Tunis. It was a very cosmopolitan place, with lively social and economic business. It bustled with excitement whenever a new trader entered the town. It was famous for its elegance and the beauty of the Soninke women. Many traders married local women and became a part of the growing wealthy class of merchants in the city during the tenth century. By this time many of the leading citizens had become Muslims, dropping their original religion.

A Spanish Arab named al-Bakri wrote an important account in 1067 of one of the Ghanas. His name was Tunka Manin, and al-Bakri wrote about how he organized his power and wealth. It is interesting that al-Bakri did not visit the kingdom but got enough information from travelers and traders to compile a book about the court of the great Ghana, Tunka Manin.

Clearly after the Islamic conquest of the eighth century many Amazigh and other ethnic groups became Muslim. They were welcomed into the capital of Wagadu. Soon the Ghana allowed the Muslims to build their own town about 15 miles away from the capital. The houses of the Soninke were built of hardened clay, wooden beams, and thatch. The successful Muslim traders built stone houses as was their custom in North Africa. Thus, there developed in West Africa cities that had two identities, a section for the indigenous people and a section for the foreigners, usually Arab traders or Muslims of other ethnic groups.

Before 1240 Kumbi Saleh was undoubtedly the largest city in western Africa. It was the seat of the king as well as of economic power. All roads led across the desert and through the forest to Kumbi Saleh. Its reputation as a city was huge; nearly 15,000 people lived there. Because it was able to support the poor with a decent living it was a highly civilized city, capable of creating communities of artisans, thinkers, and traders.

Visitors and traders found the city friendly. There was no reason for the people of Wagadu to keep others out. So long as the visitors obeyed the rules and laws of Ghana they were all right. Al-Bakri, the so-called armchair historian who never went to West Africa, says of Ghana Tunka Manin that he "is the master of a large empire and of a formidable power." How large was the empire? According to the historian it was so large that the king could put 200,000 warriors in the field, more than 40,000 of them armed with the bow and arrow. The real strength of the army of the Ghana was its reliance on the iron-tipped spears. Their weapons were more deadly than those of their neighbors and their government was able to attract far more soldiers to its side because of its wealth. No surrounding power could withstand the full strength of Ghana. It was said that "Wagadu is a lion among the wildebeest."

The Soninke rulers of Wagadu subdued the Tekrur (of modern-day Senegal) and brought them within the Ghana Empire. These people helped the empire to push its borders to the sea and to the southeastern gold mines. They controlled the principal south Sahara city called Audoghast, an important trading town frequented by merchants from the north and south. It has long since disappeared because of the many wars that were fought to capture it. However, it remains a part of the history of the Ghana Empire because from here Ghana was able to command wealth and to wield power as traders passed through its gates. Indeed, these rulers and the elites who supported them were among the most talented rulers of their time.

To be the emperor of a huge empire like Wagadu the Ghana had to have other rulers under him who could govern effectively according to his edicts and laws. Thus, councilors of state, sub-kings, and government officials, particularly those who collected tribute, were organized from the capital city of Kumbi Saleh and sent out to carry out the commands of the emperor. Governors in charge of distant provinces reported back to the emperor on a regular basis through a series of messengers who were employed to go back and forth between the province and the metropolis. Such a large empire was a political, economic, and organizational success.

One could easily ask the question, where did Ghana Tunka Manin and other emperors before and after him find the money to pay the soldiers and the court officials? It is to the words of al-Bakri that we must turn because he gives an account of how the emperor Tunka Manin ruled his court and managed his affairs.

There were two main sources of revenue. Both were forms of taxes on the people. The first kind was an import–export tax. This was a sum of goods (more likely a portion of the product or produce than money) that a trader had to pay in order to bring goods into the empire or take goods out of the empire. So if you brought gold into the empire of Ghana you had to pay a certain amount of it as taxes to the emperor. If you took out salt you had to give the emperor a certain amount of gold for exporting. The king of Ghana, said al-Bakri, "places a tax of one dinar of gold on each donkey load of salt that comes into his country." But he also "places two dinar of gold on each load of salt that goes out." Similar taxes were paid for ivory, copper, spices, or ebony. The second form of tax was a production tax. It was applied to gold alone. Al-Bakri said it this way, "All pieces of gold that are found in the empire belong to the emperor." The system of control was quite brilliant because had the emperor not taken all the gold as his then the metal would have become so abundant among the people as to become worthless. This was not so much about the amassing of gold for the sake of wealth as about the controlling of the product to hold back inflation and to maintain the quality of life in the empire.

This system of control is not foreign to governments today. It is called the monopoly system and works quite well in the area of diamonds now. The vast majority of diamonds in the world are produced by a few large companies in Africa and Russia. All of the companies that participate in this business work together; it is a cartel. They have agreed not to put all the diamonds they have mined on the table for selling and distribution because if they did it would flood the market and the prices would go down. The oil cartel is another example. The less oil out for purchase means the higher the price you have to pay for it. Monopolies have the ability to manipulate the market. The emperors of Wagadu did the same with their gold nuggets. If a person in the empire found gold it belonged to the Ghana.

Since Europe could not get gold except from West Africa and their capacity to consume the gold was greater than that of Africans, the emperor made sure that the gold for ornaments and jewelry was scare so that the price for it would help maintain the state. It was in the steady demand for gold in North Africa and Europe that the West African empires found their continuing importance as traders and merchants in the precious metal. If the Europeans needed gold for their crowns, they got it from West Africa. If they needed to make gold coins they received the gold from the mines of West Africa.

Ancient Ghana, that is, Wagadu, was the pioneer in gold trading. In that sense, the first gold traders were Africans. The success of the Ghana Empire was to inspire other people to follow its pattern and when Ghana was defeated in the thirteenth century the Mali Empire would continue the trade.

By the eleventh century, Ghana had become the envy of many nations. It would spend the next 200 years fending off its enemies who sought to take control of its lucrative trade business. The ultimate demise of Ghana would not come from a single blow by its perennial enemies from the northwest, the Mauritanian and Moroccan Amazighs, who challenged the trade routes, attacked caravans, and razed oases and towns loyal to the Ghana. By the middle of the eleventh century many citizens of Wagadu had become intimate with the Zenata Amazighs from the north. They had created an environment that was conducive to intercultural relations. Intermarriage between rich trading families from the south and rich trading families from the north was not uncommon. Wagadu had allowed the Zenata to share control of Audoghast and to rule Siljimasa independently as part of the trade route. This was an attempt to establish a beneficial relationship with the Amazighs in the north. Although Zenata Amazigh and Arab traders lived in their own cities in the empire they were increasingly becoming a part of the inner circle of the ruling clan of the Soninke. The knowledge of the habits, customs, and languages of the inhabitants allowed the merchants to gain access to intimate details of military, political, and economic behaviors of the Wagadu administration. Yet it would not be this alone that would weaken and destroy the Ghana Empire. In the final analysis, it would be a small Mali kingdom that would ultimately succeed Wagadu after the Amazighs invaded with religious zealotry.

However, before the eventuality of the victory of the Mali kingdom could take place the ground had to be prepared for the Wagadu Empire's demise. Northerners, living in conditions of poverty and envious of Ghana's wealth, sought to gain control over the empire through economic penetration and a series of religious wars. Among the Moroccans there arose a leader, one devoted to Islam, named Abdullah ibn Yasin who established a center of religious teaching called a *ribat*, or hermitage. This was a fortified religious center similar to a monastery, where his followers would be indoctrinated in his puritanical form of Islam. He was not from the Zenata group but from the Sanhaja group of Amazighs. Ibn Yasin and those who followed his doctrine came to be known as the people of the *ribat*; the name in Arabic is al-Murabethin, or the Almoravids. They taught a puritanical form of Islam and sought to force their religious doctrine on all of those who professed Islam. Ibn Yasin subdued many groups in the north, bringing them under his control and form of religion. In the meantime, the empire of Ghana had to contend with the Almoravids coming down the west coast of Africa indoctrinating the Tekrur (or Futa Toro) rulers to believe in Islam. They were among the first West Africans to accept Islam.

The Almoravids split into two groups because of internal rivalries. One group under Ibn Tashufi conquered Morocco and established the Almoravid dynasty in that country. Another group led by Abubakar bin Umar allied with Tekrur and invaded Wagadu, whose royal house still followed the traditional African religion. In 1054 the Almoravids captured Audoghast, the southern powerhouse of a city, and then two years later in 1056 they captured the mighty city of Sijilmasa, the main northern trading center for West African gold, the end city for many caravans.

Nothing seemed capable of stopping the enthusiasm of the brotherhood; the Almoravids conquered people after people and crossed over the Straits of Gibraltar and took control of al-Andalus, or Muslim Spain. Stretching itself, the Almoravid movement leaped into action again against Ghana in the south as it had taken Spain in the north. Abu Bakr, naming himself after the uncle of the Prophet Muhammad, placed himself at the head of the army of the south as it sought to conquer Ghana. Finally in 1076, after many battles, the Almoravids seized the city of Kumbi Saleh. However, it would prove much easier to capture the capital city than to hold the empire of Ghana. Resistance was constant and unrelenting. Revolts and intrigues were the talk of the day. Abu Bakr was assassinated while trying to suppress one of these revolts in 1087.

Yet the Almoravid challenge to the power of the Ghana Empire inspired other kingdoms to break away from the center. Although the Almoravids ruled for only a few years they did so much damage to the prestige and power of the Ghana Empire that it was really up for grabs among the competing provinces when they left, having taken control of the lucrative desert trade when they moved the commercial center to Walata under local pressure.

Now new powers arose asserting their own independence. They attempted to create their own spheres of influence. One was the state of Tekrur. Already strong militarily, Tekrur, ruled by the Peul, asserted its independence from Wagadu and in time refused to pay tribute to the Ghana. The people of Kaniaga, under the Soso, did the same. These actions were followed by Diara and Bambuk and other provinces. These were rebellious provinces and they exercised a certain amount of autonomy in a country as large as Wagadu, which exceeded the territory of modern-day Germany, Spain, and France combined.

What was common about these people is that each people seemed to have at its core a powerful ethnic group, perhaps even a clan within the ethnic group, that demonstrated its internal unity and military expertise. Two groups emerged to challenge the Soninke power which had been at the base of the Wagadu Empire. These were the Soso and the Peul. The Soso would turn the tables on the Wagadu Empire and take charge of the remnants of the empire. On the other hand, the Peul (singular Pula), whose name English speakers have mis-spoken for many years as Fulani, would create their own kingdoms and dynasties in the western part of the empire. Their contribution to African history is a matter of record that is worth repeating because they are deeply embedded in most of West African history after the eleventh century. The Peul were cattle-keeping farmers who shared territory with the Soninke around the Upper Niger. Their Tekrur kingdom was located in the northern part of present-day Senegal and southern Mauritania. In 1199 they also took control of the kingdom of Diara, which had been one of the important provinces of Wagadu. This gave the Peul kingdom, Tekrur, effective control of a large portion of the original Wagadu Empire. But it was not alone in its ambition.

The Soso, who had also gained their independence from Wagadu during the turmoil caused by the Almoravid wars, made their play for power as well. In 1180 a Soso soldier of the Kaniaga kingdom by the name of Diara Kante overthrew the ruling Soninke dynasty of Wagadu and one of his successors became king. His name was Sumanguru Kante.

Under the kingship of the military ruler Sumanguru, the Soso, once a subject state, seized the throne and dominated the kingdom of Wagadu. Sumanguru made himself the supreme ruler of the people who had once been under the sole authority of the Soninke Ghana. He became, in effect, the new Ghana, paramount king of kings. In 1203 he surrounded the weakened capital city of Kumbi Saleh, laid siege to it and within a matter of days claimed victory by smashing the city and destroying the royal houses of the Soninke.

Sumanguru's reign was not to be a peaceful one for he was not a peaceful man. He soon found himself engaged in battle on every front; even smaller states controlled by other Peul like the Kaniaga kingdom felt that they did not have to submit to the "king of kings."

It is fair to say that the new Ghana had two major obstacles to his success. One was the fact that the Amazigh traders who had become accustomed to certain privileges in Kumbi Saleh were loyal to the old administration and tried everything they could to undermine Sumanguru's leadership. To them, he was not the true Ghana. The second problem the king faced was the fact that a little Mandinka state called Kangaba near the headwaters of the Niger River kept sending signals that it would not be controlled by the new Ghana. Thus, the king had commercial and political problems. The response to the first issue, that of the Amazigh traders who had settled in Kumbi Saleh, was to force them to Walata, a city further north in the kingdom. Ultimately Sumanguru knew that he had to fight the people of Kangaba in order to bring this small kingdom into check or else larger and more prosperous states would seek to get from under the power of Ghana. Furthermore, the small kingdom located in what is today's Guinea was close to the gold mines and threatened the very source of the livelihood of the royal house of Wagadu.

With the flux in the Sahel region numerous kingdoms were formed and re-formed under the leadership of intelligent and brave men and women. During the twelfth century, Yenenga came from what is now northern Ghana (the modern state) and founded the Mossi nation.

This region was called Dagomba and its capital city was Gambaga. It was a wealthy state and the king of Dagomba, who was called the Nedega, invited neighboring people from the Ghana Empire to reside in his territory. Many Malinkes and people who lived to the south came and helped form the army of the Dagomba. Among the greatest fighters of the Dagomba was the king's daughter, Yenenga.

She was a charming woman of extraordinary intelligence, but also a skilled horse-woman, an accomplished javelin thrower, and an expert with spears and bows. Her father was so fond of his daughter that he refused to let her marry. He wanted the best for her and he could see her leaving the kingdom. This saddened Yenenga and she felt that she could not persuade her father to change his mind. Her mother was unable to convince the father to let her marry.

Yenenga decided to plant a field of wheat. When it was ready for harvest, she would not harvest it, but let it rot. Her father was surprised and asked her for an explanation. "You see, father," she said, "you are letting me rot like the wheat in this field." The Nedega was very upset and ordered that she be imprisoned. But Yenenga had many friends among the king's guards. One night, one of the king's horsemen helped her escape from the prison. Both rode long into the night and were later attacked by Malinke outlaws. Yenenga and her benefactor routed their attackers but the horseman paid for the victory with his life. Yenenga was now alone in the middle of the forest, many miles from Gambaga. She continued to ride north. Soon she came to a river. Braving strong currents she and her horse managed to cross it. She was exhausted from the effort and lay on the back of her horse to sleep when she saw a house. It belonged to Riale, a famous elephant hunter. Riale came to her and when he saw her he wanted her for himself. In time they had a son who came to be called Ouedraogo. Yenenga is also known as the founder of the Mossi people.

## Mali Empire: West Africa's golden era

The appearance of Sundiata Keita as the king of Mali was a major moment in the history of West Africa. Everything that had gone before him would pale by comparison and he would become the most famous personality of West Africa. According to the *djeli*, traditional historian, often mistakenly called "griot," Sundiata's history is almost magical. In fact, the *djeli*, Mamadou Kouyaté, has been considered one of the most authoritative Malian *djelis*. His account of the story of Sundiata was told by the great historian and philosopher D. T. Niane (1966). Niane retold the story and translated it into French. It has since been translated into scores of languages. Other versions of the history of Sundiata (Sun-jara, Sunjata, Keyta) have appeared but they are all based on the same oral tradition.

It is said that Nare Maghan Kon Fatta Konate, king of Mali, was the son of a long lineage of great hunters who were able to communicate with spirits that influence human life. These were the spirits of ancestors who had died and were a part of the living dead, in the traditional sense of ancestors who continue to guide and direct activities among the living, creating when called upon and appealed to in ancestral ritual the harmony of community. Nare Magan Konate was a Mande, that is, his ethnic identification was as a Mande-speaking person. This name of the people is sometimes called "Mandinka," "Manding," "Malinke," or "Mandingo." I prefer the use of the word "Mande" because it is more common among the people themselves.

Although the Islamic faith had impacted the ruling families among the Mande-speaking elite during the thirteenth century, they still believed in the traditional spirits, often mixing the principles of Allah with those of the gods of their ancestors. This had not disappeared from their belief system by the time of Sundiata. So when a hunter came to Maghan, threw the cowrie shells of divination, and read the prophetic meaning of the design that they made, the king took it very seriously. In the African context a hunter is not merely one who seeks to kill animals for food, but an adventurer, quester, knowledge seeker, who loves the search, even if it takes him to distant lands. Thus, a king would be remiss to ignore the advice of someone as knowledgeable as a great hunter.

The hunter prophesied that two hunters would come to the king with a very ugly woman, and despite her ugliness, the hunter said, the king would have to marry this woman because she would bear him the greatest king who had ever lived. The king's counselor told him that he was skeptical of this prophecy and did not believe it. Of course, the king's first wife, Sassouma Berete, did not accept the prophecy either and she was very dissatisfied.

But as the prophecy had said, two hunters appeared at the court with a hunchbacked woman. They told the king that this woman, Sogolon Kedju, was a human double of a buffalo that had ravaged the county of Do, which was to the north of Mali, and had killed citizens and animals. Hunters in African societies are often the scientists and explorers because they see many things in their travels and are able to reflect on what they discover. In this case the two hunters said that they had killed the buffalo and brought the woman to Mali. As hideous as she was, they said, she was very wise and had extraordinary powers. They offered her to the king and the king, reflecting on the prophecy, accepted her and quickly married Sogolon. Soon Sogolon was pregnant with a child.

Sassouma Berete, the first wife, was jealous. She had the right to assume that her son, Dankaran Touman, would be the next king of Mali. After all he was the first-born son. She plotted to harm Sogolon because she did not want the prophecy to come true that this woman's son would be the greatest king who ever lived. But the powers of the mysterious Sogolon were too strong to be overcome. She eventually gave birth to a son. She named the child Mari Diata, but the son of Sogolon became known as Sogolon Diata, then finally Sundiata.

So filled with hatred for this child was Sassouma that she cursed the child and her curse seemed to work; the baby was lame and turned out to be without much energy, could not walk, and was ugly on top of all that. Sassouma was gratified and quite happy. How would this boy be able to compete with her son for the title of king when the father died? She was sure that there would be no contest. Sundiata did not speak by three and could not walk. Even at seven years of age he was still crawling around on the floor. He spent his time eating. He had no young friends. It was rather pathetic. The king himself did not see how this boy would ever amount to anything and probably questioned himself many times for making Sogolon pregnant. Yet the king was a believer in the prophecy, and on his death bed he honored the prophet's prediction and gave his seemingly handicapped son a gift that signified his desire that the boy should become the king of Mali. The gift was the *djeli* named Balla Fasséké, the son of the king's own *djeli*. However, when the old king died, Sassouma Berete immediately saw to it that the elders placed her son, Dankaran, on the throne. After all, Sundiata was still crawling on all fours.

It so happened that one day Sogolon, Sundiata's mother, needed some leaves from the baobab tree for her cooking and she asked her arch rival Sassouma Berete if she could borrow some. Sassouma said, yes, but took the opportunity to insult Sogolon and her lazy, dumb, and crippled son. The insults stung deeply. They were like daggers into the very heart of Sogolon because all that Sassouma said had been whispered by others and had been said aloud by those who did not like Sogolon. She grew angry and started to cry. Her tears overwhelmed her son. He asked his mother what had happened and she repeated the incident to him, still sobbing. Looking up at her, Sundiata said, "Don't worry mother, I will get up and walk today!"

Sundiata asked the blacksmiths to make for him the heaviest iron rod that they could make, which was then carried out to the prostrate Sundiata. A large crowd of people gathered around to see what he was going to do with the iron rod. He lifted himself upright, shaking and perspiring, and in the process transformed himself into a new person. However, the iron rod was bent like a bow under the weight and strength of the young Sundiata. At that moment the *djeli* Balla Fasséké composed the song "The Hymn to the Bow," which remains a part of the oral epic still used by many Mande poets and *djelis* today.

Now the transformed Sundiata posed an even greater threat to the plotting mother of Dankaran as well as to the false king himself. Sogolon urged Sundiata to take their people, family members, into exile for safety but before they could leave, Dankaran ordered that Balla Fasseké and Sundiata's half-sister be sent on a mission to the Soso king, Sumanguru Kante, who had been threatening all the kingdoms in the region with his growing army as he tried to reinvent the Wagadu Empire. Thus, Sundiata had to leave for exile without his *djeli*. His mother convinced him that it was best for him to leave although he was furious and wanted to confront Dankaran. He left with a small entourage of people who were to serve him until he could return. He was gone for many years. He came to manhood while traveling through kingdoms hundreds of miles from his home. He learned how to speak, to negotiate, to hunt, to read the stars, to fight, and to use his ancestral proverbs for wisdom. One day in the kingdom of Mema, Sundiata saw people selling baobab leaves in the market. He asked them where they came from because there were no baobab trees in Mema. They said they had come from Mali. They told him that the evil Sumanguru had conquered Mali and had sent Dankaran into exile. Sundiata soon gathered an army and journeyed to reclaim his country. On the eve of his departure from Mema, his mother Sogolon, the once extraordinary buffalo woman, died. Sundiata was very sad.

Meanwhile, Sundiata's sister and his *djeli* had been captured by Sumanguru and held captive at his court in Soso. One day when Sumanguru was away the courageous Balla Fasseké decided to enter Sumanguru's secret chamber to see where he kept his powerful medicines. He found poisonous snakes writhing in vases and owls standing watch over the skulls of nine kings that had been killed by Sumanguru. It was a ghoulish place. There was also the biggest balafon that Balla Fasseké had ever seen. While the place might have killed any ordinary person, the young *djeli* had powers of his own so he ventured to play the balafon and it made magnificent music. This balafon charmed the snakes and owls. Unfortunately the *djeli* did not leave before Sumanguru returned and when he saw the young man in his chamber he was livid. Thinking fast, Balla Fasseké composed a praise song (from whence come the rap, calypso, and other instantaneous creative poems and songs) in honor of the king. It completely disarmed the king. In fact, the king declared that day that Balla Fasseké would be his *djeli*. One could say that this definitely meant that there would have to be a war between the king of Ghana and the new king of Mali.

And so it was that when Sundiata was returning he saw many villages and towns that had been destroyed by Sumanguru. From the remnant people of these places he recruited archers, soldiers, and horsemen as he went. At the town of Tabon, near the city of Kita, he launched a surprise attack on the forces of Sumanguru. Sundiata's forces prevailed, sending the Soso army into retreat. There was a second battle and in it Sundiata and Sumanguru came face to face for the first time. Again, Sundiata's army dominated the field through superior tactics and skill, but Sumanguru escaped. The way the historian tells it is that one moment the Soso king of Ghana was standing before Sundiata on his black-coated horse and the next instant he was standing on a far distant ridge. As far as Sundiata was concerned, the magic powers of Sumanguru were enormous, enough to make an opponent despair.

Recruiting still more troops to his side, Sundiata thought that it was not more men that he needed, but more supernatural powers, more magic, the things that made Sumanguru seem invincible. He asked his wise men to give him counsel on harnessing supernatural powers. They told him that he had to sacrifice 100 white oxen, 100 white rams, and 100 white cocks. As the ritual slaughter began, Sundiata's *djeli* and his sister escaped and arrived at his camp.

His sister recounted how she had been forced to be Sumanguru's wife and had learned all of his secrets. She told her brother that Sumanguru's sacred totem animal was the cock and it was the source of his amazing powers. This animal could destroy Sumanguru. With this knowledge Sundiata fashioned an arrow with a tip made of the spur of a white cock.

The final showdown of the two great kings came at the battle of Kirina, one of the most significant battles ever fought in Africa. On the evening before the decisive battle the two kings ceremonially declared war, each sending an owl to the other's encampment and the owls delivered the boasting messages. "I am the wild yam of the rocks. Nothing will make me leave Mali," said Sumanguru. "I have in my camp seven master blacksmiths who will shatter the rocks. Then, yam, I will eat you," said the message from Sundiata. Sumanguru said, "I am the poisonous mushroom that makes the fearless vomit." Sundiata responded, "I am the ravenous cock. The poison does not matter to me." "Behave yourself, little boy, or you will burn your foot, for I am the red-hot cinder," Sumanguru said. "But me, I am the rain that extinguishes the cinder, I am the boisterous torrent that will carry you off," said Sundiata. "I am the mighty silk cotton tree that looks from on high on the tops of other trees," said Sumanguru. "And, I am the strangling creeper that climbs to the top of the forest creeper," replied Sundiata.

This was the beginning of the war. This was the ritual ceremony of honor. It was the declaration of war in the African style, indirect, insulting, and full of innuendo. Nothing remained except the battle itself.

When the sun had got up the next day the combatants met on the battlefield. In the midst of full battle, with 60,000 men on both sides engaging each other, Sundiata let loose his special arrow with the cock's spur at the tip and it grazed Sumanguru's shoulder. It was enough for him to lose his confidence. The battle went badly for the Soso king. Victory was sweet for the young Malian king. His army pursued Sumanguru to Kulikoro but failed to capture him there and then marched to Soso, the capital, and burned it to the ground. When they entered the special chamber of the king at Soso they found the snakes almost dead and the owls flopping on the ground. It was as if someone had entered and tried to kill all of his animals, to upset his power, to destroy the source of his secret energy. Sundiata then invited the twelve kings of the savanna kingdoms to come to Kaba, an old city in Mali. There he told them that they could keep their kingdoms but that they would now join a new empire. While the leaders were confirmed in their provinces, only two bore the title of king, the king of Mema and the king of Wagadu. Sundiata became the Mansa, king of kings, and was declared Emperor of Mali. Sundiata's word became law respected throughout the twelve kingdoms and the Empire of Mali was born, stretching from the Atlantic Ocean over close to the Mossi Empire, and from the forests of the south far into the Sahara Desert, north of Timbuktu. Sundiata worked to improve agriculture by using his soldiers to clear the land and to plant rice, yams, beans, onions, grain, groundnuts, and cotton. Mali became the largest empire in Africa's history. The capital city of Mali was Niani, which is located in present-day Guinea.

The Empire of Mali was magnificent. Sundiata put his army under several valiant generals and although he often led the wars against the enemies of Mali he was not the only outstanding general of the Malian army. He had inherited a great number of the fighting men of the old Wagadu Empire and the recruits from the Wangara region also helped to enlarge the military. However, Sundiata died in 1255. At his death, Mali was the richest state in all of Africa. No state in Europe was better organized or controlled as much territory as Mali. Its wealth was the foundation upon which the succeeding rulers would build, making the Empire of Mali unparalleled in West Africa.

At its very height as an empire in the fourteenth century, Mali reached all the way from the Bure and Bambuk goldfields in the forest region to the northern "ports" of Walata and Tadmekka. It stretched from the Songhay capital of Gao to the Atlantic Ocean, taking in most of modern-day Senegal as well.

The empire had great respect from the visitors who entered its territory. In fact, Ibn Battuta, the greatest traveler of his age, who traveled to China, India, Egypt, and many other places, wrote in 1353 that he was impressed by the rule of the mansa and the ethics of the African people:

> The blacks possess admirable qualities. They are seldom unjust and have a greater abhorrence of injustice than any other people. Their sultan shows no mercy to anyone who is guilty of the least act of it. Neither traveler nor inhabitant in it has anything to fear from robbers or men of violence. They do not confiscate the property of any Arab who dies in their country, even if it be uncounted wealth.

While Islam was steadily making its move into the populations of West Africa, the traditional religion of the Malinke people was based on the idea that all human beings and animals had destinies and that the Supreme Deity set these in motion and various divine spirits and ancestors ensured that chaos would not overtake the village or farm. Violations meant that the entire community would have to sacrifice or participate in a ritual to make the universe whole again. This was the religion of most of the West African people. It was based on the idea of a Supreme Creator and numerous spirits who carried out the ordinary and daily tasks of making certain that humans remembered to do what they were supposed to do. Farmers, and the Malinke were farmers, had a particular concern that their crops would grow and that they would become successful at their work. Ancestors could be asked to assist in making sure that the harvest would be good. Life was not individual but collective, communal. The village leader, or king, was a direct descendant from the first ancestral farmer. He was called *mansa*. Thus, as under the Soninke the title for the king had been "Ghana," under the Malinke Manse it now became, that is, Mande "Mansa." Sundiata had become the first paramount Mansa, since all the other kings had given him the power, under threat of force admittedly, to become the sole Mansa. Subsequently all the rulers of the empire were called Mansa.

One should remember that the people were accustomed to paying homage to their village or town leader, who was a direct descendant of the original founder of the people. It was not a big stretch for them to accept the fact that it was possible to have a sole Mansa who would be the direct descendant of the original Malinke founder. Such a person would have religious and secular duties. This was the case with the first Mansas. They lived apart from the people in huge palaces. They were surrounded by the regalia of their office, mainly gold and precious stones. The people accepted the king as the incarnation of the first ancestor, the direct descendant of the spirit of that ancestor, in effect, a divine king, much as the Per-aa of Kemet became the embodiment of the deity. Of course with the coming of Islam this system changed. Most of the kings who followed Sundiata were Muslim; in fact some were extremely devout. Mansa Musa, who took a lavish pilgrimage to Mecca in 1324–25, years after his brother Abubakari relinquished the throne to him in order to travel across the sea toward the Americas, was one of the greatest devotees of his time.

The rulers of Mali had to tread the religious path quite lightly because although they accepted Islam the masses of the people in the empire still believed in the local deities, practiced the religion of their births, and prevented the rulers from imposing Islam on some of their domestic practices, as in the example of marriage and ancestor reverence. Yet the Arabic language and its script became instruments for administration, law, and commerce during the fourteenth century.

However, as the Arabic script became the dominant written tool among the elites, many people who could write the script, having learned it in Arabia or Egypt, or from religious leaders in Mali, were employed as administrators in the Mansa's court. They were clerks, often with the ability to use Arabic script to write the local language, just as we use the Latin script to write English. Authors who write in French, German, or KiSwahili now use the Latin script, but the language they write is not Latin. The same was true with the African clerics in the courts of Mali. They would use the Arabic script in order to write the African languages.

The *djeli* Mamadou Kouyaté is quoted in *Sundiata: An Epic of Old Mali*, as saying of *djelis*, historians of the Mali court:

> We are vessels of speech, we are repositories which harbor secrets many centuries old … without us the names of kings would vanish from oblivion, we are the memory of humankind; by the spoken word we bring to life the deeds and exploits of kings for younger generations. History holds no mystery for us; we teach to the vulgar just as much as

we want to teach them, for it is we who keep the keys to the twelve doors of Mali ... I teach the kings of their ancestors so that the lives of the ancients might serve them as an example, for the world is old but the future springs from the past.

The historian al-Umari, writing in the book *Masalik al-Absar*, said that the emperor of Mali told him the following when he visited the court of Mali at Niani:

The monarch who preceded me would not believe that it was impossible to discover the limits of the neighboring sea. He wished to know. He persisted in his plan. He caused the equipping of two thousand ships and filled them with men, and another such number that was filled with gold, water, and food for two years. He said to the commanders: Do not return until you have reached the end of the ocean, or when you have exhausted your food and water. They went away and their absence was long: none came back and their absence continued. Then a single ship returned. We asked the captain of their adventures and their news. He replied, Sultan, we sailed on, but as each of them came to that place they did not come back nor did they reappear; and I do not know what became of them. As for me, I turned where I was and did not enter the current.

The year was 1310. In the following year, Emperor Mansa Abubakari II resigned his throne and outfitted another 2000 ships with men and supplies and went himself with them across the ocean. It would be after the reign of Abubakari II that Mansa Kankan Musa took charge of the empire.

Much has been made of this fourteenth-century account of Africans crossing the sea, and rightly so. In 1920, Leo Wiener, a Harvard graduate, wrote the book *Africa and the Discovery of America*. This was to be followed by Harold G. Lawrence's 1962 book *African Explorers of the New World* and Alexander von Wurthenau's *Unexpected Faces in Ancient America* in 1975. In 1980 the Canadian writer Michael Bradley wrote his book on *The Black Discovery of America*. Perhaps the most widely read book of this genre was Ivan Van Sertima's *They Came Before Columbus*. Some European writers deny this pre-Columbian African crossing, believing that it is better to ignore it than to deal with it. Others have tried to refute it outright. However, there is a preponderance of indicators and evidence to suggest that Africans not only crossed the ocean but landed in the Americas.

The Atlantic Ocean has currents and winds that move in the same direction all year around with little or no variation. It is possible to predict the appearance of hurricanes in the Caribbean on the basis of the movement of the winds and currents from Africa to the Americas. A ship could be pulled off course and forced to one side of the ocean or the other without the possibility of resisting the currents unless it had a strong motor. Two currents that originate off the coast of Africa and flow west to the Americas are the Guinea Current and the Canary Current. The Guinea Current starts from the equator area of the continent and flows to South America just about Brazil. The Canary Current begins at the Canary Islands and flows westward to Cape Verde and then runs into the North Equatorial Current. This current, along with the northeast trade winds, could deliver a ship to North America around the Bahamas. Scientists have tested the theory of the African discovery of the Americas with many experiments. A famous one was the 1952 experiment of Dr. Alain Bombard, who sailed from Casablanca to Barbados in an African raft. Then in 1955 Dr. Hannes Lindermann sailed for fifty-two days to the South American coast from the Cape Verde Islands. Both journeys were successful. Perhaps the most famous test was that of Thor Heyerdahl, who actually made two voyages in 1969. His ships were called *Ra I* and *Ra II* and were identical to earlier African ships. The *Ra I* was built by the Buduma people out of papyrus and sought to demonstrate that a papyrus boat from the Lake Chad region of Africa could be seaworthy. It was known that these types of boats could navigate the lakes and rivers of Africa and so Heyerdahl wanted to test the theory that they could have crossed the sea. The *Ra I* fell short of its goal: leaving from Safi on the Moroccan coast it landed in Barbados. The *Ra II* was built by a Native American ethnic group called the Aymara. This ship made it from Africa to America successfully. The idea behind Heyerdahl's experiment was that if some of the simple boats of Africa could make the journey, surely it could be done by more sophisticated African ships.

African ships could have been reed boats, jointed boats, rope sewn plank vessels, double or triple canoes, wide-berthed dugouts, or long fishing boats with straw cabins and cooking facilities. Such boats had been known along the Nile and Niger rivers for thousands of years. So it is neither far-fetched nor preposterous to believe that the greatest emperor of the world, Mansa Abubakari II, could command an expedition to cross the Atlantic Ocean, which at its closest point between Africa and America is a mere 1500 miles.

Mali was at its height in the fourteenth century. Its army was professional, a large standing army, which could put 200,000 men on a battlefield in a matter of days. Battalion leaders were among the most respected men in the Mansa's government. Each battalion was comprised of an elite corps of horsemen and a large number of foot soldiers who were armed with the most advanced bows and arrows of any African army of the day. This meant that they were tipped with iron, a precious and important metal to the economy and military of the Mali Empire. The Malian blacksmiths were kept busy fashioning arms of war and implements of agriculture. Indeed, it was an empire of farmers-soldiers who were willing to defend their territory in order to be able to farm in peace. Make no mistake, Mali was ready to defend itself and on occasion to punish its enemies or its restive vassal states who refused to pay taxes or tribute. It was like many other empires in history, built and maintained by the sword.

The principal source of income was the taxation of trade. In addition to the tributes that were paid to the imperial treasury by subject states, taxes on imports and exports kept the country rich and powerful. Although agriculture was a mainstay of the rural areas, the capital city, Niani, was in the heart of a very productive agricultural belt. The people of the capital were close to the farming tradition. They were unlike the Sahelian Ghana people, who lived in the semi-desert areas; Mali extended into the Sahel but its base was the rich agricultural regions around Niani with ample rainfall, food surpluses, a diversity of foodstuffs, particularly sorghum and millet, and rivers and streams with abundant fish. In the north, the grasslands accommodated sheep, cattle, goats, and camels. Small and independent farms produced most of the food and livestock for food. People were eager to send their foodstuff to market. It was therefore important that food be traded from one region of the empire to the next. Thousands of caravans reaching from the farthest corners of the empire would enter Niani every year. One must think of the Empire of Mali as most of western Africa without boundaries and complications of visas and security arrangements that prevent people from traveling from one place to the other. In fact, if there were such complications to trade and the free movement of commerce, the Malian army would intervene. In that regard, Mali was no different from most modern imperial nations. Actually farmers were often commanded to pay a portion of their surplus to maintain the army and the court.

Agriculture was important, but gold remained dominant as a commodity that attracted the foreigner to Mali. The empire had inherited the goldfields of the previous empire and had strengthened its hold on the gold mines in the south. The miners sought to remain independent of the ruling house. Although they willingly paid nuggets to the royal court they refused to convert to Islam for the most part and sought to keep as much control of their activity as they could by refusing to work in the mines if the heavy hand of the Niani government came down upon them. Since gold was the key product for the engine of the empire the gold miners had a great bargaining chip.

During the fourteenth century a class of professional gold traders arose in Mali. They were called the Wangara in the western part of the empire and Dyula in the eastern part. It is believed that most of these traders were Mande-speaking people, although it is possible that some were Soninke and Bamana. They traded with all parts of West Africa. In fact, the Dyula are said to have penetrated as far as the Akan kingdom in present-day Ghana and added the gold mines of that region to the Malian area of influence. The Wangara and Dyula together opened trading villages and towns in areas such as Jenne, Gao, Walata, and Timbuktu.

## Mansa Kankan Musa: the traveling trendsetter

Mansa Kankan Musa is the most famous leader of the Mali Empire. He remains known more for his travel to Mecca than for anything else, although he spent considerable time, after the costly expeditions of Abubakari II, rebuilding the administrative and fishing infrastructure. Mansa Musa undertook a memorable *hajj*, or pilgrimage, to Mecca in 1324. A *hajj* is one of the five pillars of Islam. Every Muslim is required to try to visit Mecca at least once unless he is in ill health. According to the historian al-Umari, Mansa Musa's *hajj* changed the way the Empire of Mali was seen by people in other parts of the world. While Europe slept, and woke to ward off the bubonic plague, Africa produced the most dramatic traveler of the day. Here was no pauper traveling on the handouts of other people. Here was no itinerant adventurer lost in the desert. No, Mansa Musa, emperor of the mighty Empire of Mali, was arrayed in all of the majesty possible for a king of his era.

Al-Umari says that Mansa Musa took with him 60,000 people, 100 camel-loads of gold each weighing 300 lb, 12,000 servants to attend to the needs of the Mansa and his royal entourage, and 500 servants marching in front of the Mansa, each carrying a 4 lb gold staff; thousands of his subjects marched across the deserts loaded down with all kinds of provisions; and 500 more attendants walked in front of the senior wife, each with gold staffs. They crossed the Sahara and entered Cairo. Spending was lavish on the trip, so much so that when the entourage passed through Cairo it caused a depression in the value of gold. They spent so much gold in Cairo that gold lost much of its value. When the emperor and his entourage finally entered Mecca they kept up their spending ways and caused a depression in the Holy City. In fact, it is believed that the emperor's people spent so much on the trip to Mecca that they had to scramble to have enough money for the return trip.

The *hajj* brought the empire more international attention and immediately made Mali one of the wonders of the world. It is likely that the stories of Malian gold inspired international visitors and adventurers to travel to the heartland of the empire, because during the next hundred years Mali became one of the most visited destinations in the African world. From its capital, Niani, and the principal cities, Jenne, Gao, and Timbuktu, the word went out that there was no kingdom greater than Mali.

It might be said with certainty that Mansa Musa's wealth planted in the minds of the men and women of the fourteenth century legendary stories of the fabulous king of Mali. Imaginations were fired up as they would later be fired up about the possibility of El Dorado and the cities of gold in North America 200 years later.

Probably as a result of Musa's conspicuous flaunting of gold, when the ships of Portugal's Prince Henry captured Ceuta in 1415 African prisoners were obliged to tell more details of the African gold trade. Henry sent his explorers down the African coast to find a route across Africa in order to contain the spread of Islam. This strategy of containment failed as Constantinople fell to the Muslims under the Ottoman Turks in 1453. Furthermore, after the successful reconquest of the Iberian Peninsula to push out Islam and Judaism, Europeans turned toward the Americas. However, it had been the African gold of Mali that provided the initial material for European adventurism. What was soon set in motion was a slow pillaging of the African continent, to be followed by the full-blown scramble for people and wealth.

Mali, already on the cultural and political map of the geography of the African world, became a feature on the actual maps made in Europe. In 1339, Mali first appeared on a "Map of the World" as a significant empire.

Later, in 1367, a map of the world showed a road leading from Mali through the Atlas Mountains into the western Sudan. One contemporary Spanish mapmaker depicted Mansa Musa on a third map, seated on his throne, holding a gold nugget in his right hand and a golden scepter in his left, and wearing a golden crown on his head. He was truly, as al-Umari had written, the wealthiest, the most feared, and the most powerful emperor of his day.

Trade flourished between Mali and Egypt, Syria, Sudan, and Arabia. The impact of the *hajj* created a revival in Islamic education in the Mali Empire. There had already been a constant flow of Islamic travelers and imams visiting with the traders who came to Mali prior to the *hajj*. The kingdom was large, powerful, and progressive. In fact, the *hajj* was a result of the Malian Empire's impressive cultural and political reach into western and northern Africa. It could not help but attract attention. Thus, when Mansa Musa returned from Mecca and Cairo he brought back with him an Arabic library, Islamic scholars, poets, and artists, and the highly respected Muslim architect al-Sahili, who built the great mosques at Gao and Timbuktu and a royal palace. Al-Sahili's most famous work was the chamber at Niani. Indeed, it was al-Sahili's brilliance as an architect that made his style the dominant influence in the Sahel region where, in the absence of stone, the beaten earth is reinforced with wood, which bristles out of the buildings.

Because of his devotion to Islam Mansa Musa strengthened Islam and promoted education, trade, and commerce in Mali. The foundations were laid for Walata, Jenne, and Timbuktu to become the cultural and commercial centers of the western Sudan, eclipsing those of North Africa and producing literature from the Mali Empire in the fifteenth and sixteenth centuries. Diplomatic relations were established and ambassadors were exchanged between Mali and Egypt, Syria, and Morocco. Students from all over the world came to the Mali Empire to study and to learn.

Mansa Musa ruled for twenty-five years, bringing prosperity and stability to Mali and expanding the empire he had inherited from his ancestors. His interests were in agriculture and industry. It was important that the farmers were happy since most of the citizens of the empire were farmers. Yet Mansa Musa did not forget the control of the gold and salt; it was essential, fundamental for the international trade relations, that the industry of gold and salt be healthy.

Mali achieved its greatest territorial expansion under Mansa Musa. The Mali Empire extended from the Atlantic coast in the west to Songhai far down the Niger Bend to the east: from the salt mines of Taghaza in the north to the legendary gold mines of Wangara in the south. When Mansa Musa died in 1337 he had overseen an administrative infrastructure that had brought stability and good government to Mali, spreading its fame abroad and making it truly remarkable both for its expansiveness and for its wealth and a striking example of the brilliance of West African leadership.

Mansa Musa left the throne to his son Mansa Maghan I. Soon the empire began to unravel, having exhausted itself, it seemed, on the massive and extravagant spending of the previous years. Mansa Maghan continued to spend excessive amounts of Mali's wealth, leaving a weakened empire at his death around 1341 to his uncle Mansa Sulayman. Several of Mansa Musa's famous mosques are still found in Mali, yet the Empire of Mali lasted no longer than two centuries following the death of Mansa Musa.

## Neighborly disrespect

Sapped of its strength because of the raids from the Tamaschek in the north and the Mossi in the south and east, Mali fell into a downward spiral like a spinning top losing its energy. Among the nations that had constantly irritated Mali, the Mossi, from the savanna country south of the Niger Bend, had been the most united and powerful. They had a series of strong kings who never allowed them to be brought under the rule of Mali. The ruling aristocracy of the Mossi people had created a number of Mossi states that paid their tribute to the ruling king at Ouagadougou. Using their forte as expert horsemen, the Mossi raided neighboring kingdoms in search of water for their herds. Their intent was to use both cattle-raising and crop-raising as stabilizers for the economy of the state. They were able to quickly bring their peasantry up as formidable agriculturalists. The kingdom was rich because of their conquests and in 1484 they left the city of Walata, a northern point for the Mali Empire, in ruins.

As the Mossi had done in the south, the Tamascheks (so-called Tuaregs) of the north attacked the frontiers of the Mali Empire. In fact, Timbuktu, the fabled town that had feen founded as a tented settlement not far from the banks of the Niger River, became the point of entry for the Tamaschek fighters. They had long used the area as a southern grazing ground for their herds and flocks. From here one could also join the trans-Saharan caravans moving to Tripoli, Cairo, Tunis, or Casablanca. One might say that the city had been founded by the Tamaschek and they had always resented the fact that the Mande under Sundiata had taken it away from them, using it as one of the great cities of trade and commerce in the north.

Unlike the Tamascheks, who were nomadic and pastoral, the Malinke, settled and agrarian, built permanent houses for the town, established government, created institutions, settled disputes over land, and regulated the imports and exports. By the early fifteenth century the city of Timbuktu had become a major learning center for Muslim scholars, who were Malinke, Tamascheks, Amazighs, and Arabs. It was then, in 1433, that the Tamascheks laid siege to the walls of the town until they captured it. They saw the wealth that flowed in and out of the city and understood it as a source of power for themselves. They did not disrupt the town's life, but redirected the flow of taxes and tributes to themselves and away from the city of Niani, far to the south. By 1450 the city was flourishing as a major commercial center. Mali could never regain Timbuktu and this was a signal that the empire was moving toward a full and ultimate decline. Following the reign of several weak mansas and numerous civil wars, the Empire of Mali just wilted away into the Songhay Empire in 1456.

## The Songhay Empire: reclaiming a legacy

The kingdom of Songhay had increasingly exercised its own authority over its subjects, freeing itself from tribute to the Mali emperor and refusing to be brought back under the rule of the Niani government. Songhay was a small state compared to Mali but it had proved its mettle in numerous skirmishes with the Mali soldiers. Like the Mali armies, the Songhay soldiers used both iron-tipped spears and arrows as well as guns. The Songhay heartland lay along the banks of the Niger River southeast of the town of Gao.

A number of small ethnic communities occupied this region and lived together in relative harmony. There were Gao, Mossi, Sorko, and Do people. But it was the Sorko people who were able to use their industrial and technical skills to master the river and the trading activities in the middle region of the river to eventually carve out a territory under their authority. The Sorko were expert boatmen, having created canoes and river boats that could withstand the constant use on the river, and having dominated the fishing business for many years; they became experienced hunters of hippopotami.

At this time the river had an abundance of crocodiles and hippopotami and the Sorko fishermen were the most courageous at battling these dangerous animals in the river. Actually it would be their ability to fight the river creatures that would give them an advantage on the land creatures. They developed their boats for military purposes. The Sorko, united with the Gao, soon created a series of towns held together by a common language and common commercial interests. By the ninth century the name of the region was Songhay and its capital city was called Kukiya. Its most important trading city was Gao. Trade between Gao, a city with a large international population in addition to its local people, and Kukiya, a resilient and tightly run city of Songhay people, increased greatly during the eleventh and twelfth centuries. Gao seems to have had Malinke, Egyptian, and Amazigh dwellers who enjoyed the trade with the outlying Songhay merchants who came up the river. This contact brought the Songhay people into closer contact with the Muslims earlier than it did the people of Ghana, Tekrur, or Mali. Of course, at this earlier time Songhay was not a major power, just an aggregation of fishing and hunting villages along the river.

The Gao had an illustrious history from the reign of their first king, Dia Assibia. He established a dynasty that lasted for sixteen generations. The combined lineage of the Gao and Sorko was the centerpiece of the growing power of Songhay. They had merged their rituals, traditions, and families to become a united people.

The rise of Songhay power under its military kings, known as *sonnis* and *askias*, introduced a new phenomenon into the equation of African imperial authority. The Sonni dynasty, centered on the martial arts of its horsemen and its agile war canoes, used its special knowledge of the river and its adjacent land areas to overwhelm its opponents. Under the reign of Sonni Sulayman Dandi, the Songhay extended their control of the upper reaches of the Niger River and eventually controlled all of the tribute going in and out of the territory. Few fighting kings had ever been so effective in putting fear into the hearts of enemies as Sonni Sulayman Dandi. He was known for the speed of his successes in battle. It is said that his troops were so quick that they stole the day from the enemies while they were still asleep and kept them in perpetual darkness. His horsemen attacked towns from the land while his sailors attacked from the river. This trap method, where the opponent was squeezed from the land and the water, became a feature of many of Sonni Sulayman Dandi's victories. His greatness in making Songhay a mighty nation to be reckoned with was well respected by the kings who came after him. No greater king would arise in Songhay than Sonni Dandi's successor, Sonni Ali Ber, the last descendant of the Dia Assibia.

When Sonni Ali Ber ascended the throne in 1464, the kingdom of Songhay had already established itself as a force, indeed the only force that could unite all of the warring nations of the Sahel. Sonni Ali Ber took charge of an army and a nation ready for its great historical mission. One of the prizes that had never been captured by Sonni Dandi was Timbuktu. It remained almost alone of the mighty cities of the Niger without direct rule from the Songhay. Therefore, to assert his authority and to announce the power of the kingdom of Songhay, Sonni Ali Ber invaded Timbuktu in 1468 and brought it to its knees, scattering the Tamaschek administration and taking over the lucrative trading houses.

Sonni Ali Ber was a wise leader, a thinker, a philosopher, and a keen observer of human behavior. One might say that he was a psychologist and a strategist because he used his knowledge of the commercial and military ways of his enemies to his advantage. He went so far as to take an Islamic name in his attempt to placate those Africans who had become followers of Islam. However, he resisted the attempt of Islam to supplant the traditional religions of Africa. In fact, he united his empire, including the Muslim people and those who practiced popular traditional African religion, under his banner. Many Arab historians do not consider him a friend to Islam although he was nominally a Muslim himself. In fact, Kevin Shillington writes, "Sonni Ali's raids on Muslim Timbuktu, his relentless pursuits of the Tuareg [Tamaschek] and his general lack of respect for Islam led to his being highly criticized by Arabic historians" (1989, p. 103).

In a long line of warrior kings, Sonni Ali Ber was one of the greatest to sit upon the throne of an African empire. He built up a powerful army that went from conquest to conquest as he extended the kingdom into an empire. He was soon hailed as "Sonni Ali Ber, the Great!" His cavalry was well trained, disciplined, and expert. He enlarged the fleet of war canoes on the Niger River, paid his soldiers on time, and rewarded the kings who paid their tribute to him with goods from the imperial treasury. Without a question this was one of the most formidable armies Africa had ever seen. Sonni Ali Ber pushed the borders of his empire into the desert in the north and as far as Jenne in the southwest. Even the mighty Mossi were forced back south of the Niger in the late 1480s and Songhay periodically raided deep into their territory just to keep the disciplined armies of the Mossi off balance. Out of respect for the fierceness of the Mossi the Songhay Empire never brought Mossi into its ranks. The open plains of the savanna area had seen many armies swallowed up by the unrelenting might of the Mossi cavalry or the foreboding *harmattan*, the desert sandstorms, especially from January to April.

Like the battle for Timbuktu, which was a defining moment for the forces of Sonni Ali Ber, the battle for Jenne was equally important. This battle started in 1466, two years after the capitulation of Timbuktu. The people of the city knew that the time would soon come for them to defend themselves against the onslaught of the mightiest army along the Niger. They prepared for it. Oral historians reported that the Mali Empire had tried to take the ancient city of Jenne ninety-nine times to no avail. Each time the city was able to repel the attackers and continue its life. Sonni Ali Ber would not be rebuffed. He laid siege to the city, extending his attacks for a long time, trying to wear down the people's will. In fact, the siege of the walled city of Jenne was seven years, seven months, and seven days. The city finally fell to the army of Sonni Ali Ber in 1473.

In a 1906 book called *A Tropical Dependency*, the historian Lady Lugard, whose husband was governor-general of Nigeria, wrote: "At the end of the siege, the town yielded by honorable capitulation. No injury of any kind was done to its inhabitants and the seven days which are added to the period of the siege were consumed, it is said, by festivities on the occasion of the marriage of Sonni Ali with the widow of the ruler of the town who had died during the siege."

There was great respect for the people of Jenne on the part of the emperor. It was one of the most beautiful, thriving cities in the Songhay Empire and it would remain a rich trading center, bustling with activity, expressive of its wealth and industry, and full of rich traders and streets lined with beautiful private and public buildings. It was a city that rivaled Timbuktu as a center for education. Its university was a focus for medical education. Doctors at the university were even removing cataracts from the human eye at Jenne medical school. In 1485 thousands of people worked in Jenne at the university, the schools, the trades, and in commerce and business. Thus, Jenne became for the imperial government one of the great cities, alongside Gao, Timbuktu, and Kukiya.

Sonni Ali Ber's reputation as a leader is unquestioned. He had a peace-keeping strategy that started with respect for the local populations. He honored the ancestors and the traditions of Africa and saw in those who honored the same the future of the empire. He sought to re-establish the presence of African culture in education, religion, and traditions throughout the empire. In this regard, he might be said to have been a reformer. He cleared the universities of intellectuals who brought Islam and replaced them with those who practiced the African traditions. This was to create enormous resentment in the empire and bring about rebel forces within the government. By the time of his drowning death in the Niger River in 1492, he was the most powerful leader in all of Africa and one of the few leaders in the world who could be called absolute. At the time of his death he was, of course, more famous than Columbus, who would make a voyage from

Europe to the Americas in the same year of Sonni Ali Ber's death. Indeed, Spain would expel hundred of thousands of Africans and Jews in 1492 as well, but it would be the death of Sonni Ali Ber that would ultimately affect the direction of the African world. Because of his death and the consequent unraveling of the African traditional forces trying to prevent the West African kingdoms from being immersed in Islam, Sonni Ali Ber remains the standard by which much of African history is written. What if Sonni Ali Ber had been able to reverse the Islamic onslaught? What if the European slave trade had been stopped in its tracks by a unified African Empire?

Travelers from other parts of Africa and Europe reported that Sonni Ali Ber was the greatest leader in Africa. They referred to him in documents as Sonni Heli, king of Timbuktu. They also reported that his empire extended all the way to the Atlantic Ocean.

The great emperor left a highly organized and efficient government. His son, Sonni Bakori Da'as, also called Baru, came to power after him in 1492. Sonni Bakori Da'as, like his father, was nominally a Muslim but with even less religious conviction than Sonni Ali Ber. He wanted to preserve the traditional values of the people.

In less than ten months, the Muslims organized a revolution against Bakori Da'as because he sought to continue his father's assault on the foreign influences in Songhay. He was bitterly overthrown by Muhammad Toure, general-in-chief of the army of Gao, a devout Muslim. At the battle of Anfao in 1493, Sonni Bakori Da'as was killed and General Toure was crowned emperor of Songhay under the new dynastic name of Askia Mohammed Toure. The *askias* would now become the new dynasty. Askia Mohammed would rule until 1529.

Askia Mohammed wasted no time establishing his right to the throne. He made his own pilgrimage to Mecca in 1495, where he met the Sharif of Mecca and was named the Caliph of the Sudan. He strengthened the administration of the empire by consolidating the conquests, bringing in fresh recruits to the clerical offices and re-establishing Islam as the dominant religious tendency in the empire. He soon used Islam as a religious tool to justify his attack on the Mossi nation. He declared a *jihad*, a religious war, on the Mossi in 1498. The Moro Naba, the King of Kings, of the Mossi met the armies of Songhay and in numerous battles many thousands of soldiers were lost and in the end, although Mossi was badly mauled, it was not defeated. In 1505 Askia Mohammed sent another expedition to battle Mossi. He not only succeeded in subduing Mossi, but brought some of their children to Kukiya to be raised as Muslims. Battles between these two enemies would occur again over time.

Under this warrior king, Songhay was always ready to expand its borders. In 1513 the armed forces of Songhay entered the Hausa states to the southeast of Mossi and defeated most of the kingdoms along the Niger River as far as Lake Chad. Only the Kano state was not defeated. Yet, after a long siege, the king of Kano sued for peace. Askia Mohammed let the Kano king keep his throne but, of course, for a price. The Kano king had to pay an annual tribute of gold to Songhay.

It was in the same year of the defeat of the Hausa that an African born at Fez in Morocco writing under the name Leo Africanus published a vivid account of the Songhay Empire under Askia Mohammed. On the city of Timbuktu he wrote:

> The inhabitants are people of a gentle and cheerful disposition, and spend a great part of the night in singing and dancing through all the streets of the city.

Of the governor's wealth he wrote:

> The rich king of Tombuto [governor of Timbuktu] has many articles of gold, and he keeps a magnificent and well furnished court. When he travels anywhere he rides upon a camel which is led by some of his noblemen. He travels likewise when he goes to war and all of his soldiers ride upon horses. Attending him he has always three thousand horsemen, and a great number of footmen armed with poisoned arrows.

Leo Africanus was impressed by the city:

> Here there are many doctors, judges, priests and other learned men that are well maintained at the king's cost. Various manuscripts and written books are brought out of the Barbarie and sold for more money than any other merchandise. The coin of Tombuto is of gold without any stamp or superscription, but in matters of small value they use certain shells brought here from Persia, four hundred of which are worth a ducat and six pieces of their own gold coin each of which weighs two-thirds of an ounce.
>
> (Leo Africanus, *History and Description of Africa*, trans. Jay Pory and ed. R. Brown, London, 1896, vol. III, pp. 824–7, and quoted in E. W. Bolvill, *The Golden Trade of the Moors*, Oxford, 1968, pp. 147–50)

Although Askia was an able conqueror, a good administrator, and a devout Muslim, the empire was difficult to manage. Almost everywhere the king looked he saw intrigue, rebellion, and jealousies. Songhay took over the salt mines at Taghaza, reaffirmed its commitment to Islam, and collected tributes from its vassal states, and yet trouble arose in the royal family. Askia Mohammed's son, Askia Musa, overthrew his father in 1529. It was hard to see from inside the royal chambers, but Songhay was soon on a downward spiral. Dispute after dispute at the local level and at the central government level created instability. Soon the same Islamic force that had been used to overthrow the father, the power of the ulama, was used by Is'mail to overthrow Musa in 1537. Askia Is'mail freed his father from the captivity that had been imposed on him by Musa but did not give up the throne. He ruled until his brother, another son of Askia Mohammed Toure, came to power. This brother was named Askia Dawud, and he ruled from 1549 to 1582.

This was a relatively peaceful time for Songhay. The reputation of the Islamic schools grew. Indeed, in Timbuktu alone there were 150 Islamic schools. It seems that everyone who studied the Qur'an wanted to start a school, to read rhetoric, logic, philosophy, mathematics, algebra, ethics, and literature. Askia Dawud's death brought more fighting, court disputes, and royal rebellions. At this time, because of the constant communication across the desert between Morocco and Songhay, the people of northern Africa and Europe knew of the turmoil in the largest African empire in the world. There were many weak points in that empire. Morocco sent Judar Pasha across the Sahara with firearms to fight Songhay. Pasha's forces gained the upper hand on the Songhay cavalry after several battles. Finally Askia Ishaq II's forces were defeated by the Moroccan army of Pasha.

A long history of independence and the habit of freedom made the Songhay people difficult to rule. In most of the large towns such as Timbuktu, Gao, Jenne, and Kukiya, the ruling families and the religious scholars refused to cooperate with the Moroccans. Although they were also Muslims, the Moroccans had tried to assert their control over the religious centers. Many scholars were killed; others, like the famous professor Ahmed Baba, were taken away in chains and forced to live in Marrakesh alongside dozens of authors and writers. Ahmed Baba was responsible for forty-two books on different subjects. He was the most prolific writer of the Songhay Empire.

In the end the conquest did not aid Morocco as much as it had hoped. The gold trade was being diverted to a large extent by growing trade with the European states sailing around the coast of Africa. Morocco was thus deprived of the full power of the economic energy that had fueled the economies of Ghana, Mali, and Songhay. The migration of Islamic scholars from the big cities to the small villages in what might be called the "Dyula diaspora" led to Islam being practiced in the interior of the forest region as well as in the urban areas of the scattered empire.

# 9 Generators of traditional and contemporary Africa

Like whitecaps on the sea, kingdoms and empires have danced on the bosom of the African continent, expressing their individual gifts, longer than anyone can remember. Yet there have been a few distinctive political entities that have emblazoned their histories in the collective narrative of the continent's life. They have functioned so well as generators of thought, behavior, and philosophy for themselves and other societies that they can be seen as sources of many of the traditions of African culture.

## Kanem-Borno: bridging east and west

The Empire of Kanem-Borno, located in the region of Lake Chad, played a major role in the expansion of Islam in Africa. It was a combined kingdom, that is, two or more ethnic kingdoms came together under the rule of one dynastic family. The Mais (kings of Kanem) converted to Islam during the eleventh century and were subject to the Saifawa dynasty founded by the Arab hero Sayf bin Dhi Yazan. The leaders of the Kanem-Borno Empire exercised considerable authority and were devout enough to make the *hajj* to Mecca and to establish a dormitory in Cairo for students from Kanem-Borno who went to study at Al-Ahzar University.

Just like we found in Timbuktu in Mali, the capital of Borno, N'gazargamu, became the major center of Islamic scholarship in that part of Africa. Indeed, so prominent were the teachers of Kanem-Borno in religious interpretation that believers in other states considered the empire to be an integral part of the Dar al-Islam. Yaqut, a twelfth-century Greek bookseller who was sold into slavery to a Syrian merchant and was later freed and traveled to Africa, said:

> Kanem is part of the land of the Berbers in the farthest west in the land of the Sudan. Some say that the Kanem are a people of the Sudan. At the present day there is a poet at Marrakesh in Maghrib known as al-Kanimi [the one from Kanem] whose excellent work is attested to, but I have never heard any of his poetry nor learnt his proper name.

We can see that the name of Kanem was well known in the twelfth century although Yaqut got his geography and ethnology a little wrong (Kanem was not a part of the Berber lands); he announces that there was at least one famous poet from the place. It is good to observe that the scholars at Kanem were indigenous although they practiced Islam. Niane has made an excellent point on this score by saying that "the one-sided character of the Arabic written sources for the Nilotic Sudan has led to an over-emphasis on the northern factor at the expense of indigenous developments" (Niane 1997, p. 263). It is often assumed, given the diversity of the African continent, that most developments in poetry, art, science, architecture, mathematics, and literature came from outside of the local areas; to make this assumption is to stand uneasily on a precipice.

Tradition has it that the Saifawa dynasty was one of the longest-lasting dynasties in world history. Although the dynasty is said to have started under the first Mai of Kanem around 915 CE, it was in 1134 that Sayf bin Dhi Yazan, who had married into the lineage of the Mai of Kanem, created the Saifawa dynasty, which lasted until 1846, when the last of his descendants left the throne.

From what historians have been able to tell, the early state appears to have been pastoral. It was created by the grouping together of many different nomadic and pastoral peoples under the mais. Actually, they did not have a capital city during the early days and they controlled no particular trade. They were a confederation that operated under allegiance to a single leader and ruling family. However, by the twelfth century the writer al-Idrisi recorded that the towns of Manan and Njimi were occupied. In fact, the town of Njimi became the capital city of Kanem. The thirteenth-century Syrian politician and scholar Abu el-Fida, quoting Ibn Said, wrote: "Njimi is the capital of the land of Kanem. There resides the sultan of Kanem, well known for his religious warfare." One reason that Njimi became the capital city is because it was the starting point and the terminus for the caravan route across the desert to and from Tripoli and Tunis. Two cities on the Mediterranean coast had routes to Njimi. One could take a caravan through the towns of Bilma and Zawila in the Fezzan *en route* to and from the sea coast. Not only did goods travel those caravan routes, but also religion, culture, artifacts, and ideas, moving back and forth across the desert in both directions. It was not to be thought of as a one-way route. While it is true that Kanem received religion from the north, the north also received from the south foodstuffs, gold, salt, and ideas of governance.

The mais were mysterious to many of the common people. They rarely appeared in public and gave the impression of being superhuman. In fact, the fourteenth-century Syrian scholar al-Umari, who was a specialist on Mali as well, wrote:

> Their king despite the feebleness of his authority and the poverty of his soul, who has an inconceivable arrogance; despite the weakness of his troops and the small resources of this country, he touches with his banner the clouds in the sky. He is veiled from his people. None sees him save at the two festivals, when he is seen at dawn and in the afternoon. During the rest of the year nobody, not even the commander-in-chief, speaks to him, except from behind a screen.

Obviously the idea was to make the king a figure of mystery, thereby increasing the people's belief in his authority.

Mai Hume was the thirteenth ruler of Kanem but the first to make the *hajj* in the eleventh century. By the late twelfth century Islam had become the dominant religion in Kanem. This brought teachers, religious leaders, and visitors to Kanem. One Mai, Dunama Dibbalemmi, made three pilgrimages to Mecca during his reign on the throne. It was probably under his reign in the thirteenth century, around 1240, that the hostel was erected in Cairo for students from Kanem-Borno.

How did the various ethnic communities become one group? Kanem was directed by skillful leaders who made laws and decrees about intermarriage that encouraged their subjects' marriages to members of the leading families until they formed a single group speaking one language, Kanuri.

Unity gave them strength and they began to move against other groups, conquering them and subduing them for tribute. They took control of the Fezzan and established an outpost nearly 800 miles from Njimi. The Kanuri-speaking people found easy prey in the people to the north and east of themselves but ran into strong resistance from the So people in the south.

In the early fourteenth century Kanem was pressured by the Bulala people, a nomadic group, who attacked their outer flanks. Quarrels in the royal house about succession to the throne gave the title "Era of Instability" to the fourteenth century. Finally the Bulala drove the dispute-riddled royal family of Kanem out of their homeland and forced them to settle in Borno. It would take several centuries, to the time of Mai Ali Gaji in the fifteenth century, before the Seifawa dyansty would end its political troubles. He was able to stop the fighting and in-fighting over the succession and he also founded the capital city at N'gazargamu. Mai Gaji was considered one of the greatest of all Seifawa dynasty kings. Mai Ali Gaji was a warrior king of great power. He campaigned against the Hausa state of Kano and regained control over the northern trade routes across the desert. Raiders from the Middle Benue River belt were cut to pieces when they sought to attack N'garzargamu. Ali Gaji made headway against the Bulala and the next mai was able to complete the job.

Several mais came to power with the objective of defending the empire and holding back chaos from those kingdoms that wanted to revolt. Mai Idris Katarkambi (1504–26) came to power with a clear purpose: to continue the campaigns of Mai Ali Gaji against the enemies of the empire. He was able to liberate the ancient capital of Njimi from the Bulala. Another Mai, Muhammad (1526–45), had to put down a revolt by the Bulala, who had been defeated by Mais Ali Gaji and Katarkambi. He followed his victory over the Bulala by marching his army north to the important city of Aïr, which was under the control of Songhay. He took this vital city by conquest and held it to the advantage of Kanem-Bornu.

Around 1545 Mai Ali fought with the kingdom of Kebbi in Hausaland. The reason for this battle was the fact that Kebbi had begun to disrupt the caravan trade controlled by Songhay and the Tamaschek Tuaregs. When they asked for assistance from Bornu, Mai Ali took an expeditionary force around the Hausa kingdoms and attacked the Kanta (king) of Kebbi in the fortress city of Surame, west of the city of Katsina. This was a definitive victory. The Kanta of Kebbi fled but Ali also left the town and headed for Bornu. This allowed the Kebbi army time to regroup and they chased the army of Mai Ali at a place called N'guru. On the way back to their country the Kebbi soldiers were ambushed by soldiers from Katsina and their king was killed. Mai Ali died in 1546. His son was too young to be king and so Ali's nephew, Dunama, took power and reigned from 1546 to 1563. He was followed by Mai Dala Abdullah, who ruled from 1564 to 1569.

The greatest of all Mais was the noble Idris Alooma, who came to power in 1569 and established a reputation for fairness, justice, and sternness with the enemies of Kanem-Borno. Mai Idris was the young son of Ali. He became a man of tremendous vision and experience.

He lived in old Kanem, far to the east of Bornu, east of the lake, in an area still ruled by the Bulala. It is believed that his mother was the daughter of a Bulala king and had returned home when his father died. His mother, Queen Amsa, showed great courage and ingenuity in protecting the young heir during the reign of Mai Dala, who tried to kill him on several occasions because the young child was the rightful heir to the throne.

Even when Dala died in 1569 the young king could not gain his rights to rule. The power in Bornu was immediately seized by a woman, Dala's brilliant but cunning sister, Queen Aissa Killi. A war broke out among various members of the royal house and it was only after several years of instability that Idris finally won the kingship.

Idris' imam, Ahmad ibn Fartua, made his name famous. He wrote more about his ruler than any of the other imams wrote about theirs. Mai Idris Alooma did a lot of things to make his name famous. He was not sitting around asking Ibn Fartua to write about him. No, this was neither empty praises nor false propaganda. Alooma defeated the Teda and the Tuaregs, two groups from the north who had hounded the boundaries of the empire for many years. Employing Turkish infantry and musketeers who had worked in Egypt as a part of his army, Alooma was able to defeat most of his neighbors with the new weapons brought into the empire. He also used long-range camels for warfare as well as for expeditions. The Muslim officials loved him because he was a builder of mosques and a practitioner of Islam.

Probably more because of Idris Alooma than any other Mai, the world knows about Kanem-Borno. He developed political and diplomatic relations with countries inside Africa as well as outside. Fearless when he was in the right, he had a running dispute with the Ottoman Turks, who had occupied Tripoli in 1551. They would occasionally send probing expeditions into his empire. He did not like the disrespect he felt the Turks showed toward his nation and so he played off the Sultan of Morocco and the ruler of the Ottoman Empire. What he did was quite remarkable for an African leader who had little experience at manipulating world leaders. He told the Sultan of Morocco, Mansur, that he recognized him as the ruler of all Muslims in Africa. He sent emissaries to Morocco to convey this message, also sending gifts as tribute of recognition. Alooma then told this to his imam and asked that the information be broadcast throughout the Muslim world. It struck the Turks as a bold and dangerous move. Nevertheless, Kanem-Borno had an alliance with its African neighbor and this protected the nation from the wanton exercise of Turkish power. In 1603, some say 1617, the great king died, and Morocco already powerful in western Africa, consolidated its power over Songhay (see Davidson 1977, p. 102). Idris died at the head of his soldiers in one of the many battles he fought to expand the empire. He was buried in a marsh at Aloo, thus the name Mai Idris Alooma.

All African historians wish for detailed information on Kanem-Borno of the sort that we have of the Ghana, Mali, and Songhay empires because of the writings of al-Bakri, al-Umari, and Ibn Battuta, but, of course, we do not yet have it. We have enough information from travelers and tradition to say that the trade in kola, ivory, gold, salt, and people fueled a lot of commerce.

As we now know, Kanem-Borno was originally ruled by a Mai who appointed princes to govern the territories. However, this was the source of disputes, attempted coups, and succession battles, and so soon the Mais made their own servants the governors and kept the princes in exile or under house arrest. These actions were evidences of a broken society, a nation that limped like a hurt antelope toward its own demise. By the seventeenth century the Empire of Kanem-Bornu was nothing more than a collection of villages that held memories of long-past glories.

The next major feature in the central Sudan was the contest between the French and Rabih ibn Fadl Allah, the conqueror of Borno. In the late nineteenth century the French would seek to subdue most of the Sudan outside of the British sphere, including Niger, Mali, Upper Volta, and Chad. Rabih rose to leadership as a military general trading and dealing in ivory and humans. Following the creation of the Mahdist state 1885, Rabih created his own state in Bahr el-Ghazal. Although Rabih had an army and a powerful cavalry, he did not build a strong infrastructure. His main idea was to raid the surrounding villages and towns in order to gain wealth.

Using the Mahdi's credentials, Rabih considered himself a Mahdist and this allowed him to reach westward as far as Lake Chad. It was not long before Rabih had claimed all the territory he had crossed, organized a dictatorial government, and collected taxes from the surrounding peoples. He set a fixed time and amount for taxes. Although he was successful in subduing the villages around his palace, Rabih was never considered one of the people of the area. He remained an outsider to most of them. Thus, he was not loved by the people, who thought his constant raids on the villages brought about a lack of interest in agriculture.

When the French began their push into the interior they were surprised by the resistance they met from Rabih's forces. The French challenged his independence and put his armies under pressure. In April 1900 two major French armies converged and met at Borno. The battle raged heavily and Rabih was defeated and then killed by the French. His son, Fadl Allah ibn Rabih, took over his forces and retreated to northeastern Nigeria. However, he did not find solace in the move because the British who were then in charge of Nigeria refused to give him protection. The young officer was tracked and gunned down in 1901.

## Hausa states: a military phalanx

When the Seifawa dynasty moved to the south it ran into the Hausa states, a group of people comprised of city-states. The Hausa city-states of the present Nigeria came into existence around 1000 CE. It is believed that an ancestor named Bayajidda was responsible for the seven main cities of Hausa because his sons became conquerors who established these cities. One son founded the city of Biram (Garun), another founded Daura, Katsina, Kano, Rano, Zazzau (Zaria), and Gobir. They were started as small villages comprised of farmers. The Hausa people were a combination of southern Sahara nomads and sedentary farmers of the savanna. Living behind walled villages, called *birane,* the people became very close-knit. The wooden stockades that surrounded the smaller villages were mainly used for protection from raids from other villages. Occasionally they would have to protect themselves from larger armies coming from their neighbors to the south or to the north. However, the idea of walled villages or walled cities seems to have grown out of necessity. It has been practiced by many people in various regions of the world. Some of the earliest walled cities had been in the Nile Valley. But here in the broad savanna of today's northern Nigeria the Hausa states had to protect themselves from any external threat and thus became a military phalanx.

Hausa cities were formed from the merger of villages in an effort to create settlements large enough to defend themselves. Since these cities depended upon agriculture they were dedicated to the protection of the huge acreage of farmland that was a heritage of the people. Most of the farmland was walled, or at least fenced in, so that it could not be overrun by enemies or destroyed by ordinary sandstorms. The Hausa mentality was that of a caterpillar, insular, protected, and strong. However, once these city-states had created administrative cadres they moved aggressively to coordinate and consolidate their outlying lands and kingdoms.

The Hausa founded several important cities. The city of Gobir had originally been founded as far north as Aïr, north of Agades in the Sahara. It had moved southward because of the constant agitation from the Tamaschek (Tuareg) people. Gobir was a farming city but it also had extensive trade connections across the Sahara. It was the most important of the Hausa trans-Sahara trading cities. Katsina arose around the twelfth century and was incorporated into the trans-Saharan trade as one of the principal city-states. The walled city of Kano, now the largest city in northern Nigeria, was a manufacturing and craft center during the eleventh and twelfth centuries. In Kano one could find cotton-weaving, iron-making, cloth-dyeing, leather-working, copper and silver markets, and all kinds of produce from the fertile farmlands. The cities of Daura and Biram were not nearly as important as Gobir, Katsina, and Kano but nevertheless were a part of the Hausa city-state system. Zaria was the capital of a region called Zazzau, founded in the sixteenth century. According to Shillington (1994, p. 186) Zaria became a major center for the slave trade when raiding parties captured people from the Kwararafa area near the Benue River in order to export them to Borno, Nubia, and Libya in exchange for horses and guns. If this were the case it would have been an activity that occurred in the seventeenth to nineteenth centuries since in the earlier period we do not have any records of guns being used on a wide basis. So this "trade" would have been something that arrived with the expanded Arab presence in West Africa and the increasing demands for Africans to work for the Arab traders and merchants who had established large enterprises in the Hausa and Borno regions.

Islam conquered the Hausa states by the fourteenth century. That is to say, the leaders of the state were nominally Muslim, while the majority of the people remained tied to their traditional religion. It would take several Islamic revivals before the Hausa could be thoroughly converted to the religion. Indeed the city-states were quite cosmopolitan in the sense that there were many ideas, perspectives, and insights gained from the international trade as well as the internal trade. Yet it would be the Islamic preachers who would soon set the thematic agenda for the city-states. One by one they fell under the influence of the Islamic leaders.

The ruling elite of the Hausa city-states accepted taxes from the masses that lived in the interstices between city-states. Nevertheless wars occurred between them as one city emerged for a time as the dominant one, only to be replaced by another. All of these cities were active politically and socially. A great rivalry existed between them and yet not a single city could be said to dominate the entire Hausa area. There is no such thing as a Hausa empire. Ironically, the closest thing to such a conception may have occurred after Nigerian independence, when the Hausa began to see themselves as united against the Yoruba and Ibo forces in the south.

Increasingly in the fifteenth and sixteenth centuries Hausa city-states controlled the routes between the Akan goldfields and the cities of Aïr as well as the Songhay trade routes between Gao, Jenne, and Kukiya and Borno. This was important because it allowed the city-states to increase their wealth and to govern the movement of people. The countryside was often devastated by the wars that occurred because of the fighting for dominance. By the seventeenth and eighteenth centuries Islam was really entrenched in the minds of the masses. They felt that they had gained a sense of justice and righteousness that was new, revolutionary. They adopted the shari'a, the Islamic law, and condemned all forms of corruption and placed stringent rules on women and those who had become too universal in their approach to the religion.

In the sixteenth century Queen Bakwa Turunku fortified the small city of Zaria named after her youngest daughter. It became the capital of an area called Zazzau. Soon the entire region was called Zaria after the city-state. Although the city bears the name of the younger daughter it was the elder daughter who was to memorialize the city. She was the legendary Aminatu, shortened to Amina, who inherited her mother's military genius and skill. Indeed Amina was only 16 when her mother became queen.

Because of her bravery in battle, cunning in negotiations, and wisdom in managing the affairs of the city-state she was given the traditional title of honor and respect *magajiya*. She is celebrated in poetry and song as "Amina, daughter of Nikatua, woman as capable as any man."

When she gained power in the city-state one of her first acts was to fortify the walls of the city. In fact, she is called the architect of the earthen walls around Zaria, the prototype for other earthen fortifications in the land of the Hausa states. The people called her fortifications Amina's walls, that is *ganuwar Amina*. There is some controversy as to whether or not she was ever queen. It is possible that she was always a princess, but a princess who had no equal in power for about thirty-five years. Her brother Karama died in 1576 and she may have assumed the role of queen at that time. It is also likely that she could have ruled from 1536 to 1573 as some records say, which would place her prior to her brother's reign and death.

It is known that Amina was a conqueror. She understood that war could protect her people, although it had no power to establish harmony. That had to be done with diplomacy and tact. Nevertheless, she sought two achievements with her wars: first to extend Zazzau's rule over the countryside and consolidate the power of Zaria, and second to reduce the vassal states to subordination so that their allegiance would be only to Zaria. It is said that her kingdom eventually reached the sea in the west and south. The Kano Chronicle says "The Sarkin Nupe sent her [Amina] 40 eunuchs and 10,000 kola nuts. She was the first in Hausaland to own eunuchs and kola nuts."

Amina of Zaria was preeminent as a military leader and must be considered alongside the panoply of African conquerors such as Tarharka, Ramses II, Thutmoses III, Sundiata, and Sunni Ali Ber. As a female military leader she is clearly in the company of Amanirenas and Yenenga: one fought Caesar's armies and stopped them dead in their tracks as they sought to invade Nubia; the other stormed out of the grassy plains of West Africa with thousands of loyal cavalry troops to establish the Mossi dynasty. So when we speak of Amina of Zaria we must see her in the context of some of the world's greatest fighting women.

The rich history of the Hausa city-states is still being written and when the record is clear it will be shown that the Hausa people organized themselves into protective *birane* but were open to the world. Indeed, in the eighteenth century the region would experience a Dyula diaspora where people would move south to continue their livelihoods in farming. Among the Hausa, as was happening among other savanna kingdoms and nations, there was a decline in trans-Saharan travel. There had been numerous cycles of heavy activity and then of fewer caravans moving back and forth across the desert. However, a jihadist movement began to reverse the trend of the decline in the late eighteenth century. A group called the Fulani (Peul, Fulbe) gained power and leadership over the Hausa population. It had been deeply influenced by the jihadist movement elsewhere in Africa.

There were five important *jihads* in the savanna region of Africa during the nineteenth century. The first was the Futa Jalon (hilly region in the north of Guinea) *jihad*. Two key personalities emerged in this *jihad*, Ibrahima Sori and Karamoko Alfa Barry. Over the years they shared governance and influence in Futa Jalon. The area was known for its religious scholarship. It had been at the center of the Mali Empire hundreds of years earlier and now it was the key region in West Africa for Islamic training.

The second *jihad* occurred in the Futa Toro region (middle valley of the Senegal River) and was sparked when a group calling itself the Torodbe (Seekers) complained that the local Denyanke dynasty did not protect Muslims from being sent into enslavement. More conflict occurred because an Arabic-speaking group of migrants, the Beni Hassan, from Morocco, opposed the Torodbe's criticism of the Denyanke. Abdul Qadir Kan organized the Torodbe and was successful in defeating the Denyanke and the Beni Hassan. He negotiated an agreement with the French in 1786 to allow them certain use of territory so long as they guaranteed the Africans that they would not sell into slavery those who were Muslim.

The third *jihad* was that led by the Usman dan Fodio, a Fulani, whose family had migrated generations earlier from the Futa Toro region. He distinguished himself as a teacher and scholar. His students were fervent in their passion for Islam and he became known for his knowledge, spirituality, and willingness to fight for the religion of Islam. His fame soon brought him into conflict with local rulers. The leader of Gobir, Na Fata, sought to force Dan Fodio to stop preaching his doctrine but in 1804 conflict broke out between Dan Fodio's followers and Na Fata's sucessor, Yunfa.

Dan Fodio based his actions on those of the Prophet Muhammad. He faced a serious threat from Yunfa's army and decided that he needed a flight from Gobir. He regrouped his army and then declared a Jihad of the Sword, a reference to Muhammad's *hijra* to Medina. Gilbert and Reynolds are correct to assert that "Usman dan Fodio was also deeply influenced by Al-Maghili's instructions on proper Islamic governance, written for the Hausa King of Kano Muhammad Rumfa, roughly 300 years before" (2003, p. 195).

Usman dan Fodio continued to write treatises against the local rulers, especially the leader of Gobir. He had two main complaints. First, the political leaders had allowed the traditional African culture to corrupt Islam. Second, the local leaders did not protect Muslims from enslavement. By 1808 the armies of Gobir had been defeated and Dan Fodio and his followers established a new state with the capital at Sokoto. By 1814 almost all the Hausa states had been overthrown by Fulani-led *jihads*. Dan Fodio handed out flags to those who visited him seeking his help. In the end the *jihads* helped to create the largest African state of its kind at the time, the Sokoto caliphate, a confederation of city-states, each ruled by an emir (*sarki* in Hausa) who owed allegiance to the Sultan of Sokoto.

Dan Fodio did not seek administrative power as the sultan. He divided those duties between his brother and his son. In fact, his son, Mohammed Bello, became the sultan. Dan Fodio's daughter Nana Asma'u wrote poetry and essays that were aimed at ridding the region of African traditional religion. Indeed, the mixture of African and Islamic religions was called *bori*, but for the jihadists it was very bad. Teaching the women a more fundamentalist version of Islam had an effect on the children. They became willing converts to the *jihad*.

The Sokoto caliphate became a major player in the slave trade of the nineteenth century. One could say that the caliphate never thought slavery was wrong; it was wrong only to enslave Muslims. This has been an often-repeated message in contemporary Africa as well. One can see evidence in Darfur and southern Sudan regions and the southern region of Egypt of this idea of slavery for the unbeliever but freedom for the believer.

Interestingly, with Muhammad Bello, Usman dan Fodio's son, firmly in control the Sokoto caliphate extended its area, creating crises everywhere. The Shehu of Borno, ruling an Islamic state to the east near Lake Chad, wrote to Bello complaining:

> Tell us why you are fighting us and enslaving our free people. If you say that you have done this to us because of our paganism, then I say that we are innocent of paganism, and it is far from our compound. If praying and the giving of alms, knowledge of God, fasting in Ramaddan and the building of mosques is paganism, what is Islam?
>
> (Hodgkin 1969, p. 112)

Bello's reply was that of a man bent on conquest. He said that although the Shehu was a good Muslim many of his subjects were not and therefore they were open to capture and enslavement under Islamic law. Following in his father's footsteps Bello gave out flags to those who sought to join the *jihad*. A noted scholar, Seku Ahmadu Bari, from the Upper Niger River region in Mali contacted Bello and asked for a flag of legitimation. He was granted one and launched an attack on the "corrupt" and "pagan" cities of Segu and Jenne. In 1818 Bari was victorious and established a state he called Massina with a new capital called Hamdullahi, meaning "thanks be to God." Although he had received a flag from the Sokoto caliphate which suggested that he would submit to the authority of the Sultan he neverthe-less decided that he would declare himself the Twelfth Caliph. Had Bari never become a leader, no one would have doubted that he could have been a great leader. However, as a leader, he was a failure. He died in 1845 with few people recognizing his power. His son, Ahmadu II, succeeded him.

The fourth *jihad* was led by al-Hajj Umar Tal. He was born in Futa Toro and studied in Futa Jalon. He was a very religious man, taking his religion so seriously that he believed all of those who were not following his path would be eternally lost. From 1828 to 1830 he made a *hajj* to Mecca and Medina. This trip really impressed him and when he returned he started to spread the Tijaniyya Sufi Brotherhood (Tijani). Umar Tal followed the path of many young Africans who have left their homes to gain education and experience in far distant lands. Traveling to other lands is not uncommon in Africa and was not uncommon in Tal's day. On his way back to Futa Toro he stopped in what is now northern Nigeria and spent several years at Sokoto and Hamdullahi. He was convinced that he had to return home and lead a *jihad*. In the 1840s he returned to his home area and attracted a following and soon led a *jihad* against the king of Tamba. He fought against the French, who were asserting themselves in the area as well. But Umar Tal launched a campaign against the king of Kaarta, the king of Segu, which he captured in 1861.

Pumped up with pride at his accomplishments, Umar Tal turned his attention to Ahmadu II and the state of Massina. After a brutal siege for many months the state of Massina fell to Tal. He seemed ready to fight other Muslims, believing that they were incorrect in their practice. Because he was a follower of Tijani Sufism and the other leaders practiced the Qadiriyya it is likely that Umar Tal saw them as less than pious. When he died in 1863 his son, Ahmadu Seku, succeeded him and the state disintegrated from French pressure as well as lingering bitterness stirred up by his father's conquests. Little had been done to create a framework for governance.

A fifth *jihad* would occur in the Sudan. It would be led by Muhammad Ahmad, who declared himself to be Mahdi, a figure in Islamic thought who will announce the Second Coming of Christ, the defeat of the evil, and an era of righteousness, prosperity, and stability. Mahdi was first of all a nationalist. He preached that it was necessary for the Africans to drive out the "Turks," a name used generally for foreigners, because Muhammad Ali, the Albanian leader of Egypt, had invaded Sudan, seeking to enslave people in order to produce more cotton and to build up the Egyptian military. When the British took over from the Ottoman Turks they appointed General "Chinese" Gordon as governor of the Sudan. He did nothing to endear himself to the African people of the Sudan. So much resentment had built up in the country that it was only a matter of time before the country exploded.

The Mahdi preached a strong doctrine of resistance to oppression. In 1881 the British decided they had to arrest him. This proved to be a catalyst to the Mahdi's troops. In several battles the Mahdi's forces defeated the Anglo-Egyptian army. They captured a number of garrisons in the region, harassed the British army and its allies, and preached the belief in the infallibility of their objective. In 1883, the British sent 10,000 Egyptians against the Mahdists and this army was also defeated. Of course, victory after victory seemed to assure the followers that Ahmad was indeed the Mahdi. The British sent Governor Gordon to Khartoum, the capital of Sudan, in 1884 to oversee the evacuation of the city. He did not want to give up the city to the Mahdists so he decided to make a stand. The city was starved and overrun by the Mahdists in January 1885, handing Britain one of the most famous colonial defeats in history. The Mahdi died soon thereafter and the state survived under the direction of Abdullah ibn Muhammad and was not defeated until the British returned to Sudan in 1898.

## Zimbabwe: the great stone city of the south

The name "*dzimbabwe*" in the Shona language means "place of stone houses." Thus, Zimbabwe takes its name from the more than 300 places of stone houses found in southern Africa, mainly in Zimbabwe, Mozambique, and South Africa. Most of the walled stone cities are found between the Limpopo and the Zambezi rivers. Great Zimbabwe, as it is called, is the most imposing of all of the ruins named *dzimbabwes*.

Great Zimbabwe was the center of a thriving and powerful kingdom from the eleventh to the fifteenth century. It is possible that men and women of this kingdom also traded with India and China as objects from both of those places have been discovered in the environs of Great Zimbabwe.

Located on an imposing hill on the southwestern edge of a vast plateau about 220 miles inland from the Indian Ocean, Great Zimbabwe is in two main parts. One part has been called the Great Citadel because it occupies the very top of the hill and the other part, located down the hill in the meadow, is the Great Enclosure. There were buildings and two pathways up the hill in ancient time. One could easily go from the top of the hill in the Great Citadel to the Great Enclosure in thirty minutes. These two structures represent immense construction projects (Beach 1980).

There have been several theories about the Great Citadel. The Europeans called it the "Acropolis" after the Greek example. However, it is much more like a place for the king's palace and various rituals of state. It is probably not a mere fortress as some have claimed. On the vast plateau one could see many miles from the Great Citadel. It would be unlikely that any foe would choose to approach Great Zimbabwe with enmity. We have no records or objects indicating warfare in the Granite City. The passageways and rooms in the Great Citadel remind one of the ancient Egyptian passageways in various buildings, including the pyramids.

The Great Enclosure was built without cement or mortar. Its huge walls are made of stone laid like brick in regular form and fashion to a height of nearly 30 feet. In some places the walls are more than 6 feet thick. The king and his royal family lived in the Great Enclosure, surrounded by his most beautiful wives, his luxury of gold and silver and bronze. The king ate from plates imported from Persia and China according to the history written about this period. Zimbabwe is one of the handiworks of Africa that suggest the sublime and the beautiful in the straightforward sincerity of style and form that make a remarkable achievement. Some authors have said things like "Zimbabwe is one of those remarkable instances of man's handiwork from which a glamour is distilled, which emanates an atmosphere elusive alike to reason and to definition" (Caton-Thompson 1932). Or consider the statement of Maynard Swanson when he writes, "There is no geometry or regularity apparent in its physical plan or construction" (2001, p. 293). The architect Edwin Wilfrid Mallows exclaimed in 1984, "Not one straight wall, not one rectangular space, no true right angles or circles or true arcs of circles in any portion of the plan. Great Zimbabwe is devoid of geometrical control. All shapes are curving, sinuous, infinitely flexible, a purely instinctive feeling for shape ... This characteristic non-regularity alone makes the Great Zimbabwe ruins unique in the world ... It is another world of form altogether" (Mallows 1984, 39, 41, 56).

Obviously what we see in these statements are the attitudes of individuals trying to come to terms with something totally outside their experiences. Who is to say, for example, that a building *ought* to have right angles, or ought to have rectangular spaces? If one means by geometrical control doing things like they are done in the Western world then you could criticize Great Zimbabwe for not being that type of construction. On the other hand, one could also think of the Zimbabwean style as having its own form of control of spaces.

The rise of the Zimbabwean civilization can be placed between the eleventh and thirteenth centuries CE. Originally built by the ancestors of the Shona of the modern republic of Zimbabwe, the site represents an extension of the Iron Age culture of southern Africa, including the famous Leopard's Kopje, near Bulawayo, and Mapungubwe. The oldest known gold site in southern Africa was at Mapungubwe (now in the Limpopo province of South Africa) and it was here that the ancient people built their City of Gold and established their golden emblems and sacred objects as the center of their social life. The people mastered the technique of dry stonewalling for personal and animal spaces. They would have cattle enclosures made of stone or kings' homes surrounded by stone. So it should not surprise us now to discover that the Shona people used the same ideas to build the most complex structure yet found in southern Africa.

It is likely that Great Zimbabwe added to the might and majesty of the paramount king, the Mwene Mutapa. As a capital city Great Zimbabwe was well positioned between the sea and the rich mineral deposits and great source of game in the interior. At the head of the Sabi River valley, Great Zimbabwe was in a pivotal position for advancement, control, and extension of power. Cattle were basic to the early society and the people used them for food and milk. They also had good grazing lands on the plateau. There were elephants, antelope, and other game for food. In addition, they also were able to find firewood for cooking and well-watered land for cultivation of crops. This was an ideal area for a major center of activity.

Trade between Zimbabwe and the coastal areas, particularly the Kilwa Swahili culture, was frequent and helped to shape the gold and ivory trade that made Kilwa one of the richest ports in the thirteenth century.

The state of Zimbabwe probably started as a trading center. It is likely that it was a prosperous center for cattle-keeping, farming, and the gold and ivory trade. In the twelfth century it regulated the trade passing between the coast and the interior. Taxation from the trade, paid in ivory or gold, helped to keep the state afloat. The city became a seat for craft development as well as a center for cotton-weaving. Wealthy people often imported their fabrics from India. As the center of trade the town grew to control much of the surrounding territory, becoming a powerful state.

It is unclear why the site of Great Zimbabwe was abandoned around 1450. Some theorize that the timber and grazing lands had been exhausted by this time. Others claim that the area may have suffered from an epidemic of sickness that obliterated the population and sent any remaining persons out of the city. Oral tradition speaks of the lack of salt as one reason the people moved to other places. It seems to me however that the lack of salt would not be a reason to move since salt is not a staple food and the region gave forth an abundance of other seasonings for food.

If it is true that nearly 12,000 people lived in the city around 1400 it would be one of the more important concentrations of people on the African continent and one of the major cities in the world. Of course, such a population would put a strain on the economy and the ecology of the region. It is suspected that the city simply collapsed politically and socially from such an intensive use by the population.

Several states existed during this period of time and traded with the Great Zimbabwe. Among these was the trading center of Ingombe Ilede ("The Place Where Cows Lie"), situated near the confluence of the Kafue and the Zambezi rivers. This region produced fine pottery polished with graphite. Some writers believe that it may have been an outshoot of the Luangwa tradition or the Kisale region of the ancient Luba. We know from the burial sites that the people were wealthy because they buried their dead with beads and polished stones.

It is likely that much of eastern Central Africa from Zambia to Lake Malawi may have participated in the late Iron Age culture called Luangwa. It is named for the pottery from the region and seems to have spread between 1000 and 1200 CE. Iron was used quite widely in the region to make axes for clearing land for cultivation, as well as spears, arrows, and hand tools for digging. There were also instruments for ritual use made of iron. In this area of the continent there was also the herding of cattle, the manufacture of copper, the hunting of elephants, and extensive trade. Among the connections to the Luangwa tradition are the various ethnic cultures of Bemba, Bisa, and Chewa, names that appear in modern Africa.

The Bemba, Bisa, and Chewa are related in some ways to the people of central Malawi, who are descendants of the Phiri clan, which in the 1400s married into the Banda clan and formed the Nyanja. The kings of the Nyanja took the title *Kalonga*. According to oral tradition the Phiri clan came from the Luba. It is difficult to say when this migration took place but there are certain rituals that are similar to those of the Luba. By 1540 the Kalonga dynasty had founded the Lundu dynasty among the Manganja of the Shire valley and the Undi dynasty among the Chewa, who lived between the Shire and Zambezi. Few people in Africa have ever used fire as ritually as the Phiri clan. Indeed, the Kalonga, Lundu, and Undi peoples were called by others "Maravi," meaning "people of the fire." Thus, from the sixteenth century the Maravi were the most important groups down the Shire and Zambezi to the Indian Ocean.

One of the successors to the Great Zimbabwe was the Torwa state organized in the Leopard's Kopje region of Guruuswa (or Butua). The capital city, made of stone, was called Khami. It is likely that the Torwa state was an offshoot of Great Zimbabwe. This area had more terraced hillsides than in Great Zimbabwe. The stonewalling tradition was refined and perfected with the layering of differently trimmed stones. It was located in the center of the goldfields of the western plateau. Also the Torwa people were great cattle herders, and their political structure, skills, and organization were keys to the rise of Changamire's Rozvi state in the seventeenth century.

Mutapa was founded by the courageous and energetic explorer Nyatsimbe Mutota, who had taken a large entourage northward from Great Zimbabwe looking for salt. Most scholars now believe that this took place in 1420. Mutota settled his family and entourage in the area of Dande in the Mazoe valley. This region had good land, great rainfall, trees for building, and access to the Zambezi River as well as stations at Sena and Tete for trade with the Swahili merchants from the coast. Many of the coastal traders sought the copper from the inland area for their shops and for personal use in their homes and palaces.

Both Mutota and his son Matope took advantage of their favorable position between the trading routes and proximity to the trading stations to establish themselves firmly as the controllers of the area. In fact, Mutota started to build an army with which he conquered other Shona clans and took the title *Munhumutapa* (Mwene Mutapa, sometimes Monomatapa). This title means "Conqueror" and is an indication of Mutota's and Matope's relationship to the people they defeated. By the middle of the fifteenth century, Mutapa had succeeded Great Zimbabwe as the principal Shona state in the high plateau. By the 1480s tribute was being paid to the Mutapa by the kings of Uteve, Barwe, and Manyika.

In the past scholars have thought that the Great Zimbabwe and the state that surrounded it was the same as Mutapa. This is a common misunderstanding because of the fact that the founder of Mutapa came from Great Zimbabwe. Actually there was a real difference between the Mutapa state and its predecessor state Great Zimbabwe. The Mutapa kings were outsiders who used their army to defeat their subjects. This was not the case with Great Zimbabwe, which was a kingdom formed from the indigenous population, perhaps integrated with some Rozvi or Lozi from farther north. Furthermore, the Mutapa kings received regular tribute from the chiefs of northern Shona villages and towns. Of course, there was not a great stone-building tradition in the north of Zimbabwe; this was primarily a tradition of the southern and eastern Zimbabwe people.

The Mutapa's palace was made of poles and clay and enclosed by a wooden palisade. One of the most important differences between the two kingdoms, Zimbabwe and Mutapa, is that Great Zimbabwe had to import gold but the Mutapa kingdom had gold in the local area. Also, many peasant farmers paid their taxes and tribute to the king by working in the alluvial goldfields. The kings of Mutapa used this gold to trade with the coastal people for cloth and fine jewelry.

The gold trade between the Shona and the Swahili drew the attention of the Portuguese in the sixteenth century. Quite unkindly, the Portuguese sought to divert the trade from the coastal Swahili to their own trading posts along the Indian Ocean. This brought them into conflict with the Swahili. Battles raged, people were killed, and the issue was not resolved to the satisfaction of the Portuguese, who then took it upon themselves to go up the Zambezi River to find the source of the gold. In 1530 they conquered the trading towns of Sena and Tete but still believed that they could go farther and finally establish direct links with the Munhumutapa. They believed they could have even more gold if they controlled the source. Forty years later, in 1571, they sent another army into the Zambezi Valley. This army's misfortune was that it went into the valley during a drought. It never left the valley. It was defeated by the Tonga people, hunger, thirst, and disease. In 1574 the Portuguese forced the Uteve king to agree to pay tribute to them at Sofala on the Indian Ocean coast. Nevertheless, the resourceful and masterful Munhumutapa stayed beyond the reach of the Portuguese. He remained the greatest king in this part of Africa and his kingdom one of the most insular from the influence of the Europeans on the coast. Ensconced behind stone walls, protected by a vigilant army, and considered invincible by his people, the Munhumutapa could not be touched by the short arms of the Portuguese.

## The Yoruba states: art and religion born of the forest

The word "Yoruba" probably originated as a Hausa term for the people of Oyo in the western part of the modern country of Nigeria. The Yoruba represent a major language group in the southwest of Nigeria and the eastern part of the modern country of Benin, not to be confused with the Nigerian province of Benin. The Yoruba are an ancient people who likely moved to their present homeland from the east. In fact, one Yoruba historian claims that the people descended from a group of Egyptians who moved to the west (Lucas 2001). Clearly they have a strong and powerful history based on traditions, rituals, histories, orature (oral literature), and narratives of heroic deeds underlined by a philosophical worldview found in their culture.

It now appears that the formation of states in Yoruba occurred during the tenth to twelfth centuries CE. This was the time when the farmers and hunters, speaking the language of the Oyo people, gathered in small and large villages to become one of the most urbanized groups of Africans. The land was located in the savanna region between the forest zone and the ocean, where the land was fertile and the rainfall high enough for food production that included a range of cereals, root crops, and domesticated animals.

The traditions of the Yoruba say that the sky god Olorun sent Oduduwa, the founder of the Yoruba, down to earth at the city of Ife. It is often called Ile-Ife, the place where heaven came to earth. Oduduwa became the head of the first Yoruba state and then sent his sons to rule over the other states. The first *Alafin* of Oyo was one of his sons as was the first *Oba* of Benin. Another son was the first *Onisabe* of Sabe and his eldest daughter is known as the mother of the first *Alaketu* (in modern Benin, old Dahomey), while another daughter gave birth to the first *Olowu* of Owu. The tradition has continued to the present time, where the ruler of Ife is called the *Oni*, in recognition of a direct descent from Oduduwa. And the Yoruba are fond of saying, "if you do not have a past, you do not have a future."

Evidence exists to show that people have lived in the Yoruba area for a long time, as far back as the Stone Age. Archaeological evidence suggests that they were metal-workers and fine artists. Some scholars believe that they may be related to the people of the famous Nok Culture. Yoruba, a tonal language, is ancient and has acquired a strong literary status among traditional African cultures. There are many Yoruba authors and critics who study the language.

The students of Yoruba culture often say that there were two main movements of ancestors, one in the area of Ekiti, Ife, and Ijebu in the dense rainforest zone and the other toward Oyo in a region beyond the forest. Both of these migrations probably occurred around the fifth or sixth century CE.

Who were these migrants and from where did they originate? Some Yoruba legends claim that they came from Arabia, while others say that they came from the Nile Valley, probably from Egypt or Kush. One can say, however, based on the people's own statements of their history through their language and customs, that they came from the central Sudan and had felt the influence of the Nile Valley travelers or migrants, if they were not those migrants themselves. When these new people entered what became Yorubaland they brought fresh political, social, and philosophical ideas and methods of doing things with them. They formed and developed a type of government that reflected their traditions. By 1000 CE the Yoruba had perfected the town type of government, not to be confused with the common village governance found in many parts of Africa. These were urban societies with numerous artisans and clans of professionals who performed services for the state. There is no parallel to the old Yoruba city anywhere in tropical Africa. It was the special gift of the Yoruba, who shared the ability in iron-smelting, agriculture, brass-working, and art with other African groups, to make cities. Basil Davidson says it this way: "They had, of course, many villages and small settlements: *abúlé* (hamlet), *iletó* (village), *ilú olójà* (small market town); but it was in their big towns, their *ilú aládé*, that their urban achievements were greatest" (Davidson 1965, p. 120).

Consensus among historians is that the most important city of ancient Yoruba was Ife. It was the seat of the mighty kings who were said to be descended from Oduduwa and only they had the right to wear the crowns with bearded figures as an indication of their authority. It is likely that Ife had several thousand inhabitants in the twelfth century and had grown both in tradition and in numbers through the years. Indeed, this city, the "City of Heaven," was the place that was called "Ile-Ife" because it was where the creation happened. It is the center of philosophical and religious discussions and decisions and is only rivaled by the political capital of Oyo. Ife, like the other towns, was surrounded by an ancient wall as a defense. These walls were used first around family compounds and then around the cities as a whole. They kept out wild animals as well as any human intruders who wanted to do harm to the citizens.

## Farming among the Yoruba

The Yoruba were also excellent farmers and good traders, but the gift of the creative and ritual arts was at the source of their power and prestige in the region. Although they were able to gain extensive lands for farming, the rulers of the Yoruba, like many others, used taxation of the peasantry as an additional source of revenue for the state system. Wealth that came from taxation, farming, and trade helped to underwrite the large artistic culture associated with the royal houses of the Yoruba. Since religion was fundamental to the people's ambitions and aspirations, most of the art, some of the finest in the entire world, was directed toward the religious community.

Among the art produced by the Yoruba were some of the best bronze and brass images of the human face found anywhere in the world. There were terracotta sculptures, and brass and copper castings using the lost wax process. While archaeologists have dated some of these works as early as the twelfth century, it is likely from the maturity of the designs and the competence of the execution that the Yoruba were creating these works on the basis of a long-established tradition. Discovering that some works were dated to the 1100s is no indication that there were no earlier works. Remember, absence of evidence is not the evidence of absence. We have no idea what will be discovered in years to come by entirely new teams of archaeologists.

I think it is important to make several observations about the Yoruba based on what we know about their artistic developments. They obviously had a source of copper inasmuch as their art suggests possible links to the mines on the edge of the Sahara. They traveled as far as the southern Sahara to trade for copper, using food, kola nuts, and ivory for exchange. One is impressed by the beautiful images of the heads of the *onis* cast in metal. They remind one of the gold funerary masks of the ancient Egyptians. This work, extremely realistic, shows a people with enormous artistic capabilities.

One finds a very highly developed artistic culture in this part of Africa among other people as well. The Nok culture, more ancient than the Yoruba, gave the world some of the finest pieces of terracotta sculpture ever seen. The bronzes of Igbo-Ukwu show an unusual gift for the creation of beautiful works in copper alloys. It would be wrong to suggest that these techniques of metal-casting were imported from outside of Africa. Why would one want to make such an assumption in the first place? This archaeological site in southeastern Nigeria dates to the tenth century CE and may even be older. Bronze products were being created at an early period and the region also traded and interacted with areas as far afield as North Africa.

*Figure 9.1* Benin bronze, Nigeria
© Molefi Kete Asante

Archaeological finds were first discovered in 1939 when a farmer named Isaiah Anozie saw several bronze objects as he was digging a cistern to hold water in the dry season. It was not until 1959 that the site was excavated and was discovered to have been a storehouse for ritual objects (Shaw 1977). Dated to the ninth or tenth century CE, Igbo Ukwu represents one of the earliest examples of bronze-casting in West Africa.

It would be a mistake to assume that the Yoruba were only artists. They were great builders as well. In recent years it has come to light that the Yoruba may have created the largest human-made construction on the continent of Africa and one of the most massive in human history. It is called Sungbo's Eredo. A team of Nigerian and British archaeologists have dated the Eredo to about 1000 CE, thus suggesting that as the savanna empires were dominating much of western Africa the Yoruba were making their own history in the creation of the giant embankment, made from a dug-out trench, covering nearly 100 miles in a circle around the palace of the queen; the wall is 60 feet tall in some places. It was hidden by hundreds of years of rainforest growth, and scholars are still studying how an engineering feat of this proportion could have been achieved by a people who lived in the rainforest. Some people have declared that the queen responsible for the construction of the wall was none other than the Queen of Sheba. However, the dates are way off and it is more likely that this was a great Yoruba queen called Bilikisu Songbon. The legendary Queen of Sheba lived in Nubia more than 2000 years earlier, around the tenth century BCE. Sungbon's Eredo remains a great human achievement, and like so many activities in the African past we know only a small fraction of what truly happened. Nevertheless, it is a physical structure like the pyramids, the tombs in the Valley of the Kings, the Great Zimbabwe, and the Great Wall of China, and now that it has been uncovered it will occupy our thinking for years to come as the greatest monument in Africa. We will all call the massive trench and embankment the Great Eredo.

The Yoruba social structure was based on an extensive philosophical tradition which made the Great Eredo and the refined bronzes simply evidence of the people's purpose, skills, and productivity.

## The political organization

The political organization of the Yoruba states was based on a confederation of Yoruba capital towns under the leadership of the Oni of Ife. This system was kept in place by arrangements between the ruling families of the leading towns. Each state in the confederated system was permitted to run its own affairs. However, the rise of Oyo in the sixteenth century caused the decline of Ife dominance. Inasmuch as the Oni of Ife held both the political and the spiritual power of the confederation, Oyo's challenge and eventual conquest gave the Alafin of Oyo the political leadership. This was the era of heroic people who created heroic art forms and managed their confederacy on the basis of their heroic past.

One of the defining characteristics of the Yoruba Confederacy was the Ebi system of governance. It allowed the leaders of the various states to see each other as relatives and hence to govern their kingdoms and the confederation as one would govern a family. In fact, the eldest kingdom was considered the most senior and hence the one that would be called upon to settle disputes, to take political leadership, or to counsel the others to go to war. Under the Ebi system the country was therefore a family. The Oyo kingdom, being a junior kingdom in terms of age, was a contradiction to the Ebi system because of its strong political influence. It was in conflict with the Ebi system yet the two patterns of governance seemed to work by force of Yoruba creativity.

The structure of the Yoruba city was based on the family, and the patterns of the houses, including architectural styles, were related to the types of Yoruba self-rule where the kings' palaces were in the center and all other family structures radiated from the palaces. Looking at a Yoruba city the Westerner, given to the idea of individualism, would not understand the organization of the Yoruba city, where dwellings were closely packed together by family. Each family, from the elders to the youngest, lived in a cluster or compound of houses called in Yoruba *agbo'le*. Each *agbo'le* was constructed around the house of the head of its descent line, the *agba ile*. In the center of the Yoruba city stood the *oba*'s palace, the *afin*, and everything was dictated by the palace.

## The council of kings

Even in contemporary times, the *iwarefa*, the chiefs who are the leaders of descent lines, govern their own descent groups and appoint the *oba*. It was a process by which the people through their representatives elected the *oba*. Long before the Europeans came to the shores of Africa the Yoruba and other nations were practicing an open form of government understood by all and transparent to the masses. The *iwarefa* remained central to any major decision that was made for the confederation of Yoruba. Of course, now the political power of the *oba* is curtailed by the modern state system but in the past the *iwarefa* assisted in decision making and the *oba* was responsible for carrying out the decisions. Thus, a cadre of servants, messengers, and counselors served the *oba*'s palace to put into action the ideas that had been decided upon by the *iwarefa* and the *oba*. Some of the servants of the *oba* belonged to special societies or age-set groups and were able to bring about actions in support of the *oba* because they were leaders of committed followers.

There was generally a feeling of community based on the Ebi system where everyone was supposed to feel that the kings, nobles, and other authorities worked for the family. Most of the time this system worked but there were times when different towns believed that they were slighted by the central power or saw themselves in competition with other towns and this led to conflict. Mixing politics with religion was one way to keep unity since all Yoruba people tended to believe in the sanctity of Oduduwa. As children of Oduduwa they could all place their allegiance in the Oni of Ife, the direct descendant of the founder.

Yet as the Yoruba nation grew, some towns became so large that the loyalty to Oduduwa was interpreted by the nobles of those towns in their own way. In fact, you will still find that some Yoruba see Oduduwa as a man while there are a few towns that speak of Oduduwa as a woman. Furthermore, the divinities, orishas, of Yoruba take different forms depending upon certain historical, social, or philosophical interpretations by the leading authorities.

## The Yoruba religion

In the 1990s it was reported that the fastest-growing religion in the Americas was a derivative of Yoruba called Ogun. As some of the main exports of Africa to the Americas, the religious ideas, ceremonies, divinities, and rituals of Yoruba have become ingrained in the thinking of the West. When one speaks of Macumba, Santeria, Candomblé, Voodoo, and Myal, one is speaking of the impact of Yoruba. What is the source of this religion's strength?

There are several important attributes of Yoruba religion. The earliest philosophers and thinkers of the Yoruba people established the following principles:

- There is one Supreme God.
- Only two days are certain, the day you were born and the day you will die; all other days and events can be forecast and if necessary, changed.
- You are born into a specific destiny or path.
- Your spirit lives after death and can reincarnate through blood relatives.
- Divination is the instrument that will reveal your path.
- Our ancestors must be honored, respected, and consulted.
- The forces of nature live within each of us and deal with our affairs.
- You must never harm another human being or the universe, because they are you.
- Sacrifice is necessary to assure spiritual success.
- All realms of our existence must work together and be balanced.
- Character is the greatest trait for the human being.

To bring about the proper response of the human to his or her path or destiny it is necessary for the person to engage the *orishas*, the forces of nature. There are numerous forces of nature that have been identified in the Yoruba pantheon. However, the central power is *Oludumare*, the Supreme God. Among the other important *orishas* are *Obatala*, the *orisha* of harmony and purity, and the creator of humanity; *Elegba* or *Eshu*, the owner of the roads and opportunities, *Oshun*, the *orisha* of love, sexuality, and beauty; *Shango*, the purifying moral terror; *Oya*, the *orisha* of wind, fire, and power; *Yemaya*, the *orisha* of wealth and sustenance; *Ogun*, the *orisha* of promise, commitment, and war; and *Ochosi*, the seeker and searcher.

It is easy to see how the Yoruba people made anthropomorphic examples of the great abstractions of human life. In other societies, people simply drop the metaphorical identifications and name the abstraction. Thus, Elegba would not be the owner of the roads and opportunities, but rather the idea of decision making.

Ifa, the deity who was with Olodumare when the universe was formed, is the source of the wisdom of the Ifa Divination *odus*, the 256 *odus* that are used to determine how a person is applying himself or herself. In the end, the only thing that Ifa desires of human beings is to show good character. It is neither money, fame, education, nor power that works with Ifa because Ifa only wants *iwa pele*, good character.

Over the centuries the religion of the Yoruba has affected numerous peoples in the Americas and although it is not an evangelical religion in the same way as Christianity and Islam might be said to be evangelical, when people hear about Yoruba they are captivated by its magnetism and mystique.

The *Odu Ifa* is the great sacred teachings of the Yoruba. It has been codified into 256 *odus* constituting all of the principal instructions of Yoruba morality. These teachings are thought to have been compiled or created by Agboniregun, who used the name Orunmila, 4000 years ago (Karade 1999, p. 33). He was the accepted prophet of the Yoruba tradition who constructed the system of ancestral reverence and ethical teachings, basing everything on the Wisdom of the Ancients. Karade says, "Orunmila is the pivotal point of the ifa belief system and ritual ceremony" (1999, p. 33). Indeed, Orunmila ritualized the *orisha* system. In time, Orunmila became the divinity of the Odu Ifa, the sacred scriptures, and of the *babalawos*, the high priests.

As a system of divination, the *odus* are referred to during consultation with a *baba-lawo*, "father of secrets," who interprets the system of signs that are presented during divination. The Luba, Yaka, Shona, and other African people have established systems of divination using a spirit medium. However, the Yoruba rely on the interpretation of the *odus*. The universe is seen in terms of two halves of a calabash. These two halves represent the realm of living beings (*aye*), comprising all humans, animals, and plants, and the realm of spiritual powers (*orun*), which includes the 401 deities (*orisa*) and the ancestors (*ara orun*, literally "the living dead").

Since there are numerous powers that make claims on an individual, including one's family, friends, visitors, and not readily seen entities such as ancestors, deities, nature spirits, and also the powers of death, disease, and *ajogun*, "malevolent spirits," one must seek out the *ase* (*axé*) to mediate one's existence. The word *ase* means the intrinsic "power" by which a person or thing is what it is – the inherent authority of a person's or element's nature deriving from his, her, or its character, position, type, or function. Every one has an *ase*. A woman has hers, a man has his. The *orisas* have *ase*, the ancestors, rivers, forests, rulers, rain, thunder, all have *ase*. It represents to the Yoruba the ground of being, the life force, and the warrant for existence.

What one seeks to do is to navigate one's way prosperously through life, drawing on the *ase* of gods, ancestors, parents, and nature to enable one to fully realize the personal destiny (*ori inu*) that one chose before coming into the world (*aye*). Now the Yoruba believe that the only way to accomplish this is through divination based on the interpretation of *Odu Ifa*.

This massive body of literature in prose and poetry started as oral practice; indeed, many explanations, narratives, and illustrations remain in oral form, although there are some useful modern translations of the 256 main *odus* such as Maulana Karenga's *Odu Ifa: The Ethical Teachings* (Karenga 1999; also see Karade 1999) that contains the wisdom of the Yoruba. There are sixteen principal *odus*, each with its identifying sign and name and consisting of sixteen subordinate *odus*, each with its sign and name, making a total of 256 *odus*. There are also 256 *odu* signs, each associated with one of the 256 *odu* subsections and its particular story about the lives of gods, humans, and animals. The subsections are ranked in importance, a ranking said to have been determined by the order in which the *odus* – which came from *orun* and are regarded as *orisa* – arrived in *aye* and became known among humans.

Wande Abimbola, the second-ranking priest of Ifa in Ile-Ife and former vice-chancellor of the University of Ife, has written extensively on the training of Ifa priests and on the *Odu Ifa*. A youth who shows intellectual imagination at an early age will be regarded as a candidate for training to be a *babalawo*, especially if divination in a rite known as Imori ("knowing the head [*ori*]"), performed when he was a small child, revealed that he was a "child of Ifa." The youth will live with a local priest of Ifa, learning ritual procedures, memorizing passages from the *Odu Ifa*, observing divination sessions, as well as carrying out the daily chores of the priest's household. He may spend several years with his mentor. As he matures, refining his knowledge and skills, he will seek out *babalawo* in other areas for further instruction, moving from one tutor to another over a period of several years, during which time he will begin to "cast Ifa."

From Eji Ogbe:

> K'a má fi wàrà-wàrà n'okùn orò.
> Ohun à bâ if s'àgbà,
> K'a má if se'binu.
> Bi a bá de'bi t'o tútù,
> K'a simi-simi,
> K'a wò'wajú ojo lo titi;
> K'a tun bò wá r'èhìn oràn wo;
> Nitori àti sùn ara eni ni.

> Let us not engage the world hurriedly.
> Let us not grasp at the rope of wealth impatiently.
> That which should be treated with mature judgment,
> Let us not deal with in a state of anger.
> When we arrive at a cool place,
> Let us rest fully;
> Let us give continuous attention to the future;
> and let us give deep consideration to the consequences of things because of our own eventual passing.

# 10 Societies of secrets: farmers and metallurgists

Constance B. Hilliard has written eloquently that the "absence of literacy does not preclude wisdom and a reverence for knowledge" (Hilliard 1998, p. 2). Africans have maintained a thorough interaction with the environment, nature, society, and the idea of ancestral wisdom for a very long time. Societies have risen and fallen, appeared and disappeared, and yet the overarching attitudes of Africans toward human relationships and familiarity with the mysterious world of ancestors have remained intact. While groups often referred to as "secret societies," but which are really "societies of secrets," represent the accumulated knowledge of a community they are not the only sources of that accumulation. In fact, numerous empires and kingdoms, some quite quixotic, as in the case of Dahomey, and others brilliant in their execution of cultural forms, such as Edo, have interpreted their interactions with nature, relationships, and environment quite well; there is evidence, as in all societies, of some untested approaches to phenomena. Nevertheless, the kingdoms and empires presented in this chapter might be read and studied for their impact on our overall understanding of Africa. It is with this reason in mind that I have discussed these societies.

## The Edo Empire of Benin

Two regions of West Africa bear the name "Benin." One is the country once called "Dahomey," which is now called Benin. The other is a region of Nigeria which bore the name Benin for a much longer period. This section is about the Nigerian Benin. To the south and east of the Yoruba region, toward the Niger delta, lived a people whose name has been memorialized in oral and written tradition for their unsurpassed skills in architecture and art. They have been heralded as the masters of the lost wax process in bronze sculpting. These are the Edo-speaking people of Benin. By the twelfth century CE, they had developed a centralized state system to draw all of the small villages surrounding the palace into one unit. The kingship system in Benin is dated to the eleventh century, about the same time as it was being established at Ife. The current Oba traces his ancestry to the thirteenth century.

The Oba of Benin based his legitimacy on the claim that he was a direct descendant of Oduduwa, the founding ancestor of the Yoruba. There was no greater legitimacy in the realm than to be a direct descendant of

Oduduwa, hence the close relationship between the Edo and the Yoruba. Interactions between the Yoruba and the Edo people have been long and the original histories of the earliest ancestors remain locked in the forgotten past. There is a tradition, now recognized as history, that the Edo became upset with the ways of their own kings many hundreds of years ago and sent a messenger to Ife to ask Oduduwa for one of his sons to rule over them. The son who was sent was called Oranmiyan or Oronyon. His entry into the kingdom brought about a new political history in Benin. Certainly Benin developed ideas, philosophies, and skills independently of Yoruba, but they could never dissociate themselves from their Yoruba heritage. Like the Yoruba, they produced incredible art works with characteristic precision and graceful details demonstrating how the artist serves the interest of the eternal quest for harmony.

The artists and artisans of Benin became especially brilliant and excellent at working metals. One might say that "everywhere in Benin one could see the fire of the blacksmith." They produced many objects made of brass, but there is little copper found in this part of Nigeria, which means that the people of Benin had to trade with those who exchanged copper for the products of Benin. They were master architects and builders, producing some of the most magnificent structures in West Africa. The making of brass plaques to decorate the palaces of the Oba was added to the carving of ivory and other precious items for the royal houses. Thus, by the fourteenth century the customs and traditions of Benin had already been established (Ajayi and Crowder 1974).

Benin was a big city in the fifteenth century. It had a large wall and several large buildings, mainly royal, and some hundreds of smaller dwellings for the citizens. When a Dutch visitor came to Benin in the 1600s he remarked that its wide streets and fine houses were equal or superior to those in Amsterdam.

> When you go into it you enter a great broad street, which is not paved, and seems to be seven or eight times broader than the Warmoes Street in Amsterdam. This street is straight, and does not bend at any point. It is thought to be four miles [6 kilometers] long.
>
> At the gate where I went in on horseback, I saw a very big wall, very thick and made of earth, with a very deep and broad ditch outside it ... And outside this gate there is also a big suburb. Inside the gate, and along the great street just mentioned, you see many other great streets on either side, and these also are straight and do not bend ...
>
> The houses in this town stand in good order, one close and evenly placed with its neighbor, just as the houses in Holland stand... They have square rooms, sheltered by a roof that is open in the middle, where the rain, wind and light come in. The people sleep and eat in these rooms, but they have other rooms for cooking and different purposes ...
>
> The king's court is very great. It is built around many square-shaped yards. These yards have surrounding galleries where sentries are always placed. I myself went into the court far enough to pass through four

great yards like this, and yet wherever I looked I could still see gate after gate which opened into other yards.

(Dapper 1668)

This description, collected by O. Dapper who was a geographer, is an indication of a city that was well organized, balanced, structured, and grand. It was because of the good leadership of the empire that Benin city developed along lines that were recognized as those of a great city. Many kings contributed to the growth of the city but one of them was Oba Ewuare.

A stealthily creative military Oba, Ewuare created fear in the forest regions when he started attacking his neighbors and extending the borders of Benin to incorporate more farmland. His armies moved with deftness through the forest, defeating town after town and creating a kingdom that included many neighbors of the Edo. Oba Ewuare created a stable succession by having his eldest son sit on the throne, thus establishing a tradition. With Ewuare the warring clans of the Edo came under one general government, protected their borders, created institutions that revered the ancestors, and concentrated on the metal and plastic arts.

King Jacob Egharevba wrote about the royal traditions of this period in Benin history. He identified Ewuare as one of the leading Obas of all time. When he came to the throne in 1440 he came with experience, training, and wisdom. He had traveled widely in Africa, as far as Guinea to the west and Congo to the southeast. According to the record Oba Ewuare was a powerful, courageous, and wise leader. In fact:

> He fought against and captured 201 towns and villages in Ekiti, Ikare, Kukuruku, Eka, and Igbo country. He took their rulers captive, and he caused the people to pay tribute to him. He made good roads in Benin City ... In fact the town rose to importance and gained the name of city during his reign ... It was he who had the innermost and greatest of the walls and ditches made round the city, and he also made powerful charms and had them buried at each of the nine gateways to the city so as to ward against any evil charms which might be brought by people of other countries in order to injure his subjects.

> (Egharevba 1952, p. 14)

It was during the reign of Ewuare that the Benin people first saw Europeans. The Portuguese brought a ship under Captain Ruy de Siqueira into the Bight of Benin in 1472, twenty years before Columbus set sail for the Americas. Basil Davidson is correct to note that "Ewuare is remembered as an outstanding ruler not only for his conquests and breadth of contact with the world. He also presided over important political changes" (1977, p. 131). Among the political changes that Ewuare established were the State Council and the State Bureaucracy. It was the beginning of a strong central government of civil servants to assist in running the extensive kingdom.

When Oba Esaghie came to power in 1504 he took the changes that he had inherited from Ewuare and made them tradition. He added the region of Idah, between Benin and the Benue River, to the empire. But he is also remembered for being the Oba who allowed the Portuguese to establish missions in his kingdom. He received envoys from the Portuguese along his coasts and one of them, Duarte Pires, wrote to the Portuguese king in 1516 telling him how generously the Oba had treated them. Indeed, Pires reported that he had sat them at table to dine with his son. He is considered a man of learning, science, and art. Tradition has it that Oba Esaghie could speak and read Portuguese and was a master of Iwe-Uki, astrology, forerunner to the science of astronomy, the study of the universe. His reign lasted nearly half a century and he oversaw the development of Benin city into a great city of many people, institutions, and places of commerce.

The next Oba was Orhogbua, who came to the throne in 1550. Ehenguda came to power in 1578, and Ahuan in 1606. Ahuan was a scientist and had a great sense of nature. He had been a hunter as a young man and particularly loved nature. He practiced the gift of the herbalist and was skillful in making ritual objects from natural materials. These three Obas are considered among the most progressive in Benin's history. They were important in establishing the bureaucracy and political system that sustained the kingdom. When the British arrived in 1553 during the reign of Oba Orhogbua they had a Portuguese sailor with them who wrote that the Oba, like Esaghie, could read and write Portuguese. The powerful Edo merchants traded their peppercorns for English pots and pans.

Perhaps a word should be said about the trading of human beings in the Benin kingdom. One of the most misunderstood periods of African history is the role and place of Africans in the selling of Africans to Europeans. There will be more on this when we discuss Dahomey. Nevertheless when the Portuguese came into contact with Benin, the Oba was on a campaign to extend his kingdom. The Oba of Benin, the king of kings, willingly sold to the Portuguese some of the captives that had been taken in wars with Benin. This was a way to get the trouble-makers out of the region. In some instances the Portuguese exchanged people along the coast of Africa for gold. At the end of the sixteenth century Benin had exhausted its export of Africans and the major trade items between Benin and Portugal were ivory, gum, pepper, and cotton. But by this time the empire stretched across Africa from the Niger delta in the east to the swampy area of Lagos to the west. It was situated to play a key role in the interaction of Africa with Europe.

It is probably true that the bringing of European firearms into the kingdom and the exchange of war captives for foreign goods were largely responsible for the decline of Benin power. It became a weaker kingdom with the advancement of the slave trade and found itself captive to the greed of some of its own citizens as well as the imperial designs of Europe. Members of the ruling elite competed with each other for access to the gun-runners and slave traders. Such disorder meant that the general citizenry of Benin were disheartened, threatened in their liberties, and frightened for their safety and lives. The seventeenth and the eighteenth centuries were periods of great chaos along the coast and in the interior of the Benin Empire. After years of cooperating with the Portuguese and Dutch in trade, the Benin people were overcome by a punitive expedition of British colonialists in 1807, a period that began the "One Hundred and Fifty Year War of Africa" between the Europeans and Africans. But for now let us return to the end of the greatness of Benin.

When the European slave trade was prohibited on the high seas in 1807, the Europeans and Africans sought to reignite the legitimate trade that had been interdicted by nearly 250 years of slave trade. The idea was to trade raw materials or semi-processed commodities like palm oil for European goods. In fact, palm oil became the major lubricant for the industrial revolution in Europe for a time. It would later be supplanted by petroleum. At the end of the nineteenth centry, after the European Declaration of War on Africa at the Berlin Conference of 1884–85, the British had established trading posts along the coast of present-day Nigeria as within its sphere of influence. Actually the idea of "spheres of influence" was determined in Berlin and based on little more than the relative power of each European nation rather than any agreement with African nations or kings.

Against the will of African people the British, through an entity called the Niger Coast Protectorate that included the rich Niger delta, had started to establish trading posts. Using their soldiers the British through force pushed their way into the interior, defeating the armies of several coastal people until they came up against the Benin kingdom. Benin's Oba sat on a throne that had existed since the thirteenth century, the direct line of its monarchy was older than Britain's, and the Edo people were proud, independent, and intent on maintaining their sovereignty.

In 1892 they had entered into a "trade and protection" treaty with Britain. It had been promoted by Captain Gallwey on the first official visit to Benin city. He had not been the first British subject to visit the city but he was the first one to visit it in thirty years. Nevertheless, Benin was not impressed with the British designs on its territory. Trade conducted through the intermediary of the Itsekeri people, who lived along the coast, and who had been completely defeated by the British, was less profitable for the British than they wanted. The Niger Coast Protectorate sought to rival the profits of the Lagos Colony and the Royal Niger Company. Thus, a competition between British colonizers in this rich area of Africa played out to the detriment of Benin. Ralph Moor, the consul-general of the Niger Coast Protectorate, wanted to mount an armed expedition against the Benin kingdom. The British Foreign Office was reluctant to give a positive answer to Moor. He left on leave for Britain soon afterward and a newly appointed acting consul-general, James Phillips, took up the post in the Niger Coast Protectorate. The two Englishmen had met in London just before Phillips was to depart. It is likely that Moor, a man with a record of cruelty and violence against African leaders who did not submit to white authority, told Phillips what he would do if he were still in the Niger delta. But the British government was cautious about getting bogged down in military operations in the forests of Africa. They had experienced numerous defeats and many deaths in similar adventures in Africa. The record was not good, plus military expeditions were expensive and the results not always successful. In addition they had heard that Oba Ovonramwen of Benin was a very power-ful king who held his office because of his strong links to his ancestors and his commitment to following the old ways. He was a king with a big heart who filled his people's lives with joy.

When Phillips arrived at his post in Africa he was pressured by the English merchants, who wanted even more profits than they were already receiving from the trade in the Niger delta, to write to Whitehall, the government in London. Phillips wrote:

> The whole of the English merchants represented on the river have peti-tioned the government for aid to enable them to keep their trading posts open, and last but not least, the revenues of this Protectorate are suffering ... I am certain that there is only one remedy. That is to depose the King of Benin ... I am convinced that pacific measures are now quite useless, and that the time has now come to remove the obstruction ... I do not anticipate any serious resistance from the people of the country – there is every reason to believe that they would be glad to get rid of their King – but in order to obviate any danger, I wish to take up sufficient armed force ... I would add that I have reason to hope that sufficient ivory may be found in the King's house to pay the expenses incurred.

Even before the government in Britain could respond Phillips had under-taken his fateful mission. He had sent messengers to the Oba of Benin informing the King of Kings that he intended to visit Benin soon. The reply had come from the Oba, the King of Kings, that Phillips should delay his visit for some time due to the customary rituals and festivals of the Edo people during which time no foreigner was allowed in the city. Phillips felt insulted by the Oba's response requesting him to delay his visit to Benin city. After several exchanges in which the Oba did not budge Phillips decided, against the advice of an Itsekeri king, Dogho, to lead nine British officials and traders and their servants and porters to Benin city. Seven of the white men were ambushed and killed on a narrow road leading north toward Benin city. The two white survivors managed to escape and find their way south to the coast. They were shaken and had run for their lives when they saw the others cut down by the Benin soldiers.

The fact that Phillips had made a bad decision led to the punitive expedi-tion that Moor had wanted in the first place. Although Phillips had acted out of his own ambition or on Moor's advice, it was Moor who was now prepared upon his return to Africa to lead the punitive expedition, as the British called it. Within six weeks of the ambush the British mounted a massive attack on the city. They burned all of the buildings, leveled the city, raped women, smashed the heads of children against the ground, and showed no mercy to the Benin defenders. In the end, they looted the treas-ury, stealing the gold, diamonds, silver, and beads found in the Oba's palace. In addition, and worst of all, the British took all of the ivory they could find, including the sacred ivory mask icon of Queen Idia. The British punitive raid against Benin city in 1897 has gone down in African history as one of the vilest acts of aggression in world history. The theft of the treasures of Oba Ovonramwen includes the fifteenth-century ivory leopard dotted with metal spots, scores of fourteenth- and fifteenth-century bronze plaques representing different figures from ordinary life in Benin, bronze horsemen, heads surmounted by two birds, and musicians.

The British were quick to justify their actions. They argued that Oba Ovonramwen's accession to the throne was questioned by internal disagreements in the court of Benin. They argued that the Oba was stonewalling them and that he therefore needed to be taught a lesson for holding out against British authority. The Oba was deposed and sent into exile, his accumulated works of arts from many centuries were removed and many pieces eventually shipped to London, the United States, and Germany. In fact, the Germans discovered a large trove of artifacts in eastern Germany after the unification of East and West Germany. Ovonramren's eldest son was elevated to Oba upon his death.

The great treasures of African art taken from Benin will never be in one place again. Many of the works have been destroyed by ignorance, some have been destroyed by war (World War II bombing attacks on Liverpool and Berlin), and much of it has been sold to Germany and the United States. Nigeria has never forgiven the British government for refusing to return the mask of Queen Idia during the 1977 FESTAC (Second World Black-African Festival of Arts). Britain has kept its large collection of Benin art in storage since an exhibition mounted in the early 1970s. In 1980 the Nigerians had to pay more than $1,200,000 for four Benin pieces at an auction. International pressure for nations to return art taken during colonial times has intensified recently. It seems logical that many African artifacts will be repatriated to their rightful nations in years to come.

When the people of Nigeria gained independence in 1960 they had taken the most populous nation in Africa out of the British colonial empire. The agitation had been long and had involved numerous courageous individuals. The early fighters knew that the country had to be free but many of them never saw independence day. No one wanted freedom any more than Herbert Macaulay.

Macaulay (1864–1946) was a Nigerian hero who became a politician, engineer, and journalist. As the son of Thomas Babington Macaulay, a prominent missionary, and grandson of Samuel Ajayi Crowther, the first African Anglican bishop in Nigeria, Macaulay was born into a privileged household in Lagos in 1864. Like other children who attended school he completed his education in mission schools. After this, Macaulay served in one of the jobs left for Africans. He took a job as a clerk at the Lagos Department of Public Works and then for three years, 1891–94, he studied civil engineering in England. When Macaulay returned, the only position he could find was as a land inspector. His dislike for the discrimination experienced by Africans drove him to become a journalist. He wrote articles that were critical of the colonial administration and used his writing to help him organize the Nigerian National Democratic Party, on 24 June 1923. Macaulay became editor in chief of the party newspaper, the *Lagos Daily*

*News*. The British arrested him on two occasions, accusing him of fomenting anti-colonial attitudes. This did not stop Macaulay; it only infuriated him. Thus, he joined with Nnamdi Azikiwe to create the National Council of Nigeria and the Cameroons (NCNC). He remained secretary-general of this movement until his death in 1946. It would be another fourteen years after his death before his beloved country claimed its independence. Nigeria was granted full independence in October 1960 under a constitution that provided for a government modeled on the British parliament but with some measure of self-government for the country's three regions.

In fact, on the basis of the negotiations that produced the new government, the central government held power in foreign relations, fiscal policy, and defense.

Actually, the British monarch retained the position as head of state although legislative power was vested in a bicameral parliament, executive power in a prime minister and cabinet, and judicial authority in a federal supreme court. During the early days of independence the political parties reflected the personalities, individual and collective, of the three largest ethnic groups. The NPC (Nigerian People's Congress) represented conservative, Muslim, largely Hausa–Fulani interests and dominated the northern region. The NCNC (National Convention of Nigerian Citizens) was Igbo and Christian and exercised power in the eastern region; and the AG (Action Group) was a left-leaning party that was under the control of the Yoruba in the western region.

Given the political climate and the huge numbers in the northern region it was no wonder that the Africans in the north and the southeast formed the first government along conservative lines. The AG was the opposition, ably so, because of the eloquence and charisma of Chief Obafemi Awolowo. It was a Hausa, Sir Abubakar Tafawa Balewa, a Hausa, who became Nigeria's first prime minister. Nnamdi Azikiwe held the post of governor-general.

Nigeria proclaimed itself a federal republic in October 1963 with Nnamdi Azikiwe as the country's first president. In an attempt to find solutions to the tensions that were inherent in the government structure because ethnic and religious emotions were not adequately dealt with in the constitution, the leaders of government tried to create methods to lessen the difficulties. There were disparities in economic and educational levels as well as differences in the political consciousness of the populations in the north and south.

Soon the AG was maneuvered out of political power and influence by a party established by the government to be more agreeable. A political party, based in the Yoruba region and calling itself the NNDP, became dominant in the west and supported the government. Chief Obafemi Awolowo was imprisoned on treason charges that were later shown to be without any basis.

The 1965 national election introduced the elements that would lead to civil war. The northern party, NPC, went into an alliance with the Yoruba NNDP, leaving the Igbo NCNC to fend for itself and to try to recover some influence by allying with the old AG. The western region contested the elections. The AG did not believe it had lost the election. Riots broke out. As we will see later, the country was now on a straight path to civil war.

## Dahomey (Benin): the shadow kingdom

The name "Dahomey" is almost synonymous with some of the worst aspects of the European slave trade on the West African coast. It was here, more than elsewhere, that the African kings participated and collaborated with the Europeans in the trade in human beings. Unfortunately for Dahomey, a name that is now consigned to history since the country where the kingdom was located changed its name to Benin, historians still record its short history as one of the most complicated in the annals of Africa.

Dahomey was not an ancient kingdom and its radical departure from African traditions in terms of human relationships represents an odd episode even in recent African history. It was a kingdom that started quite simply as an attempt by a small Fon kingdom to survive against its larger neighbors and to consolidate its military positions on the Atlantic coast as a way to guard against slave raiders. History has shown us many actions that began with good reasons but were soon subverted to bad ends. One has every reason to believe that the Fon people did not want the invasion of their territory, the stealing of their women, men, and children, or the plunder of their villages for human beings who would be dragged in shackles to the sea coast in order to be sold into bondage. No nation would want this for its people. Every nation would do what it could to prevent this type of disaster from occurring. It was true with the kingdom of Dahomey. The Fon became militarily powerful and therefore could prevent raids on their own territory but they could, consequently, raid other territories.

Dahomey, or as it is sometimes called after the name of its capital, Abomey, has a history rich in migratory stories of Africa. Three migrations into the present area of the Fon took place to bring about the kingdom of Dahomey. The first movement was a group of Yoruba people from what is now Nigeria. A second movement of Akan people from the Asante region of present-day Ghana came into the area. Finally, a third movement of people from Alladahanu from the southeastern part of today's Togo came into the territory. This was a very significant migration because three brothers from the town of Tado entered the territory and the eldest brother became king of Allada; the others left the territory and took up kingdoms of their own, one in Porto Novo and one near Abomey. About 1645 the kingdom of Abomey conquered the neighboring kingdom of Dan and thus the country was called Dahomey, meaning "in the belly of Dan." These waves of people from about 1300 to 1600 were important in the making of Dahomey. However, these people were not a nation when they appeared initially; it would take some time before all of these people, with different languages and styles, could be molded into the Fon nation. Yet it was clear that Abomey, now Dahomey, would take the lead in this development. It conquered Allada in 1724, and in 1727 it conquered Savi, the powerful kingdom on the coast near Ouidah (Whydah). This was to prove pivotal in

Dahomey's commercial development because Allada and Savi-Ouidah were Portuguese and French coastal slaving areas where both European nations had massive trading fortresses. Dahomey was no longer the source of human capital as it had been for many years; it was now in the position to become an important player in the brutal trade itself.

In a real sense the short history of Dahomey, from 1600 to 1900, reminds one of so many kingdoms and nations that have come and gone on the earth. They served a purpose and seemed at the time of their existence to be indispensable, and just as quickly as they came, they disappeared. It seemed so with Dahomey. A kingdom strewn with blood, ritual, and sacrifice, all in the name of expansion, territory, authority, brutality, and wealth, shot across the history books with untold successes and unheard of cruelties and then became a legend to be studied and analyzed.

The 13 kings of Dahomey are recorded in history as some of the best administrators, wisest tacticians, and cruelest despots in Africa's history:

Ganye Hessu (1600–20)
Dako Donu (1620–45)
Houegbadja (1645–85)
Akaba (1685–1708)
Agadja (1708–32)
Tegbessu (1732–74)
Kpingla (1774–89)
Agonglo (1789–97)
Adandozan (1797–1818)
Guezo (1818–58)
Glele (1858–89)
Gbehanzin (1889–94)
Agoli Agbo (1894–1900)

These kings ruled as sacred beings on the throne of the Alladahanu dynasty. A king had several titles in Dahomey. He was *Dada*, meaning father of the community, *Dokunnon*, distributor of wealth, *Ainon*, master of the world, and *Jehossu*, master of pearls. Like all humans elevated by the people and revered by the masses, the king of Dahomey had mystic, religious, social, and temporal powers that could turn ruin into wealth and wealth into ruin. He was carried in a hammock or rode in a palanquin like the Asante and Egyptian kings.

Some of the kings of Dahomey were known for their wisdom, others for their guile and cunning. One could say, as it is often said of rulers who live in chaotic times, that they were only accommodating themselves to the difficulties of their years, but in some cases in Dahomey we find nothing to praise and indeed it is not a record of our present alone that affirms this but the record and history of the kings' contemporaries.

Tegbessu (1732–74) died two years before American independence. His administration in Dahomey was not enlightened; it was venal because he did not follow the path of his ancestors in simply trying to prevent the raids on Fon territory but entered into the enslaving business with the Europeans as a way of gaining wealth and influence. In effect, Tegbessu was responsible for taking Dahomey on the road toward its ultimate decline. If a *katakle* (three-legged stool) would never be able to stand on two legs, then it is equally clear that a nation cannot build a lasting legacy on slavery. Tegbessu squandered the strength and dignity of Dahomey by forging a relationship with the European nations that would make Dahomey an intermediary for the slave trade.

By the time in 1797 when Adandozan reached the throne, through intrigue and the ability to outmaneuver the rightful owner of the throne, his brother Guezo, the kingdom of Dahomey was already deeply embedded in the slave business. In fact, the coastal areas of Ouidah had attracted Portuguese, French, and Dutch traders in the eighteenth century and they were intent on expanding their operations in Dahomey. Thus, there was created on the African continent for the first time a manufactured, inauthentic African kingdom, one practicing the buying and selling of human beings for the purpose of wealth-making. Never in Africa's history had a kingdom been so totally engrossed in the business of slavery. Nowhere was there an economy that was based solely on slavery and yet here in Dahomey we have a society where the kings, obviously influenced by the possibilities of material goods from Europe, were willing to barter with their people's moral character and the physical survival of captured and kidnapped Africans from other places. Europe traded weapons for human beings. Dahomey supplied captives and got guns. The kings used the guns to expand their territories. Adandozan's collaboration with the Europeans did not satisfy all of their lust for wealth on the African coast and many of them were angered by Adandozan's brazen desire to control even more of the profits from the Europeans.

Around 1818, a Portuguese slave trader, Francisco Felix da Souza, running ships between Africa and Brazil, used his forces and cunning to assist Guezo in seizing the throne from Adandozan. Guezo proved to be a tyrannical ruler. He had inherited a strong army, which he improved, relying heavily upon the Amazons (a group of women soldiers) and the purchasing of more guns from the Europeans to solidify his position as king. Each year he organized the *huetantu*, an annual festival, where human sacrifices were offered to the gods.

Souza was rewarded with a monopoly in the entire Dahomey kingdom over the sale of captured Africans into slavery. He soon became a settled person in the Dahomey kingdom, buying nearly fifty shiploads of humans to be shipped to Brazil within two years. Soon he ran foul of Guezo and was imprisoned. He was threatened with decapitation, a favorite method of death in the kingdom, but Guezo, having heard from other whites that it was a taboo to decapitate a white man, allowed Souza to live. This proved his undoing, because through the clever manipulation of the royal family Souza was released and the king's half-brother supplied him with African virgins, and gave him the monopoly of the slave trade again and an official title as the viceroy of Ouidah. In return, Souza managed through his connections to supply his sponsor with guns and European clothing. He fathered many children by African women and left on the continent a legacy that persists till this day. As recently as 2004 Martine da Souza, who is the great, great, great granddaughter of the infamous Francisco Felix "Cha Cha" da Souza, worked as a guide in the Slave Museum in Ouidah.

Dahomey had been watched by the French for a long time, and since they already had fortresses doing business on the coast the French knew quite a lot about the habits and ways of the Fon. In 1863 the French declared that they would control Porto Novo. In 1889 they moved to occupy Cotonou. In 1892 the French declared to King Gbehanzin that they would take over the entire kingdom. The king launched a fierce counterattack against the French, but it was too late and the firepower of the brave and courageous Dahomeans too little to overcome the massive cannons of the French. It was revealed at this point that with all of the trade between Africans and Europeans the Europeans did not trade their finest weapons to Africans. In the bitter end, King Gbehanzin was deposed and exiled to Martinique. The French installed a puppet king, Agoli Agbo. The kingdom was abolished by the French in 1900. It regained its independence in 1960 and changed its name to Benin in 1975.

## The Swahili nations

The word "Swahili" is derived from the Arabic word "sahil," which means coast. When the Arabs first saw the African people living along the coast they gave these coastal people who spoke Bantu languages the name "Sahili". KiSwahili is a Bantu language to which many Arabic words have been added. This came about over a long history of trade relationships between the people. It is the adopted language of the modern nation of Tanzania.

To understand the Swahili culture it is important to start at the beginning. For millennia Africans lived along the coast of the Indian Ocean without too much interference from foreigners. Visitors from Asia and Europe found the east coast of Africa quite accessible, as they had found the west coast. In the east there were visitors from Arabia and Portugal and other countries from Asia and Europe. Soon after 622 CE and the beginning of Islam the east coast of Africa became popular with Arabs, Persians, Indians, Indonesians, and Chinese. They came to the coast of Africa looking for exotic spices, ivory, rhinoceros horn, tortoise shells, and coconuts. Soon Arab traders had made their way from Somali in the north to Pemba Island in the south. But Africa was not just a market for traders: some of the people were escaping punishment in the religious conflicts that engulfed their own lands. Nothing in the religion of the Bantu was a threat to anyone else. Africans did not mistreat, harm, or kill people simply because they did not like their religion. There was nothing called religious intolerance in the mind of Africa. Therefore, many people rushed to live on the coast of Africa. The east coast was one of the world's first melting pots. Here one could find people from all the countries of Asia and many of the European countries from the seventeenth to the twentieth century.

The Somali coast, also called Banadir, had to accommodate a large Arab and Persian population by the ninth and tenth centuries CE. The Persians came from Shiraz, a city of Iran. These visitors intermarried with Somali women and developed what was called the Shirazi culture, a combination of African, Persian, and Arab peoples. Shirazi culture was to have a major impact on coastal activities. It was between the tenth and fourteenth centuries that the term "Swahili" came into existence to define people who were African in language and phenotype but Islamic in culture and religion.

Soon the African cities of Mogadishu, Brava, and Merka became magnets for trade and centers for Islamic thought and culture. As in West Africa, particularly during the Mali Empire, the imprint of Islam on the east coast of Africa changed the culture of the people. African traders took their goods to India, Arabia, and China, and traders from those places traveled to the Swahili coast, sometimes going into the interior as far as 400 miles to trade with Great Zimbabwe. Along the coast huge towns such as Mombasa, Malindi, Lamu, Kilwa, and Sofola were beehives of trading and proselytizing.

The Banadir coastline all the way down to Sofola was nothing but one large human experiment in how much activity around trade and culture could take place without the host people losing their patience. However, the Arab traders grew sensitive to the Africans' concerns about losing property and influence to the rich traders and soon there was a movement of Arab traders to live on the offshore African islands, and the African populations of islands like Pemba, Mafia, and Zanzibar became known for their concentration of trading vessels and goods, and people to be sold into slavery, taken from the mainland. The Arab slave trade on the Indian Ocean was as onerous as the European slave trade on the Atlantic Ocean. Neither practice was pretty; both were monstrous in their brutality and exploitation of Africans.

When the history of Kilwa was written in KiSwahili in 1520 the language of the Bantu people now occupying the coast had become a sort of lingua franca for East Africa. Almost all Bantu speakers had KiSwahili as a second language or could speak KiSwahili with a little practice. Thus, the African people soon Africanized all the cultural elements that had been supplied by the Arabs and Persians. Indeed, the first sultan of Kilwa, Ali Selimani, a Shirazi, married the daughter of the African king he overthrew. His son, half African, became the second sultan of Kilwa. Over time the intermarriages between the Arab and Persian traders, men who did not bring their women on the trading voyages, Africanized the Swahili society. Although the people remained African the teaching of the Qur'an and Hadith kept the people firmly in the grip of Islamic culture. The ruling families were thoroughly Islamicized, while the masses of African people continued to practice African traditional religion.

Beginning in the tenth century CE the entire Swahili coast, called Zanj, was under the control of one king who ruled all of the coastal areas from his capital at Sofala. The people expected the king to keep a democratic government, one that served the interests of the people in the interior as well as the traders along the coast. He could be deposed by the ruling council if they felt that he had become tyrannical. This was the pattern of African governments throughout the region. By the fourteenth century there were forty towns at least that claimed to be under the authority of the ruling king. From Mogadishu in the north to Sofala these towns practiced Islam, followed the Qur'an, traded with Asia and Arabia, and engaged in raids into the interior for ivory and people who could be kidnapped and brought to the coast and sold into slavery. City-states, some with only a town where a mosque existed with a few houses, became the norm in the sixteenth century. The coast had become too long and too perilous to control as one nation. Now the Swahili culture was transformed into the Swahili states. Some of the states were built entirely of coral stone and showed great beauty. Places like Kilwa, Pate, Malindi, and Zanzibar reflected the combination of African creativity and Islamic themes in the structure and aesthetics of the buildings.

During the city-state phase most of the towns acted independently and were ruled by their own sultan. At various periods there were conflicts, rivalries, and disputes where one town would conquer another and rule over that town as well as the main capital of the sultan. This was the situation when the city of Kilwa dominated all of the land between Sofala and Zanzibar in the early fourteenth century, but after several decades of fighting and dynastic disputes the towns reasserted their independence around 1390. Soon thereafter the coast was visited by the Chinese Ming Dynasty explorer Cheng Ho (Sheng He).

Cheng Ho was a Muslim eunuch who was well suited to deal with the Islamic rulers of South Asia and East Africa (Mote 1995). He made seven voyages to South Asia and Africa. However, it was his seventh voyage that was most important for the trade between the Swahili coast and China. Cheng Ho's first long-distance voyage was in 1405–07, with sixty-two vessels carrying 28,000 men to India. During the seventh voyage in 1431–33, Cheng Ho's sailors reached far down the east coast of Africa, probably as far as western South Africa, certainly hitting Mogadishu and Malindi. Of course, the development of Chinese shipbuilding and techniques of navigation on the Asian sea routes made Cheng Ho's voyages possible. Missions from the African coast came to China four times, as recorded in Ming Dynasty records. These expeditions provided the same kind of lines of communication between Africa and China that had existed between Africa and India for hundreds of years.

## The social organization

The social organization of Swahili society was comprised of four classes: the ruling class, the merchant class, the artisans and clerks, and the manual laborers. The ruling class was made up of those who traced their descent to Arab and Persian ancestors. They were practicing Muslims. As rulers they lived in extraordinary luxury in huge ornate palaces decorated with ivory and fine woods. They wore silk and cotton garments often imported from China and ate the best vegetables and fruits produced along the coast. The ruling class was hereditary and hence all of the sultans considered themselves Arabs or Persians although they were often African in phenotype and complexion. The merchant class was both African and Arab and made up of those who owned vessels, dhows, that could ply the waters off the coast of Africa and perhaps travel to India. They were also shopkeepers who grew wealthy on the production of cotton, shell beads, and various types and colors of glass beads. The third class was made up of KiSwahili-speaking artisans and clerks, court officials, and captains of ships. Most of these people spoke both Arabic and KiSwahili and could be called upon by the merchants and ruling class to support them if necessary. However, they were not necessarily practising Muslims as were the merchants and the rulers. A fourth level was that of the manual laborers, who were most often enslaved people or servants who had been taken from the mainland and brought to the islands or indigenous people who had refused to become Muslim and therefore were outside of the benefits distributed to those who practiced Islam.

The laborers carried out all the agriculture that supported the economy. Food was produced on a scale to satisfy domestic consumption rather than commercial interests. The farmers cultivated sugar cane, figs, oranges, lemons, and many vegetables. One could find private gardens in cities such as Mombasa, Malindi, and Kilwa. Large flocks of sheep, cattle, and fowls were kept by the wealthy in the cities.

According to Seth Kordzo Gadzekpo:

> There was a lucrative trade between the Swahili coast on one hand and India and China on the other. Kilwa, Malindi, and Mombasa were great trading entrepots. Ships from India and China brought cotton cloths, silk cloths, wheat, grey/red and yellow beads, spears, axes, knives and porcelain to the Swahili ports. At the port cities of Kilwa, Malindi, and Mombasa, the goods were transported in small vessels named "Zambucos" to the Sofala coast where they were bartered for wax, gold, and especially "soft" ivory for the manufacture of furniture and handles in China.
>
> (1999, p. 112)

Without any question the Swahili coast was a major player in African history for a considerable time. By the tenth century CE local artisans were already producing iron implements and by the fourteenth century the trade between the east coast of Africa and India, Arabia, and China had been well established. The historian al-Masudi said that the people of Zanj were already wearing iron ornaments by the tenth century. The people had also learned how to use bronze and silver to manufacture goods like sword sheaths, sofas, chairs, and tables. In addition, trade with Asia brought into East Africa many products such as silk, and thus by the time the Portuguese, the first Europeans to go around the Cape of Good Hope, reached East Africa in the fifteenth century they found a long tradition of trade and commerce between Africa and Asia. It would take several hundred years before Europe supplanted Asia in the minds of the East Africans, and even when Europe occupied and controlled the eastern coast there would always be remnants of the Asian contact.

Perhaps the Asian connection was most clearly seen in the Malagasy people, whose country, Madasgascar, was an independent kingdom prior to French colonization. Located off the southeast coast of Africa in the Indian Ocean, Madagascar is the world's fourth-largest island. Nearly 20 million people were living on the island in 2006. It was comprised of African, Malay,

Indonesian, Indian, French, Comoran, and Arab ethnics and all combinations of these groups. More than half of the population consider themselves to be religiously African; others are Christians and Muslims. However, because of the strong Asian presence the cultural impact of Asia, particularly India and Malaysia, represents a major factor in the life of the country.

Although the Malagasy trace their history to the African continent, since 700 CE, when Indonesians migrated to the island, there has been a strong Asian presence. King Andrianampoinimerina (1787–1810) ruled the most prominent kingdom on the island, and his son Radama I (1810–28) was responsible for unifying the entire island. Called the founder of the Malagasy nation, Radama I enjoys a high status in the country's memory. However, the French occupation in 1885, immediately after the Berlin Conference of European Powers determined to divide up Africa, gave the Malagasy a reason to become even more unified in resistance to France.

The country of Mauritius, 560 miles to the east of Madagascar, is the farthest east of all African countries, and therefore more deeply entrenched with Asian culture than almost any other, although it changed hands between European powers several times. It was first occupied by the Portuguese in 1505, taken over by the Dutch in 1638, captured by the French in the 1700s, and conquered by the British in 1810. It became an independent country in 1968, by which time the population was thoroughly creolized. Among the Asian communities are the speakers of the Indian-derived languages of Hindi, Urdu, Tamil, Telugu, Marathi, Bhojpuri, and Gujarati. There are groups derived from Africa and Europe, plus mixtures of Chinese, Africans, and Indians. While this African nation, far out in the Indian Ocean, has the least influence from the continent, it remains firmly within the sphere of African political and economic influence. Like the nations on the continent itself, Madagascar and Mauritius, as well as Cape Verde and other islands, see themselves in the light of African heritage, even if it is no more than the migratory history of the people.

## The decline of the Christian Nubian states

About the time of the Swahili states on the Indian Ocean coast there began to be changes in the six-centuries-old arrangement between Christian Nubia and Muslim Egypt. The agreement, called the *bakt*, had kept the two nations interdependent. It was a formula for tolerance that was effective during the reign of the Fatimids in Egypt. However, the period of the Ayyubids (1171–1250) and that of the Mamluks (1250–1517) witnessed deterioration in the relationship between the two Nile countries. This was because of "the growing pressure of Cairo on a weakening Nubia and the increasing, and destructive, infiltration of Arab nomadic groups" (Kropacek 1997, p. 159).

There were two Nubian kingdoms that constituted the frontier between Egypt and Nubia: Mukurra in the north with its capital at Dunkula and Alwa in the south. The succession to the throne was matrilineal, with the son of the past king's sister being next in line for the throne.

The king of Nubia was on good terms with the patriarch of Alexandria because he was the protector of the king; they were both Christians and the Nubian king paid homage to his patriarch. Nevertheless, the Nubians increasingly became a solid force for the Fatimid rulers of Egypt; they constituted the nucleus of the Fatimid soldiers and were protected by the Nubian mother of al-Mustansir. However, when the Ayyubids came to power the Nubians attacked Egypt in 1172 and were driven back by Turanshah, the brother of Salah al-Din (Saladin). This led to the Arabization and Islamization of Nubia. It included forced intermarriage with the Banu al-Kanz, already a mixed people of Nubian and Arab descent, but now to be remixed, so to speak, with additional Arab blood. The Ayyubids and the Mamluks attacked the Bedouin nomads' *kabilas*, driving them deeper into Nubia (Kropacek 1997, p. 161).

A political mistake of massive proportions occurred when King Dawud of Nubia attacked and won an Egyptian Red Sea port. Sultan Baybars responded by sending an expedition to Dawud's capital and deposing him. His nephew Shakanda was placed on the throne and he agreed to be a vassal to Egypt. He also agreed to pay Egypt half of the income of the country. Soon the Mamluks and Arabs, the Mamluks being from Russia or Albania, turned Nubia into a country to be raided and raped (Kropacek 1997, p. 161).

King Shamamun of Nubia sacked the Mamluk garrison stationed in Nubia at Dunkula. Thinking that he might have angered the Egyptian rulers too much, he sought forgiveness of Sultan Kalaun who, because he was engaged against the Crusaders, accepted and asked the Nubians to pay tribute. When King Karanbas assumed the throne in Nubia he omitted to pay and the sultan sent a punitive expedition, along with a pretender to the throne named Sanbu, who was a Muslim. It was his installation on the Nubian throne in 1294 that marked the official beginning of the conversion of Christian Nubia to Islam. Sanbu transformed many of the main churches into mosques. He was soon defeated and killed by Kanz al-Dawla. The reaction of Cairo was to try to restore the deposed Karanbas, the Nubian king who had now converted to Islam after being held in Cairo.

Although Mukurra slipped into a form of anarchy with competing factions fighting for supremacy, the country was being changed into an Islamic country without ever being annexed by Egypt. It was undermined from without and within by the infiltration of many ethnic Arabs, who attacked every aspect of the society. Kropacek writes, "Intermarriage, which, according to the Nubian principle of succession gave the sons of Arab fathers and Nubian mothers the right to the property of their Nubian maternal uncles, accelerated Arabization and Islamization in the midst of an apparently chaotic situation" (Kropacek 1997, p. 162).

Like Mukurra, so went Alwa later. This kingdom, according to accounts of Ibn Salaym in the tenth century and Abu Salih in the thirteenth century, had 400 churches and many slave markets. Arab immigrants who had infiltrated and married locally assumed control over the pastures and ended by undermining the central authority by the last half of the fifteenth century (Kropacek 1997, p. 162). Thus, put upon by the Arabs and other African groups from the central and eastern regions of Sudan, the Alwa kingdom fell in 1504.

Soon there were no more Christian kings, but the practices of Christianity survived for years more. The Portuguese priest Francesco Alvarez, who visited Ethiopia in 1520, said that the Nubians still had 150 churches in old castles. The people of Nubia sent a delegation to the court of Ethiopia asking for Christian priests. Perhaps the Christian religion would have survived had its roots been deeper among the masses. It was a religion of the elites of Nubia, and the Coptic clergy prayed to saints of whom not one was a Nubian. Kropacek claims that "Although the frescoes in churches reveal the faces of autochthonous black bishops, the religion did not become indigenous in the sense that Islam, for example, did. That is why pre-Christian beliefs have survived there with such vigor" (Kropacek 1997, p. 163). While Nubian Christianity held out longer than Egyptian Christianity, both gave up much of their indigenous religion early to outside influences. Thus, the aggressive assault on the power institutions meant that Nubia would lose much of its character over the next few centuries.

## Asante: the kingdom of gold

The development of the Akan people into a powerful group occurred over several centuries. With the decline of the Sahelian empires of Ghana, Mali, and Songhay, especially Songhay, numerous artisans, traders, and military families moved south. The dyula, a professional class of traders from the Bamana, Soninke, and Malinke ethnic groups, migrated to the region of the Upper Volta River during the fourteenth century. They were known for trading in gold and kola nuts on a small scale but soon a people arose, probably as a combination of these remnant peoples of the Sahelian empires and indigenous peoples, and the Akan people of the forest region were born. They took charge of the gold trade and became the most aggressive merchants in the area. Later they would be implicated in the slave trade as collaborators with the Europeans and Arabs.

Like other people of the forest region the Akan were expert farmers and participated in trading as a supplemental way to obtain goods that they could not ordinarily get from farming. They were used to survival in the forest, clearing and planting small plots of land, and holding back the fast-growing brush by the slash-and-burn technique. One of the enduring characteristics of the Akan people was the strength with which they were able to hold back the encroaching forest. It took a particular genius and energy to be able to exist in the midst of an assertive forest, one ever ready to pounce upon the unsuspecting and engulf an area in green foliage.

A kingdom of gold arose from the forest floor during the fifteenth century. The Akan states, those people speaking the Twi language, became powerful as gold miners and farmers. They traded with the Wangara people of the Sahel, as well as the other forest people in present-day Ghana, Togo, and Ivory Coast. But it was in the sixteenth century that the Akan states became militarily and economically so strong that they were able to bargain with the seemingly ubiquitous Portuguese traders at the coast. Two kingdoms, Denkyira and Akwamu, were immediately seen as the leading states

*Figure 10.1* King Osabarima Nana Adusei Peasa IV, Tafohene, Akyem, Ghana
© Molefi Kete Asante

of the Akan. Already by this time the Fante kingdom, located near the coast, had exercised its political options with the Portuguese. The Fante, under King Kwame Ansah, had been badly beaten in 1482 by the Portuguese, who came ashore to establish a fortress that was called El Mina. The Fante would soon serve as buffers between the Portuguese and later the Dutch who occupied the coast and the interior peoples.

The Asante kingdom, soon to be the most feared kingdom among the Akan, originated from a collection of towns with the creativity of two extraordinary individuals, Okomfo Anokye and Osei Tutu I. The first was a philosopher-priest and the second was fated to become the founding king of the most heralded kingdom of the Akan, the Asante nation (Wilks 1975).

Of course there had been kings and priests before, but the coming together of Okomfo Anokye, who was about ten years the senior, and Osei Tutu was a replay of Imhotep and Zoser in ancient Kemet. It was necessary for a philosopher, thinker, priest, if you will, to interpret and explain the conditions, challenges, and possibilities of kingship. It was the role of the king, inherited from the ancestors, to act. Both characters played their roles expertly and with historical deftness. No other priest-philosopher among the Akan had arrived at the creative point and the intellectual vision of Okomfo Anokye.

Okomfo Anokye's birth name was Kwame Agyei, but he was also called Frempong Manso. This was in accordance with ancient African tradition. One sees the tradition of having more than one name throughout African history and Okomfo Anokye was squarely inside the circle of African thinking. The appellation "Kotowbere" is known and used among the Asante

*Figure 10.2* Professor Botwe-Asamoah with queens and princesses at Tafo, Ghana
© Molefi Kete Asante

people. His full name is sometimes given as Kwame Agyei Frempong Anokye Kotowbere. He was said to be the grandson of Amoa Gyata from Bona-Bom in Adanse, but some reports say that he may have been the son of a man named Kyei Birie and a woman named Dwirawira Kwa from Adanse-Akrokyere (Anti 1973, p. 8). Another account says that Okomfo Anokye was the son of "Ano, a quiet and physically weak father, and Manubea, an energetic, sentimental and talkative mother," who were from Awukugua in the Nifa Division of the Akuapem State (Anti 1973, p. 8). There is more to substantiate this account because of the extensive detail given about Okomfo's life in Akuapem. It is likely that numerous families sought to claim the popular priest once he had reached the level of being a national icon. However, it is most likely that he was born in the region of Akuapem. According to the local historians, when he was born in Awukugua, Akuapem, he was already holding in his right hand a short white tail of a cow. In the Twi language this is called *bodua*. The infant Anokye clenched his left hand so tightly that no one could open it. The midwife who had delivered the child tried to open his hand because she suspected that he had come into the world with something. The father was called in to assist and as soon as the father touched the left hand the child opened his eyes and stared at the father. He then opened the mysterious hand, showing it to his father and saying in the Guan language, the oldest language spoken in Ghana, "Ano, kye," meaning "Ano, see", and gave the father a talisman of herbs. From that moment he was called Okomfo, meaning priest. Another version of this story is that the mother and father

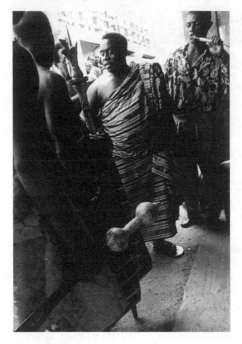

*Figure 10.3* Okyeame, royal linguist, Akyem, Ghana
© Molefi Kete Asante

went to sleep when they could not open the left hand of the child and at night the mother felt something drop on her and it was a talisman. She turned to her husband and said, "Ano, see." This earned him the name Ano-Kye, Anokye. The townspeople thought of the infant as the incarnation of the old grandfather, Obiri Agyei, a former physician and herbalist. Clearly, the tradition saw Okomfo Anokye as one who was able to perform great deeds, including miracles of nature.

In the seventeenth century the kingdom of Denkyira was the most powerful state in the interior of what is now Ghana. It controlled all the other states and was an important source for trading gold and human beings with the Dutch at El Mina. Adanse, the state that had competed with Denkyira, had been weakened by wars and internal power struggles and consequently many of the people of Adanse had moved to Asante, Kotoku, and Akyem-Abuakwa. Now Denkyira was preeminent among the Akan states.

Nana Boa Amponsem, king of Denkyira, had defeated many surrounding states and had exacted tribute from all of them. Asante did not exist as a unified state at the time, but already it was beginning to assert itself from its principal city, Kwaman, later to be called Kumasi. From this city, Kumasi, philosophers, priests, adventurers, and oral historians spread the news of the Akan heritage. They sang in Twi and the drummer played on the *fontonfrom* and *atumpan* the ancient wisdom:

> The river crosses the path,
> The path crosses the river.
> Which is older?
> The river is from long ago.

*Figure 10.4* Outdooring of a new king, Akyem, Ghana
© Molefi Kete Asante

Two events would change the history of the region: first, Okomfo Anokye would migrate to Denkyira and be forced to leave soon after, and second, Osei Tutu, the young military leader of Kwaman, would become king of a unified state after the death of Nana Obiri Yeboa. Okomfo Anokye had traveled to the state of Denkyira after leaving his home area of Akuapem, where he served under the tutelage of the priests and king of Nyanaw. It was here that Anokye first met Osei Tutu, who was his junior and had also been sent to Akuapem for education. There had been some difficulties with the officials in Nyanaw, particularly the fact that Nana Ansa Sasraku I of Nyanaw found his incredible ability to cure diseases and to prophesy correctly future events threatening to his authority as the chief spiritual and political leader. In Denkyira, Anokye ran into similar difficulties with Nana Amponsem's chief spiritual counselor, Kyerekye. He was the most famous priest among the Akan-speaking people prior to the rise of Okomfo Anokye. His professional skills as a doctor, herbalist, and prophet were well known throughout the land. But Anokye was capable of doing even more than Kyerekye and soon won the confidence of the population to the dismay of Kyerekye (Anti 1973, p. 25). Jealousy on the part of the resident spiritual leader eventually led to the dismissal of Anokye from the Denkyira court of Nana Boa Amponsem. He then made his way to the city of Kwaman and the court of the king, Nana Obiri Yeboa. Since Kwaman was still a subject state to Denkyira, the priest pushed farther north and found shelter in a small village for about a year. When he returned to

Kwaman he was sick and plagued with sores. The year was 1677 and Nana Yeboa was dead and there was a huge dispute between two royal families about who should succeed the king, each family claiming the stool. One family was the Agona line and the other was the Oyoko line. The regent after the king's death was Adu Gyamfi from the Agona line. Okomfo Anokye tried to find employment with the regency but to no avail. In a fateful decision, he went and joined forces with the opposing family, the Oyoko family, and their leader Adoma Akosua. This family had compassion on the priest, and gave him food, a house, and protection. In return he served the family with his wisdom, experience, and knowledge of nature. In addition, they asked him to help them bring the stool (the kingship) to the Oyoko family. When Adu Gyamfi heard about this arrangement he drove Okomfo Anokye away from Kwaman. He fled to Dwaben and remained in the palace of Nana Akrasi, the Dwabenhene. Anokye later had to leave and went to the town of Obi, where he remained until the time Osei Tutu I came to power. He had gone to Nyanaw for education and training and during the time that he had been away Nana Adu Gyamfi had solved the leadership dispute. In 1680, when Osei Tutu I was 36 years old, he returned from Nyanaw to assume the kingship.

Okomfo Anokye was faced with a dilemma. He had known Osei Tutu for seventeen years from the time both of them were at Nyanaw. But he had also entered into intrigues against the Agona family of which Osei Tutu was a part. Furthermore, old Adu Gyamfi was still alive and had to tell Osei Tutu of the deeds done against the family by Okomfo Anokye. Yet with a stroke of boldness and genius Okomfo Anokye left Obi and went straight to his friend, Nana Akrasi of Dwaben, and told him that Onyame, the sky god, had ordered him to make Asante a great nation. Nana Akrasi went to inform Osei Tutu of Anokye's mission. Of course the Nana Osei Tutu could decide nothing without the council of elders and could not accept Anokye's mission from God.

It was necessary for Okomfo Anokye to prove his genuineness. He could not be taken at face value. The people of Kwaman and surrounding towns had seen many charlatans come and go and so they demanded that Anokye be put to the test. Without his knowledge two small mud houses were made in which were placed two cows, one black and the other white. Okomfo Anokye was asked by the elders to tell which house held the black cow. Instead of answering the question Anokye pointed to the house in which the white cow had been placed and said that it contained a brown cow. The elders looked at each other, knowing that they had placed a white cow in the house; they opened the door and to their amazement they found a brown cow. At that point, Anokye said to them that the other house held a cow that was both black and white. They opened that door and sure enough there was a black and white cow. From this time onward, Anokye did not have to prove himself to the people of Kwaman.

The elders asked Okomfo Anokye to which clan or family he belonged and he declared that he was Agona, whereupon he was given over to the Agona to find him permanent accommodation. He was given citizenship with all its rights and he became the chief priest and king of the town of Agona.

Like many philosophers and visionaries, Okomfo Anokye spent many hours contemplating the future of his society. One day, after heavy rain accompanied by thunder and hail, Okomfo Anokye was relaxing in a chair in the antechamber of his house in Kwaman (Kumasi). He saw in a trance a great assembly of kings and elders who were all the past royalty of Asante. Near them was a large river whose waters were moving rapidly.

According to the story the meeting place was surrounded by darkness and gloom and then there arose a smoke-like cloud which covered the whole area and hung over the heads of the assembly. In an open space in front of the assemblage of dignitaries, human skulls and bones were heaped in piles with broken pieces of drums, damaged headwear, sandals with broken straps, umbrellas, and gold dust (Anti 1973, p. 29). While still in the trance, Okomfo Anokye could see a small house not far from the assembly in which Osei Tutu was seated. Then he saw a man emerge from the assembly and walk toward the small house where Osei Tutu was seated. The man was carrying on his head a stool which was lying on its side in a brass pan and which had been covered with an Adinkra cloth. The man was in motion but his feet never touched the ground and the stool he was carrying never seemed to touch his head.

Soon there was a procession of kings and elders behind the man with the stool. They entered the room in front of Osei Tutu. At this time the smoke-like screen seemed to move in such a way as to protect the stool. Just then Osei Tutu rose and stopped the procession from going any farther. When the smoke cleared the people in the procession had gone and only the man with the stool was standing with Osei Tutu, whereupon the man left the stool and disappeared. Anokye then called for Osei Tutu and the Queen Mother and related the dream to them. Soon a Golden Stool was presented to Anokye, who then presented it to Osei Tutu. Within a few days Osei Tutu and the Queen Mother of Kokofu called the other kings of Asante together and ordered them to swear an oath to the Golden Stool.

A more magical version of the Golden Stool is that Anokye brought down a wooden stool adorned with gold from the sky in the midst of thunder and hail and it floated lightly to the knees of Osei Tutu.

What we do know is that Kwaman was able, because of the genius of Okomfo Anokye, to bring three more states into its confederation because of the Golden Stool. This allowed the king of Kwaman, now called Kumasi, to become the Asantehene, that is, king of the Asante nation. He was no longer just king of Kumasi but also the ruler of several states. This also allowed the Asante to be powerful enough to challenge Denkyira. Using the wise counsel of Anokye, Osei Tutu was able to consolidate his victories against the enemies of Asante. Anokye's policy was to admit new states into the confederation on equal terms, each retaining its customs and high ceremonial days. He created the institution of a council to check the power of the king. The fear and reverence for the Golden Stool helped Anokye and Tutu organize and control the state of Asante. Thus, this powerful kingdom was the result of the philosophical and political genius of Anokye and the military and administrative genius of Osei Tutu I.

By 1700 Asante had conquered Denkyira, brought other Akan states into submission, and controlled the goldfields. Osei Tutu's successor was the fighting king, Nana Opoku Ware I (1717–50). During the reign of Nana Opoku Ware I it became the talk of the neighboring kingdoms that Asante was supreme as a military nation. They said, "Kill a thousand, and a thousand will come!"

Taking his place next to the great generals of Africa, Opoku Ware managed with his skill and the reverence he had for the Golden Stool to advance the empire in areas that it had not dreamed of in the days of Osei Tutu. He was an imperial king, expanding the boundaries of Asante to cover most of what is present Ghana. The Asante Empire stretched from the savanna region of the north to the waters of the Atlantic Ocean in the south. Shillington says that "the rulers of Asante sold their war-captives to slavers at the coast ... But they never became very dependent on the trade for royal revenue" (1989, p. 195). Neither did the Asante use enslaved persons for the mining of the gold that was the real basis of the wealth of the empire. In fact, those who worked in the goldfields had to be the ones most trusted by the Asantehene since all gold belonged to the royal house. As much as Asante was involved in the trading of war-captives it never became a society whose principal mode of production was the enslavement of others. Furthermore, chattel slavery was unheard of in African societies and remained a practice to be carried to its highest degree of inhumanity in the Americas. Asante would later fight the British in an effort to keep the Gold Coast free of colonial invasion. They would fail but in their resistance would create fear in the hearts of the whites who met them in the forest. Britain applied a form of practical politics to the conquest of the Gold Coast, but it meant that they had to ignore the concrete facts of history, which indicated that the people of the area would not long be enslaved. Indeed other kingdoms, especially of the Akan, would deal with the British colonial agents with resistance. Queen Aframoa Dipo of the Akyem refused to sign a bond with the English. Her actions wrote her name indelibly in the hearts of her people but lost the Tafo people their paramountcy among the royals of Akyem. The British, once they gained control, transferred the paramountcy to a more pliable monarch, the king of Kyebi.

## Zulu: the people of heaven

Perhaps no nation has ever been born out of warfare and blood to such an extent as the Zulu nation. Prior to 1819 it was relatively unknown even in South Africa, where it was surrounded by much older and more established states such as the Xhosa, the Swazi, and the Sotho. However, the dramatic entry of the Zulu into African history as a major player trounces all comparisons with other societies in southern Africa. Yet the origins of this state are found in the legends of the people themselves. The first name in the memory of the Zulu people is that of Luzumane, who was the father of Malandela. It is believed that Malandela was born around 1591 and lived until 1627. Malandela settled at Mandawe Hill and had two sons, Qwabe and Zulu, by his wife Nozinja.

Upon the death of Malandela the elder son Qwabe left to form his own clan. Zulu, the younger son, became the protector of his mother. He lived from 1627 to 1709. As he grew in stature, he was able to establish his own authority and gave his name to the family line, becoming the founder of the famous Zulu clan. He was succeeded by Punga, who died without a male heir and was succeeded by his brother Mageba. He inherited his brother's widow and through her left children in his brother's name, and fathered a son named Ndaba from his own wife. Ndaba lived from 1697 to 1763. His eldest son Xoko branched off to form his own Gazini clan. Ndaba was succeeded by his youngest son, Jama. Jama was born in 1727 and died in 1781 and left a minor son, Senzangakona, as heir. Because of his minority his eldest sister Mkabayi and various uncles served as regents until 1783. He ruled for thirty-three years and had many wives and scores of children, among whom were the famous Shaka, Dingan, Mpande, Mhlangana, and Sigujana, his nominated heir. At the death of Senzangakona, Sigujana became king and was promptly murdered at the age of 26. It is believed that Shaka ordered Ngwadi (also his half brother) to kill his half-brother, who lived from 1790 to 1816. This assassination would set a violent pattern that would end in Shaka's own assassination years later.

The rise of Shaka Zulu to the highest seat of authority among the Zulu was one of the most fateful moments in African history. He had been born in 1787 out of wedlock, the son of Senzangakona and Nandi. Shaka's mother had ultimately been taken as the third wife of the king, but soon after she came with her son to live in the king's compound the king exiled the two of them, when Shaka was only six years old.

As can be expected, the young Shaka had an unhappy childhood because his mother as an exile had few friends. They were finally befriended by a powerful Mtetwa king, Dingiswayo, who launched Shaka on a military career. He also helped him take the Zulu clan leadership from Sigujana.

Immediately Shaka embarked on military training with the idea of expansion of the territory by conquest. When Dingiswayo died Shaka assumed leadership of Mtetwa and took the Mtetwa army to war against all of its enemies, including the great king Zwide, king of the Ndwandwe. Having defeated Zwide, the young Shaka combined the forces of the greatest Nguni-speaking clans and created the Zulu nation.

Shaka reigned in Zulu from 1816 to 1828, twelve of the most historic and momentous years in the annals of Africa. When he died at the age of 41, assassinated by two of his brothers, Dingane and Mhlangana, and one of his closest friends, Mbopa, he had written a record of bloodshed and military conquest unheard of in southern Africa before him. It is estimated that nearly one million people were killed or left homeless by the wars of Shaka. The homeless wanderers were called "Mfengu" and became attached to groups that had not been defeated or scattered by the Mfecane.

One must be clear that Shaka was not insane or irrational; he was like all military leaders who believe that their missions are so important that they are willing to sacrifice their lives and the lives of other people to achieve their aims. To the degree that we call other generals of war (Ramses,

Alexander, Sundiata, Napoleon, Hannibal, Genghis Khan, Sunni Ali Ber) bloodthirsty and violent, we must also give those appellations to Shaka. As historians can explain some of the motivation for these violent outbursts in history, the actions of Shaka are also interpreted in the light of the threat he perceived to be sitting at the door of heaven. How to strengthen his nation and prevent its domination became his burning desire.

The word "Zulu" means "heaven" in English. The people are called AmaZulu and their country or region is called KwaZulu, literally the "place of Zulu." A number of factors contributed to the rise of the Zulu as a military nation who believed that the land, like the rain, belonged to no one. It was simply there for all to share. But this was not the philosophy of the whites who had entered South Africa at the Cape under Van Riebeck in 1652, thirty-three years after the first twenty Africans had disembarked in Jamestown, Virginia. Thus, one must set the context for the appearance of a leader like Shaka.

The whites introduced a notion of private ownership of the land that was as anathema to the Africans they met as it was to the African ancestors. This was the principal factor that would lead to disagreements between Africans and the Europeans. Van Riebeck's party met the indigenous Khoi-san and San people at the Cape. Soon they were to meet the Xhosa, who shared the same African philosophy as the Zulu, Tswana, Sotho, and Khoi-san regarding the land. The Europeans would be met by a stubborn culture born of thousands of years of experience, and even when Europe was no longer dominant politically the Europeans would remember the strength of the African will.

It is thought that Vasco de Gama visited South Africa in the late 1400s but Africans have inhabited the country since the beginning of human time. Waves of immigrants from Europe and Asia have met in the gardens, mountains, fields, towns, and villages established by African ancestors thousands of years ago. In 2006, 45 million people called South Africa home, but only the Africans see it as their original home. To the Zulu, an Nguni-speaking group, the Indian Ocean side of South Africa is home, despite the fact that the origins of the first Zulu may have been as a descendant of one of the other African ethnic groups.

I have made the preceding digression to suggest that Shaka's wars were not disconnected from the events occurring in other parts of South Africa. Already by the time of Shaka the British had pushed into Natal, seeking profits and land. Indeed, he had acquiesced in the establishment of British trading and missionary posts while trying to protect the Zulu from the fate of the Xhosa and other southeastern and southern ethnic groups that had been pacified by the wars with the whites. Zulu would not be pacified. It would not submit to the rule of the whites or become victim to the ever-widening assault on African lands.

Eventually the South African ethnic groups were caught up into one giant wheel of turbulence and chaos because of the aggressively racist policies of the European invaders. They upset the general protocols for group cooperation and community with an assertive idea of individual and private ownership of land. There is no doubt that the Africans, despite the racial and cultural differences, could have managed to live side by side with whites. What was not tolerable was the idea that whites could simply assume control over lands that other people had through common agreement seen as the land of their ancestors. Bringing in traditions of paper ownership, legal deeds, and European laws which negated the rules and principles of hundreds of years of African community, the whites soon "owned" the land of the Khoi-san and the San and were encroaching upon the lands of the Xhosa when they had to fight several wars. The English were the first whites to engage the local people in warfare. They would fight for the land. Brave Xhosa leaders met them on the battlefield many times but eventually had to allow the whites to control the land of their ancestors. The weapons of the white settlers were deadlier, although their soldiers were not braver than the Xhosa.

By the early decades of the nineteenth century the entire region of southern Africa was under reigns of terror, horror, and chaos. The white push into the interior had squeezed various ethnic groups against each other so no one could stay on his or her ancestors' land. These wars fought between 1816 and 1840 were called by the Nguni name of *Mfecane*. The Sotho called this time the *Difaqane*. Both words carry the meaning of chaos in graphic terms. The first word means "the crushing," and the second one means "the scattering." The people were crushed and then scattered. Many ethnic groups lost their homesteads, their villages, their sense of purpose, and their will to live. Only the strong survived.

The main players in the Mfecane were the Mtetwa, Ndwandwe, and Ngwane kingdoms although the military operations involved many more ethnic communities. Never before had these nations gone to war over limited resources in such a brutal fashion as at this period of instability. A domino-like effect caused by the aggressive actions of the white settlers in the south trapped thousands of people in a whirlwind of terror. In addition to the competition for resources and the Madlatule famine at the end of the eighteenth century, the region saw increasing militarization of youth and female groups used to expand the grazing lands for cattle. They would take the animals into new territories for grazing, often creating problems with neighboring people. Small kingdoms would seek the protection of larger kingdoms if they felt that their grazing lands were coveted by others.

The situation was extremely volatile between 1816 and 1819. The great military king Dingiswayo led his people, the Mtetwa, against the Ndwandwe. Then in the great battle, the last between them, the Ndwandwe seemed to have won the victory when Dingiswayo was killed and his forces scattered across the land. As history has always shown, it is in the moments between strength and weakness or weakness and strength that a catalyst appears to move the pendulum in one direction or the other. This is why the African proverb says, "one must observe not where one slips, but where one falls."

Shaka, a young lieutenant in Dingiswayo's army, rose to challenge the domination of the Ndwandwe. As the leader of the Zulu, a minor kingdom, in fact merely a collection of a few hundred people, Shaka at the head of the Mtetwa forces drove the Ndwandwe army north of the Pongola River. The war was long and devastating. It costs hundreds of lives but in the end the Zulu vanguard of the Mtetwa was successful. Remnant forces of the Ndwandwe caused havoc throughout the east central region of the continent for many years. They constituted a maurauding army of broken and defeated soldiers looking for a place to call their own.

It would not take long for the brave young general Shaka to establish himself and his kingdom as the greatest military force between the Pongola and Tugela rivers. Expanding his kingdom by incorporating smaller kingdoms into Zulu he vigorously pursued an imperial policy. The Zulu nation was comprised of a strong Zulu core but included numerous other ethnic groups. The Zulu territory was then extended north to the Drakensberg Mountains and his armies conquered areas in the south as far as the Umzimkulu River.

Shaka was a military genius who loved his people so much that he was willing to devote his life to the expansion of Zulu culture. He was also a visionary, seeking to improve the administration of Zulu. He sought to beautify the capital city, Ulundi, by creating new cattle-folds, and replacing the old latrines and building better ones farther from the palace. He also had new walls built around the city.

One factor in the power of the Zulu was the military creativity and authority imposed by Shaka. He ruled with a steady hand like that of the master djembe drummer playing the percussions in rhythm. This creativity was demonstrated in two principal ways: the invention of the short-stabbing spear called the assegai and intensive military discipline based on systems of drilling soldiers. These were innovations that led to the belief that the Zulu were invincible. With the assegai replacing the long throwing spear, where the soldiers would have to throw the weapon and then wait to see if anyone on the other side was struck before they rearmed, the Zulu soldiers could move faster and more efficiently. They combined discipline, new military weapons, and a ruthless will to victory to give them success. Shaka organized his army into regiments according to age groups and gender. Each regiment was trained with the idea of conquest.

Once a region or kingdom had been conquered, Shaka replaced the king with an *induna* (general) who was directly responsible to the King of Kings. Those who quickly accepted Shaka's rule could be made *indunas* who served the king. Those who refused to submit to the authority were killed, their families literally wiped out. In fact, entire villages were destroyed and disappeared from the earth at the hands of Shaka's troops. They gave no mercy and they asked none. Incorporating all of the young men and women of the conquered people into his own army made Shaka mighty indeed. By 1824 Shaka had insisted that all soldiers remain in the service of the state until they were in their thirties. Furthermore, they were forbidden to marry and to wear shoes. The idea behind not wearing shoes was that their feet should be tough so that they could run swiftly and feel little pain as they closed in on their enemies. Shaka was seen as the perfect model of his own teachings. He was the absolute ruler under heaven.

From time to time other leaders rose to make their mark on the history of the region. One of the most important during the early nineteenth century was a young man who had grown up during the bitter period of internecine warfare. He was both a victim and a participant. Mzilikazi, the young king of the Khumalo, became one of Shaka's closest friends and *indunas*. He had been born about 1805, the son of a chief under the paramount king of the Ndwandwe, Zwide, one of the most feared of all kings in southern Africa. When his father was killed, Mzilikazi took over the leadership of his people and moved them to Shaka's capital city, switching allegiance from Zwide to Shaka. He was allowed to form his own regiment and retain hereditary and military authority over that regiment. Shaka never allowed other kings this power once they had been incorporated into the Zulu nation. However, this exception was to prove a serious mistake for Shaka when Mzilikazi defied the king after a raid on another kingdom and refused to bring the goods his regiment had taken to Shaka. Mzilikazi saw himself as a courageous fighter and an able leader as well as the hereditary king of the Ndebele. He did not back down from Shaka but had to flee with all of his people away from the territory of the Zulu. By 1825 the young Mzilikazi was a great military king. His state was an itinerant one, on the move across the great plains and hills of South Africa, in search of a homeland. Mzilikazi gathered to himself all of the remnant people who had been made destitute by drought and war and molded them into the Ndebele nation, with the Khumalo clan as the core. This organization of scattered and broken people allowed them to protect themselves from raids by larger groups. All the people who were incorporated into this new state had to learn the Zulu language. They had to eat Zulu food, to dress like the Zulu, and to fight like the Zulu. The Tswana people called them "Matabele," but in the Zulu or Nguni language this word is "Ndebele." Mzilikazi took this integrated and indoctrinated nation north into the territory that is now called Zimbabwe. The state created by Mzilikazi was one of the first in southern Africa to be based on skills, talents, and abilities. Many of the leaders of the Ndebele were from ethnic groups other than Zulu. Thus, as some have said, the wars of the south were caused not by ethnic hatreds but by limited resources and the economic hardships that had been caused by the rampant expansion of the whites from the Cape.

Like Mzilikazi and Shaka, another king by the name of Lepoqo, called more popularly Moshoeshoe, was the son of a minor king who became famous by sheer courage, persistence, intelligence, and charisma. His Mokoteli clan had been driven out of the Caledon valley by constant attacks by the Tlokwa, Hlubi, and Ngwane. Moshoeshoe formed the Lesotho nation, which has survived as an independent country until the present time. Lesser kings saw their people expelled from their homelands and scattered over the earth. In the case of the Ngwane under Sobhuza, they had been forced across the Pongola valley and could not count on their allies to support them in their weakened state. But Moshoeshoe claimed his kingship while his father was still alive and in 1821–23 consolidated a move of the capital from the flat-topped mountain of Butha Buthe, which had been his father's stronghold, to a new site called Thaba Bosiu. He had learned a lesson very early that if his army retreated to the top of the mountain they would have an advantage on any enemy pursuing them. Thus, when he found Thaba Bosiu, which was more fortified than Butha Buthe, he was excited. It was about 80 miles away from his father's stronghold but was surrounded by steep cliffs and had few narrow paths up to the top. The fortress was impregnable to most armies unless they used modern artillery. Also like Mzilikazi he brought many different people into his nation although he was baSotho. Some of the leaders were Nguni-speaking people. Anyone who wanted to be shielded from the warfare down below could apply to become a member of the Lesotho nation. He made it a requirement for the newcomers to learn Sotho, just as Mzilikazi had required people to speak Nguni. A skilled diplomat, Moshoeshoe was able to get weapons and blankets from the British without giving up his kingdom. He invited them to come to his kingdom to teach religion but his motives seem to have been political. As long as the British saw them as peaceful people who had friendly relationships with whites they would not attack them.

Earlier, left without one of his strongest supporters and defenders, Shaka grew increasingly bitter. Those Shaka assisted, supported with his generosity, befriended when they needed to flee from their enemies, and gave access to his most important military secrets had turned their backs on him. He was saddened by the loss of Mzilikazi because more than all other *indunas* they had grown to manhood together, fought in scores of battles, their shields protecting each other, competing with each other for the bravest acts, and talking about the expansion of the Zulu nation. How could anyone be so close to him and not undersand his desire for the common good? Why would Mzilikazi defeat the enemy of the Zulu and not bring back the spoils of victory to his king? Was it jealousy? Was it the fact that Mzilikazi desired to command his own clan as Shaka had commanded the Zulu and brought them to nationhood? Did Mzilikazi think that the Khumalo clan could be so magnificent as to challenge even the mighty elephant himself? After the unsuccessful expeditionary forces sent after Mzilikazi and his clan had returned to Shaka's capital he grew even more morose. It was as if a curtain had been drawn across the stage of Shaka's life.

At his weakest moments now, with the bulk of his formidable army in battle with another enemy and away from the capital, the mighty bull was exposed to physical dangers he had not expected. So concerned was Shaka with the state of the nation, the protection of the women and children, and the training of the teenage soldiers, that he did not see the conspiracy of his own brothers against him. Shaka's assassination brought his half-brother Dingane to power as the absolute king of Zulu in 1828.

Dingane took a forceful position against the white intrusion into Zulu lands. He met the leaders of the Boer (Dutch) farmers who had begun to move into the interior to escape British domination and warned them of violating Zulu territory. When one of the Voortrekkers (Boer intruders) refused to adhere to the decrees of Dingane he was killed in an effort to stop the penetration of the whites into African lands. Soon the Boers, who had fought the British at the Cape and other African ethnic groups on their trek into the interior, declared war on the Zulu. On September 16, 1838, the army of Dingane met the Boer army of Andries Pretorius at Blood River. In one of the worst defeats for the Zulu nation the army of Dingane was defeated, losing more than 3000 soldiers. Some of the most experienced leaders of the Zulu army, men who had served under Shaka, were lost in the battle of Blood River.

The Zulu moved across the Tugela River and this river became accepted as the southern boundary of the Zulu. In 1840, a younger brother of Dingane named Mpande led a royal coup with the assistance of Boers and made himself king. For thirty-two years the Zulu neither threatened the Boers nor participated in any effort to keep them from expanding. It was a quiet time bought by puppetry, manipulation, and the selling out of the birthrights and traditions of the African ancestors. As kings adopted the religion of the invaders they no longer praised their ancestors or accepted the protocols of the past as desirous. Many of the new *indunas* would select non-Zulu names, adopt non-Zulu practices, and refuse to be identified with their ancestors.

By 1842 because of the weakness of the Zulu nation under Mpande the Natal region had become a British colony. Revival was almost necessary. It would fall to Mpande's son, Ceteswayo, a strong nationalist, to try to recoup the pride of the Zulu. So much had been lost under his father and he had grown up with the realization that the Zulu elite were annoyed that Mpande had allowed the whites to encroach on additional Zulu lands. Whites who had been able to appease the father found the son unappeasable. They feared him and when the whites could not find royal subjects who would turn against the king they prepared for battle.

Meanwhile, Ceteswayo was extending his authority over those Zulu who had refused to submit to the authority of Mpande because they considered him a puppet of white settlers. Ceteswayo found it difficult to bring some of the groups under his control but eventually was able to reshape the Zulu nation into a mighty force by offering their leaders a role in his administration. His hero was his uncle Shaka. He admired the discipline and straightforwardness of purpose that Shaka had exhibited. These were qualities that had brought Zulu respect and dignity and had caused the nation's enemies to be cautious and fearful. It was probably during the reign of Ceteswayo that the Zulu, hoping to revive their fortunes, adopted the famous Zulu Declaration (Asante and Abarry 1996, pp. 371–8).

**The Zulu Declaration (excerpt)**
I am
I am alive;
I am conscious and aware;
I am unique;
I am who I say I am; I am the value Uqobo (essence)
I forever evolve inwardly and outwardly in response to the challenge of my nature;
I am the face of humanity;
· The face of humanity is my face.

I contemplate myself and see everything in me.
I perceive; that which I perceive is form.
Form is an unchanging value.
Value is eternal consciousness;
Consciousness is that in which all things have their origin:
It does not change; it exists from eternity to eternity;
It is an infinite cluster of clusters of itself;
It is forever evolving in response to the challenge of its nature...
My neighbor has a mind;
It, also, comprehends all things.
My neighbor and I have the same origins;
We have the same life-experience and a common destiny;
We are the obverse and reverse sides of one entity;
We are unchanging equals;
We are the faces which see themselves in each other;
We are mutually fulfilling complements;
We are simultaneously legitimate values;
My neighbor's sorrow is my sorrow
His joy is my joy.
He and I are mutually fulfilled when we stand by each other in moments
    of need.
His survival is a precondition of my survival.
That which is freely asked or freely given is love;
Imposed love is a crime against humanity.
I am sovereign of my life;
My neighbor is sovereign of his life;
Society is a collective sovereignty;
It exists to ensure that my neighbor and I realize the promise of being human.
I have no right to anything I deny my neighbor.

(Asante and Abarry 1996, pp. 371–3)

By the late 1870s Ceteswayo had made the Zulu a formidable nation once again and the British were frightened that he might lead a war for Africans to regain the entire land from Natal to the Cape. Fear was palpable. Traders and merchants warned the British officials of impending doom. Missionaries told the colonial officers that they were unable to do "the work of the Lord" among the Zulu since the ascendancy of Ceteswayo. The king remained in his compound surrounded by his *indunas*, planning ways to strengthen the age-group regiments. There was no hint of aggression against the whites, only defensive strategies to keep them from further advances into Zulu homelands. Ceteswayo had seen it before; wherever the whites went they built fences and walls and kept the indigenous people from the land where their ancestors were buried.

The stage was set for one of the most dramatic battles in Zulu history. In some ways it was a stage set not by the Zulu but by the British. One of the senior members of Ceteswayo's administration had a dispute with his wife. She subsequently fled the region under the control of the Zulu and went to the British-controlled part of Natal. The Zulu *induna* went from village to village until he discovered her in one of the villages under the control of the colonial officials. He killed her in the ensuing struggle and fled to his own village under Ceteswayo. What started as a domestic dispute and ended as a murder, and should have been dealt with by Zulu law and rules, became a pretext for the British to launch a full-scale war against the Zulu nation.

Unquestionably, the battle of Isandlwana was provoked by a clear act of aggression on the part of British officials. Sir Henry Bartle Frere, the British high commissioner in South Africa, believed that he could prevent a robust, dynamic, and independent Zulu nation if he acted quickly to curtail the power of Ceteswayo. This was his chance. He used the domestic dispute and murder as a quarrel between himself and the great king Ceteswayo kaMpande. In other words, he picked a fight in the belief that the British soldiers armed with superior arms, guns and cannons, could easily defeat the Zulu army still heavily reliant on the Shakan methods of half a century earlier. In a show of arrogance, in December 1878 the British presented an ultimatum to Ceteswayo to return his *induna* for trial in the British courts. Of course, this ultimatum was rejected by the man who considered himself the King of Heaven.

Under the generalship of Frederic Thesiger, Viscount Chelmsford, the British invaded Zululand in three columns on January 10–11, 1879. Fourteen thousand troops, which included about 7000 Africans the British had collected as porters, servants, and fighters from previous wars in Africa, entered Zululand.

There were a number of skirmishes. Caught by surprise the Zulu battled Colonel Pearson's column at the Nyeazane River. The Zulu were badly beaten. The Zulu engaged the British column led by Colonel Wood in an inconclusive battle near Hlobane Mountain. The powerful central column of the British forces was under the personal command of Lord Chelmsford.

Ceteswayo's army met the British and their African allies in the foothills of Isandlwana Mountain. The battle tested men as few battles had ever done. The Zulu soldiers struck with lightning speed, taking the battle directly to the enemy. Using the assegai, the weapon that had been invented by Shaka, they cut their foes to pieces and left an awful example of mass agony lying in the hot summer sun of southern Africa. Men without legs and arms cried until they died. When Ceteswayo's soldiers surveyed the battlefield, they killed all of those who were in agony as an act of kindness. The Zulu believed that it was important that you should not allow your enemy the shame of a suffering death. This action was misinterpreted by the early British historians, who claimed that it was an "act of barbarism." Once again cultural difference between the two peoples had been interpreted by the British to their own advantage when in fact the most horrendous action was to lead men to their death because of an officially contrived pretext for war. By now it had become accepted British practice to create a pretext for war as a land-grabbing tactic.

Let us digress to look at another example of Africans defending themselves against false pretexts for war when, in fact, the objective of some whites was to steal land and resources. The case in point is when the British sappers manufactured a reason to take the land of the Tiv in Nigeria. On January 8, 1900, a week after the British had declared an entity they called the Protectorate of Northern Nigeria, a group of English sappers, along with their African porters, had been chased off Tiv land as they tried to lay a telegraph line across the Tiv farms. The Tiv vehemently opposed the trampling of their yams and other vegetables, neatly arranged, as was the Tiv custom, around their family compounds. According to Akiga Sai the British commanding officer decided that the Tiv should be "broken" for challenging white men (Sai 1990, p. 274). Furthermore, it did not look good for the British colonial self-image and for "the white man's prestige" to have challenges from people they considered to be "savages." Yet when the British sent a group to fight the Tiv they were repulsed by the Tiv, further endangering British status. In that case, as in the South African situation, the British failed to adequately assess the conditions for war. The Tiv were the first people to do battle with the colonial administration in Nigeria. Sir Frederick Lugard, the high commissioner, described the campaign as a success and depicted the Tiv as worthy adversaries who had been chastised by the Maxim gun and transformed into people who deserved to be a part of the British Empire. In fact, the Tiv were called "of a fine physique, industrious agriculturalists, and brave warriors, yet lawless, treacherous, intractable pople, unresponsive to anything, except extremely severe chastisement" (Lugard, *Annual Report of Northern Nigeria, 1900–1901*, Cd. 788–16). The Tiv resisted domination and the first Tiv–British battle led to six years of instability, strife, and skirmishes. Finally the telegraph line had to be diverted around the land of the Tiv. With much frustration the British claimed that the Tiv were a truculent people and that their territory was not safe for whites.

At the battle of Isandlwana only fifty-five British and three hundred Africans fighting alongside the British survived. It is estimated that the central column that was wiped out by the Zulu had started with a total of 2800 men. The Zulu took no prisoners. The British had never suffered such a defeat at the hands of an African people before. The defeat of the British created the false impression and misleading pejorative that the "Zulu were a warlike people." The British would use this appellation numerous times in Africa as whites used it in North America in reference to some indigenous people such as the Apache. Any people who defended themselves or their territories from whites were called "warlike" when the term could more accurately be applied to those who were trying to take the people's lands.

Five months after the defeat at Isandlwana the British organized another mission to meet the Zulu. In that campaign, the exiled Prince Imperial of France, Louis Napoleon, who was serving with the British colonial army, was killed in a skirmish with Ceteswayo's forces. The British sent in reinforcements and pressed toward the Zulu capital of Ulundi. They reached the capital city at the end of June and then prepared for a final assault against Ceteswayo. On July 4, 1879, Chelmsford forces took Ulundi and burned the city to the ground as was the British practice. The Zulu would not go away, however, and it was months before the British had sufficient confidence that they could govern Zululand. Lord Wolseley's troops captured King Ceteswayo and sent him into exile in Cape Town. His country was divided among thirteen pro-British chiefs, a deliberately divisive action on the part of the British. Indeed, the division of Zululand led to a decade of internecine warfare between the people. In 1906 there was a Zulu uprising against the rule of the British in Natal. Ultimately the British were able to gain control of the region through pitting one leader against another and doling out rewards and gifts to those who supported the British crown against their own people's interests. Those who accepted the gifts and served the interests of the colonizers were often spoken of with derision among the Zulu loyalists.

## The Xhosa Wars against invasion

A history of the Zulu, with lessons from the attendant stories of the Sotho and Ndebele, is not complete without a discussion of the Xhosa role in fighting for freedom in South Africa. The Xhosa fought many wars with the whites in a vain effort to secure their lands. In the cycle of pain that gripped the African community after every wave of white settlers, the Xhosa were intent on renewing their efforts to break the cycle. Yet each time, the whites with their firearms were able to mow down the Xhosa soldiers. This did not stop the wars and there were several battles during the white expansion.

The fierce battles called the Xhosa/British or Frontier Wars were really raids and counter-raids between two enemies. Nothing indicated a winner or a loser in this series of wars. Of course this was not to remain the case. The British introduced the idea of total war, which was alien to the Xhosa people. Even before Shaka Zulu, the British had resorted to this use of power and mass destruction. By the Fourth War with the British of 1811–12 the Xhosa knew how to protect themselves from the British, who sought to kill all the people on the Fish River. The aim of the British was to eliminate all threats to their authority by the Xhosa. Again the British found the Xhosa strong enough to prevent them from destroying Xhosa resistance and so they waited for another opportunity to attack the African forces. This would come a few years later when the British saw their opening. In the Fifth War of 1818–19, the British intervened in a war of two warring groups of Xhosa. They chose to divide the Africans and conquer, a strategy that had worked for them in other conflicts. From this point on the battles between the Xhosa and the British take on a regular pattern. The British would try to expand and the Xhosa would react. When a British military escort was killed by Africans in 1846 the British sought retaliation. The story is that a man had been accused of stealing an axe. The man fled to the Xhosa king and the king refused to turn the man over to the whites. The whites then started what was called the War of the Axe.

Unable to successfully subdue the Xhosa, the British tried a new tactic. They feared that the Xhosa would seek to retake the land the British had occupied at the Cape and so they created a barrier of empty land between the Fish and Keiskama rivers and built several fortresses to protect the Cape. They also resettled Khoi-san and Coloured people (descendants of Africans and Europeans) along the Kat River valley. This was to be a pattern repeated by the whites even into the twentieth century. The peasants who were dumped on this new land could not make it economically viable and so the colony failed. Meanwhile the Xhosa prepared for a Sixth War with the British. This war took place in 1834–35. When it was over the Xhosa had lost even more of their land, and white farmers, mainly Boers, joined the British in trekking north and east to occupy the land left by the Xhosa moving further east and northward.

It should be noted that African resistance to the white invasion was constant and vigorous. No African nations, and certainly not the Xhosa, allowed the white invaders to occupy the lands of their ancestors without a fight. Yet between 1830 and 1840 the Boers fought their way into the heart of Xhosa land. Resentment built up in the hearts of the Xhosa nation for generations. They believed that they had been robbed of their rightful homeland. Of course, the movement of the Xhosa toward the north meant that many other ethnic groups had their lands trampled upon, and the scarcity of grazing land for cattle and farming lands for the people created tensions that would lead to monumental conflict and chaos.

## The Baganda kingdom

The wars of the Nile Valley in the thirteenth and fourteenth centuries brought many refugees into what is now modern Uganda. Among these groups were the ancestors of the Baganda (singular Muganda). They comprise the largest ethnic group in present-day Uganda although they represent barely 20 percent of the population. Uganda is an immensely diverse nation. However, we owe the name Uganda, the Swahili term for Buganda, to the fact that the British authorities in 1894 gave the entire region the name Uganda Protectorate.

As we have seen in other places, the British believed that it was necessary to break the backs of the greatest powers. They had to defeat the Baganda in order to establish authority over the land. Yet they never defeated the Baganda; the British simply tried to write into law and their history a reality that would be accepted by others. The land bounded by Lake Nyanza (called by the colonial administration *Victoria*) on the south, the River Nile on the east, and Lake Kyoga on the north is the land of the Baganda. The Baganda were ruled by a powerful *kabaka* (king). They were the greatest threat to British rule in the nineteenth century and had been the strongest group in the region for centuries, though the country was home to an immense diversity of groups.

There are indications that hunter-gatherers had been in the region of the Great Lakes (the Great Lakes are Nyanza, Rutanzige (Edward), Kivu, Tanganyika, Albert, and Kyoga), including modern-day Uganda, for thousands of years. About 5000 years ago the lush pastures and fertile grazing areas in the lake region attracted numerous ethnic groups of herders and farmers. They came mainly from the north and east, probably from present-day Sudan and Ethiopia. There is some indication that the Baganda may have derived from the Luo people of Sudan. Others believe that they are remnants of people who migrated into the lake region from Ethiopia. Africans from both northern sources probably migrated into what is today's Uganda. Actually the diversity of both regions, Sudan and Ethiopia, is so great that it is difficult to say which of the ethnic groups of the regions contributed most human material to the Baganda. It is likely that the speakers of Omotic, Sudanic, and Cushitic languages all met in the fertile areas of the lake region.

Whatever the case to be made about the original people, we know that the first king of the Baganda was called Kintu and he was crowned in 1380. He was a powerful king and his history is now clouded in legendary tales of his greatness. Kintu became the first Kabaka, that is, king of Buganda.

Obviously in the area of Uganda as in all parts of Africa there was an enormous capacity for people to intermingle and intermarry. Skills such as cattle-raising and pastoral lifestyles were quickly acquired by all of the people in the region. Sharing knowledge of farming with herders was the role of the sedentary agriculturists who planted crops for their families. By the time of Kintu in the fourteenth century the people had already discovered iron-smelting. They would no longer be considered Stone Age people as the stone tools gave way to stronger, more durable equipment and tools.

As far as the archaeological record has revealed, the region remained fairly settled during the first 500 years after Kintu. The migration patterns remained as they had been in previous eras, that is, the northerners coming into the area of Buganda for settlement, farming, and grazing of cattle.

By all estimates, the Great Lakes region was the melting pot, the generator of cultures, concepts, knowledge, and people, during the late twelfth and early thirteenth centuries. It is tempting to speak of this generator in racial terms as European writers have done, but to do so would be to miss the overall historical movement that was taking place in the continent and particularly here in this region. For example, we know that the intermingling of the pastoral people with agrarian people helped to create a mighty kingdom, Bunyoro, meaning "land of the Nyoro," in the Kitara region southeast of Lake Albert. The ruling language of these people was Bantu although this may not have been their original language. Their ruling dynasties came from the Chwezi (Bacwezi) clan, descendants of some of the earliest immigrants into the area. They influenced the Baganda, who lived on the northwestern shores of Lake Nyanza, as well as the Acholi, who lived east of Lake Rutanzige.

By the fifteenth century the Chwezi ruling clan in Bunyoro and Buganda had been defeated, thrown out of power, or exhausted from juggling the demands of herders and farmers and facing the challenges of new invaders from the north and south. What we know is that another ruling family appeared in the 1400s. This was the Bito dynasty. It had fought its way to power, integrating its institutions with those of the Baganda and Bunyoro. Soon the intermarriage between the Bito ruling dynasty and the masses of

Baganda people had created a very powerful kingdom. It is this kingdom that is called Buganda and is ruled over by the Kabaka.

Most scholars believe that the Baganda occupied Buganda from the west and the east. The Busoga people from the east and the Bunyoro people from the west merged with the Bantu-speaking Baganda. Both groups are influenced by the Baganda belief in superhuman spirits such as *mizumu*, *misambwa*, and *balubaale*. The *mizumu* are ghosts of dead people because only the body rots; the soul continues to live. The *misambwa* are natural objects, stones, trees, and so forth, that have been possessed by *mizumu*. The *balubaale* are those whose exceptional characteristics in life have been carried over in their death.

The Baganda believe that the supreme being, Katonda, is also the creator of the universe and that he has neither parents nor children. Yet Katonda was believed to be one of the seventy-three *balubaale* in Buganda. In the old days there were three temples to Katonda; all had permanent officials from the Njovu clan taking care of the rituals and ceremonies. While other *balubaale* had specific functions such as being god of lightning, god of the sky, god of Lake Wamala, Mukasa, god of Lake Nyanza, Musoke, the god of the rainbow, Kitaka, god of the earth, and Musisi, god of earthquakes, the Supreme Being, Katonda, was simply the Creator. Baganda religion made the people very consistent and strong. Their faith, so to speak, was mightier than that of their enemies. There were many temples throughout Buganda. Each temple was served by a priest and a medium. Priests occupied a central role in the society and usually were called upon by the kings as well as the masses for special consultations. The kings had special shrines of worship. The royal sister was known as Nnaalinya; she always assumed responsibility for the king's temple. There is a tradition in Buganda that the Kabaka Nakibinge created the *balubaale* idea to gain control over the people's minds.

One of the most notorious Kabakas of the nineteenth century was Mutesa I. He allowed Arab slave traders to enter his kingdom and use the capital city of Kampala for slave trading. Of course, the Kabaka shared in the wealth generated by this illegal, unethical, and vile trade in human beings. The Bunyoro kingdom had its own temporary revitalization when it fought off the Ottoman Turks in Egypt to annex northern Uganda. Omakuma (king) Kabalega was the king who successfully conducted the campaign of war against the Arab slave traders.

During the mid-nineteenth century European travelers were visiting the Buganda kingdom. Richard Burton and John Speke were the first to visit the Great Lakes region in 1858. Speke, looking for the source of the River Nile, returned to the region four years later and identified for Europeans the source of the river flowing from Lake Nyanza at Jinja. On the pretext that they wanted to stop the Arab slave trade the British government decided to replace its consul to the Zanzibar sultanate, who had been in charge of British interests. Missionaries and traders, spurred on by the activities of Henry Stanley and David Livingstone in the 1860s and 1870s, went into all parts of East Africa looking for souls to save. They found resistance and defiance. Yet the convergence of European ambitions in East Africa meant that the kingdom of Buganda was under great stress. When the British government, hoping to preempt Germany, France, and Belgian king, Leopold, declared a protectorate over Zanzibar in 1890 it would not be long before the old kingdom of Buganda would also fall under the British Union Flag. Thus, by 1894 negotiations with Kabaka Mutesa placed the kingdom of Buganda under a British protectorate. About a year later Britain included all of Uganda under the administration of the East African Protectorate, which also included Kenya. Before the end of the century Britain had annexed Sudan on behalf of Egypt, thereby gaining complete control over the Nile basin.

The Kabaka retained his authority through a system of indirect rule which allowed the Baganda to be trained as civil servants for the rest of Uganda. People from the north, Acholi and Lango, were recruited by the British to serve in the armed forces, while the Baganda were the clerks, bureaucrats, and administrators who served the British interests. This pattern would be the basis for inter-ethnic conflict for many years to come. In fact, the British introduced Indians into the population initially as servants and low-level workers to work on building the railroad from Kenya to Uganda and then as middlemen merchants. The Africans flatly rejected proposals that would have them serve the British as laborers in their own country. They were punished by the colonial officials, who gave Indians the right to open stores but refused to allow Africans to have the same access to the large African markets. This action on the part of the British colonial government was to lead to more turbulent upheavals in Ugandan society.

## Congo: a basin and a cauldron

The peopling of the Congo basin came from the north and the south. It is a result of a long process of migration and integration of populations from the northwest, the north, and the southeast. Some of the earliest evidence of *H. sapiens* using tools for calculations comes from the Ishongee of the Congo. It is a calculator made from bone. Other evidence such as fishing hooks, hand axes, and stone scrapers have been found that date as far back as 28,000 years before the present. Humans have occupied the Congo basin for a very long time.

Numerous groups of small humans such as Twa and Ituri have lived in the forest areas of the Congo basin, which includes large parts of Central Africa, longer than other people who migrated from the regions of Nigeria, Sudan, and Zimbabwe (Willis 1964). The Twa and Ituri may be called the mothers and fathers of the Congo region. Crop growers entered the region in large numbers about 500 BCE. They pushed their way into the fertile lands of the Great Lakes region, penetrated the rainforests along the Atlantic coast, and occupied large tracts of savanna lands to the south of the Congo basin.

The Congo basin was a powerful engine for the rest of Africa, receiving and sending out people from various regions. Indeed settlement by the Adamawan-Ubangian linguistic family and Sudanic languages expanded into the area. Other groups such as the Banda, Ngbandi, Ngbaka, and Zande, living south of the Ubangi River, are the modern-day descendants of the ancient Ubangians, while the Alur, Mamvu, and Mangbetu seem to be descendants of migrants who came from Sudan.

Attracted to the bounty of the land and waters of the Congo basin, people kept migrating in during the course of the first 1500 years CE. Many of the people of the eastern region of present-day Congo are related to the people of Rwanda, Burundi, and Uganda, while the Mongo cluster of people eventually settled in the rainforest core of the inner basin. Around the site of modern Kinshasa the Tio and Kuba people formed their communities and traded along the mighty Congo River. During the fourteenth and fifteenth centuries, when Great Zimbabwe was at its height and other kingdoms were rising in the southern savanna, the Congo had its own historical kingdom of note.

The most famous of all kingdoms in the Congo basin was that of the Kongo (Bakongo) people. It entered the history of Africa at a crucial time and worked extremely hard to make the best life for its people at a time of high intrigue and political trickery. The kings of Kongo were often very wise and had the greatest appreciation for knowledge, science, and art. They were supporters of diplomacy and trade.

Meeting the Portuguese, the ubiquitous Europeans of the fifteenth century, the Bakongo established close relationships with their leaders. This was to prove to be an ill-advised move on the part of the Africans. Thus, when the Portuguese reached the territory around 1480 they found a willing nation of Kongo people (the kingdom included large portions of what is now Congo-Brazzaville and Angola) ready to be partners and allies. Rivals to Kongo included the Lunda kingdom and the Luba kingdom, stretching from Lake Ubempa to Mbuji-Mayi. Around the sixteenth century a brilliant dynasty came to power and united the Lunda and Luba kingdoms under its leadership; it was called the Mwato Yamvo. The kings expanded the kingdom into an empire which did not crumble until nearly a century later as it confronted the French and Belgians. The eastern branch of the empire was centered along the Luapula River in the vicinity of the active Kazembe kingdom with its Bemba royalty as its core. In this magnificently diverse region the Lunda–Luba Empire found itself challenged, until during the eighteenth and nineteenth centuries it had to give way to the supremacy of the Kazemba kingdom.

One of the worst chapters in the history of Africa was written in this central region of the continent. Two principal actions created for the Congo people a chamber of horrors. One was the trade with the Portuguese on the western side of the basin and the other was the trade with the Arabs and Swahili traders on the eastern side of the basin. This was to set the region up for a massive exploitation under the rule of King Leopold of Belgium, since he would consider Congo his personal property.

# Part V
# The time of the chaos
"Things fall apart." (Chinua Achebe)

# 11 Arab and European missionaries, merchants, and mercenaries

African history is comprised of one general African tradition and two principal invasions. Overlays of European Christian traditions and Arab Islamic traditions have given Africa a complex cultural array of ideas. Each in its own way has impacted the life of the continent. One came early and stayed late; the other came late and stayed late. Nevertheless the Christian and Islamic influences changed the structure of African behavior and created new institutions that often competed with or replaced the ancient traditions. Only one country, Benin, remained predominantly dedicated to an African way of thinking. Other nations, some too quickly, gave way to the two invasions, becoming little more than appendages to the cultural and religious traditions of other people.

When Europe entered the long sleep of the White Ages, which lasted from about 500 to 1000 CE, the Arab subcontinent was slowly awakening until the appearance of Muhammad, the Prophet of Mecca. And while Europe slept, covered by great sheets of ignorance, essentially off the stage of humanity since the massive fall of the Roman Empire, which had at one time been thought impregnable, Islam rose to international stature on the wings of the Qur'an and the swords of passionate warriors. The flight from Mecca to Medina and the return to Mecca in triumph in the seventh century gave Islam the strength it needed to promote itself as an international ideology. General El As, at the invitation of the African leaders in Egypt, came to Africa to help drive out the Romans in 639 CE. This assistance was valuable in one instance, but in another it meant that the Arabs would remain in Africa, not just as conquerors of the Romans but as occupiers of African cities and towns left by the Roman authorities without governance. The lesson Africa was to learn again was that invitations to strong armies to assist often mean that they will leave when they want to leave or, as in the case of the Arab armies of Islam, never leave. Soon Arabic was the language of the ruling elites and the religion of Islam had replaced both the African religion and the Christian religion, which had taken root on the coast at Rhacostas–Alexandria. The pattern established in Egypt would lead to a practice throughout Arab-occupied Africa: Africans who were not Muslims, and sometimes those who were Muslims, would be abused, tortured, enslaved, and have their lands extorted. Like the Europeans who would come centuries later, the Arab invaders found the African cultures too willing to acquiesce in the "magic of the book" rather than in the traditions of their own ancestors. It was a lesson that would have to be learned over and over again as the Arab vanguard, like the Europeans later, used religion as the hook that got the African bait.

## Islam in Egypt

John Jackson, one of the giants of African writing, has said that the civilizing of Europe was the mission of African Moors (Jackson 2001, p. 157). Indeed, the advent of the civilizing mission had been established long before the first corps of soldiers crossed the Strait of Gibraltar into Europe. When Muhammad started his career as Prophet in the seventh century he set in motion many changes that would affect the world. His work as Prophet is thought to have commenced around 610 CE, about the same time as Heraclius was extending his rule over the Roman Empire. Alfred Butler wrote in *The Arab Invasion of Egypt* that both Heraclius and Muhammad experienced danger and discouragement for twelve years and then emerged victorious (1992, p. 138). In 622 Heraclius began his expedition to Cilicia to rescue the Holy Rood and to retake portions of the empire from the Persians. In the same year, Muhammad made his flight from Mecca to Medina to prepare for war to conquer Arabia and take the shrine of the Ka'aba. Both king and Prophet continued to meet their foes and to win victory after victory. Muhammad wanted Rome, a believing nation, to achieve victory over the Persians, whom he considered pagans. For Muhammad, at least the Romans had become Christians, believers.

Yet with the victory of Heraclius over the Persians, the Prophet saw an opportunity to strike for empire and dominion. He was able to see both Rome and Persia, the greatest powers of the day, exhausted in their battles, and find in their exhaustion a cause for joy. As Butler has written, "the moment of Heraclius' greatest glory may well have been also the moment of Mohammed's greatest encouragement" (1992, p. 139). By 627 Muhammad had caused letters to be written, sealed with the words "Muhammad, the Apostle of God," to some of the major leaders of the world to the effect that they should proclaim allegiance to Islam and see Muhammad as the viceregent of the Most High. The letters went to princes of Yemen, Oman, Yamamay, and Bahrain; also to al-Harith, prince of the Saracens in Syria; to George, governor of Alexandria and viceroy of Egypt; to the Negus (King of Kings) of Abyssinia; to Chosroes, king of Persia; and to Heraclius, emperor of Rome. Two of the princes of Arabia, Yamamay and Bahrain, sent acceptable answers. The princes of Yemen and Oman responded negatively.

The Negus of Abyssinia sent a polite reply saying neither yes nor no. Abyssinia remained the one power that did not bow to Islam. The governor of Egypt promised to consider the message and treated the envoy Hatib with respect, sending him back with two Coptic maidens, Mary and Shirin, a mule, a donkey, and a bag of money. Accordingly, Mary, the Egyptian, became a Muslim and a great favorite wife of Muhammad. She died in 636 and never saw the enslavement of Egypt by the Arabs.

The Persian king tore the Prophet's letter to shreds and wrote orders to the governor of the province of Hamyar to send him the head of the imposter. When Muhammad heard of Chosroes' anger, he asked, "So shall God tear his kingdom like he has torn my letter?" (see Butler 1992, p. 143).

Heraclius did not take seriously the suggestion of the Arab chieftain demanding that he submit to Islam. Instead, his war-hardened legions pressed on to Jerusalem. As they were celebrating in Jerusalem the return of the cross, a cadre of 3000 Arab horsemen was crossing the desert to avenge the murder of their messenger to Rome. They would start a war, although they were badly beaten initially, that would end with the Islamic conquest of Constantinople in 1453. In that year, 831 years after the flight to Medina, the name of the Arab prophet was emblazoned on the walls of the Cathedral of St. Sophia.

*En route* to Muta, the Saracen army under Said was brutally attacked by the Christian armies. Many horsemen lost their lives and only the leadership of Khalid, henceforth called "Sword of God," saved them from utter destruction. They limped back to Medina, where Muhammad was undismayed. He put General Amir ibn al-As in charge of a small force to patrol the borders with Syria. Two conquests consolidated Muhammad's control, that of Hunain and that of Mecca. Muhammad set about trying to create an army of 100,000 but soon discovered that without the hypocrites he could muster a force of only 30,000. Khalid with a force of only 400 captured the oasis of Dumah, its chief, the castle, 3000 camels, and 400 suits of mail, and forced the chief to abandon Christianity (Butler 1992, p. 145).

The stage was set for the battle with the Romans over the African nation of Egypt. Muhammad held a solemn consecration of the Ka'aba in the spring of 632. Two months later he called for war against the Roman Empire. He gave the command to Said's son, Ousman. Three days after the appointment of Ousman, the Prophet died, but he had put into action the union of Arabia and the desire of Islam to conquer the world. When Islam had captured Damascus in Syria and Jerusalem its attention was turned to Egypt by Ousman and his warrior followers.

By the time of Ousman many Egyptian Christians, Copts, had taken on Greek or Hebrew names. Such was the case with Benjamin, the son of a wealthy Coptic family, who became the "Shepherd of the flock of Christ" and patriarch of the Copts. Beginning in 621 Benjamin, from the province of Buhaira, became identified as an assistant to Andronicus, the patriarch of the Coptic church. When Adronicus died, Benjamin, who had been nominated by Andronicus, became patriarch. He was only 35 years old; nevertheless the pallium was placed on his shoulders at St. Marks Cathedral in Alexandria. Benjamin died in 662 CE, after thirty-nine years on the seat. Thus, Benjamin served during the period of great tension between Rome and Persia over Egypt and was in office during the conquest of Egypt by the Arab armies. While it is true that Rome was not under any threat from Persia or Arabia during the initial years of Benjamin's patriarchy, by the time he died Africa was severely changed in terms of politics and religion. Butler says that with the death of Andronicus and the rise of Benjamin to the leadership of the Egyptian church there must have been faint rumors "brought by Arab caravans concerning the rising prophet of Mecca; but not the wildest dreamer could have imagined that within a period of twenty years to come the Persians would be driven out of Egypt again by the Romans, and that the restored Roman power would be extinguished and closed for ever by the ... legions of Mohammed" (Butler 1992, p. 172).

When Heraclius had returned to Egypt to defeat the Persians a second time, he named Cyrus, bishop of Phasis in the Caucasus, to the Melkite archbishopric of Alexandria. This was a terrible mistake, because Cyrus proved to be as unpopular as Benjamin was popular. To bring an unpopular European bishop from the Caucasus to Africa and make him bishop in a multicultural city was not enough for the Roman emperor; Heraclius also had Cyrus lead a campaign to stamp out the Coptic version of the religion. By his actions Cyrus made it impossible for the adherents of the Coptic faith to love Roman rule. The loathing and hatred with which he saw the people made Cyrus a tyrant who drove the people into hatred of the Roman Empire. By the actions of the Roman emperor in appointing Cyrus, and the actions of Cyrus himself in persecuting the Copts, the country was ready to be delivered up for Arab conquest. He was referred to as an evil genius, given the name al-Mukaukas by the people and made a pathetic figure in Egyptian history.

There were two fatal flaws in the decisions taken by Cyrus. In the first place he did not consult the leader of the Copts, Benjamin, who would have counseled him on his prospects in Egypt. Second, he did not consult the masses of the people of Egypt who did not live in Alexandria, but in Upper Egypt at Waset (Thebes) and cities in Middle Egypt.

When Cyrus landed in Alexandria in 631 the Coptic patriarch, Benjamin, fled. Since Cyrus' advance men had not sought him out for advice; he could only believe that they were intent on removing him from power. Some Christians believed that he was warned by an angel to leave the city because Cyrus was coming to do him and other Coptic Christians harm (Butler 1992, p. 176). Before he left he wrote to the bishops of the church in Egypt to flee to the mountains and wait for ten years because much persecution was coming to the believers. Benjamin himself left Alexandria at night with only two companions and traveled to the oasis of El Mina between Alexandria and Barca. This town was probably named for the ancient founder of the Egyptian nation, Menes, who by now had been incorporated into the pantheon as one of the saints of the church. Benjamin did not remain long at this place because the Bedouins refused to allow any rebuilding of the churches that lay in waste. He moved further south to Egypt's heartland, past the Pyramids, until he reached the town of Kus and took shelter there in a small monastery in the desert.

The great silent majority of Egyptians, black people who remained convinced that their ancient religion was correct, were not considered in the equation of power. It is easy to consider the activities of the people of Alexandria as constituting the political and social realities of the Egyptian people. However, the city of Alexandria had a large population of people of Greek, Persian, Jewish, and Roman background as well as the African population during this time. The Copts were a mixed people who had maintained the Egyptian language with Greek alphabets. Most of them were the descendants of mixed African and Greek heritages.

Now when Cyrus took over his role as patriarch of Alexandria he was also given the title of viceroy of Egypt, a civil title. Combining these two positions in one person was a way for the emperor of Rome to give the person absolute power. Cyrus claimed that he had come to Africa in peace in order to heal the rift between the Melkite and Coptic communions of the Christian church. Very few Copts believed him because they saw the terror that he inflicted upon their believers.

The reigning issue was over the nature of Christ. The Monophysites, such as Cyrus, believed that Christ had one nature; the others, mainly the Copts, believed that Christ had both a spiritual and a physical nature. Cyrus proposed a Monothelite compromise, which was rejected by the Copts. There was little difference between this idea and the idea of "one will and one operation" espoused by the Monophysites. Neither cajolery nor anger could break the will of the Copts in their faith. Thus, Cyrus resorted to harsher measures to bring about unity in the church. He essentially locked down the nation by ordering the garrisons near Memphis, Pelusium, and Athrib and Nikiou to exercise dominion over the local areas with force. There was even a garrison in Syene (Aswan). The Coptic church had not been pleased with the Persians and now they were not pleased with the state church of the Romans. Cyrus, the Mukaukas, began to persecute the Copts as early as October 631. Melkite bishops were sent to replace Coptic bishops. During this period, Benjamin remained free, moving from one hiding place to another. But the search for him was intense. He could not be found and so Cyrus attacked the Copts at every turn. It was at this point that the future of the Egyptian nation was most vulnerable to outside influences.

The movement of Islam in Arabia, already conquering the cities of Syria, did not seem so bad to the Egyptians given the life they were living under the Roman-appointed patriarch and viceroy. In fact, Butler believes that "When they heard that even the Muslims granted a measure of toleration to the Christians, the thought may have risen in their hearts that subjection to the Muslims would make life less unbearable, that the yoke of Mohammed would be lighter than the yoke of the most Christian Emperor Heraclius" (Butler 1992, p. 192). The people of Egypt wanted the Muslims to enter the country in an effort to rid themselves of the Roman oppressors. Although Heraclius had intended for Cyrus to be a peacemaker he turned into a tyrant and was largely responsible for the advance of Islam into Africa. Unable to bring about religious compromise, without a vision for religious unity other than force, the patriarch and viceroy of the country created a horrendous storm of resistance and protest. The only way that Cyrus could see to deal with the situation was to use force. Thus, he inadvertently prepared the way for the Muslims to enter the country as the people's deliverers from the Roman occupation and warring Christian forces, one side of which had been supported by the emperor of Rome while the other side was running for its own life.

General Amir ibn al-As believed that the conquest of Egypt, coming after the surrender of Jerusalem to the Muslim caliph, Omar, would be quite easy. He convinced Omar "that there was no country in the world, at once so wealthy, and so defenceless" as Egypt (Butler 1992, p. 194). He also argued that Aretion, the Roman governor of Jerusalem, had fled to Egypt in order to rally the forces of imperial Rome against the Muslims. To take Egypt, in al-As' mind, would be to greatly increase the Muslim power (Butler 1992, p. 195). Omar subsequently gave Amir al-As permission to take Egypt. Al-As marched his soldiers and horsemen, not more than 4000, from Caesarea to the Egyptian–Palestinian border. About the time he reached the border Omar sent a messenger after him with a letter that said if he had reached Egypt he should go forward, but if he had not yet crossed into Egypt he should turn back. Omar had been convinced by Ousman that this was a dangerous adventure. Knowing that the letter could only contain second thoughts on the part of Omar, the general crossed the border and then opened the letter. Whereupon he read it aloud and said to his men that since they had been ordered forward, forward they would march. From the village of Arish along the sea coast began the Great Wall of Egypt, which ran to the eastern bank of the Nile, said to have been built by Senurset, which was broken down in many places even at this time in history. It could not stop any army, although that had been its purpose when Senurset ruled in Egypt.

On December 12, 639 CE the army of General Amir ibn al-As celebrated the Muslim Day of Sacrifice in Egypt. This band of brothers, almost literally, with most of the army coming from the same clan, saw themselves as unstoppable.

Who was this conqueror of occupied Egypt named Amir ibn al-As? It is said that Muhammad praised him as the best Muslim and the most trustworthy of men (Butler 1992, p. 202). He was of the Quraish clan and was highly regarded as a person of honesty, knowledge, and valor. Perhaps the greatest distinction to be said about al-As is that he was made military commander personally by the Prophet, who is reported to have said, "I am sending you forth as commander of an army. May Allah keep you safe and give you much treasure" (Butler 1992, p. 202). Al-As answered the Prophet that he did not become a Muslim for the sake of wealth and Muhammad replied that honest wealth is good for an honest man. There is no doubt that al-As was a strong fighter and a great tactician because Abu Bakr, the successor to Muhammad, sent him on an expedition to Syria, where he also distinguished himself.

When the Arab army fell upon Egypt it first captured the fortified town of Pelusium, which seemed to be poorly defended. The city contained many monuments and churches; they were wrecked and the city was crushed after a month-long battle with the Arab army. The loss of Pelusium by the Romans was the beginning of the end of their occupation of Egypt. Cyrus, the puppet patriarch from the Caucasus, was fearful that the fall of Roman rule would be sooner rather than later. In 640 al-As' army was augmented by many Bedouins who joined his campaign against the Romans. Theodore, the commander in charge of all Roman troops in Egypt, did not immediately grasp the seriousness of the problem his army faced. It is believed that he thought of the situation as a raid of a few hundred Bedouin from the desert. He soon discovered that the land of Egypt was a prize to be fought over by the forces of Islam and the forces of Rome.

The Copts, representing the Christian church, were urged by some of their leaders to support the Muslims since both of the groups, Muslims and Christians, share a common identification with Abraham. The same could not be said for the Romans.

On the other hand the indigenous black masses were neither Christian nor Muslim. They supported neither the Copts, the Romans, nor the Muslims. The vast majority of Africans remained loyal to the ancient traditions. They were traditionalists who adhered to the principles and teachings of the ancient Egyptians themselves. Beaten down by the heavy taxation of the Greeks, Romans, and Persians, the masses of Egyptians had limited ability to rise against the foreign invaders. They were, by the seventh century CE, exhausted by the burdens of their conquerors. After all, they had left their politics and defenses to outsiders for so long they had neither the will nor the ability to defend themselves. The struggle for Egypt in the seventh century was therefore a battle between Arabia and Rome. The prize for the victors was the grandest monument to human achievement in the ancient world, Kemet. Whoever would win the battle would be able to stamp their name and culture on the traditions, history, and accomplishments of black people for hundreds of years. The long-dormant black populations of Egypt, exploited biologically, socially, and economically, would cease to exercise spiritual and intellectual leadership on a civil society that their ancestors had created in the dawn of history.

With the rise of Abu Bakr as caliph, that is, Khalifah, or successor to Muhammad, the Islamic faith took on a mission of driving every religion but Islam out of Arabia, extinguishing the art and culture that had flourished with the Christians and the Jews.

## The 150-year African–European continental war

Africans had to resist the bitter European occupation and dismemberment of the nineteenth and twentieth centuries. When the European slave trade ended in the nineteenth century Europe was not through with the exploitation of Africa. What energy was left in Africa after the cruel enslavement would now be sucked by the political and economic vultures of the European and American continents. They saw Africa as an easy prey, as Omar and General al-As had seen Egypt after the conquest of Jerusalem.

The only way to view the engagement between Africa and Europe from 1807, the date Britain banned the slave trade, to 1957, the date the Gold Coast became independent and chose the name of the ancient empire of Ghana, is as a long, bitter, continental war. A brutal war was fought between two continents over the material wealth of one of them.

Africa had not declared war on Europe, but Europe had declared war on Africa. It was not a war that would be fought in conventional terms with standing armies respecting each other; it would be a war fought from the European side with intrigue, guile, avarice, betrayal, and brutal massacres. Africa would use all of its resources to defend its people and its territory. On the African side the war would be fought with guerilla tactics, sabotage, non-cooperation with European settlers, and destruction of crops and businesses. In the end the war would exhaust goodwill and introduce more suspicion into the relationships between Africans and Europeans. When it was over, Africa would have gained its political independence from the colonizing powers but still struggle to relinquish the mental and psychological grip on the continent.

By the beginning of the nineteenth century, Britain stood alone in Europe as the master of the seas and the largest slave-running country in the world. It was without peer in the number of ships devoted to the infamous slave trade. Liverpool alone, not to speak of other English cities, was home to nearly 60 percent of all slave ships. They sailed down the River Mersey into the cold Atlantic, headed south for the west coast of Africa loaded with trinkets, beads, blankets, and bangles that the slave raiders would use to barter with various African communities in order to gain access to African villages.

Often the kings and chiefs of coastal towns would let the slavers "pass" through their own territories to raid interior villages for a few trinkets. Once they had loaded the ships with Africans, the white slavers turned toward the Caribbean islands and the Americas with their human cargo. In the Caribbean or Americas they would sell the kidnapped victims to other whites and then load their vessels with rum and cotton bound for the markets of Europe. This passage to Europe with goods to add to the riches of the slavers was considered by some of the slave ship captains as triumphal. They had made the voyage to Africa, crossed in the perilous Middle Passage, and now headed homeward. How could life be any sweeter than that for the slavers? If one takes Liverpool as an example, the slave trade had built huge companies like Cunard and had encouraged some of the most prominent citizens of the country to be involved in the slaving business. Of course there were the resisters such as William Roscoe, a lawyer who devoted most of his life to abolition.

## The stage is set

Between 1492 and 1885, Europe's continental power and reach were unchallenged by any other area of the world. Hundreds of tons of gold and other precious metals and minerals were taken out of the Americas to enrich Europe. Millions of Africans would be uprooted during this time and sent across the ocean to the Americas and the Caribbean, making Europeans who held plantations and businesses in those places rich and powerful.

This period of time was not the time of Africa's dominance, nor that of Arabia, but of European nations acting in concert in the rape of Africa. Unchecked by the moral compass that had chastened the armies of Ra under Ramses II or by the physical obstacles that had reigned in the armies of Sunni Ali Ber, the reach of Europe, because of the sea, was global.

Africa was the prize, and all important European nations were the players. Meanwhile, the unrelenting assaults of the Moroccan armies on the powerful

Songhay Empire served to offer up the prize to the quickest and most brutal European players. In shambles, because of the nearly hundred-year low-intensity war that finally ended with the overthrow of the empire in 1594, slightly over one hundred years after Columbus landed in the Americas, the Songhay Empire, successor to the Ghana and Mali empires, disintegrated and Africa's western flank was ready to be cut up between the European nations.

## The Berlin Conference

Down the Unter den Linden, at the request of German Chancellor Otto von Bismarck, came the leading figures of Europe, and some United States delegates, in the winter of 1884–85 to the Berlin Conference on Africa. It was a summit that was to have a far-reaching impact on Europe and its relationship with Africa. Already by this time European nations had robbed Africa of much of its youthful labor in the slave trade. The horrible exploitation had been laid to rest in the middle of the century with the British African Squadron patrolling the Atlantic coasts of Africa and America to prohibit the movement of slaving ships. Emancipation had occurred everywhere except Brazil by the time of the conference. The enslaved Africans would be freed in 1888 in that country.

New forms of exploitation of Africa had been found, and with the decline in the slave trade the old European traders had discovered that settlerism and colonization could add greatly to their wealth if they simply exploited the material bounty of the continent. African leaders were not involved in this decision. Europe would simply declare its stakes over Africa. Thus, the Berlin Conference was the first European conference called for the purpose of deciding the fate of an entire continent. This had not happened in the case of Asia, or of the Americas. But because of the immense size of Africa and the numerous European national interests as residuals of the slave-trading activities, the conference was conceived as a way to avoid the pitfalls of an internecine battle between European powers over Africa. After all, slavery had demonstrated the futility of European nations fighting against each other to control their interests, and the *asiento* had served as a useful tool in establishing protocols between the nations. In the interstices between the activities of the slaving companies and colonization the political situation for European nations in Africa was not altogether clear. Since slavery had ended, it seemed that the question of controlling interests in certain regions of Africa was legitimately on the table again. Furthermore, King Leopold of Belgium had claimed a personal colony nearly eighty times the size of the country he ruled in Europe. Belgium was about the size of the state of Maryland in the United States and the Congo was about the size of the United States east of the Mississippi River. Furthermore, Leopold had never traveled to Congo, yet he could exercise his personal dominion over the territory through his surrogates. It was the testimony of his surrogates that had convinced other Europeans that he should be allowed to continue with Congo as a personal colony. Later, of course, Belgium would take over the Congo as its state possession.

By the time of the conference Germany had already established its authority over areas of Togo, Cameroon, and South West Africa (Namibia). This had been something of a German sneak attack on the interests of Britain and France. The European powers were playing games of chess all over the African continent prior to this conference. France had taken over Tunisia in 1881 in order to outmaneuver Italy, which had its own eyes on that country. Egypt was deeply in debt, as Tunisia had been, and the French and English combined to exercise control over that African country in an Anglo-French pact. However, there were many instances of resistance although the Europeans had succeeded in getting a disposition from the Khedive Ismail in 1879. Ismail Pasha had been proclaimed the Ottoman viceroy in Egypt upon the death of his uncle, Said Pasha. Ismail was considered a progressive leader and was responsible for completing the building of the Suez Canal. In addition, Ismail worked to create a stronger infrastructure for the country. He was succeeded by his son, Tewfik Pasha, who was soon under pressure to hand over financial administration of the country to the foreign forces of Britain and France. Nationalists in Egypt forced the appointment of an Arabic-speaking minister of war, Ahmed Orabi. The English reaction was swift and brutal. They defeated Orabi's army at Tel el-Kabir and shelled the cities of Alexandria and Ismailiyya. Subsequently Britain gained the upper hand over France in the affairs of Egypt and appointed puppet leaders.

Chancellor Bismarck expected the European nations to establish ground rules for dealing with each other in Europe and Africa. One way to consolidate their relationship was to discuss the future of Europe in Africa. As we shall see later, the 150-year war between Europe and Africa was fully engaged by 1884. What the Portuguese had unlocked in the fifteenth century by exploring and trading with Africa, and eventually initiating the European slave trade, was now a free-for-all among the European nations. African nations and kingdoms were reacting with indignation and defiance throughout the continent in thousands of incidents of resistance to the imposition of foreign influences. These incidents were simply the continuation of the resistance that had been provoked by the slave trade itself. Given the intensification of the industrial revolution in Europe, the nations meeting at Berlin were jockeying to ensure their continued commercial advantage in the labor and raw materials markets.

Violent confrontations between European nations over territorial impositions were considered wasteful. Although it was Chancellor Bismarck's call for the conference to be held in Berlin it was the Portuguese, the first Europeans in Africa, who had insisted that an international European conference be held to sort out the various areas of European influence in Africa. Thus, representatives from Britain, Austria-Hungary, France, Russia, Germany, the United States, Portugal, Denmark, Spain, Italy, the Netherlands, Sweden, Belgium, and Turkey met between November 15, 1884, and February 26, 1885.

The marquee theme of the conference was the ending of brutality and slavery in the Congo and the promoting of humanitarianism toward Africa, but in reality the conference was about a method for dividing the continent of Africa between the European powers. There were a few empty resolutions about the welfare of Africa and ending the Arab slave trade but the central intent of the conference came out in several substantive articles. Among the main provisions of the Berlin Act, and according to the significant chapters, were the following:

### Chapter One: Relating to the Congo Basin and adjacent territories

1. The trade of all nations shall enjoy complete freedom.
2. All flags, without distinction of nationality, shall have free access to the whole of the coast-line of the territories ...
3. Goods of whatever origin, imported into these regions, under whatsoever flag, by sea or river, or overland, shall be subject to no other taxes than such as may be levied as fair compensation for expenditure in the interests of trade.
4. Merchandise imported into these regions shall remain free from import and transit duties, subject to review after 20 years.
5. No power which exercises or shall exercise sovereign rights in the regions ... shall be allowed to grant therein a monopoly or favor of any kind in matters of trade.
6. All the power exercising sovereign rights or influences in the aforesaid territories bind themselves to watch over the preservation of the native tribes, and to care for the improvement of the conditions of their moral and material well-being and to help in suppressing slavery, and especially the Slave Trade. They shall, without distinction of creed or nation, protect and favour all religious, scientific, or charitable institutions and undertakings created and organized for the above ends, or which aim at instructing the natives and bringing home to them the blessings of civilization. Christian missionaries, scientists, and explorers, with their followers, property, and collections, shall likewise be the objects of especial protection. Freedom of conscience and religious toleration are expressly guaranteed to the natives, no less than to subjects and to foreigners ...

### Chapter Two: Document relative to the Slave Trade

9. The powers which do or shall exercise sovereign rights or influence in the territories forming the basin of the Congo declare that these territories may not serve as a market or means of transit for the trade in slaves, of whatever race they may be. Each of the powers binds itself to employ all the means at its disposal for putting an end to this trade and for punishing those who engage in it.

### Chaper Four: Act of Navigation of the Congo

13. The navigation of the Congo, without excepting any of its branches or outlets, is and shall remain free for the merchant ships of all nations equally ... the subjects and flags of all nations shall in all respects be treated on a footing of perfect equality ... no exclusive privilege of navigation will be conceded to companies, corporations, or private persons whatsoever ...

**Chapter Five: Act of Navigation of the Niger**

26. The navigation of the Niger, without excepting any of its branches and outlets, is and shall remain entirely free for the merchant ships of all nations equally.

**Chapter Six: Regarding new occupations of the coasts of Africa**

34. Any power which henceforth takes possession of a tract of land on the coasts of the African continent outside of its present possessions, or which, being hitherto without such possession, shall acquire them and assume a protectorate ... shall accompany either act with a notification thereof addressed to the other signatory powers of the present Act, in order to enable them to protest against the same if there exists any grounds for their doing so.

35. The signatory powers of the present Act recognize the obligation to insure the establishment of authority in the regions occupied by them on the coasts of the African continent sufficient to protect existing rights, and, as the case may be, freedom of trade and of transit under the conditions agreed upon.

36. The powers signatory to the present general Act reserve to themselves the right of eventually, by mutual agreement, introducing therein modifications or improvements the utility of which has been shown by experience.

The Berlin Conference was one of the most arrogant acts in modern political history. Europe and its American and Turkish compatriots decided the fate of Africa without regard to African political, social, or legal rights. Indeed, African people had no rights that white nations believed they needed to heed. As Europe's usurpation became clearer to the African nations and peoples, revolts were to break out around the continent. Three new imperialistic doctrines were expounded by the Berlin Conference:

1. *The doctrine of the spheres of influence* by which Europe established its right to control the African coastline.
2. *The doctrine of effective occupation* by which Europe established the idea that it could occupy an entire country by controlling the commerce along the coast.
3. *The doctrine of European protection of its agents*, especially missionaries, explorers, and scientists who exploited the African people's resources.

Thus, Europe had justified its act of dividing the continent of Africa among the nations of Europe without ever discussing the issue with the Africans themselves. Of course, Africans could never accept this arrangement as natural, necessary, or permanent. They would agitate with increasing force for Europe to leave Africa. Nevertheless the boundaries set up by the Europeans would plague Africa into the twenty-first century. The arbitrary boundaries imposed by Europe divided nations and ethnic groups into separate governments and also brought groups that may have had enmity between them under the same government. For example, the Akan people, who had seen themselves as one common people, were divided between Ghana and Ivory Coast. The Ewe people were divided between Togo and Ghana. The Yoruba people were in both Nigeria and Dahomey (Benin). Scores of other ethnic communities were thus divided arbitrarily and without regard to history or culture. Numerous white "experts" on Africa arose to explain this policy, carry out this policy, and enforce the imperial rule of Europe in Africa.

# 12 Resisting European and Arab slave traders

Great gain was to be obtained from the exploitation of the African continent, and during the latter part of the nineteenth century the cauldron that boiled was the vast area of Central Africa. Here, in the tropical rainforest, Europeans and Arabs would risk their lives in the greedy reach for wealth and in the process inflict senseless pain on the African continent. The Congo basin quickly became an arena where the forces of Europe and the Arabs met in an attempt to subdue the massive country of Congo. Both failed, but in their failures they meted out some of the most brutal suffering ever witnessed by humans upon the innocent people of the Congo. Henry Morton Stanley, the naturalized American who had been a representative of King Leopold in the Congo, brought Leopold a handful of alleged treaties he had made with African nations giving Leopold control over the Congo basin. He had become famous as the person the *New York Herald* had commissioned to go to Africa and find the missionary David Livingstone. He then traveled across the continent from east to west, becoming the first white man to do so. When he arrived in Europe with the news of his journey and the great wealth of the Congo he could find no excitement in Britain, but King Leopold of Belgium took an interest in Stanley's work and spent some of his own fortune commissioning Stanley to work for him. Thus, the treaties that he presented to King Leopold strengthened the hand of the king when he asked the Europeans to legitimize his rule over the Congo, which he called the Congo Free State. Of course, it was not a free state; under the control of Leopold's minions it was to become one of the most brutal slave regimes in history.

Tippu Tip, an Arab trader in ivory and slaves, came to resent the fact that Stanley, because of Leopold's fortune, was able to cover a huge area of the Congo basin, in competition with his own commercial interest. He had assisted Stanley in his expedition down the Congo, and now that Stanley was back in his territory Tippu Tip felt betrayed by the opportunistic Stanley. He attacked the officers and soldiers of the Congo Free State in a war that lasted for several years. Born of an Arab father and an African mother, Tippu Tip was a considerably ruthless slave hunter himself, kidnapping and killing men and women in the Congo basin. He showed no mercy toward the Africans he captured for the slave trade. He was a Zanzibari who had established his operations along the eastern coast and into the interior. Tip had the religious fervor of the Muslim invader; his non-acceptance and non-respect for traditional

African religions, and his calculated and specific economic and political will for which religion was used as a tool against Africans whom he considered to be infidels, made him one of the most feared of all kidnappers. Tip's area of control covered nearly one-third of Leopold's claims in the Congo. By claiming that he owed allegiance to the sultan of Zanzibar Tippu Tip was able to keep the Congo Free State off its footing. By 1887 he was asked by the sultan to take over the eastern provinces of the country. Thus, Tippu Tip was given some protection from the Congo Free State forces. However, because of his brutality some of the African towns and villages along the coast converted to Islam as a way to avoid conquest. They existed under the military banner of Islam during a period of changing economic and political conditions. In my judgment this became, as it had become in other venues, one of the dangerous results of religion and race where those people who had been mixed with the Arabs, because of the economic and military advantages of the Arabs, began to feel a sense of superiority over their darker brothers and sisters. Soon these Islamized Africans sought to enslave their darker counterparts, even suggesting that they were without humanity. Because of his role in the slave trade of eastern Africa, Tippu Tip has come down in history as one of the most notorious traitors to African interests. Like King Leopold's villainous cadre who produced wealth in the form of profits for big business and salaries for the expatriates, Tippu Tip's violent merchants of death made huge profits and gave nothing but trouble to Africans (Rodney 1974, pp. 152–3). Thus, the degrading enslavement of Africans remains the single most damaging and intense system of exploitation and hatred perpetrated in the last thousand years.

Tippu Tip's concentration on the eastern coast of Africa left an opening for the Belgians, French, and English to compete for the right to exploit Africans in the Congo–Sudan region. They all wanted control of the rubber, the ivory, and the human population. Each tried to be shrewder than the next, and none of these whites felt anything about African attitudes.

Other battles took place in the Congo basin between African kingdoms and Stanley's men. In the final analysis, the Africans were neither as ruthless nor as well armed as the troops under the protection of Leopold's money. Stanley's troops attempted to teach the Africans a lesson by destroying all villages along the river. His was a brutal surrogacy, defiling the sacred places, destroying the marriage bonds between men and women, overturning the ordinary lives of Africans along the river by enslaving millions of Africans in the Congo.

As it had been from the beginning, greed drove the actions of the white men in the Congo. Rubber was the key to the attempt to subjugate the Congolese people. John Dunlop, the Irishman who invented the rubber tyre and started making automobile tyres in 1890, added fuel to the greed of Leopold and others. In fact, Dunlop, Charles Goodyear, and Charles MacIntosh all lent their names to the rubber industry. But it was Dunlop who helped to develop the Western appetite for rubber for use as tubing, insulation, and tyres.

When King Leopold had gone into debt supplying money to Stanley and his Force Publique, a sort of military police who worked as soldiers and plantation bosses, it was the need for rubber in the Western world that had given King Leopold the greatest source of revenue. Hochschild's description

*Figure 12.1*  King Leopold II of Belgium
© Bettmann/CORBIS

of Leopold's letters is graphic: "His letters from this period are filled with numbers: commodity prices from world markets, interest rates on loans, quantities of rifles to be shipped to the Congo, tons of rubber to be shipped to Europe, and the exact dimensions of the triumphal arch in Brussels he was planning to build with his newfound profits" (1998, p. 159). Leopold had almost no regard for the African people, who were literally worked to death by the Force Publique under the direction of Stanley.

By the time the African kings knew that there was no other way to prevent the conquest of the entire Congo, Henry Morton Stanley had amassed a force with more than a thousand quick-firing rifles, four machine guns, and a dozen Krupp cannons. Mass murder of the Congolese people had its own momentum. Starvation, deprivation, and abuses of all kind were heaped upon the people and they reacted with characteristic resistance, only to see their brave men and women shot down in cold blood in front of them.

## The heroic resistance of the Budja and Kuba people

Yet the resistance was brave. Nothing vile and savage could be put beyond the operators of the rubber-collecting posts. The European operators forced their police and soldiers to carry out the most heinous crimes without a sense of the humanity of the people they were humiliating and killing. In fact, if a village did not meet whatever quota was imposed upon it by Leopold's officers the Force Publique, which included many Africans from the East African coast, would be ordered to kill everyone in the village, men, women, and children. According to Hochschild, "those times when an eyewitness happened upon a pile of skeletons or severed hands, and a report survives, represent, of course, only a small proportion of the massacres carried out, only a few sparks from a firestorm" (1998, p. 226).

The brutality of the European occupation of the Congo was made graphic in Joseph Conrad's *Heart of Darkness*, particularly in the line where Conrad has Kurtz scrawl the line, "Exterminate all the brutes!" The countryside was filled with corpses, literally. In one account it is reported by the Swedish missionary E. V. Sjöblom that he saw "dead bodies floating on the lake with the right hand cut off, and the officer told me when I came back why they had been killed. It was for the rubber. When I crossed the stream I saw some dead bodies hanging down from the branches in the water" (Hochschild 1998, p. 227). It should be clear that the African people soon understood the extent of the terror that was being carried out in their country. Although there were black collaborators, those who were paid by the whites to assist in hunting down Africans, much like there had been Africans during the slave trade used as collaborators; most of these collaborators were hated by the local people. Most often the whites hired the Africans who worked for the Force Publique from ethnic groups distant from the local Congo communities.

The Congo people say that between 1894 and 1895, Knut Svensson, a Swedish officer of the Force Publique, would assemble people in villages that did not want to be enslaved in the rubber plantation business in an open courtyard under the pretext of signing a treaty or recruiting laborers, and then, without warning, open fire, killing men, women, and children (Hochschild 1998, p. 227). Africans quickly learned that they could not trust white men with guns. One officer, Charles Lemaire, wrote in his diary, the following:

> 28 March 1891 ... The village of Bokanga was burned ... 4 April 1891: A stop at Bolébo ... Since they wanted to meet us only with spears and guns, the village was burned. One native killed ... 12 April 1891: Attack on the Ikengo villages ... The big chief Ekélé of Etchimanjindou was killed and his body thrown in the water ... 14 June 1891: Expedition against the Loliva who refuse to come to the station. Dreadful weather; attack made in driving rain. The group of villages was large; couldn't destroy them all. Around 15 blacks killed ... 14 June 1891: At 5 A.M. sent the Zanzibari Metchoudi with about 40 men to burn Nkolé.
> (Hochschild 1998, p. 228)

This is not the full account of Lemaire's rather sterile reporting of mass murders, and he was only one of the many officers of the Force Publique exercising such power over people's lives. There were at least thirty-five rubber plantation posts along the river and into the interior. Just one of them is reported to have used more than 40,000 rounds of ammunition per month. The guns and ammunition were not to kill animals, but to kill people. Of course, the people knew that when whites entered the territory it meant danger, and "as news of the terror spread, hundreds of thousands of people fled their villages" (Hochschild 1998, p. 229). Unable to find the people in their villages, the whites and their collaborators would often burn the entire village to the ground, burn the crops; all the banana trees would be destroyed, and the village animals such as goats, hens, and ducks plundered, leaving no food or shelter for the people when they returned to their homes. Africans had done nothing to deserve this type of treatment. In fact, Africans had welcomed the early Europeans and Africans as trading partners, but the guile and greed of the invaders had not been anticipated by the kings and court councilors of even the mightiest of African nations. Nevertheless there were many incidents of revolt and resistance.

Numerous ethnic groups refused to honor the will of Leopold's minions who had invaded their country. The groups who fought against the whites with great heroics were the Chokwe, the Boa, the Yaka, the Budja, and the Luba. But they were not the only resisters to the encroachment upon the sovereignty of African people on their own continent. The list is long, as one would expect, but let us examine briefly a few of the incidents and wars that must be seen as legitimate examples of African resistance in the face of more deadly weapons.

The Yaka fought the whites for nearly twelve years. When they were finally defeated in 1906 they harbored a deep hatred for the savagery inflicted upon their people by Leopold's officers. Another people with a long history of achievements in politics and art, the Chokwe, fought for twenty years against the Force Publique. A policy of divide and conquer was the principal manner in which the Force Publique operated. Leopold's officers told one group that they wanted to be friends and allies and then got them to fight against another group. Just as soon as the so-called friendly ally had assisted in disarming the target group, the whites would turn against their friendly ally, perhaps using another ethnic group the same way they had used the first. Using the shifting alliances and the natural separation because of land and politics, Leopold's army was able to cover a wide territory. However, the strength of the resistance proved more determined than even the white officers could imagine. Mulume Niama, a military strategist and paramount king of the Sanga people, was not content with the way the whites had entered his country. His soldiers put up a stiff resistance to the whites. King Niama possessed a strong character, a decisive leadership style, and the ability to explain to his people the dangers that confronted them if the whites gained control. Fighting against the whites, who had artillery as well as their rifles and machine guns, the Sanga were able to kill one white officer and three soldiers. The Sanga lost some soldiers as well, but they believed they had demonstrated the ability of their army to fight with dignity. Niama led his troops to a large cave called Tshamakele. This was not a good idea because the Force Publique laid siege to the cave. They put smoke at the three entrances to the cave and then waited for a week, sending an emissary to see if the king would surrender. Niama rejected the emissary's request that he surrender. The Force Publique refused to chase the men in the cave, knowing that the Sanga knew the cave better than they did. However, the rejection of the request to surrender meant that the siege would last for another three months. When the Force Publique finally entered the cave they found 178 bodies of soldiers and the king, Mulume Niama, who had refused to be slaves for Leopold's enterprise. They preferred death to enslavement; they preferred death with dignity to life with humiliation. Quickly the Force Publique tried to seal the cave so that it would not become a place of reverence. Yet it is a place of reverence because the strength of will and determination of the Sanga soldiers and their leader, Mulume Niama, must be accepted as marks of dignity.

About this time, the Boa and Budja people united their forces, recruited 5000 troops and fought a guerilla war from deep inside the rainforest. This low-level rebellion was important in keeping the Force Publique off its guard. Nevertheless, there were so many revolts occurring throughout the country that it is impossible to say which revolts were most important for the survival of the Congo peoples.

The Budja people revolted and initially killed thirty soldiers from the Force Publique. The punitive expedition led by a white man named Edgar Canisius followed the Budja to their home villages and torched every village and every house they could find that was said to be Budja. Indeed, smoke could be seen for many miles, attesting to the cruel revenge of the whites. More than one hundred whites were killed as they used their guns to gain advantage over the Budja. In the end, more than 1300 Budja people were killed in the retaliatory strikes against the African people. It was clear that the only difference between victory and defeat was the rifle carried by the whites and their allies.

Nzansu, a Kongo king, fought against the whites who had created a caravan route near the lower Congo rapids. These caravan routes were used by porters to bring ivory and rubber from the interior to the port cities. An agent of Leopold's government, Eugene Rommel, established a post in the area without the permission of Nzansu. It was neither proper nor customary for a person to build a post on communal or ancestral land without first following the proper protocols. Since Leopold's operation needed about 50,000 people each year to work as porters, soldiers, and spies, always under the direction of whites of course, Rommel believed that his post could help provide such labor. By all accounts the labor Rommel looked for was "forced" labor, not wage labor. This presented a problem, because even the missionaries paid for their porters. Nzansu met with his councilors and decided that it was necessary to revolt against the post and so on December 5, 1893 the Africans burned the post to the ground, then moved on to two nearby white posts and killed the white officials in those stations. The action was swift and furious, like some small, rhythmic whirlwind moving around the lower Congo. A Swedish mission at Mukimbungu was spared and the missionary, Karl Teodor Andersson, wrote to his church in Sweden the following: "The leader of the rebels, Chief Nzansu of Kasi, has let us know that he does not wish harm to any one of us as we have always shown that we are friends of the black people. But to the men of the State he has sworn death. And anyone who knows of the conditions out here cannot feel surprised" (quoted in Hochschild 1998, p. 125). One can see that the objectives of the king were clear; they were not random or irrational. His aim was to punish those who had brought pain and death to his people. The caravan route was completely blocked by the action of Nzansu and his followers. This showed that the whites were not really in charge so long as the Africans flexed their united muscle to block the avaricious practices of the Europeans. Once again the aim of the Europeans was to humiliate all of the people associated with Nzansu and they began an indiscriminate assault on villages, burning them to the ground. One of the Swedish missionaries, C. N. Börrisson, commented that "It is strange that people who claim to be civilized think they can treat their fellow man, even though he is of a different color, any which way" (Hochschild 1998, pp. 125–6).

Börrisson claims that Nzansu had a good cause, as good a cause as the Swedish patriots Engelbrekt and Gustaf Wasa had had in the fifteenth and sixteenth centuries respectively when they fought the invaders of Sweden. What was the problem if Nzansu responded like a member of the royal family had to respond in order to protect his people? Insult after insult had been heaped upon the heads of the people and the king had to act. Börrisson said that Rommel had been one of the most disreputable of all officials. He had imprisoned the women of villages when the men refused to work for the whites. He had kidnapped women and girls and treated them despicably. Hundreds of women were captured and held against their will simply because the whites could not get the men to work as rubber slaves. Börrisson asks:

> What happens to all of the women who are taken prisoners? Some are set free when their husbands have done all they can to regain the one who is dearest to them. Others are forced to work in the fields and also to work as prostitutes. Our most respected men here have told us with tears in their eyes and much vexation in their hearts that they had recently seen a group of seven hundred women chained together and transported to the coast on steamboats ... So can anyone feel truly surprised that the discontent has finally come to the surface?
>
> (quoted in Hochschild 1998, p. 126)

Nzansu's guerilla army fought for five years against Leopold's Force Publique. Another people to rise against the rubber terror were the Kubas. They were led by religious leaders who believed that they would not be killed by the white man's bullets because they were protected by supernatural powers. Of course, they were mowed down by the machine guns. It was a dreadful lesson; 180 Kuba had been killed.

Since most of the ordinary troops in Leopold's Force Publique were Africans from either the east coast or the west coast of Africa, they were often ready for revolt and mutiny. It took tremendous punishments for the slightest offenses to keep the soldiers under strict discipline. One must imagine that these soldiers felt the pain of the suffering that they were inflicting on the hapless Congolese at the command of the white officers. All commissioned officers and most sergeants were whites. Tempers were often hot and anger was quick and sharp. Indeed one of the largest uprisings occurred in 1895 when a base commander named Mathieu Pelzer, an arrogant and vile man, discovered that his African concubine had slept with another man. Pelzer ordered the woman killed. He then ordered a soldier to be punished, but just as he was about to be whipped a black soldier named

Kandolo snatched the whip. Soon thereafter Kandolo led a revolt against Pelzer. He ran away into the forest. He was tracked down and wounded. Soon the soldiers found his trail again and shot him.

Kandolo, in a white uniform, riding a bull, heralded as a hero, led his soldiers to other posts of the Force Publique. They killed several European officers and for more than half a year controlled the Kasai region of Congo, fighting off all expeditions sent against them. They had successfully turned back the white-led Force Publique. Actually the Force Publique believed that many of them had joined the local population and become integrated into the local ethnic communities. They fought battles against the Force Publique for thirteen years although their leader, Kandolo, was fatally wounded in battle in 1897. Two of Kandolo's most trusted aides, Yamba Yamba and Kimpuki, became leaders of the group and fought on against the Force Publique until 1908. They killed fifteen white officers, including a 26-year-old American from New Orleans named Lindsay Burke, who had been in the Congo less than ten months.

Hochschild recounts the facts of another rebellion in the far northeast of the Congo. It occurred in 1897 and involved about 6000 soldiers and porters. They had marched to the north through thick forests for months and had been under the leadership of several whites whose hatred and dislike of blacks were obvious by their treatment of their ordinary black soldiers. Under the leadership of Mulamba, a very strong African soldier who knew the Congo terrain, and understood military tactics and strategies, the soldiers revolted and found sympathy among the local kings. They fought the Force Publique over 600 miles of forest and savanna, staging ambushes to gain ammunition and weapons, and displaying incredible courage on the battlefield.

A French priest, Auguste Achte, stumbled into their camp one day and thought that it was the camp of the Force Publique. It was well disciplined and organized, and the leaders were dressed in gold-braided officers' uniforms. They told Achte that they had sworn to kill all whites, but the leaders argued that he had never hit a black person and had never treated a black person with disrespect. They questioned a dozen or so Africans who knew the priest, and once they were satisfied that he was not a "bad" white they let him live. Mulamba said to him, "We feed you, give you coffee, and present you with a gift of ivory because you will not write to Europe that we stole from you." He was released after they held him for about five days. The African freedom fighters told the priest Achte that they had killed their Belgian officers because they treated Africans like animals; they flogged the kings and soldiers alike, and one white officer had killed sixty black men in a single day because they did not want to work on Sunday, and another white officer had whipped a soldier, rubbed salt and pepper into his wounds, and threw him alive into the Lualaba River. I am in agreement with Hochschild's assessment that the Force Publique rebellions "were more than mutinies of disgruntled soldiers; they were precursors of the anticolonial guerrilla wars that shook central and southern Africa starting in the 1960s" (Hochschild 1998, p. 129). I would add, however, that these mutinies and rebellions, as we shall see, were part and parcel of the 150-year war.

## African American witnesses

Two African Americans, George Washington Williams and William Sheppard, journalist and missionary in the Congo, defended the African people. Williams was the first person to expose the atrocities committed in the Congo. He wrote vigorously against the Congo Free State and the policies of the Force Publique, becoming the first protester against the treatment of the Congo people. He had been born in Pennsylvania in 1849 and enlisted in the 41st US Colored Troops of the Union Army, probably training at Camp Freedom in Lamott, Pennsylvania. Williams saw action in the Civil War near Richmond and Petersburg, Virginia. Not content to sit at home after the war, he enlisted in the army of the Republic of Mexico and fought against King Leopold's ambitious brother-in-law, Emperor Maximilian, who had set his eyes on Mexico. Returning to the United States, he joined the US Army and fought against the Plains Indians. He enrolled at Howard University but did not complete his course, but he did obtain a theological degree at Newton Theological Institution near Boston, Massachusetts. After a stint as a pastor at the Twelfth Street Baptist Church in Boston, he moved to Washington, DC, and started a newspaper, the *Commoner*. Unsatisfied with the challenges of being an editor, Williams went and studied law and at the age of 30 was elected the first black member of the Ohio legislature. He served only one term. Soon he was called to complete a book called *History of the Negro Race in America from 1619 to 1880: Negroes as Slaves, as Soldiers, and as Citizens, together with a Preliminary Consideration of the Unity of the Human Family and Historical Sketch of Africa and an Account of the Negro Governments of Sierra Leone and Liberia*. This massive work was published in two volumes in 1882 and 1883.

In some ways George Washington Williams was one of the first modern historians, using not only traditional historical sources but also inquiry letters to churches asking for their minutes, inquiries to army generals asking about the black soldiers, and interviews with fellow Civil War veterans. The book, all 1092 pages of it, gave Williams recognition from W. E. B. DuBois, who called him "the greatest historian of the race" (Hochschild 1998, p. 104). Williams was a multidimensional character, doing everything he could to advance the cause of African people. So when he got the chance to go to Europe to write articles for a press syndicate about slavery in the Congo, he leaped at the opportunity. By 1890 Williams had started his trip to Africa, sailing first around the continent, stopping off at various places, lecturing in Cairo at the Khedival Geographical Society and becoming a member of the Zanzibar English Club. He spent six months in Congo and was convinced that the Congo project was a humiliating one for Africans. At Stanley Falls his anger poured forth in an indicting *Open Letter* to King Leopold. He expressed his horror at the treatment of African people. Williams made the following charges in his twelve-page *Open Letter*:

1.  Henry Stanley and his white assistants had tried to trick Africans into believing that whites had supernatural powers in order to get the Congo kings to sign over their land to Leopold.

2. Stanley was not a hero, but a tyrant. Stanley had broken his promise, used profanity, had a hot temper, and took land from the people.
3. The river posts established by Leopold's army brought nothing but death and destruction to the people. These posts compelled the Congo people to furnish them with goats, fowls, fish, and vegetables at the point of guns.
4. Leopold's government was excessively cruel to its prisoners, using chains around their necks that produce sores to which flies attach themselves.
5. It was a fraud to say that the Congo Free State was producing hospitals and schools. There were a few sheds not fit for horses. He claimed that none of the officials spoke any African language.
6. White traders and officials were kidnapping African women and using them as concubines.
7. White officers were shooting villagers, to capture their women, to intimidate the survivors into working as slaves, and sometimes just for sport.
8. Instead of Leopold being a noble antislavery crusader, his government was engaged in the slave trade, wholesale and retail.

Williams was a heroic figure, opening the door for others to condemn the persecution of the Congo people. He was the first to call attention to the crime being committed against humanity. Three months after he wrote the *Open Letter* he wrote to President Benjamin Harrison of the United States reporting on the conditions in the Congo.

Another African American would encounter Henry Morton Stanley in the Congo as well. He was an explorer, intellectual, and missionary. He had gone to the Congo because of the racist planning of Alabama Senator John Tyler Morgan, who got the United States to recognize Leopold's Congo and who wanted to find a place for African Americans to emigrate. Sheppard had been born in 1865 in Virginia and had attended Hampton Institute. He then studied at the Colored Theological Seminary in Tuscaloosa, Alabama. He was a man full of energy and dynamism; this would prove to be valuable for his work in the Congo. He had saved a person from drowning, and had rescued someone from a three-story burning building, getting burned himself in the process. When Sheppard arrived in the Congo in May 1890 with a white missionary named Samuel Lapsley, he was to establish a mission at Kasai. The Presbyterians had sent Sheppard as the junior missionary to Lapsley but the conditions, situations, and physical demands of the job soon thrust Sheppard into a natural leadership position (Hochschild 1998, pp. 151–3). The Africans took to him immediately, calling him a person of grace, with a bright character and a quick mind. William Sheppard, an orator and brilliant analyst of the situation, traveled to the United States to speak out against the torture, abuse, and criminality of the whites in the Congo. Seeing himself as a Kuba person, Sheppard believed that their art, among the highest in the world, must have been the basis for Egyptian art. He identified with the culture, aesthetics, and generally good nature of the Kuba people. Nevertheless, as a missionary he remained the teacher and defender. His defense of the Kuba people against the violence perpetrated by the Force Publique earned him recognition in the West as a champion of the African people. It was fortuitous that William Sheppard learned the language of the Kuba and became the only Westerner to speak the language. In every way he was a masterful communicator. The blacks and whites liked the fact that he had such a positive attitude toward life that he made those around him happy. He rode the first bicycle in Central Africa. When he fathered a son by a local woman, he did not lose his place in the church. In fact, his son, Shapit, grew up to run the mission printing press. Hochschild's description of him is quite appropriate:

> Tall and husky, he stands among a group of black warriors with spears and shields, holding a spear himself. Or with a rifle he grins broadly, a row of men with bows and arrows arrayed beside him. Again and again, Sheppard strikes a distinctive pose. He is wearing a white sun helmet, white shirt, white tie, white linen suit, even white canvas shoes. His chest is thrust out, his hands confidently on his hips, and, amid a group of Africans, his smile is warm and proud and almost proprietary.
> (Hochschild 1998, p. 155)

To show his appreciation for the culture and traditions of the Kuba people, Sheppard traveled alone to the capital city of the Kuba. He entered Ifuca, the capital, in 1892 and was intercepted by the king's soldiers. The Kuba king, Kot aMbweeky II, had warned that he would behead anyone who entered his capital city without permission, but when Sheppard was brought before him the king was amazed that he was a black man who could speak Kuba. Immediately his counselors told him that Sheppard was a reincarnated spirit of Bope Mekabe, a former king. Needless to say, the king greeted Sheppard with a large feast and sat him on an ivory throne and put a crown of beads and feathers on his head. He was truly a Kuba now.

Not long after this event, Sheppard returned to the United States on a lecture tour. He stopped in England, where he was made a Fellow of the Royal Geographical Society. The English arrogantly named a lake that Sheppard had been the first outsider to see in Kuba country Lake Sheppard, after him. Of course, the lake had a Kuba name and the action of the Royal Geographical Society was one more way Europeans sought to grab the history and geography of Africa as their own. William Sheppard was not impressed; he knew the realities on the ground in the Congo and spent his lecture time describing the men who ran Leopold's enterprise in the Congo as a brotherhood of bandits intent on demoralizing and humiliating a magnificent people. He reminded his audiences of the words of David Hume: "Men desire and desire, and there is no end to their desire." He had seen the greed, the utter, detestable greed, of the European officials in the rainforest of Congo and believed that it was necessary, even in God's name, to stop it.

### The military response to Europe

Reeling from the onslaught of the European slave trade, African leaders and their nations were in a persistent war. Everywhere people found the will to resist. Political leaders led resistance movements, and when they were unable or unwilling to do so these movements were led by ordinary men and women, some claiming to be spiritual guides who had special insights into the military weaknesses of the whites. As in any other case of great national tragedy, the leaders of African nations and peoples tried desperately to find answers for the loss of life and land perpetrated by the Europeans. Whether a nation is attacked by terrorists and hundreds are killed as in the September 11, 2001, assault on the United States, bombed from the sky as in Nagasaki and Hiroshima, or struck by a mighty natural disaster as with the 2004 tsunami that hit southeast Asia, people immediately seek some answer in their creeds, religions, or philosophy. The masses need answers and almost always someone steps forward to explain that the people have not been abandoned by their religion. Already by the time of the Berlin Conference on Africa the people of the continent had begun their campaign for independence. They had been rocked by the horrendous slaving practices of the Europeans and now felt that they would not allow any of the European powers to have an easy time of it.

The rise of Muhammad Ahmad in Sudan in 1881 was an indication that Europe would be contested on the mother continent. Ahmad was proclaimed to be the Mahdi, the guided one whose actions are controlled by God, and soon thereafter sought to recover power for the indigenous people of Sudan. There was to be a surge of African resistance right across the continent in the last part of the nineteenth century and the first part of the twentieth.

Germany had invaded Togo and Cameroon early in 1884, months before the Berlin Conference, and by February there was a revolt against German occupation. During the same year the Somali led an armed resistance against various European powers including British, French, and Italians, all coming ashore to advance their imperial goals. One more indication that Europe would not be able to rest comfortably in its occupation was the Massingina uprising in Nyasaland (Malawi) in 1884. This rebellion struck at the heart of the colonialist project. After the signing of the Berlin agreement that divided the African continent into European zones of influence, more than twenty major rebellions occurred in Central Africa, including the countries of Angola, Mozambique, Nyasaland, Northern Rhodesia (Zambia), and the Congo. These revolts would last until the beginning of the First World War in 1914.

The British army engaged the Mahdi and General Gordon was defeated at the Battle of Khartoum in 1885. In the very next year it was France's turn to feel the sting of African anger. The heralded military general and strategist Samori Ture demonstrated both intelligence and courage in molding a disciplined force of infantry and cavalry forces to fight the French in West Africa. Using diplomacy and war, Samori Ture's army inflicted severe losses on the French, defeating them in many battles. Badly mauled in the area of Guinea and Mali, the French invaded Ivory Coast. It may have been a diversion but it did not prevent the resistance movement to the west.

In 1889 the French were met by the forces of Ahmadu Seku, the leader of the Tucolor Empire, as they aggressively sought to establish themselves from Dakar to Bamako. The French idea was to build a railroad that would give them control of the Upper Niger area through a series of forts along the railway. This violated all of the land rights of the Tucolor people. Ahmadu Seku was the son and successor to al-Hajj Umar. His principal rival in the area was Samori Ture of the Mandinka forces. They were unable to unite against the French, as both leaders were duped by the French into believing that diplomacy was working. The French would meet with Ahmadu Seku and then disregard all agreements made with him. They treated Samori Ture in the same manner. The fact of the matter was that the French had no intentions of keeping any agreements between themselves and any Africans. They did not believe they had to keep these agreements since the Africans, in their eyes, were not the same as white men.

The French had defied the treaties they made with Ahmadu Seku many times. He had even been persuaded to support the French in their war against Mahmadu Lamine's Futa Bondu state, located between today's Senegal and Gambia, in 1885–87. In a show of arrogant treachery the French army turned on Ahmadu Seku's forces in 1889, launching a surprise attach on the Tucolor fortresses and villages. What became clear in this struggle, as it would become clearer in the next few years, was that the European forces did not have more courageous soldiers, or any better generals, but were in command of greater firepower. The French used artillery that sent powerful shells into the forces of Ahmadu Seku, destroying his army, his fortresses, and his towns. Even when the French defeated the city of Segu in 1890, the Tucolor leader refused to surrender, so great was their love for their own country. They fought in retreat as far as the town of Masina and operated guerilla actions from there until 1893. Using the divide-and-conquer technique that was to work well in places where ambition was greater than loyalty, the French made Ahmadu's brother their puppet king in Masina and then Ahmadu Seku had to flee to Sokoto, where he died. His followers were divided into factions and some joined the still-resisting forces of Samori Ture, who was bent on kicking the French "infidels and heathens" out of the land.

Samori Ture is the most legendary fighter against colonial imperialism in West Africa. He was a master general, perhaps the greatest military leader in West African history, with a pedigree reaching back to the monumental Sundiata. The 30,000 soldiers under his command would have followed him anywhere to fight the enemies of Africa. His heart was not a knee; it did not bend before the French armies. Rather he gave his courage to his fighters and stood for the principles of his native country. Both his infantry and his cavalry were well armed with weapons imported from the free country of Sierra Leone or made by his own Mandinka blacksmiths. Appealing to a strong sense of Mandinka nationalism that harked back to the glory days of the Mali Empire was enough to fill his cadres with enthusiastic fighters.

French intrigue and duplicity forced Samori away from his vigilance, and the French, after a series of meaningless treaties, invaded his territory from the north in 1891. Samori did not want to meet the French army, which contained many Africans from the Senegal colony, in open battle because they had artillery and machine guns; he retreated from the capital city of

Bissandugu using a scorched earth policy. It was a tactical withdrawal that denied the French army any supplies, since the heartland of the country had been wiped clean of all crops and animals. The French were obliged to abandon their pursuit because they ran short of supplies.

Samori Ture, the daring chameleon, had escaped to reorganize his army and his empire but because he was now seen as a foreign occupier himself he was obliged to decrease the scope of his territory. The Asante Empire of Ghana, at war with the British, blocked his eastward expansion, and the Mossi Empire lay to the north, blocking further movement in that direction. Samori tried to secure a protectorate from the British, asking them to take over his empire and protect it from the French. However, because the British and the French had the same aims and interests they refused. It was left for Samori Ture to fight it out with the French. Shillington captures the last days of the Samori Ture fighting machine with these words: "In spite of being cut off from their Sierra Leone arms-suppliers, the Mandinka army still scored some important victories over the French. In the end it was famine which finally defeated Samori's troops in the mountains north of Liberia in 1898. Samori gave himself up to the French and was exiled to Gabon, where he died aged seventy in 1900" (1989, p. 309). It would be the name of Samori Ture that would inspire resistance and rebellion into the twentieth century throughout West Africa.

The French had their hands full of rebellions and revolts in West Africa. They could never speak of the lack of African resistance to conquest because their experience was nothing but one resistance movement after another as the African leaders and their armies sought to rid themselves of this unnatural imposition on their body politic. In 1891 the Baule of Ivory Coast started a resistance that lasted until 1902. Behanzin, king of Dahomey, started a resistance that lasted from 1891 to 1894, when the king was arrested by the French and deported to Algeria, where he died in 1906. A pattern of arrest and exile became the Europeans' way of dealing with the people's loyalty to their kings and leaders. This practice was followed by all of the European nations.

The French were not alone in having their plates full of resistance. The British invaded Ijebu (Yoruba) in West Africa and Uganda in East Africa in the same year, 1892. The Yoruba king, Ijebu, resisted the British invasion with an army of 7000 to 10,000 men who beat back the British forces initially. When the British brought the machine guns, the Maxim gun, to the front of the lines they were able to subdue the Yoruba. Once again it was not for lack of courage or will that the African resistance lost but for lack of the most sophisticated weapons of the day.

The year 1893 saw the French invade Guinea, declaring it a colony of the French government. A year later a Mbona religion priest led a movement in Congo, named the Massingire rebellion, that was inspired by the priestess Maria Nkoie, who was supposed to make her followers immune to the guns of the Europeans. This project failed and many of the followers of the Massingire rebellion and the Nkoie group were killed. They had managed, however, to bring fear into the lives of the invaders and to send a message to the French. An African proverb says, "One shakes a dog and one will shake the dog's owner," and here the masses had threatened the very power of the French. From that time onwards the French never allowed any indigenous spiritual or social justice group to emerge without injecting themselves into the organization. Yet Africans were so determined to find their own way to social harmony and peace that they showed courage in demonstrating new methods of resistance. However, it was the old ways that had reappeared in Ethiopia.

Thus, in 1893 the Ethiopian resistance blossomed in an effort which was to inspire the entire African continent. Diplomacy had failed between Ethiopia and Italy, and when the Ethiopian leader, Emperor Menelik II, saw that the Italians were preparing for war, he imported 82,000 rifles and twenty-eight cannons, and repudiated the broken treaty of Wuchale with the famous declaration, "Ethiopia has no need of anyone; she stretches her hands to God."

Born in 1844, Menelik II led the most successful campaign of war against a European colonizing army. His name and deeds are recorded in the soul of the Ethiopian people and he remains one of the most celebrated world leaders of all time. He served as governor of the province of Shoa for 25 years and then in 1889 became emperor. What drove Menelik II to greatness was his desire to incorporate the best technology into his country. He wanted to see Ethiopia on a par with any other nation. He built bridges, libraries, telegraph lines, railroads, banks, hotels, hospitals, schools, a mint, newspapers, and a postal system. The idea was to modernize the ancient kingdom. But this was also the era of European expansionism and imperialism. Italy had already claimed a colony on the Red Sea, Eritrea. War was inevitable, but the Ethiopian emperor believed that victory was certain.

Menelik soon saw that Italy had designs on Ethiopia. A treaty was signed in 1889, called the Treaty of Wuchale. It was written in Amharic and Italian. The Italians understood the treaty to say that all communications to foreign nations had to come through the Italians. The Ethiopians understood the text to say that if they desired they might use the Italians to communicate with foreign forces. Italy used this text to claim a protectorate over Ethiopia and it was quickly recognized by the European powers. To enforce their claim the Italians, assisted by the British and French, advanced on the town of Adowa in Ethiopia and occupied it in January 1890.

While discussing the disputed text, Menelik was importing weapons from France and Russia, and continuing to increase his control over Ethiopia, shoring up his support among the princes, and organizing his armies. Menelik's mobilization of his army and people is seen as one of the most thorough preparations for war any African nation had ever undertaken to prevent a foreign force from conquering its land. Menelik did not want to see his religion, culture, or sovereignty in the hands of another nation.

The final confrontation occurred at Adowa on March 1, 1896, and when it was over the Italian army had been decisively defeated. The Italians were forced to sign the Treaty of Addis Ababa, which nullified the Treaty of Wuchale and recognized Ethiopia's independence. Later I will show how Menelik came to see the Treaty of Wuchale as a dangerous contract which had to be rectified.

The defeat of Italy by Ethiopia, like the defeat of France by the armies of Toussaint L'Ouverture and Dessalines in Haiti in 1804, signaled to the world that Africans would defend their rights and their liberties with their blood. As historians have generally observed, the victory of Ethiopia was not an accident; it was a decisive victory, planned and executed by brilliant soldiers. It has been compared to the victories of Hannibal, Ramses II, and Tuthmoses III.

Italy totally misjudged the will of Ethiopia. The arrogance of Europe was in its expansive nature, its imperial ambition on the continent of Africa, its blatant assertion of raw brutality, without thinking that Africans would object. The mistake for Italy in the European circle of imperialists was to have drawn Ethiopia for conquest, an ancient civilization that was at one time considered by Mani, the prophet, as one of the four great civilizations of antiquity, with Persia, China, and Rome being the others.

The country of Ethiopia enjoys fertile land in the mountains, sections of the Rift Valley run through it, and it has a moderate climate in the highlands. This contrasts with the hot and dry lowlands, which are below sea level and are often victims of drought. Thus, it is a country with great varieties of landscape and topography. The same can be said about its people, who are also diverse; there are over forty different ethnic groups in the country.

Christianity was adopted by the Ethiopians in the fourth century CE and a rich culture grew up around it with the Ge'ez language, one of the oldest written languages of Africa (others being Medu Neter [Mdw Ntr] and Meroitic), as the source for illuminated bibles and beautiful art. The *Kebra Nagast*, written in Ge'ez, was the most important book of the Ethiopian religious tradition. *Kebra Nagast*, or the *Book of the Glory of Kings* of Ethiopia, is an old book. It has been in existence for at least a thousand years and contains the history of the Solomonic line of kings in Ethiopia. The book contains information about how the Ethiopians lost their own religious way in order to accept the religion of Israel. A great interest in African history was spurred in the West by the European colonization of the African continent. Many Europeans believed that the Ethiopian king, a legendary figure named Prester John, was one of the great defenders of the Christian world. This kingdom fired the imagination of Europeans engaged in a struggle with the Islamic world. Spain and Portugal sought to discover in this legendary kingdom an ally against Islam and the Ottomans.

The earliest collections of documents of the country of the Negus, meaning King, came through the writings of Francisco Alvarez, an envoy whom Emanuel, king of Portugal, sent to David, king of Ethiopia, under the auspices of Ambassador Don Roderigo de Lima. In documents detailing his mission, Alvarez included an account of the king of Ethiopia, and a description in Portuguese of Ethiopian customs and culture, which was printed in 1533. Among the most complete translations of the *Kebra Nagast* is the work by Enrique Cornelio Agrippa (1486–1535), *Historia de las cosas de Etiopía* (Toledo 1528). Other writers include the Jesuit priest Manuel Almeida (1580–1646) in his *Historia de Etiopía*, which does not appear to have been published in its entirety. Manuel Almeida was sent out as a Catholic missionary to Ethiopia, and had learned about the *Kebra Nagast*.

His manuscript is significant for an appreciation of the Ethiopian culture. His brother, Apollinare, also went out to Ethiopia as a missionary and was, along with his two companions, stoned to death in Tigre. It was not until the close of the eighteenth century, when James Bruce of Kinnaird (1730–94), the famous British explorer, published an account of his travels in search of the sources of the Nile, that some information as to the fabulous contents of this extraordinary book came to be known among a select circle of scholars and theologians. When Bruce was about to leave Gondar, the Ethiopian king Takla Haymanot had his wazir, Ras Michael, give him a copy of the *Kebra Nagast*. It is not clear who created the *Kebra Nagast*. In fact, it has not been established when it was written; however, scholars believe that it was created during the revival of the Solomonic line of kings during the reign of Yekuno Arnlak, from 1270 to 1285. Thus, Ethiopia of the nineteenth century was a country with a foundation of dignity, power, and national pride. It would not be an easy prey for any nation. Nations seeking to conquer the country should learn that lesson.

In 1868 Ethiopia was invaded by 5000 British and Indian troops sent to chastise the Negus, Tewodros II, for detaining European envoys and missionaries. After seeing so many foreign troops in his country that he could not control, Tewodros II shot himself, after being abandoned by his nobles. His weakened army had been defeated at Magdala by the British and Indians, who soon withdrew leaving Tewodros' kingdom shaken. With Tewodros' death came a power struggle that after four years eventually resulted in the rise of Kassai, the *ras*, or lord, of Tigre, one of the provinces.

Proclaiming himself Negus Yohannes IV, Kassai had to contend with many external pressures. The decade of the 1870s was a time of stiff resistance to repeated attacks by the Egyptian armies of Ismail Pasha, the Ottoman viceroy who was leader of Egypt. Pasha's dreams of a greater Egypt that included Ethiopia and the ports of the Red Sea, particularly Massawa, led him into a futile attempt to control the port city of Massawa. His armies suffered terrible defeats at the hands of Yohannes' armies. At the battle of Gura on March 7–9, 1876, the Ethiopian forces cut down the 20,000-man Egyptian army, which was led by European and American mercenaries, and routed them in an awesome show of Ethiopian military prowess. Egypt would never invade its neighbor again, with or without mercenary support.

Less than ten years later, in 1885, Italy occupied Massawa. Under the government of Prime Minister Francesco Crispi the Italian ambition turned to having its own colonial empire. With the approval of the British government, which Crispi had courted as a political ally, the Italian army garrisoned Massawa. Of course the Ethiopians found this an intolerable act of willful provocation. Ethiopians were commanded to harass the Italians whenever they moved out of Massawa and to let them have no peace anywhere in the country. Yet the Italians doggedly held on to Massawa and tried to expand their holdings in Eritrea, using all kinds of comical techniques like releasing balloons to create panic and using electric spotlights to terrify armies fighting at night. On January 26, 1887, the Italians moved a column of 550 men toward the garrison of Saati to relieve the men who had been stationed there. They were surprised in a steep, narrow, canyon-like valley, and slaughtered. It was a horrible defeat for Italy, with 430 dead and 82 wounded; only 48 men survived without any harm. The Italians called this the "Dogali Massacre": the Ethiopians saw it as one more victory against an invading foe. In some sense, this was a precursor to what would happen later to the Italian army. The Italians, full of colonial ambitions and underestimating the Africans' will to defend their nation, found themselves in a war with a determined people. Gallantry was the calling card of the day.

Beset on all sides, it seemed, by enemies wanting to conquer the ancient kingdom, Yohannes was called into battle against the forces of the Mahdi on March 12, 1889. Actually Yohannes took a force of 100,000 to Gallabat, an Egyptian garrisoned town right across from the Ethiopian town of Meterna. The idea was for Ethiopia to help relieve the trapped soldiers of Egypt and to make a way for them to receive supplies from Egypt. However, the Mahdists saw the Ethiopian army as an interventionist army, one entering a conflict that was not its own. The two African armies clashed at Gallabat in southern Sudan and Yohannes was killed. In a gruesome display of the Sudanese victory the khalifa, Abdallahi ibn Mohammad, displayed the head of Yohannes on the end of a pole. His army withdrew to the Ethiopian mountain fastnesses. Soon Ras Menelik of Shoa, Yohannes' rival, was made Negus, and crowned Menelik II at Entotto, on the southern side of the Ethiopian high plateau. He gave the town a new name, Addis Ababa, meaning "new flower," and made it an important political center.

Five hundred miles to the north, Yohannes' son, Mangasha, claimed the throne as the heir to his father. Menelik agreed to split the province of Tigre, the seat of Mangasha's power, with the Italians. He signed the Treaty of Wuchale (Uccialli) in May 1889, which ceded a portion of Ethiopian territory as far south as the Mareb River, about 50 miles south of Asmara, and the Islamic lowlands of Bogos, to the Italians. Menelik would receive from the Italians modern rifles and ammunition. The initial shipment of 5000 rifles was delivered but the ammunition had been carefully selected so that it did not fit the rifles. Additional arms were purchased from the Italians but were never delivered.

Menelik II was quickly reminded that he could not trust the Italians when they claimed under the Berlin agreement the whole of Ethiopia and moved to take the town of Adowa from Ras Mangasha, the local leader, who had been forced to share part of the Tigrean province with Italy. The Italians announced that they would remain in Adowa until Menelik II understood the Treaty of Wuchale the same way as they did. Menelik knew then that he had made a mistake in having confidence in the words of his Christian Italian brothers. As the Negus of a Christian empire, Menelik II felt betrayed by the Italians, who represented the Roman Catholic country of Italy. He would never forget the betrayal. He wrote to Queen Victoria of England saying,

I have no intention at all of being an indifferent spectator, while distant European powers hold the idea of dividing up Africa for Ethiopia has existed for the past fourteen centuries as an island of Christianity in a sea of pagans. I trust that God, who has protected Ethiopia until this day, will protect and increase her, and I have no fear that he will see it divided and handed away to other nations.

Victoria's government, that is, the British government, was a part of the Italian plot to deliver Ethiopia to the European nation. Menelik was neither afraid, nor was he overly concerned. His idea was to prepare the people and so he sent out a mobilization proclamation that included the words, "Enemies have now come upon us to ruin our country and to change our religion. Our enemies have begun the affair by advancing and digging into the country like moles. With the help of God I will not deliver my country to them. Today, you who are strong, give me your strength, and you who are weak, give me your prayers."

This is the way the fateful war began. On February 29, 1896, with supplies of food and ammunition running low on both sides, the Italian commander, General Oreste Baratieri, made the first move in the middle of the night. He sent his troops toward the Ethiopian forces. However, he failed to calculate the impact of the rough terrain, rocks, crevices, canyons, and hills, and soon his army was separated into small pockets of men cut off from each other without communication. This weakness was observed by the Ethiopian commander, Ras Makonnen (the father of Emperor Haile Selassie), who ordered his troops to exploit the fact that the Italians were in small pockets. Just as the sun dawned, troops belonging to Emperor Menelik II and Empress Taytu joined the forces of Ras Makonnen. That day, March 1, the Italians took 11,000 casualties in the worst defeat of a European nation by an African nation. Baratieri was relieved of his command and Italy experienced national humiliation. It is believed that nearly 10,000 Ethiopians also lost their lives but the victory assured Ethiopia of its independence until 1935, when Benito Mussolini again tried to defeat Ethiopia.

Ethiopia's victory made it a highly revered nation on the continent. Whites even debated whether or not it was an African nation, not wanting to concede that the Italians had been defeated by Africans. In some ways the victory of the Ethiopians held the seeds of the later discontent of those people living in Asmara and along the coast who defined themselves as Eritreans. In 1950 the UN argued that Eritrea should become a part of a federated Ethiopia. Influenced by numerous interests, in 1962 Eritrea decided to end the federation and completely unify with Ethiopia. However, this was not a political situation that all Eritreans agreed on; opponents of the union started small-scale guerrilla warfare and the Eritrean Liberation Front (ELF) was founded. Initially, the ELF was more nationalist and Islamic and received aid from Iraq and Syria. Soon more Christians began to join and the ELF became increasingly anti-capitalist. Internal divisions within the ELF led to the creation of the rival Eritrean People's Liberation Front (EPLF) in 1972, led by Osman Salah Sabbe, the former head of the Muslim League.

When the Ethiopian Emperor Haile Selassie was overthrown in a military coup in 1974 the EPLF and ELF united against the Ethiopian government. By 1976 the united Eritrean forces had pushed all government forces out of

Eritrea. There was yet another division within the Eritrean opposition as Osman broke from the EPLF and formed the Eritrean Liberation Front-Popular Liberation Front (ELF-PLF), a move that reflected personal rivalries and ideological divisions. The Ethiopians with the help of the Soviet Union and Cuba defeated the Eritreans in 1978. It was not a total victory for the Ethiopian forces and there was a return to more limited guerrilla warfare where neither side was really able to take control. There was continued fighting between the guerrillas and government forces throughout the 1980s, but eventually the guerrillas were able to gain the upper hand, scoring several key victories against Ethiopian forces. In 1991, a UN-controlled referendum allowed the people to declare for their independence, after a complete pull-back of the Ethiopian army. On May 24, 1993, the Eritreans declared their independence and named Asmara their capital. Immediately the country had to deal with the fact that the entire infrastructure of the country had been completely destroyed by twenty years of war with Ethiopia. There were displaced persons and refugees throughout the country, and a famine on top of the poor infrastructure. Nevertheless, the strategically important Red Sea ports of Eritrea were able to assist the nation in succeeding in recovery. There was still uneasiness between the two enemies. Members of both governments had worked together to topple the socialist government but could not find a common language regarding their long borders. The Badme area was heavily disputed, but it was where Eritreans positioned their border troops. A treaty made with the Ethiopians and Italians in 1903 delineated the Eritrean border in the Badme area; however, Ethiopia's claim was that the agreement with Italy was not valid because Italy had no right to the territory in the first place. The Ethiopians could not accept the fact that the new reality meant that the Ethiopians were completely shut off from the Red Sea and the Eritreans were demanding huge payments for the transit of goods to and from Ethiopia. Thus, an issue that found its energy in the early colonial or attempted colonial influence of Italy came to dominate the lives of the Eritrean and Ethiopian people for decades.

## The spirit of revolts

In the southern part of Africa, the Mashona and Matabele people rose up against the British invaders. Mapondera, a traditional leader, led a rebellion against the occupying forces of Britain. Those uprisings were put down violently but they led to the First Chimurenga under the direction of the spirit mediums Nehanda and Kaguvi. They revolted against the taxes on their homes and buildings on their land. They refused to pay the British any money for the land that was theirs as an inheritance from their ancestors. They resented the white man's intrusion into their territory and vowed to fight to the death. When they were captured in 1898 they were both given the opportunity to recant their words against the white man's religion. Kaguvi recanted and was hanged. Nehanda refused to recant, and although she too was hanged she became the most sacred personage in the history of the Mashona (Shona) people.

Other rebellions peppered the history of Africa with bitter pills for the white invaders to swallow. In 1900 Asante revolted against direct taxation, forced labor, and the introduction of Western education. In Ghana, the British were even more demanding and arrogant than they had seemed elsewhere; here they also asked for the Golden Stool, the symbol of the Asante nation. A rebellion led by the eloquent Asante Queen Yaa Asantewa of Ejisu resisted the British and maintained the sanctity of the Golden Stool. When they were forced to present the Golden Stool the Asante gave the British a gold-plated stool but kept the real stool hidden. The Asante had no intention of allowing the British the right to exercise authority over them. They vowed to stand in the way of the British quest for a West African colonial empire. The Asante Wars against the British had started in 1805 and lasted a hundred years. Although unable to supply their armies with the same caliber of weaponry as the British industrial sector, the Asante kept the British army at bay with superior courage, ingenuity, and bravery. With their power threatened and their political and military leadership compromised because their king, Prempeh I, had been tricked, captured, and exiled, Yaa Asantewa, the queen of Ejisu, called for war against the British one more time.

Frederick Hodgson, the British representative, told the people that King Prempeh I would not be released or returned; adding insult to injury, Hodgson demanded that the people surrender the Golden Stool. The soldiers went home to prepare for war.

In the evening, the chiefs held a secret meeting at Kumasi. Yaa Asantewa, the Queen Mother of Ejisu, was at the meeting. The chiefs were discussing how they could make war on the white men and force them to bring back the Asantehene. Yaa Asantewa saw that some of the chiefs were speaking with great caution. She was agitated by the fact that the great Asante nation had allowed the British to take the king to the coast. She suddenly spoke to the assembly of royal leaders from her seat, saying words such as:

> I have seen that some of you fear to go forward to fight for our King. If it were in the brave days of old, chiefs would not sit down to see their King taken away without firing a shot. No white man could have dared to speak to the chiefs of the Asante in the way the Governor spoke to you chiefs this morning. Is it true that the bravery of the Asante is no more? I cannot believe it ... if you the men of Asante will not go forward, then we will. We the women will. I shall call upon my fellow women. We will fight the white men. We will fight till the last of us falls in the battlefields.

When she finished speaking, the Asante kings vowed unanimously to fight the white men to regain their paramount king, the Asantehene Prempeh I.

The Yaa Asantewa War, as it was called, was started on September 30, 1900. It ended with the terrible defeat of the Asante and the capture and exile to the Seychelles of Yaa Asantewa. She died in the Seychelles in 1921, never to return to Ghana, yet her memory is vivid in the ritual and practice of the Asante people (Edgerton 1995).

Other revolts broke out all over West Africa. The colonizers learned that state tyranny was a cruel commerce that gave them rotten apples in return. A Zulu proverb claims that the wildebeest can see the wind, but the white man can only see which way it is blowing. And the way it was blowing in the early twentieth century was against the structures of colonial domination.

There were the Ekumeku rebellion in Nigeria, which began in 1903; the Mossi rebellions in Kouddigou and Fada N'gourma from 1908 to 1914; the rebellion of the Gurunsi in 1915–16 in Upper Volta (Burkina Faso); and the revolts of the Lobi and Dyula in Mali in 1908–9. There had been the Manjanga Rebellion in Congo starting in 1890 and lasting until 1905.

On the eastern side of the continent, Sayyid Muhammad led the Somalis in revolt in 1895 until his death in 1920. He believed that it was the legitimate right of the Somalis to govern themselve as they had from the ancient time when their country was called Punt. A revolt in Madagascar in 1904–5 was intended to bring about independence and end colonial occupation. It would take some time before the Malagasy people would gain their victory over colonialism because tyranny is always better organized than freedom. Yet freedom is an unstoppable energy that will eventually regroup and deal the final blow to the tyrant. An armed peasant rebellion called the Sadiavahe would break out ten years later in response to the cattle tax and a compulsory draft for the First World War in 1915. In 1904 the Herero people of South West Africa (Namibia) protested against the German occupation and were shot down with machine guns; 65,000 people were murdered, representing three-quarters of the Herero-speaking population of Namibia. It was the largest single massacre of Africans on the continent. The Herero people promised their children that they would not forget the time when "the blood flowed together in rebellion."

In August 2004, the German government offered an apology for the 1904 genocide during the Herero uprising against German rule. Speaking at Okakarara village, 175 miles northeast of the capital Windhoek, near where Herero resistance was finally crushed, German economic cooperation and development minister Heidemarie Wieczorek-Zeul, representing the German government, accepted the historical and moral responsibility incurred by Germans of the early nineteenth century. The paramount chief of all Herero-speakers, Kuaima Riruako, though pleased with the German move, said Herero action would not stop here because although he was happy about the apology, Germany needed to pay reparations. In September 2001, about 200 Herero under Riruako filed a lawsuit in the US court of the District of Columbia demanding $2 billion from the German government for atrocities committed under colonial rule. The US court was chosen because a 215-year-old law, the Alien Tort Claims Act of 1789, allows for such civil action. Germany insisted it would not pay reparations but declared that the country would help Namibia with its land-reform program, which seeks to buy farms from whites in order the make the land available to blacks.

Africans were not to be denied the right to protest or to fight for their freedom. The Maji Maji Rebellion sought to expel Germans from Tanganyika. It was directed and planned by the traditional prophet

Kinjikitile Ngwale. More than twenty different ethnic groups were involved in the rebellion, and it spread over 10,000 square miles. The people resented the taxation, forced labor, and oppression. This was a mass movement meant to destroy the brutal German system of colonial occupation. Karl Peters had introduced violence of the most personal kind in East Africa by killing any African king who resisted the German occupation; now the Maji Maji, meaning sacred water, movement sought to even the score and rid the country of Germans. They moved across the country with a supply of spears and arrows and *maji maji* to destroy the German forts. Wearing millet stalks around their foreheads they marched to battle as if they were invincible. They went to the main compound of the Germans at Mahenge. As soon as they came within range of the machine guns the Germans had stationed in the fortress the Germans unleashed deadly fire. Hundreds of Maji Maji soldiers fell. As quickly as one row was shot down, another would step in its place and they, too, would be cut down by the hail of bullets coming from the machine guns. When the Ngoni people heard that the Germans were being assaulted they sent an army of 5000 soldiers to join the Maji Maji. The Germans left their camp at Mahenge with the machine guns and on October 21, 1905 attacked the whole Ngoni army in their camp. Hundreds more were killed. Unfortunately the sacred water with which the people rubbed themselves could not prevent the bullets from penetrating their bodies and more than 75,000 people in all were killed by the Germans during the revenge period of the Maji Maji war. Rembe, another prophet claiming to have power to prevent the European bullets from killing a person, arose in Uganda in 1917. He had his followers drink Yakan water, which was supposed to come from a pool in Lugbara territory where a snake with a human head gave oracles. He was arrested and executed and although a dozen police were killed the revolt was quickly put down.

But nothing could prevent the Africans from rising up against their enemies. The failure of magical thinking did not mean that the people would abandon their dreams for freedom. In some ways the magical thinking was provoked by a serious search for something supernatural to deal with something that was not clearly understood at the time. Many years later, in 1987, Alice Lakwena would lead an army of 6000 into Uganda claiming that her followers would be protected from bullets if they used an ointment she gave them for protection.

Most of the revolts were not based on magic. In fact, very few of them were based on such beliefs. Bambala of Zulu led a brief uprising against the British in 1906. His revolt, like most of them, was based on a rejection of forced labor, taxation, and oppression. Mulama of Nyasaland (Malawi) led a resistance movement in 1909 and vowed to strike all the whites who had defiled the land with their violations of the sacred traditions of the Tonga people. The Sudanese people would not be satisfied with occupation by the Egyptians or the British and would revolt in 1900, 1902, and 1904. The VVS (Vy Vato Sakelike, meaning "strong and hard like stone and iron") secret organization in Madagascar started in 1913 when seven medical students founded it after being influenced by Ravelojaona, a minister, who argued that the people of Malagasy should follow the Japanese model of accepting modernism without repudiating their culture. This was considered heretical teaching by the French and they tracked down the members of the secret society and brutally suppressed the organization, killing some and locking other members in jail. In Ghana, Mensah Sarbah, the major cultural nationalist, exhorted the Ghanaian people in these words:

> it is better to be called by one's own name than to be known by a foreign one, that it is possible to acquire Western learning and be expert in scientific attainments without neglecting one's mother-tongue, that the African's dress had a closer resemblance to the garb of the Grecian and Roman ... and should not be thrown aside, even if one wears European dress during business hours – Japan having since shown it is possible to retain one's national costume and yet excel in wisdom and knowledge.
>
> (Sarbah 1968, pp. xvii–viii)

Sarbah had identified a key problem in dealing with the European invasions. It was not that their presence changed the external institutions of government but that they brought a different culture. In fact, Sarbah's concern was that the British might change the culture of the people, the thinking of the people, not just their political institutions.

By 1913 Onyango Dande in Kenya had sought to overturn the British rule in that country. Two young people, a female priestess named Siofume and a young man named Kiamba, had risen against the British in 1911; thus two years later when Dande started his movement he drew on the inspiration from the earlier resistance leaders. The Giriama of Kenya revolted against the British in 1914 and the Acholi in Uganda refused to be forced into labor. The African refusal to succumb to forced labor led the British further into the process of bringing Indians to work in East Africa.

## The swindling of land in Nyasaland, 1885–1893

John Chilembwe arose in Nyasaland just in time to fight against the crimes committed against his people by the British. In 1890, Chilembwe became a student at the Church of Scotland mission in Blantyre. It was at the school that he first observed how the British systematically robbed the African of his culture. They forced him to take a European name, to wear European clothes, and to speak English only. Bright and energetic, the young Chilembwe soaked up as much information as he could. Soon he was converted to the Baptist faith by Joseph Booth, a British Baptist missionary. Chilembwe became his assistant from 1892 until 1895. Booth appeared to be a better-quality white person than others Chilembwe had seen. Booth worked for a number of churches and had no denominational loyalty. Chilembwe became adamant that the British had to leave the country. He was a person of great African pride and found ways to connect himself to other Africans. In 1897, Booth took Chilembwe to the United States, where a Baptist church sponsored him at an African American college. At Virginia Union College he seems to have come into contact with contemporary African American political and social thinking. When he returned to Nyasaland in 1900 as an ordained Baptist minister he founded the Providence Industrial Mission, which developed into seven schools. Before and during his absence from the country the British missionaries and commercial traders were quickly swindling land from the kings of Nyasa.

White emissaries of Cecil John Rhodes, whose trust now supports the Rhodes scholarship and for whom Rhodesia was named, made twenty-three separate treaties with kings and leaders of Nyasaland. These treaties were supposedly negotiated between the African Lakes Company and the various kings of Nyasaland. Some of these treaties speak for themselves as nothing but shyster papers with farcical attempts to sound as if real negotiations had occurred. These twenty-three separate "treaties" were "negotiated" between April 21, 1885, and August 24, 1885 by an African Lakes team led by John W. Moir and his traveling witnesses, William Harkness and Alexander Carnegie Ross. They traveled from the Lower Shire valley, beginning on April 21, and moved slowly northward to Karonga, arriving on July 16, selecting and acquiring the finest, most fertile, most beautiful, mineral-laden, and commercially accessible lands in the country, before doubling back south to carefully check their work and to identify lands that they had missed on the way north. On this trip they chose holdings in Chiradzulu, Ndirande, and Soche. This team of white swindlers even managed to get to Likoma and Chisamula Islands in Lake Malawi, arriving there on July 30, 1885.

Moir, who took the African name of Mandala for negotiating purposes, claimed to have sealed contracts with all of the important kings in the region, giving him and his company, and the Rhodes interests, complete control over most of the arable land in the country of Nyasaland. The seething anger among the Africans when they learned the full extent of the swindle built increasingly until it began to boil in the conversations, activities, and attitudes of the masses of people. The old kings could not explain the swindle and the missionaries, who had supported the white traders, had no scriptural justification for what had happened. As Africans learned to read English they were shocked at what they were told the treaties meant. Below is one of the original treaties advanced by Moir to the African kings. This is the verbatim text of Treaty Number I, "negotiated" with Chief Ramakukan of the Makololo people.

Translation of Treaty No. 1
JOHN W. MOIR – called here Mandala – Manager of the African Lakes Company, Limited, and Ramakukan, head chief of the Makololo. We have met together on the 21st day of the month of April, 1885, on board the steamer "Lady Nyassa," at Tsape, on the River Shire, that we may discuss those things of mutual benefit. Having considered well, we have finished what we have arranged written here as follows:–
First – Ramakukan declares he desires the Company to continue trading. That things may continue as they are, Ramakukan agrees and

consents to Kapene's giving the country of Mandala, to be the country of the Company, that is, all the country between the two streams, Naperi and Mudi. Ramakukan also delivers over all the road from Katunga's to Mandala and Blantyre, and thence to Matope on the Upper Shire, and the country on the sides of the road; on one side twenty fathoms, and on the other side twenty fathoms. At the same time he also delivers over one square mile of land at Matope, near the village of Chigaru, on the Upper Shire.

Second – Ramakukan consents that the other Chiefs shall give their countries to the Company, and he now consents to the Treaties which shall be made in this month.

Third – In giving over the country he gives also, with his whole heart, all rights of government over the country which is now described.

Fourth – Ramakukan promises to be a good friend of Mandala, and of the Company, and to help them with all his power, and their travelers, and all their trade, and all their carriage; and he promises to punish, or to deliver up any of his people, who steal or do wrong otherwise.

Fifth – Ramakukan promises to enter into Treaty with no other European without the written consent of the Company.

Sixth – If the employees of the Company require people, Ramakukan will send people for carriage or work.

Seventh – The African Lakes Company have power to trade with all the Makololo and all their subjects.

Eighth – Because of the agreements which we have written, and because of all the rights Ramakukan has given to the Company, I John W. Moir, give him one good percussion gun, one piece cloth, one long knife, and one clasp knife. I, Ramakukan, have received all these.

Ninth – The African Lakes Company shall give to Ramakukan two pieces of cloth (each piece eight fathoms) every month, if he shall fulfil all that has been written, and if he will remain the good friend of the Company.

Tenth – The African Lakes Company have all the power to levy tolls on travelers passing on their road. Ramakukan cannot write and has put his mark on board the steamer in presence of the following witnesses:–

William Harkess, engineer of the Company; David, carpenter of the Company; Kampata, eldest son of Ramakukan, and Tom Faulkner.

At the end of the treaty was a space for signatures. John W. Moir signed for the African Lakes Company, an agent of the Rhodes–British team, and King Ramakukan made his X mark. Witnesses included three white men and Kampata, the son of the king.

Once this treaty had been signed, the parsimonious Scottish Moir made a Treaty Number 2 on the very next day, April 22, 1885, with a payment to Chief Mulilima of one piece of cloth and a pair of shoes, and to his younger brother Massea, he gave four fathoms of cloth. Up and down the country he went, delivering a piece of cloth here and there until he ran out and then had nothing to give the African kings but odd scraps. Twenty-three such treaties were executed.

The Cecil Rhodes–British government team of Sir Harry H. Johnston (Her Majesty's Commissioner), Alfred Sharpe (Solicitor of the Supreme Court of Westminster), Henry E. Scott (Medical Missionary–Church of Scotland Mission Domasi), John Buchanan (Her Majesty's Acting Consul), H. C. Marshall (elephant hunter and policeman at Chiromo), B. L. Sclater (Lieutenant RN), Lt. Commander Henry T. Keane (CO *HMS Herald*), Allan Simpson (merchant), Cecil Maguire (Captain, 2nd HC Lancers), and a number of lesser characters, went up and down the country choosing more and more land. From September 30, 1890, to July 12, 1893, they forced treaties and deeds of cession from all major chiefs in the Protectorate, which, in the meantime, had undergone a change in name to British Central Africa. This exercise formalized the earlier settler land swindle and put the full power and authority of the imperial British government behind all land acquisition and opened doors for even more demands for land in the future. Nothing had ever been so offensive to African communities as the unbridled greed that they found in the European's character.

Many of the treaties included an annual tax to be computed at the rate of 6 shillings per house, or the value of 6 shillings in foodstuffs or marketable products. They also claimed all mineral and mining rights within the territories and dictated crops, obligations, and methods of agriculture.

The Nyasaland/British Central Africa land swindle had far-reaching impact in that the forced labor demands made upon the rightful landowners, or guardians as the Africans would say, set the stage for unrest in 1911–12, the Chilembwe Uprising of 1915, unrest in 1953 and 1958–59 and the eventual ousting of Britain from its Central African territories. It is impossible to view the treaties any other way but as an unscrupulous, onerous, obscene greediness, reducing kings and their people to groveling, subservient slaves.

It was in this context that John Chilembwe, who had traveled outside the country and returned, saw himself as one of the chosen deliverers of his people. Thus, in 1915 Chilembwe organized and led a revolt against British rule. This revolt came during World War I, in protest against Malawians being conscripted in the British Army and the treatment of workers on plantations. In this same year the British had already been fighting the Germans in northern Nyasaland. The revolt began on January 23, 1915, and ended with the death of Chilembwe on February 4, 1915.

## The spiritual element in resistance

Many of the resistance movements were led by spiritual leaders because they saw the presence of whites in their country as an indication that the deities and sacred ancestors had been angered. Such signs of violation required spiritual attention. There needed to be sacrifice in order to remove the oppressive whites from the land. Spiritual leaders also had the ability to use psychological motivation to mobilize their followers against the invading forces. Much like the leaders of modern wars who insist that their forces are "invincible," or as many modern presidents of the United States who have faced war repeated to their troops and people, *ad infinitum*, "We are the strongest nation on the face of the earth," "We will not be deterred in our objectives," "We are going to kick butt," and "Our troops are the best prepared in the world." These statements were usually made to inspire and motivate the soldiers to risk their lives for their objectives. Needless to say, many of these soldiers were killed and their invincibility proved to be nothing more than the rhetoric of war. In the same way, the spiritual leaders of Africa who saw the danger of the European invasions told their people that if they went to war against the enemies of the nation, they, too, would win because the oil, water, or millet given to them by the spiritual leader would protect them from death. Of course, men and women died who faced the bullets that were fired from the European guns, as men and women have died in all wars, even those men and women whose leaders told them that they were invincible. Yet it is the brilliance of the spiritual leaders as motivators and fearless generals of war, willing in almost all cases to place themselves at the front of the lines of those who challenged the guns of the Europeans with low-technology weapons, that must be applauded in the struggle against oppression. They believed in their cause and were willing to die to prove that they were right. Their children have reaped the benefit of their sacrifice and they have placed their names in the ancestral books as brave and courageous men and women who knew that oppression was inhuman.

## Multiple strategies against European invasion

Adu Boahen, one of the most important African historians, claimed that rebellions, revolts, and insurrections against the Europeans were just one collective method of assault against the invasion. For him, these popular expressions of resistance were coupled with other forms of struggle against domination. He writes:

> Another strategy often adopted was migration or flight across international boundaries. This strategy was particularly popular among the Africans in the French, Belgian, German, and Portuguese colonies, mainly because of rampant forced labor, oppressive direct taxation, compulsory cultivation of crops, and in the case of the French colonies, the *indigenat*, that is, the arbitrary and rough-and-ready way of administering justice and the use of corporal punishment.
>
> (Boahen 1987, p. 66)

This meant that large numbers of people left one country for another if they felt overwhelmed by the oppressive conditions. They would soon discover that leaving Ivory Coast for Ghana or Northern Rhodesia (Zambia) for Southern Rhodesia (Zimbabwe) did not resolve their problems, because they would have to fight racism, discrimination, and brutality in all of the countries. Adu Boahen says that "50,000 Africans living in the Zambesi valley escaped into Southern Rhodesia and Nyasaland between 1895 and 1907. The Ovambo and the Bakongo from Angola, and the Shona and Chewa from Mozambique, slipped across the borders to Nyasaland to join their kinsmen there" (Boahen 1987, p. 66). Other Africans moved into the inaccessible parts of their country, outside the range of the white officials who had invaded. This practice was especially followed in the mountainous and forested regions of Congo and the Gambo region of southern Angola.

A culture of maroon societies had been established in the Americas during the enslavement period, and in Africa, during the 150-year African–European continental war, people used the same technique to avoid whites. Adu Boahen calls the leaders of these communities "commando leaders" (1987, p. 67), which is a reasonable term for those who led these communities. In Brazil, during the period of enslavement, the most famous leaders of the quilombos, Zumba Ganga and Zumbi, were called quilombo leaders. These terms, "commando" and "quilombo leader," speak to the martial knowledge and ability of these leaders. In addition to the revolts that seemed to occur everywhere you had oppressive conditions or the migrations that happened when people decided to place themselves outside of the authority of the Europeans, there was a passive resistance carried out by the masses of people who remained in the territories under white control. Much like the multiple levels of resistance one finds in the history of the Americas, on the African continent people mastered the technique of creating havoc for the whites. One could create many problems for whites by absenteeism from work or school, sabotaging equipment used for production, or simply rejecting any form of white institution or process that would contradict the traditional institutions. There was no way that the whites could convince the hard-core nationalists that their language was better than African language, that their food was better than African cuisine, that their dress and clothes were better than the African's and so forth. They were often adamant in their resistance to the imposition of white institutions. Nothing could please the African nationalists more than having the masses of people resist sending their children to European schools and churches. Yet this is precisely what the whites insisted on doing in order to undermine the traditional authorities. To the degree that the whites succeeded, they were able to transmit their values to the African society. In some cases, the results was deep confusion and frustration on the part of the African. One must make a distinction between the nationalists-traditionalists, rural folk, and the urban elites.

One way that the urban elite was able to advance in the colonial system was to adopt as quickly as possible the manner and behavior of the whites. They looked down on those who retained African languages and failed to learn European languages. For some of them, their names, manner of dress, religion, and houses were considered "inferior" to the whites. At the moment Africans accepted white society as "superior" to their own societies the only thing that was left for them was to make colonialism reasonable and comfortable. They wanted the whites to permit them to participate in their economic and educational institutions, they wanted to have the freedom to change churches at will as the whites had, and they wanted to be represented on the various councils and legislatures whites had created in the colonies. This was the cultural web that entrapped some Africans.

The elite used every means at their disposal to bring about reforms. They wrote columns in newspapers, novels, poetry, broadsides, plays, and pamphlets against the discrimination in the system. The Western-educated elite soon became more popular in the cities than the traditional elites. They were knowledgeable of the ways of the whites and also had access to the new technologies. Adu Boahen writes:

> Between 1890 and 1919 about ten newspapers were founded in Ghana alone, either in Accra or in Cape Coast, among which were the *Gold Coast Aborigines* (1898), the *Gold Coast Free Press* (1899), and the *Gold Coast Leader* (1902). Five were founded in Nigeria: the *Lagos Standard* (1895), the *Lagos Weekly Record* (1891), the *Nigerian Chronicle* (1908), the *Nigerian Pioneer* (1914), and the *Nigerian Times* (1910). T. Jabavu founded the first African newspaper, *Imvozaba Ntsundu* (Native Opinion), printed in both English and Xhosa; and by 1915, there were five major newspapers there. In Uganda the *Ebifa Mu Uganda* was founded in 1907.
>
> (Boahen 1987, p. 68)

All the African newspapers attacked colonialism. There was not one African newspaper that felt any good could come out of the European occupation. During this period Africans throughout the continent were reenergizing writing systems, inventing and sustaining symbolic communications created by their ancestors as a way to express truly African ideas.

## African writing systems

Saki Mafundikwa, writing in the book *African Alphabets*, makes this argument:

> If all writing is information storage, then all writing is of equal value. Each society stores information essential to its survival, the information which enables it to function efficiently. There is in fact no difference between prehistoric rock paintings, memory aids (mnemonic devices), wintercounts, tallies, knotted cords, pictographic, syllabic and consonantal scripts, or the alphabet.
>
> (Mafundikwa 2000, p. 3)

The author goes further to say:

> There are no primitive scripts, no forerunners of writing, no transitional scripts as such (terms frequently used in books dealing with the history of writing), but only societies at a particular level of economic and social development using certain forms of information storage. If a form of information storage fulfills its purpose as far as a particular society is concerned then it is (for this particular society) "proper" writing.
>
> (Mafundikwa 2000, p. 3)

Africans have produced many scripts, including of course the Mdw Ntr, the oldest writing known to humans. But in addition to this system, Africans have been inventing writing for a long time. A list of writing systems indicates that the African continent has been one of the most prodigious producers of script. Here is a list of African scripts: Vai, Mende, Loma, Kpelle, Bassa, Gola, Mandinka, Bamana, Wolof, Gerze, Fula, Bete, Nsibidi, Guro, Bamun, Bagam, Ibibio-Efik, Yoruba, and the Djuka syllabary brought by Africans to Surinam in South America. There is also a variation of Nsibidi found in Cuba (*Anaforuana*) and Haiti (*Veve*).

One of the most dramatic invention stories is that of King Njoya. He was only 19 when he assumed the throne of the Bamun kingdom. King Ibrahim Njoya, who was king of the Bamun for over forty years, was a visionary genius. Njoya wanted to have an independent system of writing, not connected to the Arabic script or the Roman script, in order to create a secret court language. Apparently Njoya was inspired by a dream, in which he was directed to draw a man's hand on a board and then to wash off his drawing and drink the water. He then asked some of his most knowledgeable subjects to draw different objects and name them. When he got the results he experimented until he had completed a writing system comprised of 466 pictographic and ideographic symbols. Afterward he established a series of schools, referred to as "book houses," throughout the Bamun kingdom, at which hundreds of his subjects learned to read and write. Court officials made collections of literature, volumes of history, customs and traditions, a book of rules of conduct for the court, a pharmacopia, and a collection of maps of the kingdom. Njoya then created a library and ethnographic collection at his palace and encouraged the development of traditional weaving

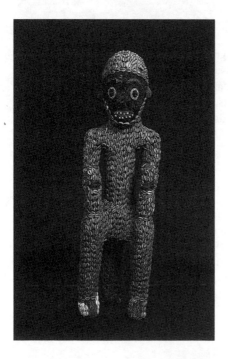

*Figure 12.2* Bamun ancestral figure, Cameroons
© Molefi Kete Asante

and dyeing under his patronage. An original intellect and a brilliant scholar, Njoya was one of the most creative minds of Africa in the nineteenth and twentieth centuries. The French despised the creations of Njoya and in an attempt to destroy his schools and achievements deposed him in 1931 and exiled him to Yaounde, where he died a humiliated and broken man two years later. Nevertheless, he had become an icon in the history of Africa. Below are some typical examples of African scripts.

## The Vai syllabary (Liberia)

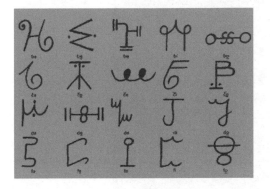

## The Mende syllabary (Sierra Leone)

This was devised around 1920 by Kisimi Kamala.

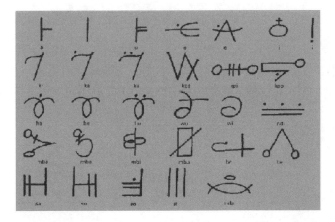

## The Bamana "Ma-sa-ba" syllabary (Mali)

A syllabary devised by Woyo Couloubayi in the Kaarta region of Mali in 1930.

## The Bamun (Sha-Mon) syllabary (Cameroon)

## The Nsibidi (Nsibiri) syllabary (Nigeria and Cameroon)

This script was invented by the Ejagham people of southeastern Nigeria and southwestern Cameroon.

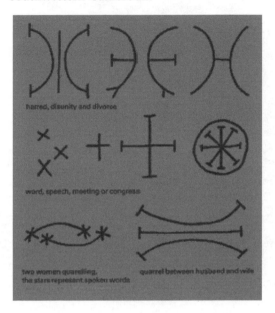

## *Nsibidi variation in the Americas*: the Anaforuana script of Cuba

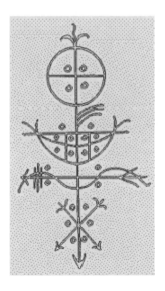

## The Somali syllabary (Somalia)

Developed by Isman Yusuf, son of the Somali Sultan Yusuf Ali, around 1930.

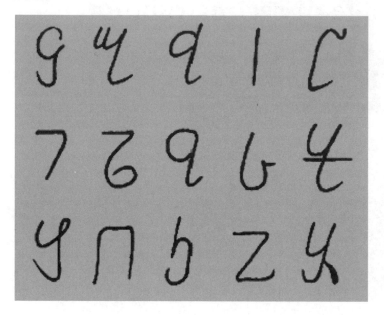

## Part VI

# The age of reconstruction

"We are the living and the dead. Let us go forth and make. Let us open a path." (Miriam Makeba)

# 13 Africa regains consciousness in a Pan-African explosion

Africa regained its political feet during the struggle for independence in the twentieth century. More than any other century in the last 500 years, the twentieth must be claimed as the century of African freedom. An explosion of freedom movements took place on and off the African continent that had direct influence on the nature of African development. This was a period when Africans took back the discussion about the future of the African continent, created world organizations to mobilize the African people, and launched indigenous groups to fight for independence from colonial repression and oppression. The giant cat was out of the bag and it would never be captured and placed in such a position again. The attendants of this freedom era were Henry Sylvester Williams, W. E. B. DuBois, Marcus Garvey, Anna Julia Cooper, Kwame Nkrumah, George Padmore, Nnamdi Azikiwe, Julius Nyerere, Haile Selassie, Gamel A. Nasser, Sekou Toure, Léopold Senghor, Patrice Lumumba, Jomo Kenyatta, Nelson Mandela, Abdoulaye Wade, Marcelinos dos Santos, Samora Machel, Robert Mugabe, Eduardo Mondlane, and scores of others. They represent Africa in all of its glory, from the discourse on freedom to the vision for a United States of Africa. To begin with, Africa needed an ideology that would drive the debate and lead to a common view of the future. This was provided by the Pan-African Congresses. Although they had their own internal and ideological issues, they were seen as catalysts. But they must be seen alongside the powerful movement of Marcus Garvey called the Universal Negro Improvement Association and African Communities League.

## The Pan-African Movement

The term "Pan-Africanism" has come to mean the unity of Africans and the elimination of white racial domination from the continent of Africa. It was this movement that generated the political discussion around African unity for most of the twentieth century. In fact, the Pan-African Congresses of the twentieth century were begun in the African Diaspora, thereby molding the discourse on Pan-Africanism in the context of world Africanity. All discussions of African unity must hark back to the days when Africans in the Caribbean and the Americas called for solidarity between all African peoples.

Coming as it did on the heels of the Berlin Conference the Pan-African Movement was rapid and determined, although the first conference lacked clarity of purpose. Henry Sylvester Williams, a Trinidadian barrister practicing in London, called the Pan-African Conference in London in 1900. Often this congress is not thought of properly as one of the major congresses because of several factors. The opening address was given by an Englishman, the bishop of London, who was considered liberal in the context of the England of the day and who wanted to see Africans educated enough to be able to have a sense of responsibility that would lead to self-government. In a word, the bishop believed that Africans were not yet ready, owing to lack of intelligence, civilization, or culture, to run governments. The conference had another problem that would be questioned by some of the more progressive forces in the African world. The thirty or so delegates petitioned Queen Victoria through the British government to look into the treatment of Africans in South Africa and Rhodesia.

DuBois led the African American delegation, which included a number of women, notably Anna Jones, who was on the Executive Committee, and Anna Julia Cooper. One of the leaders who drafted the petition to Queen Victoria was Anna Julia Cooper, the African woman from America who received a doctorate from the Sorbonne. The memorial to Queen Victoria of England included the following acts of injustice in Africa perpetrated by whites against the people:

1. The degrading and illegal compound system of labor in vogue in Kimberley and Rhodesia.
2. The so-called indenture, i.e., legalized bondage of African men and women and children to white colonists.
3. The system of compulsory labor in public works.
4. The "pass" or docket system used for people of color.
5. Local by-laws tending to segregate and degrade Africans such as the curfew; the denial to Africans of the use of footpaths; and the use of separate public conveyances.
6. Difficulties in acquiring real property.
7. Difficulties in obtaining the franchise.

In response to the memorial to Queen Victoria, her respondent wrote the following to Henry Sylvester Williams, the General Secretary for the Conference:

> Sir. I am directed by My Secretary Chamberlain to state that he has received the Queen's commands to inform you that the Memorial of the Pan-African Conference requesting the situation of the native races in South Africa, has been laid before Her Majesty, and that she was graciously pleased to command him to return an answer to it on behalf of her government. Mr. Chamberlain accordingly desires to assure the members of the Pan-African Conference that, it settling the lines on which the administration of the conquered territories is to be conducted; Her Majesty's Government will not overlook the interests and welfare of the native races.

Of course, Africans were not convinced that Queen Victoria would do anything toward alleviating the conditions of Africans in the "conquered territories." If anything, the oppression in those territories was intensified for the next few years. By the end of the First World War the map of Africa had been changed again according to the European nations that won or lost in the war. Germany had been the big loser and Britain had become the big winner.

William Edward B. DuBois, the African American scholar, attended the first conference and was impressed that Henry Sylvester Williams had thought of the idea of a meeting that would bring together important Africans from around the world. It would take nineteen years before another congress would be called. This time it would be called by DuBois himself. He had taken notes at the conference of 1900 and was in ascendance as the leading intellectual of African descent in his day. He had received a PhD in history from Harvard after studying at Berlin and Fisk. His dissertation on the suppression of the slave trade had been accepted and published by Harvard.

## The First Pan-African Congress

The First Pan-African Congress, directed by W. E. B. DuBois, was held in Paris. It represented Africa in a small way but was mainly a conference of Diasporan Africans, since of the fifty-seven delegates from fifteen countries only twelve delegates came from nine African countries. Sixteen came from the United States and twenty-one came from the Caribbean. Most of the delegates already resided in France because the United States and all the colonial nations refused to issue visas to Africans coming to the conference. The *New York Evening Globe*, February 22, 1919, described it as "the first assembly of the kind in history, and has for its object the drafting of an appeal to the Peace Conference to give the Negro race of Africa a chance to develop unhindered by other races."

Despite the difficulties experienced by the delegates; they were committed to showing the Allied Forces in the Peace Conference with the defeated Germans that Africans were ready and willing to take their territories back. This caused considerable distress on the part of the colonial powers. They had just defeated the Germans in the war and had no intention of giving any power to Africans.

The Congress delegates specifically asked that the German colonies be turned over to an international organization instead of being handled by the various colonial powers. The resolutions of the Congress said in part:

(a) That the Allied and Associated Powers establish a code of law for the international protection of the natives of Africa, similar to the proposed international code for labour.
(b) That the League of Nations establish a permanent Bureau charged with the special duty of over-seeing the application of these laws to the political, social, and economic welfare of the natives.

(c) The Negroes of the world demand that hereafter the natives of Africa and the peoples of African descent be governed according to the following principles:

1. The land and its natural resources shall be held in trust for the natives and at all times they shall have effective ownership of as much land as they can profitably develop.

2. Capital: The investment of capital and granting of concessions shall be so regulated as to prevent the exploitation of the natives and the exhaustion of the natural wealth of the country. Concessions shall always be limited in time and subject to State control. The growing social needs of the natives must be regarded and the profits taxed for social and material benefit of the natives.

3. Labor: Slavery and corporal punishment shall be abolished and forced labour except in punishment for crime; and the general conditions of labour shall be prescribed and regulated by the State.

4. Education: It shall be the right of every native child to learn to read and write his own language, and the language of the trustee nation, at public expense, and to be given technical instruction in some branch of industry. The State shall also educate as large a number of natives as possible in higher technical instruction in some branch of industry. The State shall also educate as large a number of natives as possible in higher technical and cultural training and maintain a corps of native teachers ...

5. The State: The natives of Africa must have the right to participate in the Government as far as their development permits in conformity with the principle that the Government exists for the natives, and not the natives for the Government. They shall at once be allowed to participate in local and tribal government according to ancient usage, and this participation shall gradually extend, as education and experience proceeds, to the higher offices of State, to the end that, in time, Africa be ruled by consent of the Africans ... Whenever it is proven that African natives are not receiving just treatment at the hands of any State or that any State deliberately excludes its civilized citizens or subjects of Negro descent from its body politic and cultural, it shall be the duty of the League of Nations to bring the matter to the civilized World.

The *New York Herald* of February 24, 1919, wrote:

There is nothing unreasonable in the programme, drafted at the Pan-African Congress which was held in Paris last week. It calls upon the Allied and Associated Powers to draw up an international code of law for the protection of the nations of Africa, and to create, as a section of the League of Nations, a permanent bureau to ensure observance of such laws and thus further the racial, political, and economic interests of the natives.

## Second Pan-African Congress

A Second Pan-African Congress was called for and DuBois went to work on it. The idea of Pan-Africa having been thus established, he wanted to build a true movement. This was his second conference, but the third one if we take the 1900 Congress into consideration. DuBois was concerned mainly with his own congresses and when he counted the congresses rarely spoke of the first one in the same breath. Nevertheless by the conference of 1921, DuBois' second, the idea had fully matured. DuBois arranged for a Congress to meet in London, Brussels, and Paris, in August and September 1921. Of the 113 delegates to this Congress, forty-one were from Africa, thirty-five from the United States, twenty-four represented Africans from the Americas living in Europe, and seven were from the West Indies. Thus the African representation was stronger than it had ever been. They came for the most part, but not in all cases, as individuals, and more seldom as the representatives of organizations or of groups. But DuBois believed that the movement was beginning to feel the impact of several other world actions. First of all, there was the determination on the part of elements in Britain, Belgium, and elsewhere to intensify the exploitation of their African colonies to recover money lost in the war. They did not want to see any activities that seemed political on the part of Africans. Then, too, there was the presence of Marcus Garvey, one of the most powerful anti-European orators of his day, an organizer and race-first agitator, who led a people's movement rather than a movement of intellectuals. Garvey's rhetoric frightened not only whites, but many Africans also, who were determined to wring from the whites certain concessions. He was able to galvanize the masses in ways that made the congresses of DuBois seem like elite affairs of the mind and not like the general movement DuBois had said he wanted for the Pan-African Movement. DuBois would claim that Garvey used intemperate propaganda and therefore introduced fear into the political equation.

The London meetings of the Congress were held in Central Hall, opposite Westminster Abbey, August 28 and 29, 1921. The Paris meetings were held on August 31 and September 1 and 2. The meetings were welcomed warmly to Belgium at the Palais Mondial, but opposition arose because some politicians saw it as part of the Garvey Movement. This was proof enough for some Africans that whites had no intention of seeing Africans free. If Belgians were so confounded by the meeting, thinking it was Garvey's group, then they knew little about the DuBois group nor cared to know. In fact, the Brussels *Neptune* wrote, on June 14:

> Announcement has been made ... of a Pan-African Congress organized at the instigation of the National Association for the Advancement of Colored People of New York. It is interesting to note that this association is directed by personages who it is said in the United States have received remuneration from Moscow (Bolsheviki). The association has already organized its propaganda in the lower Congo, and we must not be astonished if some day it causes grave difficulties in the Negro village of Kinshasa, composed of all the ne'er-do-wells of the various tribes of the Colony, aside from some hundreds of labourers.

The Congress in Belgium was mostly whites. It is usually not mentioned as one of the significant meetings. Nevertheless, resolutions which were passed unanimously in London criticized the practices of Belgium. This aroused bitter opposition in the political circles of Brussels, and an attempt was made to substitute an innocuous statement concerning good will and investigation which Blaise Diagne, serving the interest of Europe rather than Africa, declared adopted in the face of a clear majority in opposition.

At the Paris meeting the original London resolutions, with some minor corrections, were adopted. They were in part:

> To the World: The absolute equality of races, physical, political, and social, is the founding stone of world and human advancement. No one denies great differences of gift, capacity, and attainment among individuals of all races, but the voice of Science, Religion, and practical Politics is one in denying the God-appointed existence of super-races, or of races, naturally and inevitably and eternally inferior.
>
> That in the vast range of time, one group should in its industrial technique, or social organization, or spiritual vision, lag a few hundred years behind another, or forge fitfully ahead, or come to differ decidedly in thought, deed and ideal, is proof of the essential richness and variety of human nature, rather than proof of the co-existence of demigods and apes in human form. The doctrine of racial equality does not interfere with individual liberty: rather it fulfils it. And of all the various criteria of which masses of men have in the past been prejudged and classified, that of the colour of the skin and texture of the hair is surely the most adventitious and idiotic ...
>
> 1.  The recognition of civilized men as civilized despite their race or colour.
> 2.  Local self-government for backward groups, deliberately rising as experience and knowledge grow to complete self-government under the limitation of a self-governed world.
> 3.  Education in self-knowledge, in scientific truth, and in industrial technique, undivorced from the art of beauty.
> 4.  Freedom in their own religion and social customs and with the right to be different and nonconformist.
> 5.  Co-operation with the rest of the world in government, industry, and art on the bases of Justice, Freedom, and Peace.
> 6.  The return to Negroes of their land and its natural fruits, and defence against the unrestrained greed of invested capital.
> 7.  The establishment under the League of Nations of an international institution for study of the Negro problems.
> 8.  The establishment of an international section of the Labour Bureau of the League of Nations, charged with the protection of native labour.

DuBois ended the resolutions with the following words, "In some such words and thoughts as these we seek to express our will and ideal, and the end of our untiring effort. To our aid, we call all men of the earth who love justice and mercy. Out of the depths we have cried unto the deaf and dumb masters of the world. Out of the depths we cry to our own sleeping souls. The answer is written in the stars."

The resolutions of this 1921 Pan-African Congress went farther than the previous ones and established the concept in the mind of the world. Two civil rights organizations had been founded, the National Association for the Advancement of Colored People, and the African National Congress, that would underscore the Pan-African Movement. One had been founded in the United States and the other in South Africa.

## The Third Pan-African Congress

The Third Pan-African Congress was held in London and Lisbon. DuBois had a dispute with the Paris Secretariat of the Pan-African Movement and went ahead with a conference despite the fact that Paris wanted it delayed. The meeting was held in London and then in Lisbon in 1923. The Congress did not have proper publicity or preparation and so the London session was small and unremarked as a conference. However, the meeting of the Congress in Lisbon was more successful. Eleven countries were represented, mainly from Portuguese Africa. The Liga Africana (a great association of Africans in the Portuguese-controlled territories with headquarters in Lisbon) was in charge. It was a federation of all the indigenous associations scattered throughout the five provinces of Portuguese-controlled Africa.

The following demands were made in the name of Africans at the Lisbon meeting:

1. A voice in their own government.
2. The right of access to the land and its resources.
3. Trial by juries of their peers under established forms of law.
4. Free elementary education for all; broad training in modern industrial technique; and higher training of selected talent.
5. The development of Africa for the benefit of Africans, and not merely for the profit of Europeans.
6. The abolition of the slave trade and of the liquor traffic.
7. World disarmament and the abolition of war; but failing this, and as long as white folk bear arms against black folk, the right of blacks to bear arms in their own defence.
8. The organization of commerce and industry so as to make the main objects of capital and labour the welfare of the many rather than the enriching of the few.

## The Fourth Pan-African Congress

The Fourth Pan-African Congress was held in New York in 1927. Thirteen countries were represented although African representation was small. There were 208 delegates from twenty-two American states and ten foreign countries. Africa was represented by representatives from the Gold Coast,

Sierra Leone, Liberia, and Nigeria. Chief Amoah III of the Gold Coast spoke to the Congress. Among the resolutions were the following points about what Africans needed:

1.  A voice in their own government.
2.  Native rights to the land and its natural resources.
3.  Modern education for all children.
4.  The development of Africa for the Africans and not merely for the profit of Europeans.
5.  The reorganization of commerce and industry so as to make the main object of capital and labour the welfare of the many rather than the enriching of the few.
6.  The treatment of civilized men as civilized despite difference of birth, race, or colour.

Even as much as DuBois tried to keep the movement alive, he realized that the Pan-African Movement had been losing ground since 1921. Marcus Garvey had outmaneuvered the movement by his mass movement, which attracted more than 10 million people as paid members by 1925. DuBois struggled to remedy the decline of the movement by calling a conference in 1929 for Tunis. Elaborate preparations were begun, but then the French government very politely but firmly informed DuBois that the Congress, this Pan-African Congress of Africans, could only take place at Marseilles or any French city, but not in Africa. In addition to this political blow, the Great Depression brought all plans to an end.

## The Fifth Pan-African Conference

The Fifth Pan-African Congress was held in Manchester, England, in 1945. It had been called for by an assembly of African trades union representatives attending a meeting in England. After consultation and correspondence with a number of individuals a Pan-African Federation was organized to sponsor the Congress.

The West African Students Union of London (WASU) was one of the principal groups backing a call for the Congress. These students had been influenced by the Marcus Garvey Movement in the 1920s and believed that it was now necessary for Africans to stand up for themselves. It was no longer reasonable or correct to ask or beg whites for anything; if anything, Africans had to project themselves as capable of handling their own affairs.

The Fifth Pan-African Congress was in many ways the most historic because the figures who assembled went on to make history during the next two decades: DuBois, Padmore, Nkrumah, Amy Ashwood Garvey, Kenyatta – all were outstanding delegates. The Fifth Congress was the spark plug for decolonization in Africa and in the Caribbean. It marked a significant advance in the participation of workers in the Pan-African cause. It demanded an end to colonial rule and an end to racial discrimination. It established the African vanguard against imperialism and for human rights.

The Pan-African Congress manifesto economic demands were keys to a new construction of the international world. By 1945 DuBois was an active 73, and the honorary chair of the meeting. Amy Ashwood, Marcus Garvey's first wife, presided over the first session. However, what was so powerful about the Manchester Congress, coming on the heels of war in Europe, was the fact that a new generation of continental leaders was being trained and readied to take over the continent. The Pan-Africanists from the continent of Africa, including Kwame Nkrumah and Jomo Kenyatta, would take vision of independence to their people with a new fire.

Nkrumah soon became the major voice and organizing spirit of Pan-Africanism. He revered the legendary W. E. B. DuBois; although they differed on some issues he exemplified the African proverb that "a person who pays respect to the great paves the way for his own greatness." It would be Nkrumah, as Botwe-Asamoah (2005) and Poe (2003) understood in their books on Nkrumah, who would become the leading edge for the ideological and philosophical interpretation of the liberation struggle. He would show both organizational ability and intellectual discipline. Botwe-Asamoah writes:

> In 1945, DuBois had invited Nkrumah to the membership of the international committee, which drew up the four resolutions on the colonial question for the United Nations; these resolutions became part of the UN's Charter on the Declaration of Human Rights. Also Kwame Nkrumah and DuBois authored the two declarations at the the Fifth Pan-African Congress.
>
> (Botwe-Asamoah 2005, p. 9)

Poe writes confidently that

> Nkrumah's political currency increased through his association with this historical conference. Nkrumah's ability to organize and articulate the interests of the liberation movement impressed a number of intellectuals and labor organizers, who would come to affect the history of Africa and the world.
>
> (Poe 2003, p. 89)

In the late 1940s and 1950s Nkrumah promoted the idea of an independent West African Federation, seen as the first step toward a United States of Africa. When, in March 1957, he became leader of the newly independent state of Ghana, one of his first ideas was to use his new position to help other Africans transcend the old colonial boundaries and work toward uniting the continent. He convened a Conference of Independent States in 1958, though at that stage there were only eight independent countries in Africa. He also went immediately to the aid of independent Guinea when France victimized it for rejecting membership of the post-colonial African franc zone. Nkrumah and the Guinean leader Sekou Toure agreed on a union of their two countries, which they hoped would prefigure wider African unity. His vision was profound, a worthy successor to the work of DuBois and Garvey, both as a continental and as a student of African liberation.

## The African National Congress

On January 8, 1912, the African National Congress was born in South Africa out of a united effort on the part of Africans in the four distinct regions of the country to protest to the imperial government of Britain against the treatment Africans received at the hands of the whites. Britain refused to hear the delegation that had traveled to London and told them to go back to South Africa and work with the whites. Instead the Africans formed the African National Congress. Originally called the South African Native National Congress until 1923, the organization's first president was John Dube and the poet and author Sol Plaatje and Albert Luthuli, a future Nobel Peace Prize winner, were some of the founders.

A year later the African National Congress sent a delegation to Britain to protest against the Land Act of 1913. Among the delegation were outstanding names like Msane, Dube, Mapikela, Rubusana, and Plaatje. They concluded that they had to prosecute their own cause, and from the inception of the ANC the organization represented traditional and modern elements, mineworkers and farmers, urban and rural people, although women were only made affiliated members in 1931 and full members in 1943.

The creation of the ANC Youth League in 1944 by several young members including Nelson Mandela, Walter Sisulu, and Oliver Tambo suggested that a new, more energetic generation would be committed to a mass action against the white minority regime. Allied with the Natal Indian Congress and the Transvaal Indian Congress in 1947, the African National Congress effectively broadened its base and its opposition to the white government. When the Afrikaner political group voted overwhelmingly for the National Party in 1948 and created a policy called apartheid, it signaled to the ANC that the struggle would be difficult. Africans and Indians were removed from electoral rolls; residence and mobility laws were tightened so that blacks could not participate in political activities. These laws were unfair and unethical and went against all the traditions of the African people since nowhere in the African world had people been restricted because of their race or color.

By June 1952 the ANC had joined with other groups in a defiance campaign against the restrictions. They deliberately violated the laws, following the example of Mahatma Gandhi's passive resistance to the British colonial forces in India. The whites simply passed new laws prohibiting meetings. In a June 1955 Congress of the People, the ANC-led coalition of groups against apartheid adopted the Freedom Charter, the fundamental document of the anti-apartheid struggle. The Freedom Charter was a progressive document calling for equal rights regardless of race. The whites struck at the heart of the movement by arresting 156 members of the ANC in 1956. After they were tried for treason the 156 were acquitted five years later.

The African National Congress became increasingly interested in alliances with Indian and white members and groups who were committed to the same principles. This led to a split, with a faction under the guidance and direction of Robert Sobukwe called the Pan-Africanist Congress.

It is important to understand that the history of the African National Congress is one of campaigning against all the discriminatory practices of apartheid. The group fought the Pass Laws, which required blacks to carry an identity card at all times to justify being in so-called white areas. The first ANC campaign against the Pass Laws was to begin on March 31, 1960. But in the most violent confrontation at the time, the PAC had held peaceful protests on March 21, 1960 and had pre-empted the ANC. The non-violent protesters were attacked by the white government, and sixty-nine people were killed and 180 injured in what was called the Sharpeville massacre. It would prove to be one of the icons of the struggle as Africans reminded each other to "never forget Sharpeville!"

The ANC and PAC were banned from all political activity by the white regime. They went underground to keep their work alive. International opposition to the apartheid regime increased in the 1960s and 1970s. African independence was breaking out all over the continent, African Americans were on the move politically and socially, and the air was pregnant with the prospects for liberation in South Africa. Albert Luthuli, the leader of the ANC, won the Nobel Peace Prize in 1960, a feat that was to be repeated by Nelson Mandela in 1993.

Nelson Rolihlahla Mandela would become the icon of the African National Congress for many years, fueling the resistance with his Masai-like discipline and his brazen attitude toward punishment. Nothing distracted him from the ultimate goal and he could not be persuaded to turn back from victory. He was born in Transkei, South Africa, on July 18,

*Figure 13.1*  Nelson Mandela, 1990
© David Turnley/CORBIS

*Figure 13.2* Mandela's name on a street in Guadeloupe
© Molefi Kete Asante

1918. His father was Chief Henry Mandela of the Tembu. Mandela himself was educated at University College of Fort Hare and the University of Witwatersrand and qualified in law in 1942. He joined the African National Congress in 1944 and was engaged in resistance against the ruling National Party's apartheid policies after 1948.

In a dramatic show of moral leadership the ANC joined with other anti-apartheid groups and adopted the Freedom Charter on June 26, 1956, at a Congress of the People in Kliptown.

### The Freedom Charter

*We, the People of South Africa, declare for all our country and the world to know:*

> that South Africa belongs to all who live in it, black and white, and that no government can justly claim authority unless it is based on the will of all the people;

> that our people have been robbed of their birthright to land, liberty and peace by a form of government founded on injustice and inequality;

> that our country will never be prosperous or free until all our people live in brotherhood, enjoying equal rights and opportunities;

> that only a democratic state, based on the will of all the people, can secure to all their birthright without distinction of colour, race, sex or belief;

> And therefore, we, the people of South Africa, black and white together equals, countrymen and brothers adopt this Freedom Charter;

And we pledge ourselves to strive together, sparing neither strength nor courage, until the democratic changes here set out have been won.

### The People Shall Govern!

Every man and woman shall have the right to vote for and to stand as a candidate for all bodies which make laws;

All people shall be entitled to take part in the administration of the country;

The rights of the people shall be the same, regardless of race, colour or sex;

All bodies of minority rule, advisory boards, councils and authorities shall be replaced by democratic organs of self-government.

### All National Groups Shall Have Equal Rights!

There shall be equal status in the bodies of state, in the courts and in the schools for all national groups and races;

All people shall have equal right to use their own languages, and to develop their own folk culture and customs;

All national groups shall be protected by law against insults to their race and national pride;

The preaching and practice of national, race or colour discrimination and contempt shall be a punishable crime;

All apartheid laws and practices shall be set aside.

### The People Shall Share in the Country's Wealth!

The national wealth of our country, the heritage of South Africans, shall be restored to the people;

The mineral wealth beneath the soil, the banks and monopoly industry shall be transferred to the ownership of the people as a whole;

All other industry and trade shall be controlled to assist the well-being of the people;

All people shall have equal rights to trade where they choose, to manufacture and to enter all trades, crafts and professions.

### The Land Shall Be Shared among Those Who Work It!

Restrictions of land ownership on a racial basis shall be ended, and all the land re-divided amongst those who work it to banish famine and land hunger;

The state shall help the peasants with implements, seed, tractors and dams to save the soil and assist the tillers;

Freedom of movement shall be guaranteed to all who work on the land;

All shall have the right to occupy land wherever they choose;

People shall not be robbed of their cattle, and forced labour and farm prisons shall be abolished.

### All Shall Be Equal before the Law!

No-one shall be imprisoned, deported or restricted without a fair trial; no-one shall be condemned by the order of any Government official;

The courts shall be representative of all the people;

Imprisonment shall be only for serious crimes against the people, and shall aim at re-education, not vengeance;

The police force and army shall be open to all on an equal basis and shall be the helpers and protectors of the people;

All laws which discriminate on grounds of race, colour or belief shall be repealed.

### All Shall Enjoy Equal Human Rights!

The law shall guarantee to all their right to speak, to organise, to meet together, to publish, to preach, to worship and to educate their children;

The privacy of the house from police raids shall be protected by law;

All shall be free to travel without restriction from countryside to town, from province to province, and from South Africa abroad;

Pass Laws, permits and all other laws restricting these freedoms shall be abolished.

### There Shall Be Work and Security!

All who work shall be free to form trade unions, to elect their officers and to make wage agreements with their employers;

The state shall recognise the right and duty of all to work, and to draw full unemployment benefits;

Men and women of all races shall receive equal pay for equal work;

There shall be a forty-hour working week, a national minimum wage, paid annual leave, and sick leave for all workers, and maternity leave on full pay for all working mothers;

Miners, domestic workers, farm workers and civil servants shall have the same rights as all others who work;

Child labour, compound labour, the tot system and contract labour shall be abolished.

### The Doors of Learning and Culture Shall Be Opened!

The government shall discover, develop and encourage national talent for the enhancement of our cultural life;

All the cultural treasures of mankind shall be open to all, by free exchange of books, ideas and contact with other lands;

The aim of education shall be to teach the youth to love their people and their culture, to honour human brotherhood, liberty and peace;

Education shall be free, compulsory, universal and equal for all children; Higher education and technical training shall be opened to all by means of state allowances and scholarships awarded on the basis of merit;

Adult illiteracy shall be ended by a mass state education plan;

Teachers shall have all the rights of other citizens;

The colour bar in cultural life, in sport and in education shall be abolished.

### There Shall Be Houses, Security and Comfort!

All people shall have the right to live where they choose, be decently housed, and to bring up their families in comfort and security;

Unused housing space to be made available to the people;

Rent and prices shall be lowered, food plentiful and no-one shall go hungry;

A preventive health scheme shall be run by the state;

Free medical care and hospitalisation shall be provided for all, with special care for mothers and young children;

Slums shall be demolished, and new suburbs built where all have transport, roads, lighting, playing fields, creches and social centres;

The aged, the orphans, the disabled and the sick shall be cared for by the state;

Rest, leisure and recreation shall be the right of all;

Fenced locations and ghettoes shall be abolished, and laws which break up families shall be repealed.

### There Shall Be Peace and Friendship!

South Africa shall be a fully independent state which respects the rights and sovereignty of all nations;

South Africa shall strive to maintain world peace and the settlement of all international disputes by negotiation – not war;

Peace and friendship amongst all our people shall be secured by upholding the equal rights, opportunities and status of all;

The people of the protectorates Basutoland, Bechuanaland and Swaziland shall be free to decide for themselves their own future;

The right of all peoples of Africa to independence and self-government shall be recognised, and shall be the basis of close co-operation.

Let all people who love their people and their country now say, as we say here:

**THESE FREEDOMS WE WILL FIGHT FOR, SIDE BY SIDE, THROUGHOUT OUR LIVES, UNTIL WE HAVE WON OUR LIBERTY.**

## Umkhonto we Zizwe

When the ANC was banned in 1960 for trying to carry out the Freedom Charter, Nelson Mandela argued for the setting up of a military wing within the ANC. In June 1961, the ANC executive considered his proposal on the use of violence and agreed that those members who wished to involve themselves in Mandela's campaign would not be stopped from doing so by the ANC. After all, the regime's violence against the masses of South Africans had become endemic. The ANC went underground. It was no more visible on the surface as a civil rights or resistance organization, but it kept on doing its work. Once underground the ANC decided that it had to use sabotage to keep the fight against the regime strong. They had to target and sabotage the government's resources and equipment, avoiding bloodshed at all costs. The Umkhonto we Sizwe, literally the Spear of the Nation, had become effectively the military wing of the ANC in 1961. Soon after the forming of the military wing, its first leader, Nelson Mandela, was arrested again in 1962. Several other members of the ANC were arrested as well. On June 12, 1964, eight of the accused, including Mandela, were sentenced to life imprisonment. From 1964 to 1982, Mandela was incarcerated at Robben Island Prison, off Cape Town; thereafter, he was at Pollsmoor Prison, nearby on the mainland. Lots of protests broke out around the world in an effort to end apartheid and the minority regime in South Africa. Winnie Mandela, the wife of the jailed Nelson Mandela, kept his name and story alive in the press and the hearts of the people. She was the visible power inside the country for the ANC during the 1980s, keeping alive the campaign to free her husband. However, Oliver Tambo and the ANC leadership were deeply committed to both armed and political struggle from the outside as well.

During his years in prison, Nelson Mandela's reputation grew steadily. He was widely accepted as the most significant black leader in South Africa and became a potent symbol of resistance as the anti-apartheid movement gathered strength. He consistently refused to compromise his political position to obtain his freedom. Nelson Mandela was released on February 18, 1990. After his release, he plunged himself wholeheartedly into his life's work, striving to attain the goals he and others had set out almost four decades earlier. In 1991, at the first national conference of the ANC held inside South Africa after the organization had been banned in 1960, Mandela was elected president of the ANC, while his lifelong friend and colleague, Oliver Tambo, became the organization's National chairman.

In 1990, F. W. de Klerk unbanned the African National Congress and the Pan-Africanist Congress. In April 1994 the coalition of the South African Communist Party, the Congress of South African Trade Unions, and the ANC won a landslide victory in the general election. Nelson Mandela was appointed the first black president of South Africa.

But the struggle in South Africa had been long and it had not been simply the victory of the ANC. Numerous forces and parties had created an internal situation in the country, obviously driven by the ANC and PAC, that led to the revolutionizing of the masses, particularly the students. Numerous South African leaders emerged as participants in the struggle for transformation.

Bishop Desmond Tutu was one of the most important voices. Combining a Christian zeal with an African reasoning and cultural consciousness, Tutu articulated a new approach to the question of relationships. The term "*ubuntu*," from the Zulu and Xhosa languages, meaning a union of allegiances and relationships, became an operative term for the new country.

Indeed, Tutu was made an archbishop of the Anglican church and remained committed to the ideology of *ubuntu* even though the Truth and Reconciliation Committee which he headed caused lots of controversy in the nation. There were those who believed that the Commission's job was to "black"wash the crimes of the whites against the black masses. They did not think it was a legitimate move for the government of South Africa since so many people had suffered at the hands of apartheid. Nevertheless, Tutu and the Commission were operating on different principles than even those established by the white Christian religion and expounded from the pulpits of South Africa. The Commission took an African view, based on sharing and promoting humanity with and among all; this *ubuntu* was the central moral ethic of the Commission.

Tutu was later to say of *ubuntu*:

> A person with ubuntu is open and available to others, affirming of others, does not feel threatened that others are able and good, for he or she has a proper self-assurance that comes from knowing that he or she belongs in a greater whole and is diminished when others are humiliated or diminished when others are tortured or oppressed.
>
> (Louw 1998)

The Zimbabwean scholar Stanlake Samkange had expressed a similar philosophy, claiming that *ubuntu* was a Bantu philosophy based in the African's response to the environment. In South Africa, largely made up of Bantu-speaking people, *ubuntu* was clearly the most authoritative philosophy of modern times. It emphasized the need for unity or consensus in decision making, as well as the need for a suitably humanitarian ethic to inform those decisions.

Thus, the concept of *ubuntu* speaks of the person and his or her multiple relationships with others, and stresses the importance of ubuntu as a spiritual concept, stating that while the Zulu expression *umuntu ngumuntu ngabantu* ("a person is a person through other persons") may have no moral connotations in the context of European culture, in the African world it suggests that the person one is to become by behaving with humanity is an ancestor worthy of respect or veneration. Those who uphold the principle of *ubuntu* throughout their lives will, in death, achieve a unity with those still living, thus completing the circle of life.

## Mangaliso Robert Sobukwe and the Pan-Africanist Congress

Mangaliso Robert Sobukwe, founder of the Pan-Africanist Congress, was born in Graaff-Reinet in 1924. Most of the young African children who were educated went to missionary schools. Sobukwe attended church mission schools and then the venerable Fort Hare University. It was here that he first showed an interest in politics and became secretary-general of the African National Congress Youth League.

Although the school had white teachers, Sobukwe showed courage in arguing against racism and white supremacy in his classes and in the public places on the campus. When he graduated from Fort Hare, Sobukwe taught at Standerton, near Johannesburg, and at the University of the Witwatersrand.

The events in South Africa sharpened his mind and fired in him an emotion that was so passionate and powerful that he knew that apartheid had to end for his people to gain self-confidence, economic development, and social freedom. He became more politically active, outspoken, and fearless, and soon identified with the members of the African National Congress, who were committed to blacks demonstrating self-determination and self-definition. He became one of the leading African nationalists within the ANC. In 1958 he split with the ANC to form the PAC, an exclusively African organization which he hoped would lead the battle against apartheid. In 1959 he was elected president of the Pan-Africanist Congress. In his view it was not proper for whites or Indians to assume the burden of leadership fighting against white domination; blacks had to take the lead.

On March 21, 1960 – the day of the Sharpeville massacre, when blacks were gunned down in the streets – Mangaliso Robert Sobukwe was arrested on charges of incitement to riot and revolt outside a police station in Soweto. He was sentenced to three years' imprisonment. When that sentence expired, he was detained under a special amendment of the Suppression of Communism Act and held on Robben Island for six years.

On his release in 1969, the white minority regime expressed its fear of him by serving him with a five-year banning order and sent him to Kimberley. Just as soon as the first banning order was completed, a second five-year banning order was served on him in 1974. Nevertheless, Sobukwe used his time wisely and became one of the icons of the resistance movement. He completed an economics degree by correspondence with London University and then qualified as an attorney in 1975.

Mangaliso Robert Sobukwe is acknowledged as one of the sources of inspiration for the Black Consciousness movement, which grew to strength under Bantu Steve Biko in the 1970s. Sobukwe had argued that Africans had to prove to themselves and to the world they could stand on their own feet. To do this, African people had to liberate themselves without the help of non-blacks. Sobukwe was a humble man with a brilliant mind and reverent dignity. When he died in 1978 he left a void in the country but had become a spirit of great power.

## The Sharpeville massacre

One cannot forget that the Sharpeville massacre that electrified the nation happened because young students refused to submit to apartheid's demands and rules. Although it is true that there was opposition to the government's policies by the African National Congress (ANC), there was some resentment and reaction by members of the ANC called "Africanists" who wanted more direct confrontation with apartheid. The ANC had developed a Freedom Charter in 1956 which had committed itself to a South Africa which belonged to all the people. Yet the peaceful march that had occurred in June 1956 led to the arrest of 156 anti-apartheid leaders and the treason trial that lasted until 1961.

The Africanists followed a philosophy that an assertive African nationalism was needed to mobilize the country against racism and apartheid, and they advocated a strategy of mass action (boycotts, strikes, civil disobedience, and non-cooperation).

Although the PAC and the ANC did not agree on policy, they both fought for the rights of the masses; nevertheless, they became increasingly competitive, with each party seeking to attract the masses. The ANC planned a campaign of demonstrations against the Pass Laws to start at the beginning of April 1960. Not wanting to be seen taking a back seat, the PAC announced a similar demonstration, to start ten days earlier, thus hijacking the ANC campaign.

The Pan-Africanist Congress called for "African males in every city and village ... to leave their passes at home, join demonstrations and, if arrested, to offer no bail, no defence, and no fine" (Mazrui 1982, pp. 269–70).

On March 16, 1960, Sobukwe wrote to the commissioner of police, Major General Rademeyer, stating that the PAC would carry out a five-day, non-violent, disciplined, and sustained protest campaign against the Pass Laws, starting on March 21. At a press conference on March 18 Sobukwe further stated: "I have appealed to the African people to make sure that this campaign is conducted in a spirit of absolute non-violence, and I am quite certain they will heed my call. If the other side so desires, we will provide them with an opportunity to demonstrate to the world how brutal they can be."

The white police did not disappoint the militant resisters. They showed the world not only their savage brutality but the will to shoot down innocent people. Sixty-nine people were killed and more than 180 people were injured. It was the single most violent day in the struggle. As could have been expected, the violence on the part of the police electrified the movement as thousands of young people became leaders overnight.

The names of the young leaders of South Africa are illuminated in gold in the minds of the people. With the rise of Black Consciousness came a young man, Bantu Stephen Biko, who was thrust into the international arena by his courage, brilliance, and skill.

## Bantu Stephen Biko and Black Consciousness in South Africa

On December 18, 1946, a child was born in the township of Ginsberg, on the edge of King William's Town, in the Eastern Cape of South Africa. There was every indication from the time he entered school that he would be trouble for the apartheid system of racial oppression in South Africa. He did not know why he should submit to the rules against protest as a school child. He was expelled from his first school, Lovedale, for anti-establishment behavior and was then sent off to a Roman Catholic school in Natal. He graduated from school and entered the University of Natal Medical School, African Section, and showed promise as a future doctor and medical leader. However, at the medical school he became involved with the National Union of South African Students (NUSAS), an organization that was considered progressive. But the union was dominated by white liberal students who refused to view the rights and needs of black students as important. It did not take long for Biko to resign and in 1969 he founded the South African Students' Organisation (SASO), which devoted itself to providing legal aid and medical clinics for disadvantaged black communities. SASO had a profound impact on many young students. Biko had the idea that blacks must help themselves and not depend upon whites, who had abused and violated the rights of blacks, for anything; indeed Biko and his comrades created an organization that took on much of the political philosophy of Robert Sobukwe's Pan-Africanist Congress. However, SASO was limited in its scope and could not deliver the message that Biko had increasingly come to represent of resistance to apartheid.

Thus, in 1972 Bantu Stephen Biko was one of the founders of the Black People's Convention (BPC) working on the social and economic development of black people around Durban. The BPC effectively brought together nearly seventy-five different black consciousness groups and associations, such as the South African Students' Movement (SASM), which played a significant role in the historic uprisings of 1976, the National Association of Youth Organisations (NAYO), and the Black Workers Project (BWP), which supported black workers whose unions were not recognized under the white racist minority regime. Nothing so electrified the young people as the demonstration against apartheid education when the young Hector Petersen, only 13 years old, became a martyr of international resistance to oppression. This demonstration on June 16, 1976, became an uprising by thousands of students demanding an end to a discriminatory education system and specifically to be allowed to be taught in the language of their choice. The march started off peacefully, with students marching from Naledi High School to Orlando Stadium, gathering more students from high schools along the way. When they made it to Matsike High (now Orlando High), police intervened and ordered the children to disperse. They started singing *Nkosi Sikelele* and before they could be dispersed, police opened fire. Young people, alongside some older veterans who protested against the reckless abuse of human rights, marched in the face of tear gas, bullets, batons, singing brave songs that transformed into a phalanx of extraordinary courage and defiance. It was said by one observer that "Comrade Hector Petersen, the young martyr, aged only thirteen, was the first victim of wanton savagery, and when he fell, he lay there in rivulets of blood and tears, while a weeping father hauled home his own daughter's corpse." Mbuyisa Makhuba picked the limp body of Hector from the ground and walked away with it. He was only 18. After that day he went underground and was never heard from again. Sam Nzima, who was a photographer who captured the event, then drove Mbuyisa, Hector, and his sister Antoinette to the Naledi Clinic, where Hector was declared dead. Hundreds of people were killed in Soweto that day as Bantu education was doomed by the courage of the students and the savagery of the killers. They fell, that day, but they let loose a swirling turmoil of tornadic black fury rising to fever pitch. Through their courage and their fight against an evil system people like Hector Petersen and other defiant young warriors lost their lives so that others might be liberated.

This was the arena, the time that made Biko the defiant one, the interpreter of the youth spirit in South Africa. Bantu Stephen Biko was elected as the first president of the BPC and was immediately dismissed from medical school. The young man who had shown so much promise and had been a leader among students and who could have become a buffer between the black masses and the white ruling class chose to throw his lot in with the masses of his people. He started working full time for the Black Community Programme (BCP) in Durban a key unit of the Black Consciousness movement. But because of his activities against apartheid in 1973 the government banned him. Under the "ban" Biko was restricted to his home town of Kings William's Town in the Eastern Cape; he could no longer support the BCEP in Durban but was able to continue working for the BPC: he helped create the Zimele Trust Fund, which assisted political prisoners and their families. (Biko was elected honorary president of the BPC in January 1977.) He had many supporters in the township of Ginsberg and this allowed him to continue his work influencing young people who were not banned. Nevertheless, he was detained, interrogated, and threatened four times between August 1975 and September 1977 under anti-terrorism legislation meant to keep blacks from protesting against oppression.

On August 21, 1977, Biko was detained by the Eastern Cape security police and held in Port Elizabeth. From the Walmer police cell in Port Elizabeth he was transported for further interrogation at the security police headquarters. On September 7 the police reported that Biko sustained a head injury during interrogation, after which he acted strangely and was uncooperative. The white doctors who examined him naked, lying on a mat and manacled to a metal grille in a stark cell, disregarded overt signs of neurological injury. The situation grew more bizarre as the days passed and he was held in isolation. By September 11, 1977, Steve Biko had slipped into a continuous, semi-conscious state and the police physician, believing that Biko was near death, recommended a transfer to hospital. His captors, however, transported Biko nearly 750 miles to Pretoria – a 12-hour journey which he made lying naked in the back of a Land Rover. A few hours later, on September 12, alone and still naked, lying on the floor of a cell in the Pretoria Central Prison, Bantu Stephen Biko, one of South Africa's greatest heroes, died from brain damage. His passion had been cruel, brutal, uncivilized, and representative of the disfigured consciousness of a mad racial domination.

The South African Minister of Justice, James Kruger, initially suggested a cover-up by saying that Biko had died of a hunger strike and that Biko's death "left him cold." The hunger strike story was dropped after the black press and international media pressure, especially from Donald Woods, the editor of East London's *Daily Dispatch*, suggested that it was a cover-up. The inquest revealed that Biko had died of brain damage, but the judge failed to find anyone responsible, ruling rather that Biko had died as a result of injuries sustained during a scuffle with security police while in detention. There was no one to give Biko's side of the story and no policemen could come forth with injuries said to be sustained in the scuffle with Biko.

The circumstances of Biko's death, with deliberate attempts to explain his death on his own actions, created a whirlwind of demonstrations, protests, and denunciations of the white regime. Biko was immediately made a martyr for justice and freedom. He sparked young people of South Africa to call for an end to apartheid; many joined the Black Consciousness Movement, others resorted to becoming members of the ANC's armed wing. There could be no justification for such brutality and violence against people fighting for their rights. The moral position was on the side of blacks as never before and the end to apartheid could be seen clearly in the regime's inability to control its own people from criticizing the system.

The government responded to its death knell in the only way that it knew; it banned a number of individuals (including Donald Woods) and organizations, especially those Black Consciousness groups closely associatiated with Biko. The United Nations Security Council responded by finally imposing an arms embargo against South Africa.

The family of Bantu Stephen Biko sued the state and won a damage settlement in 1979 of R65,000, then equivalent to $25,000. He left a wife and two sons.

The three doctors connected with Biko's case were initially exonerated by the white South African Medical Disciplinary Committee. It was not until a second inquiry in 1985, eight years after Biko's death, that any action was taken against the doctors. The police officers responsible for Biko's death applied for amnesty during the Truth and Reconciliation Commission hearings which sat in Port Elizabeth in 1997. The Biko family did not ask the Commission to make a finding on his death; however, the Commission did report on it with the following account:

> The Commission finds that the death in detention of Mr Bantu Stephen Biko on 12 September 1977 was a gross human rights violation. Magistrate Marthinus Prins found that the members of the SAP were not implicated in his death. The magistrate's finding contributed to the creation of a culture of impunity in the SAP. Despite the inquest finding no person responsible for his death, the Commission finds that, in view of the fact that Biko died in the custody of law enforcement officials, the probabilities are that he died as a result of injuries sustained during his detention.
>
> (*Truth and Reconciliation Commission of South Africa Report*,
> London: Macmillan, March 1999)

## The ANC dominance in South Africa

While the ANC remains the dominant party in South African politics increasingly the leadership recognizes the need to accommodate all elements of the South African population. Thus, the ANC had a coalition with the Inkatha Freedom Party in the 1995 and 1999 elections in the Kwa-Zulu Natal region. However, in the 2004 election the Inkatha Freedom Party joined with another party, the Democratic Alliance. But the ANC was able to gain against all opposition in the election, with Thabo Mbeki receiving overwhelming approval from his nation.

## The Mau Mau revolt in Kenya

The Mau Mau revolt refers to a movement by Kenyans to throw the British settlers off the land. It started in 1952 and lasted until 1960. The movement created a rift in the white community, pitting white settlers against the Home Office in London and British officials in Kenya. The stage was set for the independence of the Kenyans by the Mau Mau revolt.

It is hard to say what the term "Mau Mau" actually meant. In fact, there has always been controversy about its meaning. It is the name of a range of hills in Kenya but may also be an acronym which stands for the KiSwahili "Mzungu Aende Ulaya, Mwafrika Apate Uhuru," which translates to "White man go back home and let Africans get independence."

At the core of the movement were the Kikuyu, with support from members of the Embu and Meru ethnic groups. Most Kikuyu called the group "Muingi/Movement," "Muma wa Uiguano/Unity Oath," or "the KCA", for the Kikuyu Central Association that motivated the insurgency.

There were many reasons for the revolt. One reason was economic but the principal reason was the abusive and discriminatory policies and behavior of the British settlers. The occupation of "stolen" land by the Europeans had become a bitter bone of contention as the people did not feel that the whites ever intended to leave the land that they had gotten with force. The very best land in the highest areas of the country, where the climate is cool compared with the rest of the country, had been taken by the whites. By 1948 more than one million Kikuyu had been forced off their land into an area that was roughly 2000 square miles while 30,000 whites occupied 12,000 square miles! The most fertile agricultural lands were in the hands of the whites.

This was clearly an example of the whites coming with the Bible and exchanging their Bible for the land of the people. When the whites first came, as the adage goes, "the Africans had the land and the whites had the Bible, but after a few years the blacks have the Bible and the whites have the land." This was clearer in Kenya than in any place in West Africa and it represented the intent of the whites to make Africans tenant farmers on their own land. There was no way for blacks to make money or to pay the taxes that the whites imposed without working for whites. In the 1940s settlers demanded more and more labor with more and more days devoted to working the settlers' farms if the Africans wanted to work on their own patch of land. In other words, the whites would not allow the Africans to do subsistence farming for their own families unless they worked long hours for the white farmers first. Whites wanted to turn the farmers into forced agricultural laborers, slaves on the land, and this created a bitter hatred of the white settlers. By 1953 half of the Kikuyu had no claim to their ancestral lands at all. Poverty worsened, unemployment was rampant, social and mental disorientation occurred, and the small territories reserved for Africans were overpopulated. While it is true that some Kikuyu had been granted a few more rights than the masses in an effort to divide the group, the main battle of the Mau Mau was against the white settlers. It was a "land movement."

Around 1947 the General Council of the Kikuyu Central Association, which had been banned by the white settlers, took a decision to campaign against the land grab of the whites. The members were bound together through a blood oath ritual that was traditional among the Kikuyu. The oaths were initially meant for civil obedience but as the movement advanced the members of the Mau Mau took oaths that obliged them to fight and kill Europeans.

Trade unions in Nairobi called for a boycott when the white-run city council was granted a Royal Charter for Nairobi. They paralyzed the city and proved a great headache for the white colonial government. Radical African nationalists clashed with Africans who saw themselves as loyalists to the British colonial administration. A movement calling itself the "Forty Group" was born of ex-army types who had been circumcised in 1940. They demanded, through the Kenya Africa Union, that the colonial administration remove the discriminatory legislation to the inclusion of Africans on the Legislative Council. They wanted a new proposal to be adopted that would give the five million Africans fair representation on the Legislative Council. The colonial government proposed a system that had the following provisions:

30,000 whites would receive fourteen representatives;
100,000 Indians would receive six representatives;
24,000 Arabs would receive one representative;
five million Africans would receive five representatives to be nominated by the government.

It was obvious that the people had to confront the unfair situation. A central committee was created in 1951 by urban radicals to organize the oath campaign and to form armed squads to enforce policies, protect members, and kill informers and collaborators. Activists killed their opponents, burned the houses of Europeans, hamstrung their livestock, and sabotaged the white farmers by burning their crops.

Jomo Kenyatta, who had been elected president of the Kenya Africa Union, was pressured by the British to give speeches condemning the Mau Mau. The idea was to threaten him if he did not speak out against the Mau Mau, but because Kenyatta, as clever as his enemies, did not speak forcefully against the Mau Mau, the British assumed that he was a member, perhaps the leader, of the group.

Plots to kill Kenyatta were soon discovered. However, before he could be killed, Kenyatta was arrested by the British authorities, who declared that

*Figure 13.3* Jomo Kenyatta, African nationalist leader, during a press conference in which he argued for Kenya's independence, November 1961

© Bettmann/CORBIS

he was the head of the Mau Mau. The arrest gave Kenyatta more charisma. He was seen as a lion of courage, trumping all instances of weaknesses in the masses. The people found inspiration in his discipline, intelligence, and commitment, although his leadership of the Mau Mau was disputed. Nevertheless, Britain had unwittingly played into his hands and made him the uncontested leader of the Kenyan masses.

White settlers had 100 Kikuyu leaders arrested with Kenyatta and then went on to arrest another 8000 in the next twenty-five days. The British thought that this would decapitate the revolt but two weeks after the arrests the revolt intensified. An Emergency was declared and the British sent planes, the 2nd Battalion of the King's Rifles, and the cruiser *Kenya* to Mombasa harbor. They feared, because of the people's anger, a wholesale killing of whites, which did not materialize.

Nevertheless by January 1953 the central committee had taken new action renaming itself the Council of Freedom with two wings, an active and a passive wing. The passive wing would supply weapons and equipment and the active wing, called also the Land and Freedom wing, would actually carry out actions against the white colonial regime. They were equipped with *simis* (longswords), *kibokos* (rhino hide whips), and *pangas* (machetes). Some tried to make their own guns but many of them exploded when they were fired. They had nearly 500 guns anyway and enough courage to carry them for a long time.

They were successful with the masses, who gave them food and clothes. The Land and Freedom army killed collaborators and attacked isolated farms. They would travel in bands of about 100 men, moving back into the forest to protect their secret headquarters after they had raided a farm. They had a cell structure that allowed them to know who was operating in what theater of the conflict. They had judges who could hand out fines to those who associated with those who were not Mau Mau. The three most active Land and Freedom wing leaders were Stanley Mathenge, Waruhiu Itote (General China), leader of the Mount Kenya Mau Mau, and Dedan Kimathi, leader of the Aberdare Forest Mau Mau.

The British reacted to the Mau Mau by using Africans who had been converted to Christianity as part of the official security force. This became the Kikuyu Home Guard in 1953 and the aim of this group was to infiltrate the Mau Mau and lead espionage activities and punitive raids against them. On March 26, 1953, nearly 3000 Mau Mau attacked the village of Lari, which had been known for supporting the British, and killed seventy people. This raid was used by the British media to paint an image of the Mau Mau as bloodthirsty.

The whites tried to disguise themselves as Africans in order to avoid the Mau Mau. They even used the disguises to capture and kill Kikuyu. More than 125 were killed in the sweep of Aberdare Forest by British soldiers. The white settler regime arrested thousands of people, holding 77,000 Kikuyu in camps and instituting a compulsory villagization that removed more than one million Kikuyu. In 1954 the British killed twenty-four of forty-one cell leaders and arrested more than 5500. Dedan Kimathi was the last Mau Mau to be captured, on October 21, 1956. He was captured in Nyeri with thirteen of his fellow Mau Mau compatriots. He was hanged in early 1957, effectively ending the revolt that had set Kenya on the road to self-determination and independence within three years. A parliamentary conference in Janaury 1960 agreed that Kenyans should have a government based on "one person, one vote" majority rule.

The brutality of the British revenge killings and hangings was beyond reason. For example, the Mau Mau killed thirty-two settlers, but the British security forces may have killed 50,000 Africans. Only sixty-three British soldiers were killed, three Asians, and 524 African collaborators. Nevertheless, the British hanged thirty-five Mau Mau in the first eight months of the Emergency, and by 1954 had hanged 756, with 508 of them being hanged for offenses less than murder. By the end of the Emergency more than 1000 African revolters had been hanged. An interesting comparison is the fact that only eight guerillas were hanged during the Zionist rebellion in Palestine around the late 1940s (Elkins; Anderson).

## The Algerian National Liberation Front (FLN)

On November 1, 1954, the Algerian Front de Libération Nationale (FLN) guerrillas launched a series of precision attacks against the French colonial administration. The assaults against the police posts, military installations, warehouses, communications facilities, and public utilities shocked the French authorities and sent a wave of jubilation through the indigenous population. The war against France had begun in earnest. Ben Bella, a brilliant activist and intellectual, created the FLN as an underground movement to combat the *colons* (colonials) who held power and prestige over the masses of Algerians. The colonials were mainly white French who were in the service of the French colonial service. Operating from Cairo and Algiers, Ben Bella and eight other leaders – Ait Ahmed, Mohamed Boudiaf, Belcacem Krim, Rabah Bitat, Larbi Ben M'Hidi, Mourad Didouch, Moustafa Ben Boulaid, and Mohamed Khider – were the main leaders of the Algerian War of Independence. They were the *chefs historiques*, the historical chiefs, of the movement. Representatives from the FLN broadcast a proclamation calling upon all Muslims in Algeria, Arab and African, to rise up and help restore the Algerian state, sovereign, democratic, and social, within the framework of the principles of Islam. The French minister of the interior, later to become president, François Mitterrand, replied to the FLN that the only possible negotiation was war. This set the stage for further confrontation. In the mind of Mitterrand Algeria was a departement of France and constituted an integral part of the French Republic. The Algerians, according to Mitterrand, had been French for a long time and were irrevocably French. Mitterrand's position was adamant that between Algeria and metropolitan France "there can be no conceivable secession." The idea of the FLN was different. They saw the French as colonizers who had occupied the country, imposed new values, and created the conditions of oppression for the masses.

The leaders of the movement established six military regions of the country, called *wilayat*, and appointed six internal leaders to direct the six regions. The External Delegation in Cairo led by Ben Bella, Ait Ahmed, and Mohamed Khider was dedicated to gaining arms and funds for the *wilaya* commanders, as well as supplies and foreign support for the rebellion. The FLN was an outgrowth of the Revolutionary Committee of Unity and Action, which had been underground since Ben Bella was forced out of the country in 1952. After two years of steady preparation, by November 1954 the FLN was ready. The Proclamation of November 1, 1954, was certain in its objectives, which had to be met by "all possible means until the realization of our goals." Indeed, the framers of the Proclamation sought to minimize all ethnic and clan issues by steering clear of the problems that had plagued the movement against colonialism. They wrote:

> To this end, we insist on specifying that we are independent of the two clans that are fighting over power. Placing national interest above all petty and erroneous considerations of personality and prestige, in conformity with revolutionary principles, our action is directly solely against colonialism, our only blind and obstinate enemy, which has always refused to grant the least freedom by peaceful means.

Like lightning the FLN movement, with its Proclamation as its flag, spread its attacks across the country, killing European farmers and forcing the others to seek refuge in Algiers, where the old French colonialists called for the government to take harder measures against the guerrillas. Soon the French community had acquiesced as colonial vigilante groups, with the tacit approval of the authorities, went on the hunt, *ratonnades* (rat-hunts, meaning killing of Arabs), against the Muslim community and suspects.

The vigilantes demanded that the French government protect their proper-
ties and lives by calling for a state of emergency, the arresting of all those
who called for separation from France, and the death penalty for those who
committed politically motivated crimes.

Increasingly the FLN sought to force the French colonists to feel the
vengeance of the insurgency. They attacked the town of Phillippeville in
August 1955 to bring the struggle to the ordinary French people. It was a
bloody attack against women and babies, maimed and healthy, young and
old; 123 people died. Prior to this time the FLN had only attacked military
and government targets, but the change in tactics caused alarm in the
French community.

Jacques Soustelle, the French governor-general, called for more repressive
measures against the FLN. In retaliation the French claimed to have killed
1273 guerrillas; however, the FLN said 12,000 Muslims were slaughtered in
the orgy of death carried out by the French authorities and vigilante groups.
There was no longer any neutral ground; war was declared by both sides
and the battle of Algeria had begun.

The French forces numbered nearly half a million in Algeria by 1956,
including nearly 150,000 Algerian Arabs who served in the French army.
Air and naval units were rushed to the war theater and elite units of the
airborne and Foreign Legion entered the fray as France sought desperately
to maintain the African colony of Algeria.

Becoming more organized and deliberate, the FLN created a military
wing called the Armée de Libération Nationale (ALN) that used hit-and-run
tactics against the French. They specialized in ambush, night raids,
concealed bombs in public places, and the avoidance of direct clashes with
the main French forces. They knew that they could not confront the firepower of the French. Raids on armories and police stations helped them to
obtain more weapons but the real strategy of the leadership of the FLN was
to frustrate the French in the areas where they were weakest. They would
attack factories, official cars, colonial farms, and military encampments and
then merge back into the community as ordinary Algerians. The ALN used
kidnapping, ritual murder, mutilation, violent home invasions, and small
bombs in public places against collaborators, traitors, and French officials
of both genders. The idea was to totally disrupt the society so that no one
was safe. All Arab and African colonial officials serving the colonial regime
were suspect and could be kidnapped and killed as examples of traitors.

The FLN soon controlled certain areas of the country, including mountainous areas south of Algiers and Oran. The organization set up a military
administration that was able to collect taxes, supplies, and recruits. In
1957, the French commander in Algeria, General Raoul Salan, challenged
the FLN with the *quadrillage*, dividing the country into sectors to be policed
by permanently garrisoned troops in each sector. There was also a ruthless
French campaign to suppress the rebel operations by bombing villages that
were suspected of sheltering and supplying the insurgency. Entire villages
were placed under French army supervision to deny the FLN any support
among the rural people. More than two million Algerians were removed

from their villages during the three-year period between 1957 and 1960. They were resettled in the open plains, away from their mountain homes, and most found the conditions abysmally poor.

Stung by the loss in Indochina at Dien Bien Phu in 1954, the French public grew weary of the war in Algeria by early 1960. Charles de Gaulle used the word "self-determination" in reference to Algeria in a speech and caused turmoil in the ranks of the Algerian colonialist community. They felt they had been betrayed and so they staged insurrections against the French-controlled Algerian government in January 1960 and April 1961. Internal divisions were now reducing the political will of the French government to prosecute the war. De Gaulle did not feel that the French government should keep fighting the war for the economic interests of the colonial class (*colons*) in Algeria. He abandoned that idea and sought to negotiate with the FLN. Talks had started in 1961 but they were actually realized effectively on March 12, 1962, at Evian, when it was agreed that the colonials had equal legal protection with Algerians over a three-year period in respect of property, and participation in civic affairs and in cultural and civil rights. Europeans would have to become Algerian citizens or be classified as aliens at the end of three years. This was approved by the French electorate, with 91 percent of the votes cast in favor.

On July 1, 1962, six million Algerians out of a total electorate of 6.5 million voted almost unanimously for independence after eight bloody years of revolution. Almost a million people had lost their lives through the war, starvation, or deprivation. Thus, 132 years after the French had entered the African country it was now independent.

## Frelimo and the Mozambican war of independence

The father of Mozambican independence, Eduardo Chivambo Mondlane, was the fourth son of a Tsonga king. He was born in 1920 during the time that the Portuguese controlled his country. He was a shepherd until the age of 12, tending his family's sheep as a young boy during which time he came to love the beauty of his country. When he entered college in Johannesburg, South Africa, at Witwatersrand University, he was expected to be an outstanding student but the white minority National Party came to power in 1949 in South Africa and Mondlane and other blacks were expelled from the university. It was then that Mondlane found his way to the University of Lisbon, where he formed the first Mozambican student union. However, Portugal was awful toward African students in the 1950s and Mondlane withdrew from the university after one year because of the discrimination he felt there. At the age of 31, he applied to and was accepted by Oberlin College in Ohio. He enrolled and obtained a degree in anthropology and sociology in 1953. He also took graduate courses at Case-Western Reserve University in Cleveland, Ohio.

Never one to let Mozambique leave his thoughts, even while thousands of miles away, Mondlane worked for a while as a teacher in the United States but was always committed to the freedom of his people. His dislike for the Portuguese control of Mozambique was rooted in his hatred of the racist policies and attitudes of the colonialists and also the authoritarian style of the Portuguese government.

On June 25, 1962, three regionally based nationalist organizations – Mozambican African National Union (MANU), National Democratic Union of Mozambique (UDENAMO), and the National African Union of Independent Mozambique (UNAMI) – fighting against Portuguese colonialism combined their forces to form one front. Thus, after the Frente de Libertação de Moçambique or Frelimo was founded in June 1962, the leaders of the organization selected Mondlane to be its first president. He founded the headquarters at Dar es Salaam, close to Mozambique, and started to build the organization's military wing.

However, in 1969 a bomb was planted under Mondlane's desk at Frelimo's headquarters in Dar es Salaam and he was killed. His assassination galvanized many Mozambicans, who saw him as a martyr for their independence. When the military wing went into action it was able to wrest the northern and central regions of the country away from control by the Portuguese. With 7000 guerrillas against a force of 60,000 Portuguese troops, Frelimo's military wing was able to outmaneuver the Portuguese army in most important battles during the 1970s. By 1975 Portugal was willing to negotiate with Frelimo over the independence of the country. The Universidade Lourenço Marques' colonial name was changed to Universidade Eduardo Mondlane, located in the capital city of Maputo, which was also changed from the colonial name of Lourenço Marques. Samora Machel, one of Frelimo's most celebrated heroes, was the first president of the Republic of Mozambique. Almost immediately the reactionary forces, mainly controlled by white farming interests with support from minority white regimes in South Africa and Rhodesia, created chaos by arming a group calling itself Renamo. It was a brutal war by surrogates of the white regimes. They burned granaries, bombed communication facilities, and killed many professional people. Yet Frelimo was able to subdue the rebels and get a peace treaty in 1992. The country had been nearly destroyed by two wars, one with the Portuguese and one internally with the surrogate army supplied by the white South African and Rhodesian regimes. Nevertheless, although many services were disrupted and the infrastructure of the country was badly damaged by the internal struggle, Samora Machel held the nation together using the socialist rhetoric and doctrine of Frelimo. He was killed in a suspicious airplane crash and Joaquim Chissano was elected to lead Frelimo and won election in 1994 as president.

## Angola national liberation

The war for liberation in Angola was long and bitter. Rarely has a nation suffered so much pain in being born as Angola in the struggle from 1961 to 1974 for liberation and freedom. Portugal, one of the poorest countries in Europe, was fighting to maintain control over two of its most lucrative colonies, Mozambique and Angola. By virtue of its size, location, natural wealth, and proximity to Europe, Angola was Portugal's major prize in

Africa. Thus, Portugal rejected the idea of independence for Angola, seeing it as a part of the Portuguese economy that was indispensable to the life that the Portuguese people lived both in Portugal and in Angola. Of course, this belief by the Portuguese had little to do with what the Africans themselves believed about self-governance and independence. The role of the colonialist is always to interpret reality from his or her perspective and to see the interests or values of the colonized as unimportant in the scheme of things.

Meanwhile, three independence movements emerged to fight against the Portuguese: the Popular Movement for the Liberation of Angola (MPLA) led by the poet Agostinho Neto, the National Front for the Liberation of Angola (FNLA) led by Holden Roberto, and the National Union for the Total Independence of Angola (UNITA) led by Jonas Malheiro Savimbi. Each group had its external supporters and suppliers. They were initially regionally based groups, operating on the basis of strong ethnic orientations, but they sought to expand from their bases as the struggle deepened. There was no way that a movement could win without allies and supporters from other regions. Although the MPLA was concentrated around the Luanda region and had backing from the Kimbundu and Lusofied intellectuals in the capital city, it was also a movement that resonated with the progressive, socialist organizations fighting against all forms of oppression elsewhere. On the other hand, the FNLA was centered among the Bakongo in the north of the county and supported by the United States and Congo-Kinshasa, and the UNITA movement, concentrated among the Ovimbundu in the middle of the county, was supported by South Africa and China. It would eventually, after Angola was independent, receive support from right-wing groups in the United States to fight against the MPLA and its socialist agenda.

In 1961 a group of protesters allied with the MPLA attacked several police stations and prisons in order to free African political prisoners who had been arrested by the Portuguese authorities. Cotton workers in Malanje province attacked colonial officials, public buildings, and a Catholic mission. Violence broke out all over the province and sporadic attacks happened in other parts of the country. Many rich Portuguese farmers and officials repatriated to Portugal out of fear for their lives. Whites who were not wealthy enough to repatriate were left to fend for themselves and began to form groups to defend their privileges in Angola.

An intensification of the violence in the northwest part of the huge country meant that whites were not safe anywhere. Fear had been defeated in the hearts of Africans, and the Angolan masses, like historic masses before them, turned on their oppressors with a mighty fury. Over a period of three days Africans from the Bakongo region in Uige province attacked isolated white farms and towns in forty coordinated raids, killing hundreds of Portuguese settlers. In Cuanza Norte province, other African groups fought with the European farmers and officials in the rural areas. They objected to the oppressive conditions of labor, the discriminatory practices, and the racist insults hurled by the whites. In the next few months tension ran high and violence kept occurring throughout the country and near the border with the Congo. As the Portuguese army reacted by raiding suspected rebel villages the character of the movement changed to be exclusively a Bakongo uprising.

As was the European pattern in colonialist regimes, the Portuguese responded with the usual brutality and reprisals in an effort to strike fear in the heart of the Angolans. They organized vigilante groups to terrorize African villagers, to isolate leaders and murder them and their followers, and to demonstrate that they were willing to protect their racial privilege. The Portuguese vigilante groups were not controlled by the military or civilian authorities; these were groups filled with revenge and hatred seeking only to reestablish what they realized they had lost: the element of fear in the African. Now it seemed that, arbitrary as the violence measured out to the Africans was, it was not enough to deter the uprising. Both groups felt that the time was nearing for inevitable showdowns over the control of the country.

More than 40,000 Africans were uprooted during the rebellion of 1961. Many people migrated out of Angola to Congo; others were killed; many starved or died because of disease brought about by the disruptions caused by the rebellion. Africans who were sympathetic to the Europeans, called *assimilados*, were also killed. Some of the *assimilados* had jobs working for whites as overseers, managers, and administrators. They feared for their positions and their livelihood. Therefore, many of them called for a halt to the rebellion and support for the Portuguese officials.

The Portuguese response to the uprising was described as wholesale bombing of innocent people. They used their air power to attack many villages, driving people out of their homes and across the borders to Congo. This action was criticized by a United Nations investigation and the indiscriminate bombings caused a mobilization of the masses and helped the liberation groups find recruits.

Trying desperately to hang on to its colony, the Portuguese government sought to improve the country by paving more roads (increasing the paved road network by 500 percent in a few years), and by stimulating economic growth among Angolan farmers. Coffee producers were supported and compulsory cotton cultivation, which was like enslavement, was abolished. This did not satisfy the liberation groups, which now felt the need to push on for independence. It was a matter of "too little, too late."

In 1974 a coup d'état in Portugal brought a military government to power that had tired of the war, the killing of innocent people, and the maimings and deaths of Portuguese soldiers and civilians. The Portuguese sued for peace and at the Alvor Accords in 1974 handed over power to a coalition of the three liberation movements. There remained strong ideological differences between the groups as well as tough personality issues between the leaders. Eventually armed conflict between the groups broke out, with UNITA and the FNLA seeking to take control of the capital city of Luanda from the MPLA. Since Luanda was the base of the MPLA, it was essentially in control of the majority of the infrastructure and the political machinery of the nation. The white regime of South Africa sent troops into the southern part of Angola in alliance with the UNITA forces, the Mobutu government sent forces in support of the FNLA, and the Cuban government sent troops in support of the MPLA in 1975. However the MPLA, with the support of the Cubans and a strong ideology for complete independence, maintained control of Luanda and the Cabinda oil fields. By November 11, 1975, the MPLA was ready to declare independence, and the Portuguese abandoned the capital the same day. UNITA and the FNLA went to the interior and formed a coalition government in the city of Huambo. Agostinho Neto was elected the first president of Angola and the country was recognized by the United Nations in 1976. When Neto died of cancer in 1979, the planning minister, José Eduardo dos Santos, became president. The country would see many more years of struggle before the ultimate victory of the MPLA over all of its enemies and an attempt to stabilize the nation. From the perspective of Angolans the solidarity of the Cuban forces enabled Angola to defeat the rebel forces in the south of the country. Cuba, a small island nation in the Caribbean, had found two sources of solidarity with the Angolans. In the first place, the country had taken a socialist path; second, the Cuban leader, Fidel Castro, defined Cuba as an Afro-Latin country rather than a Latin American country. The majority of the troops who volunteered to fight in Africa were of African origin. In total, more than 50,000 troops from Cuba assisted the Angolan government. The battle for Namibia and South Africa would intensify and those victories would help to bolster the southern African region.

Bristling with violence in the daily lives of the Africans, southern Africa was a cauldron of hate. Few individuals could have used the offices of president and world citizenship as effectively as the founding president of Zambia, Kenneth Kaunda, who was in the thick of the southern African war.

Born on April 28, 1924, Kenneth David Kaunda became the founding father and first head of state of the Republic of Zambia (formerly Northern Rhodesia). He was the youngest of eight children born at the Lubwa Mission Station in Northern Rhodesia to a religious family. His father, the Reverend David Kaunda, was an ordained Church of Scotland missionary and teacher. His mother was one of the first women teachers in the country. He was encouraged by his parents to search diligently for knowledge in the pages of all of the books available to him. This was good advice because the young Kaunda took it, and very early there was a mark of excellence in the work he did. He excelled at Munali Secondary School in Lusaka. After graduating, he earned a teaching certificate and returned home to take up the post of headmaster at Chinsali Mission.

However, in 1949, Dr. H. Kamuzu Banda, later to lead Malawi (which was formerly called Nyasaland), Harry Nkumbula and others intensified their fight against Britain's imposition of Federation for Central Africa, and what in 1953 was to become the Federation of Rhodesia and Nyasaland. Twenty-five-year-old Kenneth Kaunda toured Northern Rhodesia with a guitar, singing original freedom songs, inspiring the people to resist the British. In the process, he was able to help establish 116 chapters of the African National Congress (ANC), the oldest human rights organization in southern Africa. In 1953, the ANC membership elected him secretary general of the party. Of course, as leader of the ANC he was to run foul of the British, who promptly imprisoned him in Lusaka.

Kenneth Kaunda used his time in prison to formulate and develop the revolutionary political concept that eventually was called "Zambian humanism," an expression of faith in the common men and women and a belief in non-violent attainment of all goals. Probably about the time Martin Luther King, Jr. was being influenced by the model of Gandhi, who had helped lead the Indians to freedom, Kaunda was also reading and learning from the same literature. He left prison determined to live an exemplary personal life, renouncing all forms of indulgence including tobacco, rich, unhealthy food, and alcohol in any form. He became a vegetarian. He sought to lead a life of spirituality, moderation, and morality.

Kaunda split with the ANC and formed the Zambia African National Congress (ZANC), which was quickly banned by the colonial authorities. He was first restricted then rearrested and placed in Salisbury (Harare) prison. He suffered a recurrence of tuberculosis. Nine months of prison solitude, controlled at all times by his strict personal discipline, allowed him to make a full recovery and when he was released in 1960 he immediately formed and became president of the United National Independence Party (UNIP), the political party that ultimately, working with Dr. Banda's Malawi Congress Party in Nyasaland, overthrew the Federation of Rhodesia and Nyasaland. He was elected a member of the Legislative Council of Northern Rhodesia and minister of local government and social welfare in the coalition government of the United National Independence Party and the African National Congress in 1962. In 1963, with Zambian independence on the horizon, he became prime minister, and on October 24, 1964, Kenneth David Kaunda became president of the new Republic of Zambia.

He worked with his usual passion and dedication, often eighteen to twenty hours a day. He was known for playing music for relaxation. However, there was little time to rest because the situations in South Africa and Zimbabwe had to be resolved and Kaunda was dedicated to seeing all of southern Africa free of colonialism.

He became Chairman of the Frontline States, a coalition of states at the boundary with South Africa, Namibia, and Zimbabwe whose aim it was to overthrow minority white rule. His leadership, the many meetings, negotiations, and deals he brokered, were critical to the release of Nelson Mandela and the transformation in South Africa. Viewing himself as a spiritual man, Kaunda wrote on many subjects, but most frequently on non-violence and freedom.

# Part VII

# The time for consolidation

"Nothing remains except to
do Maat"

# 14 Africa consolidates independence

At the beginning of the twenty-first century Africa remained the least-explored continent, as it had been at the beginning of the twentieth century. Nevertheless, it had also been the continent most exploited. The frontiers of economic exploitation, indeed the new loci of competition among world powers, were the areas of Africa that remained underdeveloped in terms of material resources.

Africa was at once both thrown into the global economy but restrained by former colonial powers from full participation by its people on an equal footing with the Western world. Africa therefore remained an area for the exploitation of raw materials and the consumption of processed goods from elsewhere. The struggle over the vast quantities of African resources engaged and engages forces from every part of the earth. Unfair competition threatens African farmers in the world market. In places such as Mali and Guinea where cotton farmers grow good-quality crops they find that they are unable to compete with the farmers in countries like the United States because the American government gives subsidies (money) to American farmers who produce a certain amount of cotton. Without such subsidies from their own governments the African farmers seem unable to compete, when in fact they could compete quite easily if the American farmers were not afforded advantages by the American government. African integration into the world system is unequal and often unfair, and yet through the use of processed products Africans are sharing in the world economy as consumers.

## Africa and the Second World War

Germany, England, Italy, and France interfered in the lives of Africans during the Second World War. All of these powers were colonial nations bent on conserving their African colonies and preserving their white privileges in black countries. France and England declared war on Germany in September 1939, and this meant that the war against Fascism would involve the African continent because most of the parties held colonies in Africa. Fascists believed in military force, autocratic or dictatorial government, the inferiority of minority peoples, and the destruction of socialism.

By May 1940 most of the major industrial nations had taken sides. The Italians under the military dictator Mussolini came into the war on the side of Germany. They were soon to be joined by the Japanese government, claiming power over the nations in the Pacific. By June 1940 the powerful German army had overrun France and installed a puppet government at Vichy in southern France. This led to a French underground resistance movement. A French general, Charles de Gaulle, formed a Free French government in exile. Thus, the Vichy and Free French governments would have to struggle over the African colonies.

Almost a year later the Germans engaged the Soviet Union, effectively bringing it into the war. In 1941 the Japanese struck Pearl Harbor in Hawaii, showing their military reach into America's Pacific rim, but also bringing the United States into the war. In 1942 the Japanese overran Malaya, Burma, and the Dutch East Indies, creating hostilities by the British and Dutch against the Japanese. It does not take a great imagination to see that the whole world seemed to be coming loose at the joints, except in Africa. Europe, Asia, and North America were heavily invested in the war from 1939 to 1945; not so the majority of Africans.

The Italians invaded Ethiopia in 1935 with the purpose of teaching a lesson to the only nation, Ethiopia, that had defeated its army. Although Italy was a relatively weak power in Europe it believed that it, too, deserved to have African colonies.

## The era of the political giants

One could easily say that it was a period of ingenuity, courage, audacity, and will because it was a time when mortals thought that, using their intelligence, wisdom, and power, they could bring about an African resurgence. Of course, they sought every avenue of victory, examining the past for directions for the future, learning from their experiences with European colonialism, applying the proverbial wisdom from the oral traditions of the ancestors passed down through contemporary elders, and yet they often failed to achieve the goals they so eagerly strove to fulfill. Who were these leaders and what were their deeds?

There were several African leaders who arose in the 1950s and 1960s that laid the foundations for the current African reality. Their names are the most heard and discussed on the continent even now and the impression they made on their peers and on posterity is long and enduring. Like some gold nuggets dropping out of a massive cosmological pan, the names and personalities that sought to transform a continent continue to shine: Nasser, Nkrumah, Nyerere, Senghor, Lumumba, and Kenyatta.

## Gamal Abdel Nasser and the Colonels' Revolt

Nasser was born in the northern city of Alexandria in Lower Egypt, the son of a postal official. He soon left Alexandria for the much larger city of Cairo, living with his uncle, who was active in politics against the British colonial forces. When he entered the army he soon earned a major's commission and was in the war against Israel in 1948. Nasser and his men were trapped for several months after the war ended in what was called the Faluja pocket. They were eventually allowed to leave and return to Egypt when a cease-fire agreement was reached. Nasser never forgot this experience and used it in his own preparation for taking power. As a lieutenant colonel in the army he created a group called the Free Officers Movement, a group of military officers under the age of 35 who sought to bring new ideas into the army. They had felt betrayed by the British-supported King Farouk I of Egypt. In one sense, all of these officers were from peasant and poor backgrounds. They did not identify with the upper classes of Turkish-, Albanian-, or British-influenced leadership. In fact, they believed that Farouk was ineffective because he did not feel the passion and emotion of the masses of Egyptians. Therefore, they led a military coup on July 23, 1952, and overthrew King Farouk. The person who was ostensibly given power was General Muhammad Naguib. But it was soon revealed that he was a figurehead in order to keep the armed forces supportive of the coup since it was organized by junior officers. Nasser, who was named the minister of the interior, was the mastermind behind the coup. It did not take long for Nasser to manage the arrest of Naguib, blaming him for supporting a secret organization called the Muslim Brotherhood and an attempt on his life. The Muslim Brotherhood wanted to bring Shari'a law and Islamic principles to government. Nasser, on the other hand, wanted to ensure that no religious group would see itself as a political party. All political parties, if they existed, had to be non-religious. Thus, this set him on a direct confrontation with the Muslim Brotherhood, a confrontation that would last for many years in Egypt, even after Nasser.

On February 25, 1954, Nasser became premier of Egypt. He had his opposition and detractors seeking to control the military, but Nasser was able to win the struggle for absolute power in the country. He arranged an election two years later and the only candidate was Nasser. He became the second president of Egypt. Immediately he centralized the Egyptian state, increasing presidential power, instituting land reform, and nationalizing industry. In addition, Nasser was able to appeal to the masses with massive public works projects such as the Aswan High Dam.

## Nasser as Visionary

The Egyptian people believed that Gamel Abdel Nasser was a visionary, and they also believed that he reclaimed Arab heroism. Both of these reasons might be given for his celebration in Egyptian history because they are wrapped in the nature and character of the man himself. As a visionary, Nasser embodied the idea of a united Arab nation as well as the uniting of the African continent. The reality of both of these visions rested on the integrity of Nasser's character, that is, his ability to see these visions brought into existence. The people of Egypt and other parts of Africa came to believe that if anyone could fulfill the dream of African unity or Arab nationalism, it would be Nasser because of his strong rhetoric on both

*Figure 14.1* Egyptian president Gamal Abdel Nasser, December 1964

© Bettmann/CORBIS

issues. He was not without his detractors, and there were attempts on his life. But the fact that he escaped the death traps and death plots against him, including an actual shooting on October 26, 1954 where the shooter, Mahmoud Abd al-Latif, missed his target giving Nasser an image of invincibility. He was always capable of cloaking himself in the emotions of the Egyptian nation with the claim that he and the people were one. Indeed, nothing could be so powerful in Nasser's arsenal of rhetorical stratagems as his ability to demonstrate that the desires of the Egyptian people and his desires were one and the same. The phrase "all of you are Gamel Abdel Nasser" would be heard more than once in his career.

Arab nationalism had waned prior to Nasser's takeover of Egypt. There was not one country that could have been said to advance Arab nationalism among the Arab people. All of the countries were colonized or the pawns of the Western powers. In Egypt's case, the king had been under the influence of the British and the only organized resistance that captured a part of the Arab sentiment was the Muslim Brotherhood. The problem for progressives, and those who saw a larger vision than the religious one, was that this was a fundamentalist organization and the political leaders of Egypt had no intention of allowing it to become the dominant national or international voice of the country. As the leader of Egypt, Nasser pursued the Muslim Brotherhood because he believed that it was behind the various coup attempts. Many members of the brotherhood were arrested.

This situation provided Nasser with the precise conditions he needed for extending his claim to be the protector of Arab Nationalism. He wanted to see a combination of Arab nationalisms brought into one large political or national union. Thus, he led several attempts to achieve this result. By 1958 he had forged an agreement with Syria for unity with Egypt. This was the first United Arab Republic. Nasser worked hard to include Yemen in the merger, but the entire project was dissolved after three years and Egypt returned to its African roots. The political problems, not to mention the cultural issues, seemed insurmountable even with the same religion.

Nevertheless, Nasser did not give up on the dream of a larger Arab nation with Egypt at its center. Another union was later tried with Libya and Sudan. The outcome of this venture was the same as the earlier one with Syria and Yemen. In the end, the credentials of Egypt as the leader of the Arab world would be established, and the image of Nasser indelibly stamped in Arab history.

## The West and Nasser

Nasser's promise on January 16, 1956, that he would "liberate" Palestine set in motion numerous international forces against Egypt. In the first place, his vow coming less than ten years after the European nations, led by Britain, had worked to establish Israel, created immediate repercussions in the international community. It was, so to speak, a wild card in the political arrangement of nations.

Nasser went further later in the year and denounced the economic arrangement Britain and France had with the Suez Canal. Nasser announced that he would nationalize the canal since Britain had decided not to assist Egypt in building the Aswan High Dam. In Nasser's formulation he would use the fees from the Suez Canal to help fund the construction of the Aswan High Dam.

Neither Britain nor France appreciated what they considered to be Nasser's appropriation of the canal. A military campaign led by Britain and France and supported by the young Israeli nation forced the Egyptians to retreat from Port Said in a matter of days. Nasser's response, in Cold War terms, was to ask the United States and the Soviet Union, two superpowers, to support Egypt's claim and force the British and the French to back down. This action on the part of Nasser was significant because it drew the two competing powers into an international diplomatic contest to win influence in the African region. Israel was pressured to withdraw and the French and British also withdrew their armies. Israel received a promise that it would not be attacked by Arab fedayeen units originating in Egypt and Egypt was able to exercise more sovereignty over the Suez Canal.

Nasser became a national hero and was heralded as the victor in the Suez Canal conflict. Not only had he secured the rights of Egypt to funds from the Suez Canal, but he had also established relations with the Soviet Union and the United States, breaking the bonds of Britain in a new alignment of foreign policy. No previously colonized nation had resisted the former colonial nation with such success as Egypt. The excitement was palpable. Nasser was the inspiration for new revolutionaries. Cairo was the hotbed of Arab nationalism and the leaders of other national movements moved to the city to be close to the seat of resistance to colonial oppression. They were there like students at the feet of a great scholar to gain any information, insight, and support they could, for their own future exploits.

Nasser was a political and military activist in the interests of the "Arab Nation." This was his vision and he largely provoked the Six-Day War in 1967. He made a number of demands, including that the United Nations leave the Sinai Peninsula and that the peninsula be returned to Egypt. He then blockaded the Israeli port of Eilat, near the northern end of the Gulf of Aqaba, and persuaded Jordan and Syria to join him in united Arab action against Israel. Israel's offensive in the Six-Day War routed the Arab forces. When Nasser recognized that his armies could not defeat Israel, he sought to resign from office. The people declared him to be a hero and he stayed in power. He led the nation during the 1969–70 war as well, but he died of a heart attack just weeks after the end of the war on September 28, 1970. The man who succeeded Nasser, Anwar Sadat, had been one of the young generals who had looked up to Nasser as a great hero. While Nasser's legacy is more than of a military leader who brought some pride to the Arab people by leading them in wars, actually wars that Egypt did not win, Sadat remains Eygpt's most highly recognized leader of international stature. Unlike Nasser he did not build a great Aswan High Dam, but he tried to build political relationships that would allow the Arab people to live in peace with the Jews. This was not an objective universally respected by the Arab Egyptian people and Sadat was assassinated following a peace agreement with Israel.

## Kwame Nkrumah dreams of African unity

Kwame Nkrumah was born on September 21, 1909, and named Francis Nwia-Kofi Ngonloma. He would change not only his name but the course of

*Figure 14.2* Egyptian president Anwar Sadat at a Foreign Affairs Committee meeting, February 1978
© Wally McNamee/CORBIS

*Figure 14.3* President Kwame Nkrumah of Ghana arrives in London to attend the 1961 Commonweath Prime Ministers' Conference
© Hulton-Deutsch Collection/ CORBIS

African history during his lifetime. When he completed the famous Achimota School in Accra, he took courses at the Roman Catholic Seminary, Amisano. Teaching at the Roman Catholic school in the historical Akan state of Akyem he became enamored with education. Nkrumah, by all accounts, was a magnetic teacher, often demonstrating the characteristics that would make him one of history's most charismatic leaders.

There were two principle decisions made by Nkrumah that transformed him from one of the usual students who left the colony to attend school abroad only to return to serve the interests of the colonizers. The first decision was made in 1935 when Nkrumah went to the United States to attend Lincoln University in Pennsylvania, the first college established in the United States for Africans and African Americans. He obtained a BA from Lincoln in 1939 and an MA in education from the University of Pennsylvania in 1942; the next year he received a MA in philosophy from the same university. It was his lecturing at Lincoln University that brought him to the attention of many of his contemporaries. As he had done at the schools of Akyem, so he did at Lincoln. He challenged the students to look beyond the immediate condition of the African world and visualize what could be possible in a free, independent Africa where each person would take his or her station in life and show absolute determination to exhibit excellence in everything. Nkrumah believed that the African American suffered the same lack of cultural esteem, ignorance of African contributions and history, and dependence on the whites that had plagued many African nations. African students in the United States and Canada began to consult him about the future of their studies and the future of Africa. Nkrumah was elected president of the African Students Organization and was soon considered the intellectual father of pan-Africanism in Africa. He was greatly influenced by W. E. B. DuBois, whom he considered his mentor, and became the most outspoken proponent of a continental African strategy for pan-Africanism.

The second critical decision Nkrumah made was to leave the United States in 1945. He went to England, the colonial power that controlled the Gold Coast, to seek admission into the London School of Economics. However, when he arrived in London it seemed that another purpose was waiting for him. George Padmore asked him if he would assist in developing the Fifth Pan-African Congress, which had been called by DuBois and some other eminent people of African heritage. The young Nkrumah leaped at the opportunity and was immediately thrust into leadership roles in the planning and execution of the Congress. He came to the attention of many people because of his dedication to the work of the Congress. The experience at the Manchester Pan-African Congress lit a fire under him and he took on the decolonization of Africa as his principal objective in life. He was elected vice president of the West African Students Union, a position he took seriously, using every opportunity to write to European colonial administrators, politicians, and statesmen about the need for African independence. No one had ever seen the continent in such clear terms as Nkrumah right after the Manchester Pan-African Congress. It was as if a veil had been lifted from his eyes and he vowed to use his intelligence and ambition in the interest of the continent. It was a rare desire in an era that was increasingly becoming victimized by the material wealth that individuals could amass if they were not distracted by the political objectives of independence. Nothing would stop Nkrumah because he believed, as his elders had said at Manchester, that the Second World War had exhausted the European nations and they could not fight against the gathering momentum for freedom.

Two years after Manchester, he returned to the Gold Coast to become a member of the leading anti-colonial party, the United Gold Coast Convention, led by the venerable Akyem intellectual Joseph B. Danquah. He was not well pleased, to put it mildly, with the gradualism of the UGCC. He did not believe that Britain would grant independence on the basis of the UGCC's petitions and pleadings with the colonial office. There had to be a more aggressive stance toward the authorities. Nkrumah formed his own party, called the Convention People's Party (CPP), with the express purpose of "self-government now!" He left the UGCC in 1949 and near the end of that year he declared a campaign of "positive action," a mass movement of ordinary people based on boycotts, work slowdowns, strikes, civil disobedience, and public rallies. The idea was to demonstrate how inept and weak the British colonial adminstration was in the face of the power of the people. He was arrested within weeks of calling for positive protests. The British authorities sent him to prison in January 1950.

Nkrumah and his colleagues had made the situation quite untenable for the British. The decision was made to leave the Gold Coast. In the 1951 election for seats in the Legislative Assembly, under the colonial administration, Nkrumah won a seat to the body while still in prison. In fact, his political party won thirty-four of thirty-eight seats on the Legislative Assembly. He was released from prison in February 1951 and the governor, Charles Arden-Clark, recognizing the immense popularity of Nkrumah, asked him if he would lead a government in cooperation with the British with an eye to independence. Nkrumah agreed to this arrangement, and after several years with the status of "half free and half slave" the country became independent on March 6, 1957, and was renamed Ghana, after the ancient West African empire. The masses referred to Nkrumah as "Osagyefo," meaning "victorious leader." He became the prime minister, that is, with the head of state remaining in Britain. However, in 1960 Ghana was declared a republic and Kwame Nkrumah became the first president of Ghana. Three years later, because of the philosophical and ideological position of Nkrumah on pan-Africanism, Ghana became, in 1963, one of the charter members of the Organization of African Unity.

Earlier Nkrumah had invited W. E. B. DuBois to Ghana as a permanent citizen of the African world. DuBois had been asked to organize the *Encyclopedia Africana*, a project which he started before his death in August 1963. Ghana memorialized DuBois by claiming the house he lived in as a national monument. Both DuBois and his wife, Shirley Graham, are entombed in the grounds of the last home they had together.

Like several of his contemporaries Nkrumah was an intellectual with his own vision of Africa. He understood the impact of capitalism on Africa and believed that it would have a lingering effect for a long time. The capitalists had exploited the people and appropriated the resources of Africa and the only way Africa was to advance was to wrench itself from the capitalist's noose and find an accommodation with socialism because it would respect the values of the African people, if designed along African ways. Kwame Nkrumah did not believe in pipe dreams; it was clear to him that socialism was not a panacea for all of Africa's problems. It was only one way to challenge the people to examine themselves to see if it were possible for Africa to raise itself from degradation and demoralization. He believed it was possible; that is why Ghana honors him with monuments and statues today even though he had his detractors and enemies. Perhaps his most telling contribution to Africa was the proper analysis of the imperialist damage to the social fabric of the continent. He believed that the imperialists had sought to weaken the value structure of Africa as well as the desires of Africans. On the other hand, he had come to believe that socialism, particularly if it respected the Afrocentric way of being and living, could move Africa forward.

Nkrumah insisted that Ghana needed to have an industrial base devoted to the livelihood of Ghanaians and not to the old colonial interests. The colonial trade system would never allow the people to become economically independent. If he could encourage the business leaders to reduce their dependence on foreign capital, the nation could become independent in fact. Of course, economists now believe that the turn away from the cocoa sector, which had been a strong economic sector, toward a more industrialized sector crippled both. Ghana spent lots of money on massive public works during Nkrumah's time and the elites remained dependent on Western imports.

Although Nkrumah remained the intellectual and spiritual leader of the pan-Africanist idea in Africa the economic downturn in his own country weakened his ability to put into play many of his ideas. There was an attempt on his life and some political unrest because many thought that the country had spent too much money on large industrial projects such as the infrastructure at the port, factories, ships, highways, and official buildings and not enough on the subtler aspects of development such as education, health, and quality of life. It pained Nkrumah that the people were not able to see the long vision of his political project and how much he loved Ghana and Africa. Yet the unrest was unabated. It was exacerbated when he established Ghana as a one-party state with himself as president-for-life in 1964.

On February 24, 1966, while Nkrumah was on a state visit to Beijing and Hanoi, the government of Ghana was overthrown by a United States-sponsored military coup d'état. The American ambassador, a man of African origin, was used to help bring down one of the first African countries to gain independence. His actions were widely condemned in speeches and articles by African Americans. Nkrumah had found that he had enemies within and without his government. He never returned to Ghana but was well received by many other governments, including the government of Guinea, where Sekou Toure, the president of Guinea, named him the co-president of the country in an act of authentic African brotherhood. Fearful of the West because of its role in his overthrow he went to Romania to seek medical treatment and died there on April 27, 1972. He was initially buried in his home town of Nkroful but the government of Ghana later transferred his remains to a beautiful national memorial tomb in Accra, the capital of Ghana.

In memory of his struggle and the tremendous energy Nkrumah put into the Pan-African Congresses, a Sixth Pan-African Congress was held in Dar es Salaam, Tanzania, in June 1974. There had been an intense campaign to have this meeting in Tanzania, considered at the time the vanguard country of African revolution. Walter Rodney, the Guyanese intellectual, was living in Tanzania and pushed hard for this conference. Rodney also developed a reputation as a pan-Africanist theoretician and activist. He had political access and political relationships with those who were struggling to transform Africa and to snatch control of Africa from external forces. He was very close to some of the leaders of liberation movements in Africa and also to political leaders of popular organizations of independent territories. Together with other pan-Africanists he participated in discussions leading up to the Sixth Pan-African Congress. Before the Congress he wrote a piece: "Towards the Sixth Pan-African Congress: Aspects of the International Class Struggle in Africa, the Caribbean and America." The Sixth PAC, as it came to be called, had potential to be the greatest meeting of its kind because it was the first such congress held on the African continent and many nations were now independent. However, because of the great diversity of political views, international agendas, and foreign meddling, the congress did not produce the vision that had been hoped for. One observer, the venerable John Henrik Clarke, observed:

> what could have been the most important Pan-African Congress and the first to meet on African soil was the Sixth Pan-African Congress. It was the largest and most diverse of these meetings. It was unwieldy and

very little was accomplished. Too many Africans from different parts of the world and from within Africa itself came with different agendas. Not much was achieved except some good and bad conversations and an unfortunate fight over ideologies.

His assessment became the semi-official conclusion about the meeting. Essentially, the congress demonstrated that more work had to be done to prepare the African world for a profound discussion of political ideologies that competed for the attention of the independent states.

Five years later, in 1977, there would be a meeting in Lagos, Nigeria, called the Festival of Black and African Countries. More than 100,000 delegates would gather to celebrate the achievements of the African peoples. Some of the same arguments that appeared at the Dar es Salaam Pan-African Congress came into focus at the Intellectual Colloquium. The principal issues in Lagos were similar to those at Dar on representation, culture, politics, and economics. The drama was created by two incidents, each demonstrating the fundamental problems of bringing large groups together without a preparatory meeting. There was a mixture of government officials representing nation-states and Africans from the Diaspora representing no states. The latter included Africans from Brazil, the United States, and England. There were also Africans from the Caribbean who did represent states, such as Jamaica and Trinidad. However, some continental Africans had difficulty considering the Diaspora as a part of the African world. This was highlighted when the Brazilian Abdias do Nascimento, one of the great African Brazilians, was challenged because he did not represent the Brazilian government and according to some should not have a seat at the table. Instead the seat was occupied by the white representative from Brazil, while the leading black intellectual from that country was confronted by some of the continentals. His case was taken up by others from the Diaspora, including the leader of the American delegation, Maulana Karenga, who argued that it was not the intention of Diasporans to have continental Africans declare who was and who was not an African. Nascimento also got up and in a brilliant speech defended his position, claiming that the government of Brazil was racist and did not speak for the interests of black people. In the end, the leaders of the colloquium had to seat Abdias do Nascimento as well as the official Brazilian delegate. The second issue was the language issue. Wole Soyinka, a Nigerian of Yoruba ethnicity, proposed the KiSwahili language as a lingua franca for Africa. Many Africans from othe ethnic groups wondered aloud why the language should be KiSwahili, some proposing their own languages, and Yoruba people contending that Soyinka had forgotten his roots. He argued and was supported by others that KiSwahili is an international language spoken by millions of people although the ethnic group for which it is named is very small. In the end, this was resolved in support of the KiSwahili language with a recommendation that all African nations support the teaching of the language. The issue of the Arabic-speaking countries was also resolved, with those countries taking their seats at the table of African intellectuals.

## Julius Nyerere and the ideology of African socialism

Julius Kambarage Nyerere was born on April 13, 1922. His father, Mzee Burito, was a sub-king of the Zanaki. When Nyerere was born the country was called Tanganyika and it was under the British, who had managed to wrest it from the Germans during the First World War.

There was something in the young man Kambarage that others saw and appreciated. He was a born teacher. Like many of his contemporaries he believed that one answer for the development of Africa was the education of the masses. He began teaching long before he had completed his college work. The idea was to teach what one knew to those who knew less. It was this willingness to share with the less well educated that earned him the nickname "Mwalimu," meaning "teacher" in the Swahili language, because he enjoyed the idea of sharing his knowledge with others. There were other teachers but there was something special about the genius of Mwalimu. When he went off to study economics at the University of Edinburgh the community expected great things. Mwalimu could compete with the best students and would not let the people down.

Upon his return to Tanganyika he co-founded the Tanganyika African National Union (TANU) and later merged it with the Afro-Shirazi Party of Zanzibar to form the powerful party Chama cha Mapinduzi (CCM) or People's Revolutionary Movement. There was no question in his mind that any party that emerged as a vanguard party had to offer employment, work for social equality, create opportunities for equitable distribution of resources, and seek the independence of Tanganyika.

Tanganyika achieved independence in 1961 and Nyerere became prime minister. When the government merged with Zanzibar to form the new state of Tanzania, Nyerere was elected the first president of Tanzania. Almost as soon as he came to power Nyerere implemented a socialist agenda. His idea was to create a massive transformation where the masses of people would immediately become empowered with sustainable economic development. He has been trained in economics, believed in the power of the economic moment to change societies, and had useful advisors and other ideological supporters like Mohammed Babu, who insisted on the economic change for everyone.

To bring about the desired change, Nyerere used some of what he saw in the Chinese model, adapting it where necessary. He sought closer ties to the Chinese than to the Russians, Americans, or British.

The Tanzanian economic policy was the collectivization of the agricultural system, known as *ujamaa* or "familyhood." In Nyerere's terminology this was not socialism as it had been preached by Marx or any other European, it was an idea of family economics such that the foundation for it was African values. People sometimes called him an African socialist, but it was to the traditional ways of life and the values he had learned as a young man to which he wanted his country to return. He believed that social and economic life should be structured around the *ujamaa*, or extended family, found in traditional Africa. He believed, based on what he had learned from his village elders, that *ujamaa* had existed before the arrival of the European imperialists.

By returning to the state of *ujamaa* the people would soon lose sight of the capitalist model. In effect, Nyerere was convinced that Africans were already, recently socialists; all that they needed to do was return to their traditional mode of life and they would recapture it. By repudiating capitalism the masses would have enough to eat and no one would be hungry or lack for basic needs. The government also instituted a policy that said no one could have more than one house to live in. It was an ideal situation, based on the values of *ujamaa*, but unfortunately the inability of the government to overcome the realities of the global economy doomed the project. Under Julius Nyerere, Tanzania went from being the largest exporter of agricultural products in Africa to being the largest importer of agricultural products in Africa. Disappointed in the fact that his *ujamaa* program did not improve the Tanzanian economy, Nyerere told his party that he would not run for reelection in 1985. With his usual candor and straightforwardness, he said in his farewell speech, "I failed. Let's admit it."

Nyerere was respected by his peers, elevated by the masses, and revered as an elder statesman of Africa. He traveled and spoke at many conferences and for numerous universities. He was one of the founding members of the Organization of African Unity in 1963 and played a major role in overthrowing the oppressive dictatorship of Idi Amin in Uganda.

## Léopold Sédar Senghor

Léopold Sédar Senghor was born in 1906 in Joal-la-Portugaise, a small fishing village about 70 miles south of Dakar. His father, a wealthy merchant, was of noble descent among the Serere. His mother was Peul, and he was proud of his

*Figure 14.4* Léopold Senghor, president of Senegal, 1962
© Bettmann/CORBIS

heritage, combining two of the many groups of Senegal in his lineage. The first seven years of his life Senghor spent in Djilor with his mother and maternal uncles and aunts, learning many of the traditions and customs of the Peul. At the age of 12, he attended the Catholic mission school of Ngazobil, where he excelled in literature. He also studied at the Libermann Seminary and Lycée Van Vollenhoven, completing secondary education in 1928.

He won a state scholarship and was sent to Paris to attend the Lycée Louis-le-Grand in 1931. This was during the period of the Harlem Renaissance and Senghor heard of the movement while in Paris and read many of the writers. He was truly impressed with the way the African American poets of the Harlem Renaissance captured the essence of the African experience in the United States. Of course, he knew the French poets and writers such as Rimbaud, Mallarmé, Baudelaire, Verlaine, and Valéry. Among Senghor's friends were young Africans from around the world, like Aimé Césaire of Martinique and Léon Damas of French Guiana, with whom he would forge an intellectual camaraderie and create the idea of *Négritude*. Georges Pompidou, who became president of France, was also a long-time friend. Senegalese figured quite prominently in French society as scholars and soldiers; in 1932 Senghor was granted French citizenship, following a tradition that had been highlighted by Blaise Diagne. He served in a regiment of colonial infantry and in 1935 he obtained the *agrégation* degree in grammar.

Subsequently, Senghor worked as a teacher at Lycée Descartes in Tours from 1935 and then he taught for the Paris school Lycée Marcelin Berelot. When World War II started he joined the French army. After being captured by the Germans, he spent eighteen months in a camp as a prisoner of war. During this period he learned German and wrote poems, which were published in *Hosties Noires* (1948). In 1944 Senghor was appointed Professor of African languages at the Ecole Nationale de la France d'Outre-Mer. Senghor's first collection of poems, *Chants d'ombre* (1945), was inspired by the philosopher Henri Bergson. This was the period of the war but it was also a period of creativity for Senghor. In 1945 and 1946 Senghor was elected to represent Senegal in the French Constituent Assemblies. With Senghor's help Alioune Diop, a Senegalese intellectual living in Paris, created in 1947 *Présence Africaine*, a cultural journal, which had on the advisory board French intellectuals like Jean-Paul Sartre, André Gide, and Albert Camus. In 1948 Senghor was made a professor at Ecole Nationale de la France d'Outre-Mer. From 1946 to 1958 he was continuously reelected to the French National Assembly as a representative of Senegal. When he broke with Lamine Guèye, an ally of the French socialist, Senghor created a new political party, BDS (Bloc Démocratique Sénégalais). He married in 1948 Ginette Eboué, the daughter of a prominent Guyanese colonial administrator. They had two children; the marriage ended in divorce. Senghor's second wife, who was French, had her family roots in the Normandy region. When Senegal joined with the Sudanese Republic to form the Federation of Mali, Senghor became president of the federal assembly. In August 1960 Senegal separated from the federation and Senghor was elected its first president. He received several international awards as a writer, including the Dag

*Figure 14.5* Goree Island, Senegal
© Molefi Kete Asante

Hammarskjöld Prize (1965), the Peace Prize of German Book Trade (1968), the Haile Selassie African Research Prize (1973), and the Apollonaire Prize for Poetry (1974).

Senghor's poems, written in French, have been translated into several languages: Spanish, English, German, Russian, Swedish, Italian, Chinese, Japanese, and others. In his poetry Senghor invites the reader to feel the nearly mystical, supersensory world of Africa. His non-fiction includes writings primarily in linguistics, politics, and sociology. His philosophy and the concept of *Négritude* has received international attention. After leaving the presidency in 1980, Senghor divided his time between Paris, Normandy, and Dakar. Like Nyerere before him, Senghor demonstrated that not all of the independence presidents wanted to be presidents-for-life. In 1983 Senghor was elected to the Académie Française. He died in France on December 20, 2001.

## The assassination of hope: the killing of Patrice Lumumba

Patrice Emery Lumumba, one of Africa's most iconic leaders was born on July 2, 1925, the same year as the African American nationalist leader, Malcolm X. Much like Malcolm X, Lumumba would make an indelible imprint on his time. He would become one of Africa's most ardent nationalist leaders in his short career and establish himself as a revolutionary with an immense optimism for his country, the Democratic Republic of the Congo. When the country declared its independence in June 1960 it was Lumumba who was named prime minister, a post he would hold less than a year, being forced out of office in September 1960 and ultimately being assassinated in January 1961.

*Figure 14.6* A 1960 picture of Patrice Lumumba
© –/BELGA/epa/CORBIS

## The creation of a Revolutionary

There are many lessons in the life and death of Patrice Lumumba. He was born in Onalua in Kasai province during the Belgian rule of the Congo. The young Lumumba was educated at a Christian missionary school and later worked as a clerk and journalist in Leopoldville (Kinshasa) and Stanleyville (Kisangani). Early in his life he exhibited elements of flexibility, literacy, independence, and a fierce will to do justice and bring harmony and peace to his society. As a person with a dominant personality in discussion and debate, Lumumba became the regional president of a Congolese trade union and joined the the Belgian Liberal Party in 1955. It did not take long for the colonial authorities to arrest him. He was charged in 1957 with embezzlement and kept in prison for one year.

Prison gave him time for political reflection. He knew that freedom would not be handed to the Congolese without agitation and resistance. It was Patrice Lumumba's ambition to agitate and organize for freedom. Since he was one of the few Africans with some form of education in the Belgian Congo, he spent considerable energy seeking ways to create change in his country. Thus, upon his release from prison he helped create the Mouvement National Congolais in 1957. Two years later the Belgian government announced a five-year path to independence. In the meantime, they arrested Lumumba again because of his political activities, and in the December 1959 local elections the MNC won a convincing majority despite Lumumba being under arrest. This was reminiscent of the situation that occurred in Ghana when Kwame Nkrumah's party won while he was imprisoned by the British. The results of this Congo election forced the authorities to initiate a conference on independence in 1960. At the conclusion of the conference it was decided that independence should be brought forward to June l960 with elections to be held in May of the same year. Nothing could have shocked the African community more than this move by the Belgians, although some believed that the Belgians knowing that they had not prepared Africans for leadership, were simply playing a political game. It was thought that the Africans would seek to create a government, fail, and have to call the Belgians in to fix the situation. This did not happen. The first government was formed by Lumumba and the MNC on June 23, 1960 with Lumumba as Prime Minister and Joseph Kasavubu as President. The new Congo government was heralded by Africans and progressives everywhere as a major offensive against all forms of colonialism.

Nevertheless, there were inherent problems in the governing of such a vast and wealthy land. With a lack of educated Congolese to assume control of ministerial posts to direct government offices, Lumumba's rule was defined by political and ethnic unrest, international intrigue, Belgian paternalism, and serious economic and political disruption in the rich province of Katanga.

Moise Tshombe, leader of Katanga, declared with Belgian support, Katanga independent of the national government in June 1960. What had seemed like a Belgian determination to allow Congo to be independent when the elections were moved to 1960 seemed now to have actually been a plot to rob the Congo of its most economically viable region. The Belgians saw Katanga as one of the provinces where the whites could fall back into a bunker position and still remain firmly in control of the economy of the country. Tshombe was convinced that the Belgians would have supplied him with all of the resources he needed to fight against the central government. There was now a monumental challenge to the independence that Congo had gained.

United Nations troops were sent to assist Lumumba's undertrained army and yet the fighting continued because they did not supply enough troops. At this critical juncture Lumumba asked the Soviet Union for aid. In September 1960, Joseph Kasavubu, the president, dismissed Lumumba, the prime minister, from government, a crude act of dubious constitutionality; however, in retaliation, Lumumba sought to dismiss Kasavubu from the presidency. Thus, only sixty-seven days after he came to power, Patrice Lumumba, the symbol of national hopes, was out of office.

On September 14 a coup d'état headed by a former policeman, Colonel Joseph Mobutu (who would later gain notoriety as President Mobutu Sese Seko), and supported by Kasavubu was successful. Lumumba was outmaneuvered and arrested by Mobutu on December 1, 1960. When Mobutu's forces captured Lumumba he had been smuggled out of his house at night in the car of a visiting diplomat friend and was being taken on the road toward Stanleyville (Kisingali). Mobutu's troops in hot pursuit eventually trapped Lumumba on the banks of the Sankuru River. The world waited to hear what had happened to the prime minister, who was taken to the town of Port Francqui and flown to the city of Leopoldville (Kinshasa) in handcuffs like a common criminal. It represented one of the lowest points in African political history. Mobutu, a man of limited education, declared that

Lumumba would be tried for inciting the army to rebellion because he had appealed to the army to the constitutional right of the prime minister.

Now was set into place an ordeal that created consternation in world politics. Lumumba asked the local United Nations troops to protect him from his enemies. National sovereignty had dissolved into a series of political quarrels. The UN refused on orders from headquarters in New York to come to his assistance. When he got to Leopoldville he appeared beaten and humiliated before journalists and diplomats from around the world.

In an effort that was considered half-hearted and suspicious, Dag Hammarskjöld, the secretary-general of the United Nations, made an appeal to President Kasavubu to treat Lumumba according to the due process of law. The Soviet Union immediately responded by denouncing Hammarskjöld and the Western powers, including the United States and Belgium, for being responsible for the arrest of Lumumba. The government of the Soviet Union demanded that Lumumba be immediately released.

On December 7, the United Nations Security Council was called into session to consider the Soviet demands that Lumumba be released and restored as head of the Congo government, that Mobutu's forces be disarmed, and that all Belgians be evacuated from the Congo. Lumumba had shown himself to be a friend to the Soviet Union, a socialist and anti-imperialist, and the Soviet Union believed that the Western powers were intent on keeping the wealth of the Congo out of the sphere of communist influence. Valerian Zorin, the Soviet representative, refused the United States' demands that he disqualify himself as Security Council president during the debate. Dag Hammarskjöld tried to answer the Soviets' attack against his policies by saying that if the United Nations force withdrew from the region, "I fear everything will crumble." Following a UN report that Lumumba had been mistreated by Mobutu's forces, Lumumba's followers threatened on December 9 that they would arrest all Belgians and "start cutting off the heads of some of them" unless Lumumba was released within 48 hours.

The seriousness of the situation was intensified by the announcement of the withdrawal of their United Nations' Congo contingents by Yugoslavia, the United Arab Republic, Ceylon, Indonesia, Morocco, and Guinea. The Soviet pro-Lumumba resolution was defeated on December 14 by a United States-led United Nations Security Council vote of eight to two. On the same day, an American-supported resolution that would have given Hammarskjöld increased powers to deal with the Congo situation was vetoed by the Soviet Union.

As the situation deteriorated in the Congo, Lumumba's followers demanded his release and the forces under Mobutu intensified their attacks on Lumumba's people. In one of the more chaotic scenes on early African television news, Lumumba and his compatriots were humiliated at Mobutu's villa, where soldiers loyal to Mobutu beat the elected prime minister in full view of television cameras.

The entire country seemed to be coming apart at the seams. On January 17, 1961, Prime Minister Lumumba was then transported from the military prison in Thysville, near Leopoldville, to a more distant and supposedly secure prison in Jadotville in Katanga province. In a murderous plot, Lumumba and his fellow prisoners, Maurice Mpolo and Joseph Okito, were beaten several times by provincial police upon their arrival in secessionist Katanga. The Belgians, who had resented Lumumba's independent mind, his spirited defense of African rights, and his efforts to retain the unity of Congo, demanded a decisive ending to the conflict. They had insisted that Lumumba be sent to President Tshombe of the unilaterally declared state of Katanga. Lumumba had been brutalized on the flight to Elizabethville near Jadotville. Once in the hands of the Katangese soldiers commanded by Belgians he was driven to Villa Brouwe before being taken to Jadotville. He was guarded and brutalized still further by both Belgian and Katangese troops while President Tshombe and his cabinet decided what to do with him.

So deep was the hatred stirred up against Lumumba that the people who persecuted him did not know anything other than the fact that it was now possible to abuse a person who had once been elected to head the nation. It was almost as if the violence was directed against the will of Africans to be free; the assaults on Lumumba, Mpolo, and Okito were vicious and cruel.

With evil incarnate revealed in the plot to prevent the rise of another charismatic African who had the best interest of the African people at heart, the forces of iniquity bundled Lumumba into another convoy and headed for the countryside. By now, he was quite hungry, unshaven, in severe pain from all of the bruises that had gone untreated, and in an impossible state of psychic terror that his own people, with the collaboration of the Belgians, could treat him as if he was an enemy of the state, when in fact he was its best hope. That night, when the convoy drew up beside a large tree, three firing squads had been assembled, all commanded by a Belgian. Another Belgian had overall command of the execution site. Lumumba and two other comrades from the government were lined up against a large tree. President Tshombe and two other ministers were present for the executions, which took place one at a time. That night Congo was plunged back into the shadows of King Leopold's era when Africans had no rights that needed to be respected and where self-hatred was real, dangerous, and rampant. It would take many years for the country to rise above the catastrophe of chopping down the tallest trees.

After the night-time murders of January 17, 1961, the officials of Katanga said nothing for three weeks. Rumors took on a life of their own. When the deaths of Lumumba and his two compatriots were announced on the Katanga radio it was said that he had tried to escape and enraged villagers had murdered him and his comrades. This was a lie but it would be many years before the lie was uncovered. Belgium admitted in 2002 that it had been culpable and apologized to the Congolese people. The Belgians took "moral responsibility" and an "irrefutable portion of responsibility in the events that led to the death of Lumumba." United States government documents revealed that the Central Intelligence Agency, while it knew of the Belgians' plans, had no direct role in the murders.

## The Nigerian Civil War and the road to legitimate authority

Nothing indicates the difficulty of establishing legitimacy and positive government in the nations created out of the boundaries made by Europe more than the Nigerian Civil War, which lasted from 1967 to 1970. Indeed, as we now know, Nigeria, like other nations, was an artificial creation of the colonial era. Numerous ethnic groups were included within the boundaries of the country. Because of the tensions that existed between these groups and the inability of the Western-style government to accommodate the diversity, it was inevitable that there would be problems.

It is possible to say that the Nigerian Civil War was an ethnic conflict with political and economic implications. The fact that the conflict led to the self-proclaimed secession of the southeastern provinces of Nigeria, called the Republic of Biafra, identifies ethnic conflict as a concrete issue.

The colonial society was primed for conflict. When Nigeria got its independence in 1960 it was a mammoth country of more than 400 ethnic groups, with bulging populations in the three major regions of the country. A nation created by agreement between European nations who had little interest in the ideas of Africans was simply waiting for an explosion. At independence, the 60 million people of Nigeria included the major groups of Hausa-Fulana, Yoruba, and Igbo. Many smaller groups lived within the boundaries of these three general regions.

At independence the Hausa and Igbo created a conservative political alliance which ruled Nigeria from independence to 1966. Such an alliance kept the Yoruba from power. Thus the northern region and the southeastern region had effective control of the country. The well-educated Igbo people benefited from this political alliance. The Igbo were in many important posts in the country.

Although the Yoruba supported a progressive, socialist, reformist party called the Action Group, which showed antipathy toward the Muslim northern bloc, they believed that they deserved better representation. A "palace coup" in the western region led to a more conservative group in the west which sought to enter alliance with the Muslim-dominated north. This new alliance, named the Nigerian National Alliance, threatened to roll back the gains of the Igbo elites.

During the elections of 1965 the Nigerian National Alliance of the Islamic north and the conservative forces in the west contested the elections against the United Progressive Grand Alliance of the Christian southeast, some progressive elements of the west, and some northerners. The Nigerian National Alliance won an overwhelming victory under the leadership of Sir Abubakar Tafawa Balewa. Immediately, members of the United Progressive Grand Alliance claimed widespread electoral vote rigging.

Discontent with the elections led to a military coup on January 15, 1966, by a cadre of junior army officers, mostly majors and captains. When the dust cleared and the leadership emerged General Aguyi Ironsi, the head of the Nigerian army, ascended to the position of head of state for Nigeria. There was a perception based on reality that the coup benefited mostly the Igbo people because the coup plotters and General Ironsi were Igbo. Ironsi added to the suspicion by promoting many Igbo officers at the expense of

Hausa and Yoruba officers. This created harsh feelings and bad blood between members of the armed forces.

Consequently, few people were surprised when a little over six months after the first coup, on July 29, 1966, northern officers executed a counter-coup. It was led by a Lieutenant Colonel Murtala Muhammad, himself a future leader of the country, but the coup leaders placed in power Lieutenant Colonel Yakubu Gowon. Soon ethnic tensions reached fever pitch throughout the country as discussions and debates about the merits of coup politics entered every corner of the public and private life of the relatively new Nigerian body politic.

In the north the coup and counter-coup tensions brought about large-scale massacre of Igbo people living in the Muslim north of the country. Many Igbo people had migrated there as teachers, doctors, merchants, and store-keepers but saw their dreams go up in smoke and many of their fellow Igbo Christians killed. This led to a massive exodus of skilled Igbo people from the north back to their southern homeland. Large discoveries of oil in the southeastern part of the country suggested to the southerners that they could be independent and self-sufficient, given the natural resource and their educated population. However, since they were not in control of the central government they were frightened that their resources would be used to support the rest of the country rather than the southeast. Fear of punishment by the northerners now in control of the state led to political preparations for dealing with the exclusion of the Igbo people from power positions.

In such an atmosphere it was almost predictable that a charismatic leader would arise to point out that the political situation suggested secession as the only alternative to subjection at the hands of the Muslim north. Thus, the appointed military governor of the Igbo-dominated southeastern region, Colonel Oumegwu Ojukwu, citing the Muslim massacres of Igbo citizens and electoral fraud, proclaimed with the support of the southern parliament the secession of the southeastern region from Nigeria as the independent Republic of Biafra, in the early morning of May 30, 1967. Only four countries recognized the new republic. There were reports of personal animosity between Gowon and Ojukwu, some people believing that Ojukwu resented the fact that Gowon was not the next officer in line to the deposed Ironsi and should not be the head of state. Ambition was said to play a part in Ojukwu's call for an independent Biafra. Whatever the personal motivations, the fact remains that the decisison to take Biafra out of the nation created the drama that led to civil war. The Nigerian government launched a "police action," using the armed forces to retake the secessionist territory. The Nigerian army met with difficulty in gaining territory at first and the international sentiment seemed to turn in favor of Biafra because of the northern massacres and the inability, it seemed, of the Nigerian army to penetrate the defenses of the smaller Biafran army. Times of stress, tension, or war on a national level tend to create conditions for extraordinary leadership and the Biafran troops led by a brilliant tactician and brave commander, Colonel Banjo, crossed the massive Niger River and entered the mid-western region of Nigeria, launching attack after attack on targets close to the capital city of Lagos.

Such a bold move by Colonel Banjo's forces brought about a quick reorganization of the Nigerian forces, which led to a counter-offensive that stopped the penetration of other regions of Nigeria by Banjo's lightning assaults. Soon the Biafran army was reluctant to fight, particularly when they did not have proper equipment, resources, or leadership. They were pushed back into their heartland. Ultimately the capital city of Biafra, Enugu, was captured by the Nigerian army and the entire core territory was surrounded with the aid of air, naval, and land blockades. There was constant resistance and guerrilla action from the Biafran core territory.

The Igbo, Ijaw, and Ibibio people of the region learned to improvise and create their own supplies and equipment, build bridges and roads, and repair airplanes. Then a stalemate occurred from 1968 onward. It seemed that the Nigerian government, even with its best officers, one called the Scorpion, could not make advances into the remaining areas of Biafran territory. There was a looming humanitarian crisis in the territory that was receiving sympathy from the international community and campaigns to end the war were mounted in the United States, Europe, and the United Nations. Nigerian forces sabotaged Biafran farms and images of starving children suggested to the world that genocide was occurring. Numerous Europeans organized blockade-breaking relief flights into Biafra, carrying food, medicines, and weapons. Biafra also had foreign mercenaries fighting on their side, which is said to have lengthened the war. Indeed, the international meddlers had predicted an oil boom in the southeast of Nigeria had Biafra won. There was eventually an oil boom anyway, but the agents who supported the dismemberment of Nigeria had their own pockets to line rather than any altruistic motive for their support.

By 1970 the war had exhausted much of the treasury of Nigeria, depleted Biafra's international aid, and done great political damage to the proud Nigerian people. The leader of Biafra, Oumegwu Ojukwu, escaped to Côte d'Ivoire and a final surrender of the Biafran forces by General Philip Effiong, deputy to Ojukwu, to the Nigerian army took place. There were no reprisals as predicted by some people and attempts were made at reconciliation.

Nevertheless the toll of the war was great for the young country. More than a million lives were lost, money from industry, particularly the oil industry, was lost, the infrastructure of the nation was badly damaged in the southeastern region, and thousands of children died of starvation. In a heroic attempt to restore peace and credibility the Nigerian reconstruction, using the oil money, was swift; however, the old ethnic tensions did not dissipate. Several military governments succeeded the Gowon administration. Protests continued in southeast Nigeria against the governmnent's use of the southeast's resources without putting development in the region at the top of the priority list. Everyone in the southeast felt they were being denied a fair share of oil revenues. Laws were passed mandating that political parties could not be ethnically based.

The Biafran War, or the Nigerian Civil War, was finally put to rest when on Monday, May 29, 2000, the *Guardian of Lagos* wrote that President Olusegun Obasanjo commuted to retirement the dismissal of all military

*Figure 14.7* Nigerian president Olusegun Obasanjo at the opening session of the OPEC summit in Caracas, September 27, 2000

© Reuters/CORBIS

persons who fought for the breakaway state of Biafra during the Nigerian Civil War. In a national broadcast, he said that the decision was based on the principle that "justice must at all times be tempered with mercy." This could have been interpreted as an attempt to give confidence to the Igbo as members of the nation, but it was also a way for Obasanjo to bring the war to closure. It had lingered too long as a cleavage between the peoples of the country. Igbo people had felt that they had been mistreated by the government. With Obasanjo's action the resurgence of pro-Biafra sentiment among a section of the Igbo was dampened. Nigeria could praise itself in the manner of the African wisdom saying "lizard that jumped from the high iroko tree to the ground and declared that for such a feat he would praise himself if no one else did."

Numerous Nigerian writers, journalists, and scholars were created intellectually out of the political cauldron of the situation, that is, their memories had been stamped with the necessity to seek unity and union. Among the luminaries that came to the front were Chinua Achebe, Eghosa Osagie, Akin Euba, Adeniyi Coker, Ola Rotimi, Wole Soyinka, Doyin Abiola, M. K. O. Abiola, Molara Ogundipe, Ihechukwu Madubuike, Ugorji Ugorji, Chinweizu, Emeka Nwaidora, and scores of other men and women of distinction.

Chinua Achebe is one of the greatest novelists of the century. His strong narrative style as in *Things Fall Apart* has classified him as one of the best storytellers in African history. Wole Soyinka, a Nobel Prize winner for dramatic literature in 1986, is in the top echelon of world literary figures. Nigeria is a country with thousands of learned men and women whose commitment is to find unity and peace. Ken Saro-wiwa, the firebrand agitator who was executed in southeastern Nigeria in the 1990s while campaigning to stop the pollution, exploitation of the land, and devastation of the lives of the people of his region, was also one of these people. Also there was the genius Chinweizu, the journalist, who fought against all kinds of oppression, mainly mental, in order to assert the truth of an African reality. Chinweizu's first large-scale work, *The West and the Rest of Us* (1975), is a historical account of Western domination of the developing world, especially of Africa. An impressive work of synthesis, the book strongly critiques Africa's governing elites and argues for dissolution of dominant Eurocentric values and a reconstruction of African society through the establishment of pan-African political and economic unity.

Like Chinweizu on the literary front, Fela Anikulapo Kuti on the musical front sought to stretch the cultural case so that Africans would be the leaders of their own sound. His music was political and the 77 albums and 135 songs produced by Fela represent a political testimony. He was born in Abeokuta, Nigeria, in 1938, and soon became a singer, musician, and composer. His intention was to use his art to fight for the common people. This led to him being criticized, harassed, and even imprisoned by the Nigerian government. When he died in 1997 he was only 58 years old but he had made himself immortal by his constant struggle against all forms of oppression.

## The Libyan *jamahariya*

The history of Libya in Africa is long. In fact, it is a history that parallels that of Kemet and Nubia in antiquity. One reads of the Libyans in the Egyptian texts and it appears that even if they may have originated somewhere else they have been in the territory for a very long time. During the course of history at one time or another the indigenous Libyan African people have been conquered and settled by Greeks, Turks, Romans, Arabs and Amazighs.

The occupation and control of the country by the Ottoman Turks from the sixteenth century until 1911, when the Italians took Libya from the Turks as a last-ditch effort for Italy to occupy an African colony as other Europeans had done, was a defining historical moment. What it represented was the fact that the Ottoman Turks had done very little to preserve the ancient civilization of Libya or to suggest that the African population express its profound historical tradition apart from Islam.

From 1945 to 1951, Libya was under a United Nation Trusteeship as the Italian government lost the colony during World War II. It became an independent nation, with a king of Turkish heritage. The country's history and that of Africa changed when a Berber military officer, Colonel Mu'ammer al-Gaddafi, led a military coup d'état that overthrew King Idris in 1969.

Gaddafi pursued a policy of nationalizing the resources of the country, purging the nation of Western influences, and taking over the military establishment of the country for the interests of the Libyan people. British and American forces were compelled to leave bases which they had occupied since defeating the Italians. In addition, thousands of descendants of Italian settlers were forced to abandon their homes in Libya.

Taking on a pro-African stance, Gaddafi increased oil exports to other African nations, took over the majority stake in all foreign oil companies, and began incentives for Libyans and others to refine and distribute oil. This is not

*Figure 14.8* Libyan leader Mu'ammer Gaddafi at Itehadeya Presidential Palace in Cairo, February 2005
© Khaled El-Fiqi/EPA/epa/CORBIS

all that Gaddafi has changed. He has made Libya essentially self-sufficient in food by developing agriculture, encouraging farmers to adopt cooperative methods, and utilizing desert areas by pursuing water development policies.

Colonel Gaddafi is well known for his support of liberation movements; this has earned him many enemies but also a lot of respect. Taking an activist foreign policy, Libya occupied a section of northern Chad, inspired a Chadian civil war, injected many troops and arms into the country, and played the role of sponsor of the Chadian ex-president, Goukouni Oueddi. The ex-president was supported by 5000 Libyan troops, who controlled the north of the country as a consequence of a military and political stalemate reached in 1983; the rest of the country was controlled by Hissene Habre, who was supported by 3200 French legionaires. Soon after the stalemate, Libya and France agreed to withdraw their troops because neither country wanted to risk a direct confrontation and so secret talks were held in September 1984. The French withdrew from the country but the Libyans did not leave immediately and so the French troops were ordered by their government to return. The French troops managed to push the Libyans back into the resource-rich Aouzou Strip region of Chad. In the Aouzou Strip were deposits of gold, uranium, cassiterite, and bauxite.

There was another reason for Gaddafi's policy toward Chad. He wanted to create a pan-African union with another country. He had tried this with Tunisia, Sudan, Morocco, and Egypt. There was an additional point in his philosophical direction. He wanted to demonstrate that Africans and Arabs could live in a single nation. Always a visionary, Gaddafi created revolutionary committees staffed by persons with strong political credentials and a people's army.

Gaddafi has taken a leadership role with the African Union, being one of its chief sponsors in the 2002 creation of the union to replace the Organization of African Unity. In his capacity as an elder statesman of Africa he frequently lectures other African leaders about their responsibility to the continent. He has poured millions of dollars into the building of African unity, African consciousness, and the elevation of Africa's role in the world. At the African Leaders Summit of 2005 held under the auspices of the African Union in Sirte, Libya, Colonel Gaddafi told the leaders that there was no reason for Africa to have to call upon outsiders to police the continent when Africa had more than 2½ million men and women under arms itself. The problem, he concluded, was that there was no single government of Africa that could command those troops in the interest of a united Africa.

## When Africa creates its own chaos

It is easy to see that international and external forces create chaos in Africa without seeing that in many cases African people must be held accountable for the lives and philosophies of the continent. Whether it is genocide, enslavement, abuse of women, or political corruption, Africans must be in the position to condemn human outrages that exist in the name of the people of Africa. Take the Rwandan situation as an example.

Here was an organized slaughter of roughly one million ethnic Tutsis and their Hutu supporters within a period of one hundred days in 1994. There are all kinds of explanations, critiques, and justifications, as one would expect. There are those who bring history to bear on the explanations, saying that the Tutsis were placed in positions of influence in the military and bureaucracy during the days before independence, and that when independence came, since the Hutus were the majority, they were able to elect their people to office. This angered the Tutsis, who were now out of power without a European sponsor. So it is claimed that when the Hutu president's plane was shot down over the country it was an action perpetrated by the Tutsis. They were blamed for the death of the president, who had been elected by the majority of the people in the country. Thus, one must assume that there was an ethnic element to the slaughter; however, that is not the whole story. What appeared to be spontaneous and uncontrollable attacks upon the ethnic Tutsi minority may have been planned and systematically carried out by the ruling authorities. The Rwandan genocide stands out as historically important not only because of the massive number of people who were killed in such a short period of time but also because of the way Europe and America responded to the atrocities. In spite of the intelligence provided before the killing began, and international news media coverage reflecting the true scale of violence as the genocide unfolded, virtually all Western nations refused to intervene. The United Nations itself refused to allow its peacekeeping operation in Rwanda, under General Roméo Dallaire, to take positive action to bring the killing to a halt. There were bitter recriminations and enough blame to go around in the world for allowing the murders to continue. President Bill Clinton of the United States went to Rwanda and apologized for the inaction of the United States government during the crisis.

The expatriate rebel Tutsi movement known as the Rwandese Patriotic Front led by Paul Kagame overthrew the government and seized control of power to bring an end to the murders. In the aftermath of the genocide, sporadic reprisals were often taken against ethnic Hutus, causing hundreds of thousands to flee into eastern Democratic Republic of Congo.

It will be a long time before the memory of the violence is erased, if ever. Rwanda is a small country and no sector has been left untouched by the genocidal eruption, which caused untold suffering. No tribunals, no juries, and no historians will ever be able to adequately record what happened during that fateful year; 1994 will live in the memory of the nation and in the memory of African people as one of the worst years in history, when black people destroyed other black people in pursuit of revenge. Chaos reigned and the reining in of it took the efforts of a small, committed cadre of men and women who believed that it was possible for Hutu and Tutsi, relatives who had similar histories, similar religions, and one language, to live in harmony in a beautiful and storied land tucked in the Great Lakes region of Africa.

Three other wars have resulted from the genocide in Rwanda. The First and Second Congo Wars and the Burundian Civil War were all a part of the same social and political malady that degenerated into mass insanity.

The First Congo Civil War lasted for two years, 1996–1997, and led to the overthrow of President Mobutu Sese Seko by rebels backed by two foreign powers, Uganda and Rwanda. Laurent-Desiré Kabila declared himself president and changed the name of the nation back to Democratic Republic of the Congo. The first war set the foundation for a Second Congo War, which started on August 2, 1998. Mobutu had controlled Zaire since the overthrow of the popular Patrice Lumumba. There was tremendous pressure on Mobutu to liberalize the country but ultimately he was unwilling to implement broad reform, alienating allies both at home and internationally.

A long and bitter resistance to Mobutu's rule continued throughout the country with the exception of Mobutu's home region. Opposition included Marxists and various ethnic and regional minorities opposed to the dominance of the Kinshasa region over the rest of the nation. Kabila, and ethnic Katangese, had been fighting the Mobutu government for decades. Once the Rwandan genocide occurred and resulted in the flight of more than two million Hutu refugees from Rwanda after the Tutsi-controlled Rwandan Patriotic Front took over the country in 1994, pressure was put on the eastern front of Congo. Among the refugees in Congo were members of the Interahamwe, militia groups linked to political parties who took part in the genocide. They set up camps in eastern Congo from which they attacked both Rwandan Tutsi and those Tutsis living in Congo, who are called the Banyamulenge. Mobutu supported the Hutu extremists for political reasons and did little to prevent Congo from being used by the Hutu. When the vice-governor of South Kivu province issued an order in November 1996 ordering the Banyamulenge to leave the country or face the death penalty, they exploded in rebellion. Now the anti-Mobutu forces combined to form the Alliance of Democratic Forces for the Liberation of Zaire (AFDL).

The AFDL received the support of the leaders of African Great Lakes states, particularly Paul Kagame of Rwanda and Yoweri Museveni of Uganda. Some of Mobutu's forces joined with Laurent-Desiré Kabila's forces as they marched from the east on the city of Kinshasa. Resistance crumbled, Mobutu's forces fled, and Mobutu himself had to pack up and leave the country. Kabila took power on May 17, 1997. Once Kabila was in power the political situation changed dramatically. He quickly became suspected of being an authoritarian. Many of the democratic forces abandoned him.

There was renewed conflict with the minority groups of the east, who demanded autonomy. Kabila turned against his former Rwandan allies when they showed little sign of withdrawing from his Congo. He accused them and their allies of trying to capture the region's mineral resources. Furthermore, his overreliance on the Rwandans for political and military control caused the pro-democracy forces to accuse Kabila of being a political puppet of Rwanda. In August 1998, Kabila removed all ethnic Tutsis from his government and ordered all Rwandan and Ugandan officials out of the DRC. The two countries then turned against their former client, sending troops to aid rebels attempting to overthrow Kabila. This brought about the Second Congo Civil War.

The Second Congo War took place largely in the territory of the Democratic Republic of the Congo. It lasted from 1998 to 2002. Peace has been elusive. It was the widest interstate war in modern African history, involving nine African nations (Congo, Rwanda, Uganda, Burundi, Zimbabwe, Angola, Namibia, Tanzania, and Zambia), as well as twenty armed groups. It was the first truly continental African war. Some have referred to it as Africa's World War. The International Rescue Committee estimated that 3.8 million people died, mostly from starvation and disease brought about by the deadliest conflict since the Second World War. Millions of people have been displaced, have lost their farms and homes, and are in asylum in other countries.

Despite several partially successful peace initiatives and agreements that led to an official end to the war in 2002, many of the armed groups have not disbanded and a reduced level of fighting continued as late as September 2005.

The situation in Congo has often been quite confusing, with troops from Rwanda and Uganda fighting against each other, ethnic Hema and Lendu people at war with each other, and various national armies trying to sort out the proper villains and good guys. Amid these complexities, the new President Joseph Kabila, the son of the previous president, has tried to breathe new life into the peace accord reached in 1999. The United Nations accused Uganda of systematically plundering Congo's vast natural resources and selling them to outside nations. The entire region has been greatly devastated by the military might, often by surrogates, placed at the disposal of the numerous warring parties.

The Burundi Civil War can be traced to some of the same unsettling problems that affected Congo and Rwanda. Burundi's first multiparty national elections were held on June 27, 1993. At that time Melchio Ndadaye of the Front for Democracy in Burundi won the presidential election, the first person from the Hutu ethnic group to become the president since the country secured independence in 1962 from Belgium. Hutus are the majority ethnic group, at about 85 percent in the country, but the government was dominated by Tutsis, through the Union for National Progress. However, on October 21, 1993, Ndadaye was murdered in a coup d'état by Tutsi military officers. This produced an immediate outbreak of violence on the part of the Hutu people resulting in many deaths. Actually the Hutu sought revenge in an attempt to retain their control of power. The National Council for the Defense of Democracy, also called Forces for the Defense of Democracy, was the major Hutu rebel group in the country. The capital of Bujumbura became the center of political and military action in the country.

## Indigenization of Christianity

In Africa, only Ethiopia, Egypt, Libya, Tunisia, Nubia, and Congo had Christianity before the seventeenth century. Only Ethiopia maintained Christianity from the earliest times and developed a hierarchy that represented the indigenization of the Christian faith. During the period of the European slave trade and colonization, European missionaries brought Christianity as one instrument of control to the continent. They came with the Bible and the gun and used both to conquer the territories of Africa. These missionaries were the first line of offense for the European culture and they generally tried to organize local congregations along the lines of those they knew in their home countries, but by the end of the nineteenth century many African Christians, accusing Europeans of apostasy, had formed independent denominations.

There were two important movements among the African Christians. The first, often referred to as Ethiopians, tended to follow the pattern of church organization bequeathed to them by the missionaries, and their desire for independence represented resistance to foreign missionaries, who were often the epitome of racism. Thus, between the period 1884 and the First World War in 1914, new African churches flourished as Ethiopianism reached a high point. A second movement was commonly called Zionism in southern Africa, tracing its origins to the Christian Catholic Church in Zion City, Illinois, in the United States. Their emphasis was on divine healing and the building of sacred cities free of sin and sickness.

During the twentieth century and into the twenty-first century the expansion of Christianity in Africa appears to be the result of the missionary efforts of the African independent churches or AICs (sometimes called African instituted churches, or African indigenous churches). They tend to flourish because of the power and influence of charismatic prophets and prophetesses, who express a unique relationship to divinity and a special knowledge of the power of God. These groups have usually developed outside of the attention of the more traditional Christian denominations such as Baptists, Catholics, Presbyterians, Lutherans, and Methodists, and so their history is not well known or well recorded. However, it is impossible to write the history of Africa without mentioning the impact these churches have had on the masses of people. Some countries such as Uganda and Kenya have seemed especially ripe for groups such as the Lord's Army of Resistance, led by a prophetess who for a period of time in the late twentieth century brought havoc to villages in Uganda. Other groups such as Luo Nomiya, Legio Maria, Musanda Holy Spirit (Roho), Ruwe Holy Ghost (Roho), Mowal, Singruok, Luong Mogik (God's Last Appeal), Fweny, African Israel Nineveh, and Musanda Christian Church have proliferated in western Kenya. In West Africa one finds the Celestial Church of Christ, the Nigerian Pentecostal Churches, the Christ Army Church, the Redeemed Christian Church of God, and the Cherubim and Seraphim Movement. In Ghana, the Church of the Lord Aladura and other groups have tended to blend Pentecostal ideas with those of African-originated churches. Among the Douala people in Cameroon is a group of nearly one hundred denominations, called coastal healers, devoted to a practice of healing. They are sometimes referred to as the New Religions Movement (NRM). Many AICs have created their own sacred places, and the concept of Cura Divina in the Christ Apostolic Church is a West African phenomenon. But the phenomenon of African independent churches is not simply an East African or West African one; it is all over the continent. In southern Africa one can now find the Sweet Heart Church of the Clouds (Umutima Uwalowa wa Makumbi), sometimes referred to as Mutima Church or Ba Emilio Movement after the name of the founder, Emilio Mulolani Chishimba, in Zambia. Also in southern Africa one can find the amaNaaretha or Isaiah Shembe Movement among the rural Zulu people of Natal.

In some instances, the growth of the indigenous or independent churches can be tied directly to political or social conditions. For example, Rwanda initially had few indigenous churches since the people who did not practice traditional African religion were almost all Roman Catholics until the genocide of 1994. Hutu and Tutsi practiced the same religion and went to the same masses. Since the time of chaos, however, there has been an explosive growth of African-originated churches.

More established traditional churches such as the African Orthodox Church or Ethiopian Orthodox Church have generated newer movements like the Ethiopian Catholic Church in Zion, the Oruuano Church, and the Church of Africa in Namibia. Some indigenous churches, however, have shown an unusual flexibility to work with minor spiritual movements from the West such as the Harrist Church in the Ivory Coast, the Spiritual Healing Church of Botswana, and the Church of Moshoeshoe in Lesotho, which have held joint programs with the Mennonite missions. Who is trying to influence whom?

Of course many of these churches take their inspiration from the traditional religious practices of African societies. For instance, the Legio Maria Church of Kenya has *jucheckos* or "sniffers" whose job it is to sniff newcomers at the entrance to discern if they have evil intentions. This is not a historical Christian practice but it is something that some traditional healers are able to do.

## The Négritude movement

Closely identified with the African intellectuals Léopold Senghor, Aimée Césaire, Léon Damas, and Jacques Rabemanajara, the Négritude movement has roots deep in the international African world. In 1921 the Afro-Cubans started a movement called Negrismo which celebrated African music, rhythms, art, folklore, and literature. Jacques Roumain the Haitian published the journal *La Revue Indigène* to begin the indigenism movement in the Antilles. By 1930 the poet Léon Damas was ready with *Pigments*, called the Manifesto of Négritude, which claimed that "the white man kidnapped blacks and killed our people and that they now want to bleach us and make us white but we only want to be black." Soon after Damas' book was published, he met with Léopold Senghor and Aimée Césaire, also students in Paris, to discuss an ideology that would promote African culture. Damas was from South America, French Guiana; Césaire was from Martinique; and Senghor was from Senegal.

A journal called *La Revue du Monde Noir* was published in 1931 that led to the creation of a club where black writers could meet, but a more revolutionary group published *Légitime Défense*, a Marxist journal written mainly by Martinican students. Both groups demanded the attention of the African students, until in 1934 the "three fathers" edited the journal *L'Etudiant Noir*, with the aim of breaking down national barriers between African students on the continent and in the Diaspora. In 1939, Aimée Césaire published his *Cahier d'un retour au pays natal* (Notebook of a Return to My Native Land) and used the word *Négritude* for the first time. Senghor became one of the principal interpreters of the concept of *Négritude*, explaining that it was meant as a celebration of African heritage without regard to boundaries and nationalities.

Around 1950, Paris received another group of students who came near the end of the varsity years of the *Négritude* leaders. They included Cheikh Anta Diop, who had come a year or two earlier, Joseph Ki-Zerbo, and Abdoulaye Wade. These were to become some of the most recognized scholars in the African world. Diop pursued his studies in physics and then in other fields, including history and linguistics; Ki-Zerbo became a historian; and Wade went into the field of economics. In addition, Ki-Zerbo and Wade were members of the Movement for African Liberation, a student group devoted to the ultimate liberation of the African continent. It was started in 1958, with Ki-Zerbo serving as the overall president and Wade serving as the leader of the Senegalese section. These were not the Négritudinists and they made a point of speaking about the realities of the conditions on the continent. They wanted political, social, and economic liberation, insisting that cultural liberation was a product of free people. As we have seen with the icons of the Négritude Movement and the Movement for African Liberation, the continent has not been short on heroes. Indeed, almost every era has had its African leader who stepped forward in an attempt to transform the political and economic realities of the people on the continent.

## Robert Mugabe as an iconic symbol for resistance: the turn to the East

President Robert Mugabe's defiant trip to China in July 2005 was meant to send a signal to the West that he saw China as an important ally in the future of Zimbabwe. Although he had agitated Britain and the United States by moving against the white settlers who had occupied the land of the Shona people for more than one hundred years, he remained popular among the African people.

Mugabe is seen as a national hero among Zimbabweans and one of the key leaders of Africa by many young people of the continent. By opening the door to more intensive trade with China, Zimbabwe circumvented the stranglehold placed on its economy by the United States and Europe and redistributed the land the whites had occupied illegally since 1898 to the masses of poor Zimbabweans, who had been robbed of their birthright when the whites invaded and took the land from their ancestors at gunpoint. Robert Mugabe instituted a "Look East" policy that broke the hundred-year dependence on the West for his country. He has aggressively sought relationships with Arab and Asian countries during the first part of the twenty-first century. A symbiotic relationship between Zimbabwe, with the world's largest reserve of platinum, strong copper, nickel, and uranium deposits, and other minerals, and China, the world's fastest-growing economy, became a hallmark of the Mugabe campaign for Chinese support. Other countries in Africa such as Sudan and Angola also have powerful relationships with China. Perhaps Africa and Asia will be able to build political and economic relationships on foundations of equality and equanimity in ways that Europe and Africa have been unable to do because of enslavement and colonization. This is not to say that there will not be strong relationships between certain sectors in Africa and Europe. The world is interconnected and dynamic and no continent or nation can stand apart from the movements of history. Clearly, however, the future of the African continent will involve an increasingly conscious relationship with Asia as more countries wean themselves away from the vestiges of colonial Europe.

## Sudan: in search of harmony

Sudan, Africa's largest country, has rarely seen peace since independence. There was a peace agreement between the southern Sudanese insurgents, the Anya Nya, and the Sudan government in 1972. The conflict was resumed in 1983 and turned the south into a battlefield. The government was unable to establish full control over the country until an agreement in January 2005 between the Southern People's Liberation Movement and the Sudanese government. It must be accepted that the SPLA leader John Garang sought diligently to ensure that, even with the brutality in the civil war, no group engaged in struggle with another should create hostilities so vile and obscene that they would not be able to find mutual confidence when peace came. When he died soon after the end of the war, he had achieved national stature for his devotion to freedom, yet there remained the social elements on the ground that had to be worked out.

The grounds for the conflict were complex. They were religious, regional, and economic. In fact, the southern part of the country is the breadbasket of the nation, the mineral-rich region, especially for oil, and the area of the most politically progressive population. It is quite easy to think that the conflict in Sudan is basically one between two religions or between people who have two different responses to culture. There are elements of religious and linguistic conflict in the problems that have imperiled the country but these are often surrogate issues for the deeper economic conflicts. Who shall control the energy outputs, the economic resources, and the wealth of the nation? Although it is easy to see that the northern region is based on Arabic and the Islamic faith, while the south tends to use African languages and cultures, each area remains quite diverse in its own character. There are Muslims, a few, in the south, and there are non-Arabic-speakers and Christians, a few, in the north.

Sudan is such an old country it has old problems. The insurgency in the south that drained so much energy and cost nearly two million lives had its origins in pre-independence Sudan. On August 18, 1955, the Equatorial Corps, a military unit composed of southerners, mutinied at Torit. They refused to surrender to Sudanese government authorities, and many mutineers disappeared into hiding with their weapons, marking the beginning of the first war in southern Sudan. By the late 1960s, the war had resulted in the deaths of about 500,000 people. Nearly a million people in the south hid in the forests or escaped to refugee camps in neighboring countries. By 1969 the rebels were able to obtain weapons and supplies from outside the country. It is believed that Anya Nya weapons came via Ethiopia and Uganda. Anya Nya also purchased arms from Congolese rebels. Government operations against the rebels declined after the 1969 coup, and subsided with the Addis Ababa accords of 1972. These accords promised autonomy for the southern region.

The Sudanese civil war erupted again in 1983 when President Nimeiri imposed Shari'a law, an Islamic code, and had caused the death of more than 1.5 million Sudanese by 1997. The principal insurgent faction is the Sudan People's Liberation Movement (SPLM), a body created by the Sudan People's Liberation Army (SPLA).

The SPLA was formed in 1983 when Lieutenant Colonel John Garang of the SPAF was sent to quell a mutiny in Bor of 500 southern troops who were resisting orders to be rotated to the north. Instead of ending the mutiny, Garang encouraged mutinies in other garrisons and became the effective leader of the rebellion against the Khartoum government. Garang, a Dinka born into a Christian family, had studied at Grinnell College, Iowa. He was quite familiar with the United States, also studying at Fort Benning, Georgia, and earning an advanced economics degrees at Iowa State University. It was estimated that at the time of the 2005 agreement there were more than 100,000 soldiers committed to the SPLA. After 1983, the SPLA split into three main factions: the SPLA Torit faction led by John Garang; the SPLA Bahr-al-Ghazal faction led by Carabino Kuany Bol; and the South Sudan Independence Movement led by Rick Machar. These internal divisions had to be overcome in order to bring about the peace treaty of 2005.

The SPLM/A and its northern allies in the National Democratic Alliance (NDA) carried out successful military offensives in areas along the borders with Ethiopia and Eritrea. In 1996 the US government decided to send $20 million of military equipment through the "front-line" states of Ethiopia, Eritrea, and Uganda to help the Sudanese opposition overthrow the Khartoum regime. US officials denied that the military aid for the SPLA and the Sudanese Allied Forces (SAF), described as "non-lethal" – including radios, uniforms, boots, and tents – was targeted at Sudan, although it seems unlikely that there would be other targets. In some reports the Pentagon and the CIA considered Sudan to be second only to Iran as a staging ground for international terrorism.

The peace treaty of 2005 called for John Garang to become vice president of the Republic of Sudan. In late July 2005, about three weeks after he had started to serve in office, he was killed in a Uganda helicopter crash in bad weather. Hundreds of thousands of people came out to see his body as it was paraded through the streets of Juba, the largest city in southern Sudan. His body was taken to the small Old Saints Cathedral.

Garang will remain alive through his vision, thoughts, and principles because he fought for those who had been marginalized in their own country. Although his death stunned the continent and devastated his followers, his contribution made him one of Africa's foremost charismatic personalities. Some feared that the January 2005 accord to end twenty-one years of north–south civil war would be broken.

The Sudanese government, however, under President Bashir, in a show of north–south unity brought former fighters from Garang's Sudan People's Liberation Movement/Army (SPLM/A) to join Sudanese army pallbearers to carry his coffin. Garang's former enemy then partner in the peace, Sudanese President Omar Hassan al-Bashir, received the coffin off a plane with South African President Thabo Mbeki and UN envoy Jan Pronk. The Sudanese government immediately announced that Garang's successor would be Salva Kiir, who has promised implementation of the peace accord. Sudanese intellectuals like Mou Thiik and the venerable Francis Deng would have major roles to play in a more authentic union of Sudan.

At the start of the twenty-first century Sudan has also had to deal with the problem of Darfur. Like many of the issues in Sudan this problem does not seem to have a recent past, but a distant one. The people of Darfur, a north-western region of the country, unlike the people of the south who fought the central government for more than twenty years, are Muslims. The southern-ers were largely African traditionalists and Christians. However, the people who are being persecuted in Darfur are African and Muslim. They have accepted the same religion and the same practices as the Muslims in the government, but they are ethnically and culturally African, meaning that their first languge is an indigenous African language. On the other hand, the region of Darfur also includes a group of Arab nomads who graze cattle and camels over the farm lands that are ancestral lands to the Darfur people. In 1987 nearly thirty groups of Arabs formed an alliance to penetrate the lands of the Fur people. They succeeded in creating a backlash as the African groups formed organizations, the Sudanese Liberation Army and the Justice and Equality Movement, both linked to the politician Hassan al-Turabi, to fight for their rights and to defend their lands. Bloody conflicts ensued, so much so that by 2006 thousands of mostly Africans had been killed in a continuing war cast in the light of land grazing versus land farming rights.

Sudan is 52 percent African and about 39 percent Arab, yet the Africans have struggled to effectively express themselves in the country. More than two million people have been displaced and nearly 400,000 killed in a form of genocide reminiscent of various ethnic cleansing campaigns in other arenas of the world. A group of Arab militias, calling themselves the Janjaweed, has organized with what appears to be the support of the government to assault Africans in Darfur. Janjaweed militia would enter a village, burn it to the ground, rape the women, kill the men, and move to the next village. An international movement to stop genocide in Sudan has been launched by the African Union and the United Nations to save the people of Sudan.

Thus, while in the south the issue was an imposition of Arab religious nationalism on a country that was majority black and African, in the west the issue is one of land and water, but has become one of ethnic cleansing. Those who classify themselves as Arabs often do not look any different from those who classify themselves as African. It is more a language reality where those who speak Arabic are considered Arabs while those whose first language is an African language are Africans despite their Muslim religion. Sudan's only hope is a non-religious, non-sectarian nationalism based upon goodwill for Sudan. Clearly, the imposition of one religion or another will not create conditions for unity of the huge nation.

## The capitalist road: example and demise in Côte d'Ivoire

Côte d'Ivoire, as a former French colony, had inherited from France at the time of independence the halo of economic success. There were French cafes on the main boulevards, French boutiques downtown in Abidjan, the capital, and French diplomats and officials who called the capital city their own home at the time of independence. In many respects, Côte d'Ivoire was one of Africa's best examples of the capitalist paradigm.

The appearance of Félix Houphouët-Boigny as leader of the new independent country signaled to the French a continuation of the "special" relationship that had been encouraged between the two nations. Félix Houphouët-Boigny, son of a Baule king, formed the first union of cocoa farmers in 1944 with the aim of securing better working conditions from the plantation owners and better prices for the small farmers. Houphouët-Boigny soon rose to prominence and within a year was elected to the French Parliament in Paris. A year later the French abolished forced labor on the plantations. He was a favorite of the French politicians, a partner in money and power; ingratiating himself into the French upper classes and power elites, Houphouët-Boigny soon abandoned his more radical political stance in support of the farmers, in order to curry favors with the French authorities. The French reciprocated by making him the first African minister in a European government. By the time France was willing to give Côte d'Ivoire its independence, there was no one to compete with Félix Houphouët-Boigny. He became the father of independence in 1960 and worked to keep the country in the armpit of France.

However, like other colonized regions of Africa, Côte d'Ivoire was an artificial nation that had been created from several significant ethnic groups held together by the power of the French government. It was the sheer audacity of Houphouët-Boigny's personality that replaced the French government and held the country together during his regime. But the problems of ethnic and regional politics were present, though suppressed during Houphouët-Boigny's time. The nation had been molded together with portions of Baule, Kru, Senufo, Lobi, Malinke, and scores of other smaller ethnic populations. In effect, the French had maintained power by including in their colony not one dominant group but several ethnic groups as a way to balance power. However, they passed this power to a Baule whose ancestors were the same as the Asante of Ghana, who lived across the border. Houphouët-Boigny was therefore an Akan. But other groups of Ivorian Africans had large portions of their populations in other countries as well. The Lobi are found in Mali, the Kru in Liberia, the Malinke in Guinea, and the Senufo live also in Burkina Faso. The fact that the country of Côte d'Ivoire comprised of these groups attest to its diversity and energy. But capitalism also created enormous tensions, fissures, and cultural disorientations in this richly endowed land located in the rainforest to Sahel zone of West Africa. There were many ethnic migrations as well as ethnicities that had been incorporated into the French colony when it was administered by France. This multiculturalism with external links, so to speak, in other countries served as both a strength and a weakness to the country's political administration.

Two critical factors led to the decline of Ivorian power at the turn of the century: (1) the overwhelming dependence on French largesse; and (2) the smoldering fires of ethnic tensions. When France invaded the country in the 1840s and forced local chiefs to give French commercial traders a monopoly along the coast, it was the first step to France's ultimate control of the economy of the area. The second step had to be military and the French built naval bases to keep out non-French traders as they began a systematic brutal conquest of the interior. The Mandinka army put up a very stiff resistance that lasted for several years in the 1890s before the French were able to subdue it. On the eastern side of the country, the Baule led a guerrilla hit-and-run campaign against French interests that lasted until 1917.

Once the French had "pacified" the various ethnic groups they sought to control the economy by dictating the exports from the country. The exports were largely cocoa, coffee, and palm oil crops planted along the coast. Soon Côte d'Ivoire had the largest white settler population in West Africa. The French were not just bureaucrats; they were settlers who intended to make a living for their families in the country. Neither the English nor the French were able to secure a strong settler foothold in other West or Central African countries. However, in Côte d'Ivoire the French eventually owned a third of the cocoa, banana, and coffee plantations forcing the Africans into a quasi-slavery. This despised system of forced labor became the hallmark of the French occupation.

Many people were angered by the French occupation, by their arrogance, and by their belief that they deserved privilege in an African country. At that time it was the most prosperous country in West Africa. More than 40% of the region's total exports came from Côte d'Ivoire. Houphouët-Boigny's government gave farmers good prices to further stimulate production. Coffee production increased significantly, catapulting Côte d'Ivoire at the time into third place in total output behind Brazil and Colombia. Cocoa did the same; by 1979 the country was the world's leading producer of cocoa. The country also became Africa's leading exporter of pineapples and palm oil. Much of the success had to do with the French export policies, external economic connections to European markets, and the settlers' desire to demonstrate that they could transform the country to surpass neighboring African countries that had forced Europeans to leave. It was different in Côte d'Ivoire where the French poured into the country. The French community grew from 10,000 in 1960 to more than 50,000 by the late 1970s. They came as teachers, bureaucrats, advisers, and agricultural and industrial managers. The twenty-year growth rate of nearly 10% was the highest of the non-oil exporting countries during the same period.

The seeds of political trouble existed because Houphouët-Boigny ruled with an iron hand. In effect, the democratic idea was suppressed in the country in order to advance the capitalist economic agenda. The leaders of the country did not want to have any free expression, that is, any criticism of the conditions of the country. There was no free press and only one political party. Houphouët-Boigny also used millions of dollars were spent transforming his village, Yamoussoukro, into the new capital. He built the largest cathedral in the world in the village, creating consternation in the country and showing that he had little appreciation for the African religious culture. What if he had erected in his hometown the largest, most expressive, modern shrine to African Ancestors? His political regime soon became the butt of jokes because of the way he spent the money generated by the economy. But then came the terrible recession of the early 1980s. In addition, a drought in the country sent shockwaves through the Ivorian economy. Furthermore, the overcutting of timber and collapsing sugar prices forced the country's external debt to increase threefold.

When hundreds of civil servants went on strike in 1990 it was clear that the shine had worn off the Ivorian economy. Students protested the government's handling of the budget, corruption caused by French bribes to Ivorian politicians and officials, and the lack of democracy. Student demonstrations would be repeated in years to come and the fissures in the nation would rupture at the turn of the century pitting northerners against southerners, farmers against business people, and nationalists against conservatives. By the time of Houphouët-Boigny's death in 1993, the country had turned to multiparty democracy and the hand-picked choice, Henri Konan Bédié, became its leader.

In October 1995, President Bédié overwhelmingly won reelection against a disorganized and unfocused opposition. He tightened his hold over political life, sending several hundred opposition supporters to jail. Taking on the armor of a dictator, Bédié made the fatal mistake of so many African leaders, he sought to crush all opposition. Yet it appeared that the economic outlook was improving because inflation decreased and the foreign debt was being dealt with because of the economic upturn. Bédié squandered this opportunity by playing partisan ethnic politics that further opened a major rift in the nation. The politically astute Houphouët-Boigny had been very careful to avoid any ethnic conflict and he had left access to Ivorian nationality open to immigrants from Burkina Faso, Guinea, and other nations. On the other hand, Bédié emphasized the concept of "Ivority" (*Ivoirité*) to exclude his prime rival, Alassane Ouattara, who had only one parent of Ivory Coast nationality, to run for future presidential election. This inauthentic principle, given the nature of African nations created by colonizing countries, was to shatter any real sense of unity in the nation. The idea that only those born in Côte d'Ivoire could hold political office or serve in the military was anathema to the pattern that had been established under Houphouët-Boigny.

The country blew up in a military coup in 1999 that saw General Robert Guéi take office. Bédié fled into exile in France. The coup had the effect of reducing crime and corruption. However, an election was held in October 2000 in which Laurent Gbagbo ran against Robert Guéi for the presidency. There was a lot of unrest during the campaign and Guéi's attempt to fix the election led to a new public uprising, resulting in 180 deaths and his swift replacement by the election's likely winner, Gbagbo.

Once again Alassane Ouattara was disqualified by the country's Supreme Court, which based his ineligibility on his Burkinabé nationality. The disqualification of Ouattara sparked street battles in which his supporters, mainly from the country's Muslim north, battled riot police in the capital, Yamoussoukro. Furthermore, on September 19, 2002, troops mutinied and gained control of the northern part of the country. And in the metropolis of Abidjan, the police headquarters was seized by the rebels and former president Guéi was murdered alongside fifteen persons in his home. During the outburst, Alassane Ouattara took refuge in the French embassy. So much unrest occurred, some of it unfocused, that in the melee, a military coup was attempted. Many opponents of Gbagbo were summarily executed by vigilantes.

A cease-fire was called but proved short-lived and fighting over the prime cocoa-growing areas resumed. France sent in troops to maintain the cease-fire boundaries, and militias, including warlords and fighters from Sierra Leone and Liberia, took advantage of the crisis to seize Ivorian territory. A major row occurred when French soldiers were killed and the French destroyed the Ivorian air force by attacking fighter planes on the ground. Gbagbo was furious but was unable to respond in kind. His supporters felt that the French had shown their hand to be on the side of the rebels. Nevertheless, by January 2003, President Gbagbo and rebel leaders had signed accords creating a "government of national unity." Curfews were lifted and French troops cleaned up the lawless western border of the country.

The government has proved extremely unstable. In March 2004, 120 people were killed in an opposition rally. A later report concluded the killings were pre-planned. Though UN peacekeepers were deployed, relations between Gbagbo and the opposition continued to deteriorate. Obviously the French have a large stake in the country due to the tremendous amount of French resources spent there, but they also recognize the danger of losing out to a newly found nationalism that is based on the anti-French attitudes of the youth. Retreating from the brink of national disaster is not easy and yet it appears that the country may have found its footing in the recent past.

## The socialist rhetoric and reality in Mozambique

Samora Moïsès Machel was born in 1933 and educated in Catholic schools in Mozambique. It did not take him long to feel that he had to fight against the Portuguese occupiers of his country. Machel attended Catholic school but when he was not in class he had to work in the fields. He studied to become a nurse, one of the few professions open to Mozambican blacks at that time. He began his first political activities in a hospital, where he protested the fact that black nurses were paid less than whites doing the same job. He later told a reporter how bad medical treatment was for Mozambique's poor by saying, "the rich man's dog gets more in the way of vaccination, medicine and medical care than do the workers upon whom the rich man's wealth is built." This established his perspective on class distinctions in a capitalist society. Having come from a poor peasant background, Machel found the teachings of Marx quite useful for an understanding and appreciation of the persecution and oppression of the Mozambican masses. He made his life the revolution against the Portuguese. It could be said that rebellion against Portugal was not new to Samora Machel. His grandparents and great grandparents had fought against the Portuguese in the nineteenth century. In 1962 Machel joined the Front for the Liberation of Mozambique (Frelimo), as it was called, dedicated to creating an independent Mozambique. In 1963 Samora Machel left Mozambique and traveled to several other African nations, where he received military training. In 1964 he returned to Mozambique and led Frelimo's first guerrilla attack against the Portuguese in northern Mozambique. He led the guerrilla forces in 1968 and became the president of the organization in 1969. Machel was a field leader with his men, leading them in combat and sharing their dangers and hardships. This made him a special guerrilla leader. He was not giving interviews in some safe haven but was actively involved with the war against oppression. He believed in guerrilla war and Frelimo's army established itself among Mozambique's peasantry. He was a revolutionary who was dedicated not only to throwing the Portuguese out of Mozambique but also to radically changing the society. He said, "of all the things we have done, the most important – the one that history will record as the principal contribution of our generation – is that we understand how to turn the armed struggle into a Revolution; that we realized that it was essential to create a new mentality to build a new society."

Machel's objectives were realized when the revolutionary army weakened Portugal, and after that country's coup in 1974 the Portuguese were forced to leave Mozambique. The new revolutionary government, led by Machel, took over on June 25, 1975. Machel became independent Mozambique's first president and was affectionately referred to as "President Samora" because of his relationship with the common people. Committed to creating a Marxist state, Machel was faced with extreme economic difficulties, including dependence on a hostile, minority-regime South Africa, unreliable Soviet aid, civil war in neighboring Rhodesia (now Zimbabwe), and a South African-supported guerrilla resistance in his own country. He was one of Africa's most popular leaders and he retained that popularity throughout his rule. Machel put his revolutionary principles into practice. He called for the "nationalization" (government ownership) of the Portuguese plantations and property. He moved quickly to have the government establish public schools and health clinics for the peasants. He called for Frelimo to organize itself into a Leninist party. Clearly, Samora Machel saw himself as an internationalist who supported and allowed revolutionaries fighting white minority regimes in Rhodesia and South Africa to operate within Mozambique. Soon after Mozambique's independence both of these countries attacked Mozambique with an anti-Frelimo organization called the Mozambican National Resistance (Renamo). Machel's hostile and more powerful neighbors strangled the Mozambican economy, yet he would not renounce his support for the revolutionarities of Zimbabwe and South Africa. Renamo's activities included the killing of peasants, the destruction of schools and hospitals built by Frelimo, and the blowing up of rail lines and hydroelectric facilities. It was one of the chief examples of what can happen when the blandishments given by the West are accepted as more important than human freedom. Machel fought against these tendencies, trying to teach his people how to become self-sufficient and powerful.

Samora Machel was killed in an airplane crash on October 20, 1986. Although several years before the plane went down Machel had signed a non-aggression pact with South Africa, many Mozambicans believed that the white minority South African government caused the plane to crash. On October 6, 1986, just two weeks before the crash, South African soldiers were injured by land mines near the spot where the borders of Mozambique, South Africa, and Swaziland converge. The fact that Machel's plane crashed almost in the same place where the South African soldiers were injured made many people believe that the South Africans were behind the crash. It is still unresolved. Some still believe that it may have been the work of white agents, shooting the plane down, while some think that it was an accident in bad weather.

Nelson Mandela gave a speech at the unveiling of the Samora Machel Memorial at Mbuzini on January 20, 1999. He said:

> As we struggled, twelve years ago, to comprehend the tragedy that had befallen us all, our only certainty was that the peoples of Mozambique, South Africa, Africa and beyond, had been robbed of a giant. We mourned with Mozambique for the loss of a statesman, soldier and intellectual who we claimed as our leader too. He was taken from us even as a new southern Africa was struggling to be born amidst the death throes of the colonial and apartheid order.

# 15 Toward a United States of Africa without compromise: creation of the African Union

In 1948 Cheikh Anta Diop, a young Senegalese, proposed to a group of African students in Paris that the new intelligentsia should work toward an African renaissance. The basis of this renaissance in Diop's mind would be a new construction of the sciences and social sciences disconnected from the theories and doctrines of white racial superiority that had led to enslavement and colonization. Finding inspiration from the Négritudinists, including his fellow Senegalese Léopold Senghor, Cheikh Anta Diop believed that they were correct to call for an appreciation of things African but that they needed to have a scientific foundation. It was his mission, as he understood his role at the time, and as he said to Alioune Diop, the editor of *Présence Africaine*, to provide a platform from which new energies toward African renaissance could be launched.

Cheikh Anta Diop was born in Caytou, near Diourbel, in Senegal in December 1923. Senegal was still a French colony. The title "Cheikh" was given to establish him as a legitimate heir to the great tradition of Islamic scholarship and intellectual erudition that had emerged among the Mourides. Although he was born into the religion, he more often expressed a free-thinking philosophy that was not tied to any particular tradition. Nearly the entire continent of Africa, with the exception of Ethiopia and Liberia, was in the grip of a fierce European colonization when he was born, and his family was caught right in the middle.

Resistance had been suppressed and the progressive forces were waiting for another good day to begin the push for the removal of the colonial forces. But for the moment, during the harmattan of 1923, one could hear only the voice of an infant crying in the night, a sign of the arrival of a disturber of the hegemonic "peace" that had been established by Western scholars and European colonialists.

In Europe, by the time of Diop's birth, Germany had been defeated in the First World War, and France was in ascendancy. Perhaps some French even dreamed of a return to the period of Napoleonic glory. Nothing seemed to stop French arrogance in its conquest of African territory. Having defeated the forces of Lat Dior and pushed through the railroad from Senegal to Mali, the French had connected two parts of its vast African holdings. Soon after the birth of Cheikh Anta Diop, the suppressed spirit of the people, despite the efforts of the French to split off Blaise

Diagne, became another season of underground resistance by the Mourides brotherhood.

Diop was descended from a famous and important Mourides family. His grandfather, Mor Samba Diop, was the leading imam of the region, and an opponent of French colonialism. His father died when he was very young and it was his formidable mother, Maguette Diop Massamba Sassoum, who had a major role in shaping his early life and providing him with a vision for a united Africa.

Madame Diop was a brilliant woman, gifted with intelligence, integrity, and political savvy. She sent her son to school in the city of Diourbel. He spent considerable time learning from the learned men of the Mourides order of Islam. This was the tradition of his family. He would travel in the company of his grandfather between Diourbel and the holy city of Touba in the Senegalese interior. Having personally traveled that road I know that the journey must have been considerable in the days of Diop's youth. Nevertheless, Touba was for all practical and religious purposes equal to any city in the world as a center for debate, scholarship, and high learning. Cheikh Anta Diop was a scion of this tradition.

There was in Senegal, among the Mourides elite at the time, a strong educational culture and the young men who participated in it were some of the most noble in Senegalese history. Among the youth of Cheikh Anta Diop's day was Cheikh M'Backe, the grandson of Cheikh Amadou Bamba, founder of the Mourides. M'Backe was also the inheritor of the leadership of the Mourides. Known for his erudition, scholarship, and openness to new ideas, Cheikh M'Backe, who died in 1978, had been a long-time friend to his cousin Cheikh Anta Diop, who would live until 1986. Although their paths diverged in terms of the religious tradition they would always be friends, arguing over the political and social issues of the day. Both had inherited the idea that Africa could be united under its own banner from their ample intellectual and political heritage. Nothing would keep either of them from asserting the notion that Africa owed nothing in particular to Mecca that could not be found in Touba or any of the other sacred sites on the continent.

The younger Cheikh Anta admired the political wizardry and religious acumen of his older cousin yet he was never to become an imam or spiritual leader of Islam himself. He would, because of his outlook on life, become a devoted follower of science and inquiry. His inclination was to physics, but he would acquire sociology, anthropology, philosophy, linguistics, and skills in radiocarbon dating.

Cheikh Anta Diop also befriended and attended school with Mor Sourang, son of a wealthy businessman, and Doudou Thiam, who became the head of Senegalese diplomacy. Both were long-time acquaintances who can be said to have had an impact on the quickness of the young Diop's mind. Mor Sourang served the political establishment with his brilliant construction of diplomatic positions in the interest of the country.

However, it was the relationship between Cheikh Anta Diop and Cheikh M'Backe that was one of close friendship and fraternity in the interest of an African vision. Cheikh M'Backe was descended through his mother from

Lat Dior Ngone Latyr Diop, who was the last Damel of Cayor, that is, the last of the emperors of the Wolof Empire, who had fought the French to his death. According to Pathe Diagne the nickname for Cheikh M'Backe was "The Lion of Fatma" (Diagne 2002, p. 11). In fact, Cheikh Anta Diop was to name one of his children after M'Backe. Diagne believes that this was a formative relationship on Diop. Indeed, if one looks at the evidence it seems that the older Cheikh M'Backe was a key influence on the developing ideology of Cheikh Anta. During the time of their youth it was Cheikh M'Backe who took the lead in exposing Cheikh Anta to pan-Africanism and the possibility of defeating French colonialism (Diagne 2002, p. 11).

It was under the tutelage of Cheikh M'Backe that Cheikh Anta learned the dangers and terrors of French domination. Of course, this was not a one-way relationship even though the older man was quite influential. Cheikh M'Backe was impressed by the brilliance, eagerness to learn, and discipline of the young Cheikh Anta, who asked him many questions and demonstrated very early the type of inquisitiveness that was necessary for superior scholarship. Always respectful of the elders, the young Diop often sat with them while they discussed religion, politics, and history. Never one to assume an arrogant role in conversation with the elders, he practiced restraint, reflection, and repartee, though of course not on the elders but mentally, thinking, planning how to answer difficult questions by listening to their discourses. He made a habit of trying to find the best metaphors, stories, and traditional proverbs to make arguments. This reflection would follow him throughout his life and he would possess the same humility of character until his death.

Cheikh M'Backe believed that the capacity of the young Cheikh Anta to master the proverb wisdom of the elders and the knowledge of the imams indicated a bright destiny for the young man. He encouraged him to study diligently and to apply himself wisely. Thus, Cheikh Anta attended the French school at Diourbel but then in the 1940s went to the Lycée Faidherbe in St. Louis, at the Island of Sor, where Cheikh M'Backe was living at the time. He excelled as a student and in his chores while studying at the Lycée.

St. Louis was the colonial capital of Senegal. It was the place where the French had established their zone of comfort. It was the intellectual hotbed of the colonial administration but also the place where Africans from all over the French territories gathered to discuss the future of the colonies. From Mali, Côte D'Ivoire, Guinea, Algeria, Mauritania, Chad, Niger, and Upper Volta, now Burkina Faso, the intellectuals came to St. Louis because that is where the debate over the French colonial presence was most intense.

Diop's presence in St. Louis was beneficial to his intellectual growth because it allowed him to see how the French educated the Senegalese and this inspired in him a desire to resist the French colonial system. He saw the inequality, the misuse of African women by French men, particularly the creation of the large mulatto population, which did not exist in Dakar. He observed the divide-and-rule strategy of the French, who sought to emphasize ethnic differences between the African people. Thus, before Dakar emerged as the seat of power, St. Louis, to the north of Dakar, was the

cosmopolitan capital of the French African world. It had all of the contra-
dictions of such a city and they were not lost on the young Diop.

He was literally formed in the crucible of the St. Louis of 1940–50.
Among the pan-Africanists who visited the city was one of the most powerful black intellectuals of his day, Edward Wilmot Blyden. He found a
community of young Senegalese who were devoted to revolutionary change
in their condition. Blyden may have met Babacar Sy, Lamine Gueye,
Ngalandou Diouf, Mar Diop, Cekuta Diop, Raoul Lonis, Lamine Senghor,
Emile Fauré, Adolphe Mathurin, Kojo Tuwalu, and Kouyate Garang. There
is no indication that Diop met with Blyden, but the environment of St.
Louis at that time makes it possible. Here was the leading pan-Africanist in
the continent, having been in Liberia for a long time, coming to the French
colonial capital to talk to the young African intellectuals of the day. It is
certainly not out of the question for Diop to have met with him in the
company of all the other young men of the day. The environment itself,
above all the context, the political atmosphere, was hot with discussion and
discourse; it was just this milieu that helped to make Cheikh Anta Diop.

It is believed that he was also exposed to the work of Marcus Garvey in
St. Louis. A Senegalese named Sar Djim Ndiaye, who knew Cheikh Anta
Diop, gave an interview a few months after the death of Cheikh Anta Diop
in 1986 in which he said that he had gone to distribute Marcus Garvey
information in St. Louis in the 1920s and 1930s, and his friend Sama Lam
Sar recalled that the influence of Marcus Garvey was very strong in St.
Louis in the period 1930–40. When I visited the tomb of Cheikh Anta Diop
in 1990 at Caytou I was told by the elders of the village that Cheikh had
been greatly influenced by Garveyism. I have never seen this reported in any
of Cheikh Anta's own writings. According to Diagne (2002, p. 13) Diop
was also influenced by the militant nationalism of Adama Lo and Lamine
Gueye, who became a deputy of the Palais Bourbon. Without question Diop
was conversant with the works of Eric Williams, Jacques Price-Mars,
Richard Wright, Louis Achille, Léopold Senghor, and R. Ménil while he was
at St. Louis. Of course because he was a subject of France he was also over-
exposed to the French philosophers, poets, scientists, and novelists. He
knew French culture, it would be said, as well as any French person. Yet he
would find his mission in the defense of African culture in the midst of the
often brutal, unending quest for French domination.

There had been a tradition among the French-speaking Africans of defending the African race. In 1920 the *Messager Dahoméen* was published by Max
Bloncourt and L. Hunkanrin with the idea of correcting some of the false
information about the black world. Additional books and articles were also
published in this line, including *Ligue Universelle de Défense de la Race
Noire* in 1924 by René Maran and Kodjo Tovalou, who were influenced by
Marcus Garvey. So huge was the shadow of Garvey that he cast his influence
on Africans who spoke French, Portuguese, Spanish, and English.

Diop had his own ideas about the renaissance of Africa. For him, it was
possible to suggest a cultural unity of Africa that was manifest in everything
Africans did. Furthermore, pre-colonial Africa took its energy and resources

from this commonality of experiences. The books, *The Cultural Unity of Black Africa* and *Pre-colonial Black Africa,* as they were called in English, sought to establish the particularity of the African commonality. Africans expressed their relationships to nature and people in much the same way. This was not to say that other people did not hold similar values, but to identify common traits among African cultures. For Diop, as a pan-Africanist, it was necessary and useful for scholars to reevaluate the relationship of African societies to ancient Egypt. Thus, Egypt becomes a necessity for a complete historiography of the African continent without which it would be impossible to understand African history.

## The birth of the African Union

The African Union was born at the seminal assembly of African states, held in July 2002 in South Africa. At that meeting the old Organization of African Unity was retired and a new more dynamic organization was brought into existence along the lines of continental unity. The OAU had been in existence since May 1963. It was the brainchild of the early independence thinkers: Kwame Nkrumah, G. A. Nasser, Milton Obote, Ben Bella, and Julius Nyerere. It had also received the support of Emperor Haile Selassie of Ethiopia, who had made Ethiopia's capital, Addis Ababa, the home of the OAU as it would become the headquarters of the African Union. Although the OAU had started with an auspicious beginning, it had quickly run into factional disputes. Milton Obote, the Ugandan president, had taken upon himself the task of rebuking the United States for its role in supporting white regimes in Africa and discriminating against African Americans. It was a welcomed assertion of African leadership in the African American community. However, it created immediate problems and difficulties for Uganda as the United States moved to isolate President Obote. In fact, Obote, it is believed, may have issued the letter to President John Kennedy on behalf of certain member states of Africa. His ambassador to the United Nations, Apollo K. Kironda, wrote to the American president saying "Your pronouncement, albeit belatedly, showed that it is your view and intention, as President of the United States of America, to make it possible for every American, irrespective of his race, colour or creed, to enjoy the privileges and facilities of being an American without fear of interference and reprisals" (letter, June 17, 1963).

Kennedy's people rejected the letter from Uganda. The reason for the rejection of the ambassador's letter on behalf of Milton Obote had been that Obote had written a previous open letter to the president of the United States in which he explained that the foreign ministers of Africa had passed resolutions condemning the Republic of South Africa and its apartheid policies, and condemning the racist policies of the Portuguese in Angola and Mozambique and of the minority white settlers in Southern Rhodesia, but one feels that there is an iron curtain which has been drawn over the events that had been taking place in Birmingham, Alabama, in the United States.

Instead of replying to the Ugandan president, a memorandum from William H. Brubeck, executive secretary, Department of State, to McGeorge

Bundy under the heading "Inadvisability of replying to the Uganda Prime Minister's Open Letter of May 23 to the President concerning the Racial Situation in Birmingham" accused Uganda of essentially trying to stir up trouble. Pressure was apparently put on the other African nations and they did not adopt what the United States saw as the critical Ugandan approach to the racial problem in the United States. President Obote may have demonstrated his finest international intentions with his firm stand against racism and apartheid at this moment. He pointed to the hypocrisy of the American government in trying to project leadership in the work of democracy and freedom while blacks were being murdered in Alabama. However, Obote and his nation would suffer as a result of attempts to undermine his legitimacy and the leadership of the Ugandan nation. This dispute with the United States was to be a sword that would create controversies and factions between the nations as the Cold War would cause African nations to take sides. With the establishment of the African Union, an organization devoted to the integration of Africa into one nation, the leaders of Africa expected a new energy to reduce friction and factions.

The principal feature of the African Union is development. What was at stake in the creation of the Union was the authority and control of the development agenda for Africa. It was clearly understood by the member states that they must take responsibility for the continent and not allow outside nations and forces to influence the development process. At independence, nearly all the states of Africa and their leaders were saddled with debts made by the colonial governments. This meant that they could only concentrate on defining political and social relationships between states with great difficulty.

No individual African country was in the position to advance against the Western interests that discriminated overtly against them. In some cases, in 2005, some European countries would pay African oil exporters only $27 a barrel while it was selling on the world market at $60 a barrel. Consequently, since 1960 many bold attempts have been made to organize and direct African aspirations toward a greater political unity based on freedom, equality, and justice.

What was necessary at this juncture, according to most observers, was a cadre of African leaders who were willing to use political capital to demonstrate the capability of Africa to be competitive and to work for progress. Individual countries had made great strides.

South Africa is thought to have one of the most progressive constitutions of any nation on earth. Senegal, under the leadership of President Abdoulaye Wade, positioned itself as a cultural leader in the African world, pushing for the integration of the African Diaspora into the African Union. Key players such as Cheikh Tidiane Gadio, the senior minister for foreign affairs, and Ambassador Amadou Bocoum, who was consul to the United States in New York prior to becoming Senegal's ambassador to India, made enormous inroads into the diasporic communities during the early part of the twenty-first century. President Wade, demonstrating his commitment to African unity, said on November 12, 2005, "If we could unite Africa tomorrow, I would gladly serve as Governor of Senegal" (Abuja Conference on the

*Figure 15.1* Abdoulaye Wade on the campaign trail in March, 2000 © Patrick Robert/Sygma/CORBIS

African Union, Abuja, Nigeria, November 12, 2005). This is the kind of statement for development and progress that must be made by all of Africa's leaders. It is a selfless, non-chauvinistic position. Nigeria, the most populous nation in Africa, is yet to express the full weight of its intellectual and political capital in the interest of the United States of Africa but all indications are that under President Obasanjo it has made more progress in that direction than ever before. Of course, Libya has been a perennial player in the interest of African unity, expressing its view publicly and also putting its finances to work for these interests. Indeed, the mantle of pan-Africanism and African unity has passed from Nkrumah and Nasser to Wade and Gaddafi.

During the period of the OAU the continent was obliged to have numerous waves of regional integration initiatives in order to combat the real challenges of globalization, imperialism, and continental or national marginalization. What the African Union has understood and what the movers of Africa have argued, however, is that Africa's decision has to be a continent-wide union with the cooperation and support of the willing Diaspora. The African Union is the direct descendant of the plethora of initiatives for regional union.

## Regionalism as prelude to union

The African states' economies were structurally disarticulated at independence; some remain in a weak position. They did not relate to each other but had been developed as colonial aggregations connected to the umbilical cord of colonial metropolitan centers. They were often antagonistic toward each other because of the connections to the metropolitan centers of the former colonial states. It is to be understood as something that was quite natural in the sense that these new nations had little else to go on initially.

However, it became a problem when Zambia could not sell copper to its neighbor Congo without first going through London or Congo could not sell oil to Zambia without going to Belgium or France. What was disturbing to most observers was the fact that individual states of Africa seemed content to surrender their development agenda to external development agencies and foreign nations.

After independence the political elite sought regional cooperation and tended to favor ways to maximize their relations with the former colonial powers. Thus, the first stage of African integration arrangements concentrated on trade promotion through trade liberalization schemes based on the creation of free trade areas.

It was clear to most political observers that among the key constraints that were characteristic of African economies forcing regional integration were the relatively small-scale economies, the lack of rational organization in the economies due to the colonial inheritance of dependence, and the import of intermediate and capital goods. These factors created many combinations of nations, among which is the Customs and Economic Union of Central Africa (UDEAC, 1964), later the Central African Economic and Monetary Community (CEMAC) and all of the following:

- the East African Community (EAC, 1967–77), now the East African Cooperation;
- the West African Economic Community (CEACO, 1972);
- the Economic Community of West African States (ECOWAS, 1975);
- the West African Economic and Monetary Union (UEMOA, 1990);
- the Preferential Trade Area (PTA, 1980) now the Common Market for East and Southern Africa (COMESA, 1999);
- the Southern African Development Coordinating Conference (SADCC, 1980), now the Southern Africa Development Community (SADC, 1992);
- the Union of Maghreb Arab States (UMA, 1988).

Despite the proliferation of regional integration institutions on the African continent, the expected benefits have eluded the continent. It was assumed that the international order would significantly help to alter the African condition; this did not happen. Internationalism became the call word and the catch-phrase of some African economies, perhaps as leaders believed this would allow them to obtain resources from the West. This also proved futile.

What is clear is that African states seemed content to surrender their development agenda to external development agencies and foreign consultants. What is hoped is that the creation of the AU will have a moderating influence on this type of behavior.

One might recall that the Lagos Plan of Action, which was the implementation of the Monrovia Strategy for the Economic Development of Africa (adopted in July 1979), attempted to create integration and planned development. At the time, the Lagos Plan of Action (LPA) was the most comprehensive and systematic statement of the vision of Africa's leaders on the development of the continent. The plan caused Africa's patrons to be upset, but the LPA agreed that Africa's economic problems were partly caused by Africa's dependence on foreign agencies and opening to economic and political exploitation, thus the necessity for self-reliance. The Bretton Woods institutions and the West did not accept the approach of the Lagos Plan. This caused some African leaders to disavow the plan. Because they were too dependent, some of the African nations had to reform their economies along the lines suggested by the Bretton Woods institutions.

## NEPAD: new partnership for Africa's development

The NEPAD strategic framework originates with a mandate given to the five initiating heads of state (Algeria, Egypt, Nigeria, Senegal, South Africa) by the Organization of African Unity (OAU) to develop an integrated socioeconomic development framework for Africa. The 37th Summit of the OAU in July 2001 formally adopted the strategic framework document. It was a visionary document, adopted with the idea of delivering the continent from the bondage of dependence on European and American aid and grants for development because the African leaders recognized the impossibility of developing the continent in Africa's interest if dependence on the West continued at the same pace as before. They were intent on discovering a new approach to the development of the industrial and information sectors of Africa.

NEPAD was designed to address the continuing challenges facing the African continent: issues such as the escalating poverty levels brought on by poor distribution and lack of transportation networks, capital underdevelopment, lack of educational and informational capabilities, lack of clean water, and the continued industrial marginalization of Africa needed a new radical intervention, spearheaded by African leaders, to develop a vision that would ensure the necessary revival and renewal of the African continent.

NEPAD'S objectives were straightforward in that they included the eradication of poverty, placing African nations individually and collectively on a path of sustainable growth and development apart from linking Africa's growth to Western exploitation of African resources, enhancing the beneficial integration of Africa into the global economy, and accelerating the empowerment of women.

In order to effect the changes necessary to bring about the sustainable growth of the continent and change the material conditions of the people, the African leaders agreed that there were some fundamental principles that had to be accepted:

- good governance as a basic requirement for peace, security, and sustainable political and socio-economic development;
- African ownership and leadership, as well as broad and deep participation by all sectors of society;
- anchoring the development of Africa on its resources and the resourcefulness of its people;
- partnership between and among African peoples;
- acceleration of regional and continental integration;

- building the competitiveness of African countries and the continent;
- forging a new international partnership that changes the unequal relationship between Africa and the developed world;
- ensuring that all partnerships with NEPAD are linked to the millennium development goals and other agreed development goals and targets.

Africa's leaders sought to create a holistic, comprehensive response to the needs of the continent in order to ensure sustainable growth and development. Clearly, there remain many goals to be met: more critical problems in governance, human rights, health and welfare issues, and ideas of decency in political relationships; yet the Kilimanjaro of decisions about the future of Africa has been scaled and NEPAD is an opportunity for the leadership of Africa to view the entire landscape of the continent as it works toward the goals of integration of states and of the states into the global economy of the future. But in order to bring into existence this new realm of sustainable growth, Africa would need to insure that there will be:

- peace and security;
- democracy and good political, economic, and corporate governance;
- regional cooperation and integration;
- capacity building.

In addition, there must be a concentrated effort to bring into existence policy reforms and increased investment in the following priority sectors: agriculture; human development with a focus on health, education, science and technology and skills development; improving infrastructure, including information and communication technology (ICT), energy, transport, water, and sanitation; promoting diversification of production and exports, particularly with respect to agro-industries, manufacturing, mining, mineral beneficiation and tourism; accelerating intra-African trade and improving access to markets of developed countries; and protecting and enhancing the environment.

What the leaders sought to do with their document and the visionary framework that it implied was to suggest that the states had to:

- increase domestic savings and investments;
- improve management of public revenue and expenditure;
- improve Africa's share in global trade;
- attract foreign direct investment;
- increase capital flows through further debt reduction.

No one could predict the future of the project or determine what the immediate outcomes of NEPAD would be, but the creators of the framework believed that Africa would become more effective in conflict prevention and the establishment of enduring peace on the continent by adopting principles of democracy and good political, economic, and corporate governance. They wanted to see the protection of human rights, effective poverty eradication programs, and increased levels of domestic savings, as well as investments, both domestic and foreign.

The framework called for Africa to achieve the desired capacity for policy development, coordination, and negotiation in the international arena, as an assurance that it would have a beneficial engagement in the global economy, especially on trade and market access issues. This was the only way that genuine partnerships could be established between Africa and the developed countries based on an acceptance of a genuine mutual respect and authentic accountability. Among the main operational goals is the carrying out of action in some short-term regional infrastructure programs, particularly covering transport, energy, water, and sanitation. The ideas were important in the context of growing challenges to the health of African people. For example, the HIV crisis has struck Africa perhaps harder than any other continent.

## The HIV crisis

Africa remains the region of the world that is most affected by HIV and AIDS. An estimated 25.4 million people were living with HIV in 2005. In one year the epidemic claimed the lives of an estimated 2.3 million people in Africa. Around two million children under 15 are living with HIV and more than twelve million children have been orphaned by AIDS. Some countries are affected more than others. In some African countries, the epidemic has grown even though their governments have campaigned for safe sex. Some countries have seen a sharp rise in HIV prevalence among pregnant women. In Cameroon the HIV rate more than doubled to over 11 percent among those aged 20–24 between 1998 and 2000) and the country is now coping with the fact that there is an epidemic. Rates of HIV infection vary greatly between countries.

In Somalia and Gambia the prevalence is under 2 percent of the adult population, whereas in South Africa and Zambia the rate is about 4 percent. In four southern African countries, the national adult HIV prevalence rate has risen higher than was thought possible and now exceeds 24 percent. These countries are Botwsana (37.3 percent), Lesotho (28.9 percent), Swaziland (38.8 percent), and Zimbabwe (24.6 percent). West Africa is less affected by HIV infection, but the prevalence rates in some countries are creeping up. In West and Central Africa HIV prevalence is estimated to exceed 5 percent in several countries, including Cameroon (6.9 percent), Central African Republic (13.5 percent), Côte d'Ivoire (7.0 percent), and Nigeria (5.4 percent). Until recently the national prevalence rate had remained relatively low in Nigeria, the most populous country in sub-Saharan Africa. The rate has grown slowly from 1.9 percent in 1993 to 5.4 percent in 2003. But some states in Nigeria are already experiencing HIV prevalence rates as high as those now found in Cameroon. Already around 3.6 million Nigerians are estimated to be living with HIV.

HIV infection in eastern Africa varies between adult prevalence rates of 2.7 percent in Eritrea to 8.8 percent in Tanzania. In Uganda the country-wide prevalence among the adult population is 4.1 percent.

The prevalence of HIV infections among a country's adult population – that is, the percentage of the adult population living with HIV – is a measure of the overall state of the epidemic in a country. But it does not tell if the infection is recent or occurred a decade ago. Member states of the African Union recognize that HIV/AIDS impacts on Africa's economic development, and in turn this affects Africa's ability to fight against the virus.

## The NEPAD umbrella

NEPAD came into existence as a program of the African Union designed to meet its development objectives. The highest authority of the NEPAD implementation process was the Heads of State and Government Summit of the African Union, formerly known as the OAU.

The Heads of State and Government Implementation Committee (HSIC) comprises three states per AU region as mandated by the OAU Summit of July 2001 and ratified by the AU Summit of July 2002. The HSIC reports to the AU Summit on an annual basis.

The steering committee of NEPAD comprises the personal representatives of the NEPAD heads of state and government. This committee oversees projects and program development for the continent, country by country. The NEPAD secretariat coordinates and implements the main humanitarian and commercial projects.

Along with the NEPAD initiative came a call for Africans in the Diaspora to be included in the African Union as a sixth region. The protocols for effecting this reality have proved to be quite complex. However, key members of the African Union, including Senegal, South Africa, and Nigeria, remain committed to the idea that Africans who are the descendants of those who were taken from the continent against their will should have a place in the assembly that represents the African world.

A series of conferences, first initiated by President Abdoulaye Wade of Senegal, took place in New York and Dakar in 2003–04 toward the aim of developing conversation about the inclusion of Africans in the Americas and Europe in the African Union. Ultimately the African Union under the leadership of President Alpha Oumar Konare took leadership for the continent and accepted the proposal, originally created by Dr. Cheikh Tidiane Gadio, Senegal's indefatigable senior minister for international affairs, for an African intellectual conference as a prelude to more detailed discussions about incorporating the Diaspora into the African Union as the sixth region.

Thus, the First Conference of Intellectuals of Africa and of the Diaspora organized by the African Union in collaboration with the Republic of Senegal was held at the Hotel Le Méridien, in Dakar, Senegal, on October 6–9, 2004. Nearly 700 intellectuals and men and women of culture from Africa and its Diasporas in North, Central and South America, the Caribbean, Europe and the Arab world attended the conference.

The meeting was graced by the presence of heads of state, heads of government or vice-presidents of South Africa, Cape Verde, Mali, Nigeria,

Uganda, Senegal, and the Gambia. Also in attendance were representatives of other member states' governments, as well as of the international organizations and of the United Nations. The general theme was "Africa in the 21st Century: Integration and Renaissance." To facilitate deliberation, this general theme was divided into six sub-themes, namely:

1. Pan-Africanism in the twenty-first century;
2. contribution of intellectuals of Africa and of the Diaspora to the strengthening of African integration in the global context of the twenty-first century;
3. relations between Africa and its Diasporas;
4. the African identity within a multicultural context;
5. the place of Africa in the world;
6. Africa, science and technology: stakes and prospects.

The Bureau of the Conference was elected by acclamation in a meeting at the headquarters of the African Union by a select group of scholars:

| | |
|---|---|
| chairperson | Mr. Adigun Ade Abiodun |
| vice-chairperson | Prof. Iba Der Thiam |
| vice-chairperson | Ms. Martha Johnson |
| vice-chairperson | Mr. Edem Kodjo |
| vice-chairperson | Ms. Zen Tadese |
| rapporteur | Mr. Théophille Obenga assisted by Mr. Alioune Sall |

The conference in Dakar on October 9, 2004, was opened with an address by Alpha Oumar Konaré, chairperson of the Commission of the African Union, who expressed his immense joy at participating in the event. He paid a well-deserved tribute to Maître Abdoulaye Wade, president of the Republic of Senegal, and brother leader Mu'ammer al-Gaddafi, whose nation made a major contribution to the African Union for the conference. Gaddafi has always been active in support of the unity of Africa, and his presence, through his surrogates and representatives as well as his own address to the delegates, was felt in the discussions and discourses of the conference.

Chairperson Konaré discussed the resistance demonstrated by the peoples of Africa and called upon Africans to create and resist at the same time as paying attention to the new world modalities. He cited several challenges facing Africa such as development financing, developing African languages and indigenous knowledge, integrating science into culture, the struggle for integration which defines Africa without reference to its linguistic or geographical particularities, and contributing to implementation of programs initiated by the African Union and NEPAD.

President Wade also recognized "brother" leader Gaddafi of Libya for supporting from the outset the idea of a Conference of Intellectuals of Africa and of the Diaspora. Wade also noted that Alpha Oumar Konaré had run the affairs of the continent in an able manner as befitting Africa. But then, as an intellectual himself, trained in economics and history, President

Wade laid down his challenge to the assembled intellectuals. He first traced the events leading up to the Conference, with special mention of the First Congress of Black Writers and Artists held in 1956, and the first meeting of African Intellectuals held in 1996.

Wade spoke fervently of the founding fathers of pan-Africanism and their successors, who had a firm commitment to the cause of Africa. Highlighting the pivotal role to be played by the Diaspora, Wade recalled the initiative to declare it as the sixth region of Africa, with a coordinator and a representative to the African Union in charge of relations with the Diaspora.

A presidential roundtable featured several presidents, including Thabo Mbeki (South Africa), Yoweri Museveni (Uganda), Pedro Pires (Cape Verde), Amadou Toumani Toure (Mali), and Abdoulaye Wade (Senegal). In addition, Mrs. Isatou Njie-Saidy (vice-president of the Gambia) and the representatives of the heads of state of Algeria and Gabon also participated.

President Thabo Mbeki made two points: first, that the conference belonged to the intellectuals rather than to the heads of state; and second, that the one common denominator among all those present was the commitment to changing Africa for the better.

Libyan leader Muammar Gaddafi made the following points:

*Language*: We should rehabilitate African languages by choosing three or four of them, with specific alphabets that are not tied to the Latin alphabet, which deforms our native languages. He warned that if we lose our languages we will lose our origins, our roots, and our cultures.

*African religion*: We should go back to our roots, and by that token reach out to our original religions.

*African housing*: We need to rehabilitate and preserve traditional African shelters because they are suited to our climatic conditions.

*African traditions*: These should be preserved, including our own cuisine.

*Africa's stability*: Gaddafi praised the founding fathers of the OAU who liberated their people from the yoke of colonialism and said power should be handed to the people, who are the sole custodians of legitimacy, through the People's Congresses.

*Figure 15.2* African National Congress leader Thabo Mbeki, September 1993
© Louise Gubb/CORBIS SABA

*Unity:* Africa must unite so as to acquire greater negotiating powers; the leader suggests one minister of trade, one minister of foreign affairs and one defense minister for the whole continent, as well as one African Congress with real powers.

The *African Diaspora* should assist Africa and contribute to its economic development.

Clearly, Gaddafi was the one African president who had a full-blown Africa-centered approach to the continent and its problems. He understood the full implications of the idea of unity in the context of that which places Africans at the center of their own history. This is not to say that President Pires of Cape Verde or President Museveni of Uganda did not have useful ideas; it is just that Gaddafi seems to have captured the spirit of the intellectuals assembled at Dakar.

Eleven intellectuals, from diverse parts of the African world, were chosen to make major plenary addresses on the six key themes of the conference. They were Tony Martin, Elikia M'Bokolo, Suleymane Bachir Diagne, Mahmood Mamdani, Samir Amin, Théophile Obenga, Adigun Ade Abiodun, Thandika Mkandawire, Mamadou Diouf, Henri Hogbe Nlend, and Molefi Kete Asante. Respondents and participants elaborated on the ideas presented by these intellectuals in an effort to discover common ground and project future activities. Several women respondents spoke on the African Union's protocol for a 50–50 representation between men and women on all AU programs. They decried the fact that only two women were given major roles as lead intellectuals or respondents on the themes. The leadership accepted the criticism led by Professor Sheila Walker and vowed to implement the African Union's policies in the future.

In the end, President Wade said that the rediscovery by Africa of its Diaspora was like when one discovers a lost sheet of music. On the other hand, one can say that the Diaspora itself has lots of work to do to reconnect itself to its roots. These measures are being taken in South, Central, and North America as well as in the Caribbean, Europe, and the Arabian Horn. In fact, after the Dakar meeting of African intellectuals there were numerous initiatives carried out throughout the African world. Two issues came to the forefront after the Dakar conference. First, non-government organizations in several nations sought to interject their ideas into the discourse around the integration of the Diaspora into the African Union; this was especially true regarding groups representing constituencies and political persuasions from the United States; second, tensions between members of the African Arab delegations and Diasporan delegations from Brazil, Cuba, the United States and the Caribbean, especially Trinidad, had to be mediated and carefully dealt with as issues of representation, political orientation, heritage, and citizenship were all on the table after the meeting.

The government of Brazil, with the second largest number of African people, agreed to sponsor the Second Congress of African Intellectuals, in July 2006. President Lula of Brazil asked the ministries of culture and foreign affairs to coordinate the work with the African Union.

Throughout the African world, that is, on the continent and in the Diaspora, groups of scholars and diplomats met during the early part of the twenty-first century to design strategies for implementing a United States of Africa. One of the principal committees sought, under the authority of the African Union, to draft a Preamble to the Constitution of the United States of Africa that would point the continent and its Diaspora in a rational direction. One such proposal was commissioned as follows:

### Draft of a preamble to the Constitution of the African Federative State or United States Of Africa

The nations, kingdoms, territories, and peoples of Africa with respect to the ancestors dedicate themselves to the united interest of African people.

We declare a commitment to freedom, harmony, order, balance, justice, and reciprocity in all our relations with each other.

We are a collective people with long traditions in intensifying a common bond, therefore we obligate ourselves to the African community with a persistent vigilance to hold back chaos.

We declare human rights to be universal, irrespective of place of origin, ethnic identity, gender, or religion.

There is nothing more important for our unity than a commitment to continental national character, the centerpiece of a constructive advancement toward the fulfillment of our peoples' hopes and desires.

We emphasize the common destiny of the African continent, the inculcation of a revolutionary, social, and economic transformation based on African principles, and the intent to defend the continent from any colonial domination.

We enter this pact with each other willingly, believing that humans are essentially good, that truth and justice are sources of strength, and that our posterity will value the traditions unlocked by our union.

# Appendix 1
# Chronology of Africa

35 million years ago: African and Arabian tectonic plates begin to separate, creating the Great Rift Valley

30 million years ago: *Aegytopithecus*, a possible candidate for the earliest ancestor of hominids and pongids, exists in the Fayum Depression in Egypt

10 million to 4 million years ago: Hominids move from the forest to the savannas of East Africa

8 million years ago: Hominids and pongids separate

7 million years ago: *Sahelanthropus tchadensis* lives in modern-day Chad

4.5 million years ago: *Ardipithecus ramidus* lives in Awash area of modern-day Ethiopia

3 million years ago: *Australopithecus afarensis* lives in Ethopia and Chad

3 million years ago: Sahara Desert is fertile and rich land with tall trees and green meadows

2 to 3 million years ago: *Homo habilis* alive

2.3 million years ago: *Homo erectus* survives in Asia as recently as 53,000 years ago

250,000 years ago: Appearance of *Homo sapiens*, possessing language and the ability to name

50,000 years ago: Cave paintings show organization of settlements and establishment of group life

50,000 and 12,000 years ago: Wurm/Wisconsin glaciations do not affect Africans directly

38,000 years ago: Blombos Cave, in South Africa, has decorated ochre blocks and polished spearheads

26,000 years ago: Evidence of fishing hooks, hand axes, and stone scrapers in the Congo basin

10,000 BCE: People arrive in the Nile Valley before this time and introduce ideas of using wild grasses as food, and new religions as well as clan deities

10,000 BCE: Africans perfect the techniques of hunting, fishing, and gathering and are at the dawn of farming

8000 BCE: Rise of the Gerzean culture period

6000 BCE: End of Weichsel/Wisconsin/Wurm Ice Age results in population displacement

6000 BCE: Africans began living by the planned cultivation and harvesting of food

6000–1000 BCE: Sahara Desert expands

5000–4000 BCE: Rise of the Badarian culture period

4000–3000 BCE: Rise of Kush

3800–3100 BCE: Oldest tombs appear in Qustul in Nubia showing evidence of the first monarchy in Kush

*Figure A.1* Liberian presidential candidate Ellen Johnson Sirleaf smiles at supporters at Unity Party headquarters in Monrovia, Liberia © Nic Bothma/epa/CORBIS

3400 BCE: Unification of Kemet, which consists of 42 different ethnic groups, under the rule of Per-aa Narmer; unification lasts 3000 years

3400 BCE: Writing invented in Kemet and appears on many surfaces, most popularly papyrus

3400–2700 BCE: Thinite Period, consists of the first two dynasties

3400–2600 BCE: Archaic Period

3300–3200 BCE: Writing found on a group of small bone or ivory labels

3200–3000 BCE: Protodynastic Period

3100 BCE: Cuneiform writing in clay tablets in Mesopotamia, modern-day Iraq

3100–2890 BCE: First Dynasty of Kemet

3000 BCE: Natural change of climate: Sahara dries up and entire communities virtually disappear

3000 BCE: Peoples migrate to form the Sahelian peoples on the edge of the rainforests and the Amazighs in the north

3000 BCE: Lush pastures and fertile grazing areas of the Great Lakes region attract numerous ethnic groups of herders and farmers from the north and east

2920–2575 BCE: Early Dynastic Period in Kemet

2890–2686 BCE: Second Dynasty in Kemet

2686–2613 BCE: Third Dynasty in Kemet

2685–2000 BCE: Old Kingdom in Kemet

2667–2648 BCE: Saqqara Pyramid constructed as a step pyramid, the oldest form of architecture

2613–2494 BCE: Fourth Dynasty in Kemet, dominated by the building projects at Giza

2560 BCE: Pyramid known as the Great Pyramid built for Per-aa Khufu

2498–2345 BCE: Fifth Dynasty in Kemet

2414 BCE: Ptahotep, the father of ethical doctrines, wrote the first book on what it means to grow old

2345–2183 BCE: Sixth Dynasty in Kemet

2200 BCE: Collapse of the central government in Kemet

2200–2040 BCE: First Intermediate Period in Kemet

2183–2160 BCE: Seventh and Eighth Dynasties in Kemet

2160–2125 BCE: Ninth and Tenth Dynasties in Kemet

2125–1985 BCE: Eleventh Dynasty reunites the country

2061 BCE: Per-aa Mentuhotep II, the Great Unifier, comes into power and is renamed Nebhotepre, the Son of Ra, then Sematawy, He who unifies the Two Lands

2040–1785 BCE: Middle Kingdom in Kemet

2040–1785 BCE: Classical period of Kemetic history so-named as a result of the following publications: the *Coffin Texts* on the coffins of Meseheti and Djefaihapy, *Instructions of Kagemni*, *Maxims of Djedefhor*, *Admonitions*, *Instructions for Merikare*, *Maxims of Ptahhotep*, *Kemyt*, *Satire of Trades*, *Instructions to the Vizier*, *Prophecy of Neferti*, *Loyalist Instruction*, *Instructions of a Man to his Son*, *Instructions of Amenemope I*, *Drama of the Coronation*, the *Memphite Drama*, the *Tale of Isis and Ra*, the *Tale of Horus and Seth*, the *Destruction of Humanity*, *Dispute of a Man with his Ba*, the *Teachings of Khakheperreseneb*, and more written documents such as letters, administrative texts, autobiographical accounts, historical notes, medical and mathematical treatises, veterinary fragments, poetry, and priestly rituals

2040–1785 BCE: Kemet conquers Nubia

1996 BCE: 256 Odus of Yoruba compiled or created by Agboniregun, or Orunmila

1991 BCE: Sehotipibre, a national philosopher, argues that loyalty to the king is the most important function of a citizen

1991 BCE: Amenemhat, the first cynical philosopher, warns his readers to be wary of those who call themselves friends

1991–1802 BCE: Twelfth Dynasty in Kemet

1991 BCE: Sobekneferu, first certain female ruler of Kemet

1990 BCE: Merikare, a philosopher, writes on the value of speaking well and using common sense in human relationships

1962 BCE: Per-aa Amenemope assassinated

1802 BCE: Thirteenth Dynasty in Kemet

1800–1600 BCE: Second Intermediate Period

1700–600 BCE: Height of kingdom of Kush

1633 BCE: Hyksos control the north of Kemet

1570–1085 BCE: New Kingdom in Kemet founded by Ahmose

1570 BCE: Royalty and nobles receive grand ritual burials similar to those the Per-aa received

1570 BCE: Per-aa Ahmose comes into power at the age of 10

1559 BCE: Kemet engages the Nubians and Hyksos in battle

1458 BCE: Per-aa Hatshepsut's (woman reigning as a king) reign ends and Per-aa Tuthmoses III regains the throne at the age of 22

1400 BCE: Amenhotep, son of Hapu, a priest, vizier, philosopher, and master of the ancients is the second living human in Africa to be deified

1370–1352 BCE: Rise of Per-aa Amenhotep, the wealthiest and most feared of all kings, challenges the ruling theocracy

1378 BCE: Per-aa Amenhotep IV becomes king in his own right

1340 BCE: Duauf, an educational philosopher, cherishes the idea of learning and writes that the young must learn to appreciate books

1300 BCE: Per-aa Akhenaten, born Amenhotep IV, believes that the god Aten is the sole god, changes the religious doctrine of Kemet and moves the capital city

1318–1316 BCE: Per-aa Ramses I reigns, beginning construction of the massive hypostyle hall at Karnak

1318–1298 BCE: Per-aa Seti I reigns, dealing firmly with revolting nations in Asia by dividing his armies and building the temple of Ausar at Abydos

1316 BCE: Nineteenth Dynasty in Kemet

1298–1232 BCE: Per-aa Ramses II, the Great, reigns, both a magnificent leader and commander-in-chief, first to build a temple for a woman

1277 BCE: Hittite king sends a silver tablet to Ramses swearing eternal peace, the treaty lasting for 50 years

1200 BCE: Knowledge of iron smelting spreads from East Africa to other regions of Africa and the world, giving Africans authority over the land, but also a transformation in warfare

1000 BCE: Sahara too dry to sustain a huge population

1000 BCE: By this time, Kush has conquered all of Nubia

1000–900 BCE: Napata Dynasty in Nubia, often referred to as Kush

780–760 BCE: King Alara reigns in Nubia

760–747 BCE: King Kashta, named Maatre at coronation, reigns in Nubia, extends the rule of Kush to modern-day Aswan

730 BCE: Tefnakht attempts to challenge Piankhy

747 BCE: Piankhy marries daughter of Alara and becomes Per-aa, eventually ruling over Nubia and Kemet

750–590 BCE: Resurgent kingdom in Kemet

700–600 BCE: Phoenicians settle in Carthage on Africa's north coast

690 BCE: Per-aa Sennacherib murdered by his sons

690–664 BCE: Taharka reigns as Per-aa

671 BCE: Esarhaddon, an Assyrian, invades Kemet directly and forces many Delta princes to take on Assyrian names and rename their towns

666 BCE: Ashurbanipal, king of Assyria, leads army pillaging as far south as Waset

620–600 BCE: Per-aa Anlamani rules Nubia and Kemet

609–594 BCE: Per-aa Psammetichus I and Neko attempt to push the boundaries of Kemet into Asia but fail

605 BCE: Nebuchadnezzar, heir to the throne of Babylon, meets the forces of Kemet in Carchemish and destroys them

600 BCE: Thales of Miletus, a Greek philosopher, is the first Greek philosopher to study in Kemet

600–580 BCE: Per-aa Aspelta rules Nubia and Kemet

594–588 BCE: Per-aa Psammetichus II reigns in Nubia and Kemet

588–568 BCE: Per-aa Apries reigns in Nubia and Kemet and is overthrown when the people of Kemet become outraged after the failure of an expedition

525 BCE: Persia invades Kemet, becoming the third force to invade the Nile Valley from the outside

518 BCE: Darius I comes to Kemet from Persia to settle some unrest the Persian governor cannot handle

510 BCE: Carthage signs trade treaty with Rome

500 BCE: Camel replaces the horse as the main mode of transportation

500 BCE: Crop growers enter the Congo region in low numbers

500 to 200 BCE: Axumite Empire enters Dawning Era

491 BCE: Darius I defeated at Marathon

491 BCE: Xerxes arrives in Kemet

480 BCE: Syracuse army defeats Carthaginian army, preserving Sicilian city-states

450 BCE: Herodotus goes south up the Nile as far as Elephantine

415–413 BCE: Peloponnesian War, Athenians attack Syracuse

409 BCE: Hannibal destroys city of Himera and takes Selinus

406 BCE: General Himilco destroys Acragas, modern-day Agrigento

400 BCE–350 CE: Kush demonstrates power through architecture

400 BCE–1400 CE: Kush occupies Jenne-Jeno, a major trans-Saharan trade area on the Niger River in ancient Mali

378–361 BCE: Per-aa Nectanebo reigns in Egypt

361–359 BCE: Per-aa Teos reigns in Egypt

348 BCE: Carthage signs new trade treaty with Rome

341 BCE: Per-aa Nectanebo II deserted by Greek mercenaries and defeated by the Persians

341–338 BCE: Per-aa Artaxerxes III Othos terrorizes his own people, the people of Kemet

338–335 BCE: Per-aa Oarses follows his father's footsteps and terrorizes the people of Kemet

335–332 BCE: Bogoas, a eunuch, poisons Artaxerxes and Oarses and offers the throne to Darius III Codoman, who accepts and forces Bogoas to take his own poison

310–307 BCE: Agathocles, lord of Syracuse, threatens Carthage and other African shore towns

306 BCE: Carthage signs trade treaty with Rome

300 BCE: Ghana is formed by a group of people (probably Soninke) and forms a trading kingdom near the upper waters of the Niger

285 to 247 BCE: Greek Per-aa Ptolemy II Philadelphos builds the Pharos in Alexandria and is a patron of the library

284–275 BCE: Queen Bartare reigns in Nubia

264–241 BCE: First Punic War, Carthage loses all possessions in Sicily

247–222 BCE: Greek Per-aa Ptolemy III Euergetes reigns while Kemet faces famine

218–201 BCE: Second Punic War, Carthage is defeated

218 BCE: Hannibal begins his quest for victory

216 BCE: Rome meets Hannibal in battle

212 BCE: Hasdrubal defeats Roman army

210 BCE: P. Cornelius Scipio recovers what Romans had lost and takes Carthago Nova

209–182 BCE: Greek Per-aa Ptolemy V Epiphanes attempts to restore ancient temples in Kemet

207 BCE: Carthaginians lose almost all dominions in Spain

204 BCE: Scipio conquers Spain from Carthage

200 BCE to 99 CE: Axumite Empire enters Glowing Era

196 BCE: Hannibal escapes Carthage and joins Antiochus in Ephesus

183 BCE: Hannibal poisons himself to avoid death by the sword of another

177–155 BCE: Queen Shanadakete reigns in Nubia, the first significant female ruler in world history

160 BCE: South wall of the funerary chapel of pyramid N11 at Meroe shows an inscription of Nubian Queen Shanadakete, the painting showing her husband seated behind her

149–146 BCE: Third Punic War resulting in total destruction of Carthaginian power

122 BCE: New city, Colonia Junonia, founded where Carthage stood, but soon fails

99–84 BCE: Queen Amanirenas reigns in Nubia, fights Caesar's army and keeps Nubia free from Roman control

51 BCE: Greek Per-aa Ptolemy XIV ascends throne with wife/sister Cleopatra VII Philopates, serving as puppets under protection of the Roman Senate

45 BCE: Cleopatra has Ptolemy XIV poisoned and her son Ptolemy XV elected to the co-regency

36 BCE: Cleopatra has third child by Mark Antony, Cleopatra Selene, while Mark Antony marries Octavia

30 BCE: Mark Antony loses the battle of Actium

30 BCE: Octavian claims the title "Emperor Augustus" and brings Egypt into the Roman Empire as a province

30 BCE: Cleopatra dies and Rome rules Egypt

26–20 BCE: Queen Amanishakete reigns in Nubia

First century CE: Plutarch writes the best-recorded version of the legend of Ausar

25–41 CE: Queen Amanitore reigns in Nubia

83–115 CE: Queen Amankihatashan reigns in Nubia

99–900 CE: Axumite Empire Brilliant Era, and Axum is deeply Christian

100–200 CE: Nubia becomes occupied by Nobatae

139 CE: Record of the synchronization of the first day of the solar year and the rising of Sirius

220 CE: Axum rises to power as an empire

280–300 CE: Heliodorus, a Greek, writes a historical novel, *Aethiopica*

290 CE: Axumite Empire defeats Nubia and becomes the greatest empire in Africa at this time; begins to use natural resources for everyday purposes such as minting coins

300s CE: Ethiopians adopt Christianity as official religion

350 CE: Axumite Empire defeats Meroe

421 CE: Roman emperors tear down Carthaginian temple dedicated to Tanit

439–533 CE: Carthage becomes the capital of the Vandals

500–1000 CE: Europe enters the White Ages when a fog hovers over learning and small communities of priests keep literacy alive

528–575 CE: Axumite Empire invades Arabia and rules Yemenite area

533 CE: Carthage recovered for the Byzantine Empire by Belisarius for 150 years

610 CE: Muhammad's work as a prophet begins

622 CE: Muslim era

622 CE: East coast of Africa becomes popular with Arabs, Persians, Indians, Indonesians, and Chinese and becomes a melting pot for those facing religious persecution in their own countries

622 CE: Heraclius begins expedition to Cilicia to rescue the Holy Rood and take portions of the Roman Empire back from the Persians

622 CE: Muhammad makes flight from Mecca to Medina to prepare for war to conquer Arabia and the shrine of the Ka'aba

629 CE: African leaders in Egypt invite General Al-As to help drive Romans out of Africa

631 CE: Cyrus, leader of the campaign to stamp out Coptic religion, lands in Alexandria causing the Coptic patriarch, Benjamin, to flee, and begins persecuting the Copts (October) while searching for Benjamin

632 CE: Muhammad calls for war against the Roman Empire

639 CE: (December 12) General Amir ibn al-As celebrates the Muslim Day of Sacrifice in Egypt

640 CE: Amir's army expands as many Bedouins join the campaign against the Romans

651 CE: Makurra kingdom of Nubia defeats the Muslim army

698 CE: Carthage destroyed by the Arabs and rebuilt under the strict influence of the Arab Muslims

700 CE: Arabs have succeeded in taking all of North Africa as Africans who maintain their traditional beliefs become exhausted by the burdens of their conquerors

700 CE: Indonesians migrate to the island of Madagascar, where the Malagasy already live

800 CE: By this time the area between the Niger River and the town of Gao, the most important city, was known as Songhay, with the capital city as Kukiya

900 CE: Beginning of formation of states in Yoruba

900 CE: Persians from Shiraz marry Somali women and develop the Shirazi culture

900 CE: Zanj, the entire Swahili coast, is controlled from Sofala

900s CE: People of Zanj are already wearing iron ornamentation

909 CE: Amazigh Shiites, the Fatimids, pull together the Amazighs and Tamascheks and take North Africa back from the Arabs

1000 CE: Hausa city-states came into existence in present Nigeria

1000 CE: Mais, kings of Kanem-Borno, convert to Islam, Mai Hume being the first to make the *hajj* to Mecca

1000 CE: Sungbos' Eredo constructed in Nigeria

1000 CE: Yoruba perfect the town type of government

1000 CE: Zimbabwe is a thriving and powerful kingdom through the fifteenth century, with its rise between the eleventh and thirteenth centuries

1000–1200 CE: Much of eastern Central Africa from Zambia to Lake Malawi participates in Luangwa, the later Iron Age culture

1054 CE: Almoravids capture Audoghast, a powerhouse city in Ghana

1056 CE: Almoravids capture Sijilmasa, the main northern trading center for West African gold

1067 CE: Al-Bakri, a Spanish Arab, writes about Tunka Manin, a Ghanaian

1076 CE: Almoravids capture Kumbi Saleh

1087 CE: Abu Bakr assassinated while trying to suppress a revolt

1100 CE: Al-Idrisi writes that Manan and Njimi in Kanem-Borno are occupied

1100 CE: Rise of Katsina, a principal city-state in the trans-Saharan trade, and Kano becomes established as the largest city in northern Nigeria, with a manufacturing and craft center

1100s CE: Nigerian Benin develops centralized state system to draw surrounding villages into one unit and develops kingship system

1100s CE: Ife develops kingship system

1134 CE: Sayf bin Dhi Yazan marries into the lineage of the Mai Kanem and creates the Saifawa Dynasty in Kanem-Borno, which lasts until 1846

1171–1250 CE: Period of the Ayyubids

1172 CE: Nubians attack Egypt when Ayyubids come into power

1180 CE: Soso soldier overthrows Soninke dynasty of Wagadu

1199 CE: Peul takes control of kingdom of Diara, an important province of Wagadu

1200 CE: Allah is the supreme ruler in Egypt

1203 CE: Sumanguru declares himself in Ghana and surrounds Kumbi Saleh and destroys it

1240 CE: Until this time, Kumbi Saleh in Ghana is the largest city in western Africa, fending off enemies who want access to its lucrative trade

1240 CE: Hostel erected in Cairo for students from Kanem-Borno

1250–1517 CE: Period of the Mamluks

1255 CE: Sundiata Keita, emperor of Mali, dies

1270–1285 CE: Kebra Nagast, the Book of the Glory of the Kings of Ethiopia, created during the revival of the Solomonic line of kings during the reign of Yekuno Arnlak

1294 CE: King Karanbas' installation to the throne in Nubia marks the conversion of Christian Nubia to Islam

1300 CE: Mali Empire at its height, while the Arabic language and script become instruments for administration, law, and commerce

1300–1384 CE: The Arab Chihab Addine Abul-Abass Ahmad ben Fadhl al-Umari writes information about the great Malian Mansa Kankan Musa and records his interviews with Mansa Kankan Musa about his brother, Abubakari II, the previous *mansa*, who may have reached the Americas before Columbus

1300 CE: Kanem pressured by Bulala people, and Kanem-Borno undergoes "era of instability"

1300 CE: Islam conquers the Hausa city-states

1304 CE: The Arab Abu Abdullah Muhammad ibn Battuta, also known as Shams ad-Din, visits the lands of every Muslim ruler of his time, travels across Africa, and dictates his accounts, which become known as the Travels (*Rihala*) of Ibn Battuta

1311 CE: Emperor Mansa Abubakari II sends one thousand boats across the Atlantic; in 1312 he abandons his throne and sets sail with another thousand boats

1324 CE: Mansa Kankan Musa, leader of the Mali Empire, takes a *hajj* to Mecca but does so with the style of a king, bringing international attention to Mali

1332–1395 CE: Ibn Khaldun writes *Muqaddimah* or "Prolegomena," an analysis of historical events that creates and continues stereotypes but sets a list of rulers in Mali until 1390

1337 CE: Mansa Musa dies, leaving the throne to his son Mansa Maghan, who allows the empire to unravel

1339 CE: Mali first appears on a "map of the world" as a significant empire

1367 CE: World map shows road from Mali through the Atlas Mountains into the western Sudan

1380 CE: Kintu, the first king of Baganda, is crowned

1390 CE: Cheng Ho (Sheng He) of the Chinese Ming Dynasty visits the Swahili coast after the city-states reassert their independence

1400 CE: Timbuktu becomes a major learning center for Muslim scholars

1400 CE: Mai Ali Gaji ends political troubles of the Seifawa Dynasty of Kanem-Borno

1400s CE: Phiri clan marries into the Banda clan and forms the Nyanja

1400s CE: Kingdom of Asante rises

1400s CE: Bito dynasty rises to power in Baganda and Bunyoro

1420 CE: Nyatsimbe Mutota founds Mutapa in the area of Dande in the Mazoe Valley

1415 CE: Portugal captures Ceuta and forces African prisoners to reveal details about the African gold trade flaunted by Mansa Musa

1431–1433 CE: Cheng Ho's sailors reach as far down the coast as western South Africa

1433 CE: Tamascheks seize Timbuktu

1440 CE: Oba Ewuare reigns in Nigerian Benin

1440s CE: Portuguese ships land on the West African coast and take several dozen Africans to the king in Lisbon

1450 CE: Site of Great Zimbabwe is abandoned

1453 CE: Constantinople falls to the Ottoman Turks

1456 CE: Mali wilts away into the Songhay Empire

1464 CE: Sonni Ali Ber ascends as king of Songhay

1466 CE: Battle for Jenne (which the Mali Empire had tried to take 99 times) takes 7 years, 7 months, and 7 days to fall to Sonni Ali Ber

1468 CE: Sonni Ali Ber invades Timbuktu

1472 CE: Portuguese bring a ship to the Bight of Benin, exposing Nigerian Benin people to Europeans for the first time

1480 CE: Kongo people willing to build partnerships with Portuguese

1482 CE: Diogo Cão, a Portuguese sailor, visits the mouth of the Congo

1482 CE: Portuguese begin to build fortress at El Mina, in modern-day Ghana

1484 CE: Mossi leave the city of Walata, a northern point for the Mali Empire, in ruins

1485 CE: Thousands of people employed in Jenne at the university, and in schools, the trades, commerce, and business

1480s CE: Sunni Ali Ber forces Mossi back south out of Niger

1485–1554 CE: Leo Africanus, also known as Al-Hasan ibn Muhammed el-Wazzan ez-Zayyat, writes of his journeys in Africa in *The History and Description of Africa*, which also includes an impressive account of the ancient city of Timbuktu

1492 CE: Sonni Ali Ber drowns in the Niger River, his son, Sonni Bakori Da'as becomes king, the quest to end Islamic onslaught ends and Africa is not unified

1492 CE: Spain expels thousands of Africans and Jews

1492 CE: Columbus sails to the Americas and convinces Europeans to risk their money and their lives to take Africans to the Americas and enslave them

1492–1885 CE: Europe's continental power unchallenged by any area of the world

1493 CE: Sonni Bakori Da'as is overthrown by Muhammed Toure, a Muslim and general-in-chief of the army of Gao, and killed at the battle of Anfao

1493 CE: Muhammed Toure takes the dynastic name Askia Mohammed Toure and rules the Songhay Empire until 1529

1493 CE: First European settlement founded at Isabella on the north coast of Hispaniola, near Puerto Plata

1495 CE: Askia Mohammed makes a pilgrimage to Mecca and strengthens Islam as the dominant religious tendency in the Songhay Empire

1496 CE: Christopher Columbus' brother Bartholomew discovers gold in the Ozama River valley and founds the city of Santo Domingo

1498 CE: Askia Mohammed declares a *jihad* on the Mossi

1500 CE: Zazzau region founded, and the capital, Zaria, becomes a major center for the slave trade in the seventeenth century and eventually the name for the region

1500 CE: Hausa city-states control the routes to Akan, Aïr, Gao, Jenne, Kukikya, and Borno

1500s CE: Rise of Oyo in Yoruba causes decline of Ife dominance

1500s CE: Portuguese divert Shona and Swahili gold trade to the Indian Ocean and battle with the Swahili

1500s CE: Akan states become militarily and economically strong

1500s CE: Mwato Yamvo dynasty comes into power in Lunda-Luba Empire

1504 CE: Fall of the Alwa Kingdom in Nubia

1504 CE: Oba Esaghie comes into power in Nigerian Benin

1504–1526 CE: Mai Idris Katarkambi reigns in Manem-Borno, liberating Njimi from the Bulala

1505 CE: Askia Mohammed sends a second expedition to battle Mossi and succeeds

1505 CE: Mauritius occupied by Portuguese

1513 CE: Armed forces of Songhay defeat Hausa states of the Niger River as far as Lake Chad

1513 CE: Leo Africanus writes an account of the Songhay Empire

1520 CE: History of Kilwa written in KiSwahili

1520 CE: Francesco Alvarez, a Portuguese priest, visits Ethiopia and claims they still have 150 churches in old castles but not among the masses

1526 CE: Mai Muhammed stops revolt by the Bulala

1527 CE: Malandela settles at Mandawe Hill and has two sons, Qwabe and Zulu, the founder of the Zulu clan

1529 CE: Askia Musa overthrows his father, Askia Mohammed

1530 CE: Portuguese travel up the Zambezi River and conquer trading towns of Sena and Tete and establish links with Munhumutapa

1536–1573 CE: Amina may have reigned as Queen of Zazzau

1537 CE: Ismail overthrows Askia Musa and frees his father

1540 CE: Kalonga dynasty founds the Lundu dynasty among the Manganja of the Shire valley and the Undi dynasty among the Chewa

1545 CE: Mai Ali of Kanem-Borno fights with kingdom of Kebbi in Hausaland

1546 CE: Mai Ali dies

1546–1563 CE: Dunama reigns in Kanem-Borno

1549–1582 CE: Askia Dawud reigns in the Songhay Empire

1550 CE: Oba Orhogbua reigns in Nigerian Benin

1551 CE: Ottoman Turks occupy Tripoli

1553 CE: British arrive in Nigerian Benin and trade pots and pans for peppercorns

1564–1569 CE: Mai Dala Abdullah reigns in Kanem-Borno

1569 CE: Dala Abdullah dies and the reign of Kanem-Borno is seized by his sister, Queen Aissa Killi

1569 CE: Mai Idris Alooma, the greatest of all *mais*, reigns in Kanem-Borno and establishes a reputation for fairness, justice, and sternness

1571 CE: Portuguese send another army into the Zambezi Valley but are defeated by the Tonga people

1574 CE: Portuguese force Uteve king to pay tribute at Sofala on Indian Ocean coast

1578 CE: Oba Ehenguda reigns in Nigerian Benin

1582 CE: Askia Ishaq II's forces are defeated by Moroccan army of Pasha

1594 CE: Overthrow of the Songhay Empire

1600 CE: Nigerian Benin exhausts its export of "trouble-making" Africans and trades only natural resources for foreign goods with the Portuguese

1600 CE: Rise of Changamire's Rozvi state

1600 CE: Ganye Hessu reigns as king of Dahomey

1600s CE: Denkyira, in Ghana, controls all other states in Ghana and is an important source for trading gold and humans with the Dutch at El Mina

1602 CE: O. Dapper, a geographer from the Netherlands, describes Nigerian Benin as a well-organized, balanced, structured, and grand city

1603 or 1617 CE: Mai Idris of Kanem-Borno dies and Morocco consolidates its power over Songhay

1606 CE: Oba Ahuan reigns in Nigerian Benin

1620 CE: Dako Donu reigns as king of Dahomey

1632 CE: Twenty Africans disembark in Jamestown, Virginia

1638 CE: Mauritius taken over by Dutch

1645 CE: Kingdom of Abomey conquers the neighboring kingdom of Dan and calls the new country Dahomey, meaning "in the belly of Dan"

1645 CE: Houegbadja reigns as king of Dahomey

1652 CE: Van Riebeck leads whites into South Africa at the Cape, introducing the idea of private ownership

1665 CE: 200 years of Portuguese influence weakens Congo kingdom, which falls into warring factions

1677 CE: Nana Obiri Yeboa, of the Asante people, dies

1680 CE: Osei Tutu I assumes kingship of the Asante

1685 CE: Akaba reigns as king of Dahomey

1700 CE: Asante conquers Denkyira, brings other Akan states into submission, and controls the goldfields

1700s CE: Mauritius captured by French

1708 CE: Tegbessu reigns as king of Dahomey

1717 CE: Nana Opoku, the fighting king, reigns over the Asante

1724 CE: Dahomey conquers Allada, the kings of the two nations being brothers

1727 CE: Dahomey conquers Savi and positions itself to be an important player in the slave trade

1740 CE: Tegbessu reigns as king of Dahomey and enters into the enslaving interest to gain wealth and influence, trading humans for weapons in order to capture more Africans from other places

1774 CE: Kpingla reigns as king of Dahomey

1786 CE: Abdul Qadir Kan negotiates an agreement with the French to avoid selling Muslims into slavery as a result of the second *jihad* in the Hausa city-states

1787 CE: Andrianampoinimerina reigns in Madagascar

1787 CE: Senzangakona and Nandi give birth to Shaka, who rises to the highest seat of authority in the Zulu clan

1787 CE: Americans hold Constitutional Convention

1787 CE: British help 400 freed Africans from the United States, Nova Scotia, and Great Britain to return to Sierra Leone to settle the "Province of Freedom," which became Freetown

1789 CE: Agonglo reigns as king of Dahomey

1792 CE: Freetown becomes one of Britain's first colonies

1797 CE: Adandozan reigns as king of Dahomey

1798 CE: Napoleon's army uncovers the Great Sphinx and the French seek to subdue most of the Sudan outside of the British sphere, including Niger, Mali, Upper Volta, and Chad

1791 CE: Africans revolt against the French in Santo Domingo and choose as leader Toussaint L'Ouverture

1804 CE: Conflict breaks out between Dan Fodio's followers and Na Fata's successor, Yunfa, in the third *jihad* in the Hausa city-states

1805 CE: Mzilikazi, leader and creator of the state of Zimbabwe, is born

1805 CE: Asante Wars against the British until 1905

1807 CE: European slave trade prohibited on the high seas

1808 CE: Armies of Gobir have been defeated and Dan Fodio establishes a new state with the capital at Sokoto

1810 CE: Radama reigns in Madagascar

1810 CE: Mauritius conquered by British

1811–1812 CE: Fourth War with the British

1814 CE: Nearly all the Hausa states overthrown by Fulani-led jihads

1814 CE: *Jihads* help create largest African state of its kind at the time, the Sokoto Caliphate

1815 CE: Francisco Felix de Souza, a Portuguese slave trader, assists Guezo in seizing the Dahomey throne from Adandozan

1816–1840 CE: Mfecane wars fought is South Africa

1816 and 1819 CE: Dingiswayo leads the Mtetwa against the Ndwandwe

1816 CE: American Colonization Society sends its first ship, the *Elizabeth*, to Liberia with 88 emigrants, three white officials, and supplies, even though the Malinke already lived there

1818 CE: Seku Ahmadu Bari attacks cities of Segu and Jenne, establishes the state of Massina, and declares himself the twelfth caliph

1818 CE: Guezo reigns as king of Dahomey

1818–1819 CE: Fifth War with the British, British intervene with two warring groups in Xhosa, and divide and conquer

1821 CE: Moeshoeshoe, founder of the Lesotho nation, moves capital to a mountaintop for protection

1824 CE: Shaka Zulu demands all soldiers remain in the service until their thirties

1827 CE: Fourah Bay College is established in Sierra Leone and is the leading college for English-speaking Africans on the west coast

1828 CE: Shaka Zulu is murdered by his own men, and his half-brother Dingane becomes king of the Zulu

1828–1830 CE: Umar Tal makes a *hajj* to Mecca and Medina, begins spreading the Tijani and became convinced to lead the fourth *jihad*

1834–1835 CE: Xhosa's Sixth War with the British

1838 CE: (September 16) Boer army of Andries Pretorius defeats the Zulu nation at Blood River

1840 CE: Dingane's brother Mpande becomes king of the Zulu nation and does not stand up to the Boers for 32 years

1840 CE: France invades the Côte d'Ivoire

1841 CE: Liberia is turned over to Joseph Jenkins Roberts, the first governor of African descent

1842 CE: Natal region becomes a British colony

1844 CE: Menelik II, governor of the province of Shoa in Ethiopia, leads the most successful campaign of war against a European colonizing army

1846 CE: British military escort killed by Africans, British start the War of the Axe

1847 CE: Liberia writes a constitution and becomes an independent republic

1849 CE: George Washington Williams is born in Pennsylvania and becomes the first African American protester of the treatment of the Congo people

1858 CE: Glele reigns as king of Dahomey

1858 CE: Europeans Richard Burton and John Speke visit the Buganda kingdom and Great Lakes region in search of the source of the Nile

1861 CE: Umar Tal attacks and captures the king of Kaarta, the king of Segu, and seizes the state of Massina

1862 CE: Said Pasha finds a stele describing Piankhy's victory over Tefnakht

1863 CE: French declare control over Porto Novo

1868 CE: Ethiopia invaded by 5000 British and Indian troops

1868 CE: Rise of Kassai, the *ras*, or lord, of Tigre, an Ethiopian province

1870s CE: Kassai submitted to repeated attacks from the Egyptian armies of Ismail Pasha

1870s CE: (late) Mpande's son, Ceteswayo, rejuvenates the Zulu nation

1876 CE: (March 7–9) Battle of Gura, Ethiopia defeats the Egyptian army, which is led by European and American mercenaries

1878 CE: (December) Ceteswayo rejects British ultimatum to return his *induna* for trial in British courts

1879 CE: (January 10–11) British, under generalship of Frederic Thesiger, viscount Chelmsford, attack Zululand

1879 CE: Chelmsford forces take Ulundi and burn the city to the ground

1881 CE: British try to arrest Muhammed Ahmad (Mahdi), the leader of the fifth *jihad*

1881 CE: France takes over Tunisia

1881 CE: Muhammad Ahmad, proclaimed to be the Mahdi, rises in Sudan and seeks to recover the power of the indigenous people

1882 and 1883 CE: George Washington Williams writes *History of the Negro Race in America from 1619–1880. Negroes as Slaves, as Soldiers, and as Citizens, together with a preliminary consideration of the Unity of the Human Family and Historical Sketch of Africa and an Account of the Negro Governments of Sierra Leone and Liberia*

1883 CE: British send 10,000 Egyptians to attack the Mahdists in Sudan, but are defeated

1884 CE: Governor Gordon sent to Khartoum to oversee evacuation of the city and decides to take a stand

1884 CE: Germany invades Togo and Cameroon but the people revolt in February

1884 CE: Massingina uprising in Nyasaland (Malawi)

1884–1885 CE: (November 15, 1884, to February 26, 1885) Berlin Conference, Europe declares war on Africa, dividing Africa among the European powers

1884–1914 CE: African churches flourish in Ethiopia

1885 CE: French occupy Madagascar

1885 CE: Khartoum is starved and overrun by Mahdists in 1885

1885 CE: Creation of the Mahdist state

1885 CE: Rabih ibn Fadl Allah, the conquerer of Borno, creates his own state in Bahr el-Ghazal

1885 CE: Italy occupies Massawa

1885–1893 CE: "Treaties" negotiated in Nyasaland between the African Lakes Company and various kings of Nyasaland allow British to swindle land from Nyasaland

1885–1887 CE: Ahmadu Seku, leader of Tucolor Empire, supports the French in their war against Mahmadu Lamine's uta Bondu state

1887 CE: Sultan of Zanzibar asks Tippu Tip, a half-African half-Arab Muslim slave hunter, to take over the eastern provinces of Zanzibar

1887 CE: Ethiopians defeat Italians in the "Dogali Massacre"

1888 CE: Enslaved Africans emancipated in Brazil

1889 CE: French army turns on Ahmadu Seku forces

1889 CE: Gbehanzin reigns as king of Dahomey

1889 CE: French occupy Cotonou

1889 CE: The Tucolor Empire, led by Ahmadu Seku, aggressively seeks to establish itself from Dakar to Bamako

1889 CE: (May) Italy claims a protectorate over Ethiopia after the Treaty of Wuchale (Uccialli), which cedes a portion of Ethiopia to Italy

1890 CE: Italians, with the British and French, advance on the town of Adowa in Ethiopia and occupy it

1890 CE: John Dunlop, an Irishman, invents the rubber tyre, fueling the Western need for rubber from the Congo

1890 CE: British government declares a protectorate over Zanzibar

1890 CE: George Washington Williams sails to Africa to write about slavery in the Congo under Henry Morton Stanley

1890 CE: William Sheppard, an African American, goes to the Congo as a missionary and returns to the USA to lecture about the slave conditions of the Congo

1890 CE: French defeat city of Segu, but the Tucolor leader refuses to surrender for the love of his country

1890–1919 CE: Ten newspapers founded in Ghana, five in Nigeria, and one in Uganda

1891 CE: French invade the Mandika territory, led by Samori Ture, who retreated so the French would not gain any advantage

1891 CE: Baule of Ivory Coast starts resistance that lasts until 1902

1891 CE: Gbehanzin, king of Dahomey, starts resistance that lasts until 1894

1892 CE: British invade Ijebu (Yoruba) and Uganda

1892 CE: Nigerian Benin enters a "trade and protection" treaty with Britain

1892 CE: French declare to King Gbehanzin that they will take over kingdom of Dahomey

1892 CE: William Sheppard enters the capital of Ifuca in Kuba and is accepted by the king

1893 CE: Chief Nzansu of Kasi leads African rebellions against Leopold's Force Publique

1893 CE: French invade Guinea and declare it a French colony

1893 CE: Ethiopian resistance blossoms

1894 CE: Agolio Agbo reigns as king of Dahomey, but is a puppet for the French

1894 CE: British authorities name Uganda region Uganda Protectorate

1894 CE: After negotiations with Kabeka Mutesa, British place kingdom of Buganda under British Protectorate

1894–1895 CE: Knut Svenson, a Swedish officer of the Force Publique, assembles people who do not want to be enslaved in the rubber plantation business in an open courtyard under the pretext of signing a treaty or recruiting laborers and then kills them

1895 CE: Britain includes all of Uganda, including Kenya, under East African Protectorate

1895 CE: Kandolo, a Kuba, leads a revolt against Mathieu Pelzer, a Force Publique base commander, and continues to lead the Kasi region of the Congo for half a year

1896 CE: Menelik II defeats Italian army in Adowa and Italians sign Treaty of Addis Ababa nullifying Treaty of Wuchale

1890–1905 CE: Manjanga Rebellion in Congo

1890s CE: (late) Britain annexes Sudan on behalf of Egypt, gaining complete control over the Nile basin

1895–1907 CE: 50,000 Africans in Zambesi Valley escape to Southern Rhodesia and Nyasaland

1895–1920 CE: Sayyid Muhammed leads Somalis in revolt

1897 CE: Kandolo is fatally wounded and two of his trusted aides, Yamba Yamba and Kimpuki, take over and continue to revolt against the Force Publique until 1908

1897 CE: Mulamba, an African soldier serving under white soldiers, leads a revolt against the Force Publique

1898 CE: British defeat Abdullah ibn Muhammed

1898 CE: French defeat Samori's troops when they succumb to famine

1898 CE: Nehanda and Kaguvi, leaders of Zimbabwe's First Chimurenga, are captured by the British and hanged for fighting against the unjust laws imposed by Britain and after Nehanda refuses to accept Christianity

1900 CE: British declare Protectorate of Northern Nigeria

1900 CE: English sappers chased off Tiv land, Tiv people resist domination and engage in the first Tiv–British battle, which leads to six years of instability

1900 CE: Two French armies converge and meet at Borno, defeating and killing Rabih of Borno

1900 CE: The Asante revolt against direct taxation, forced labor, and introduction of Western education

1900 CE: Fadl Allah ibn Rabih takes over Rabih's forces and retreats to northeast Nigeria

1900 CE: (September 30) Yaa Asantewa War, Asante are defeated

1900 CE: Chilembwe, a Nyasaland native who studied in Britain and the United States, founds the Providence Industrial Mission in Nyasaland

1900, 1902, and 1904 CE: Sudanese revolt against occupation by the Egyptians and the British

1900 CE: Pan-African Conference in London

1901 CE: French abolish kingdom of Dahomey

1903 CE: Ekumeku rebellion in Nigeria

1904 CE: Herero people of Southwest Africa (Namibia) protest German occupation

1904–1905 CE: Revolt in Madagascar

1905 CE: Germans attack Ngoni army in their camp

1906 CE: Zulu uprising against rule of British in Natal

1906 CE: Lady Lugard writes *A Tropical Dependency*

1908–1909 CE: Lobi and Dyula revolt in Mali

1909 CE: Mulama of Nyasaland leads a resistance movement

1908–1914 CE: Mossi rebellions in Kouddigou and Fada N'gourma

1911 CE: Siofume, a female priestess, and Kiamba, a young man, rise against British in Kenya

1911–1912, 1953, and 1958–1959 CE: Political unrest in Nyasaland

1912 CE: (January 8) African National Congress, originally the South African Native National Congress until 1923, is created in South Africa

1913 CE: Seven medical students, influenced by Ravelojaona, a minister, start the VVS (Vy Vato Sakelike) in Madagascar but are suppressed by the French

1913 CE: Onyango Dande seeks to overturn British rule in Kenya

1913 CE: African National Congress sends delegation to Britain to protest the Land Act of 1913

1914 CE: Giriama of Kenya revolt against British

1914 CE: Sadiavahe, an armed peasant revolt

1914 CE: Revolts against Europe subside when the First World War begins

1915 CE: Chilembwe Uprising against British in Nyasaland

1915 CE: British fight Germans in northern Nyasaland

1915–1916 CE: Rebellion of the Gurunsi in Upper Volta (Burkina Faso)

1917 CE: Rembe, a prophet claiming to have to the power to prevent European bullets killing a person, rises in Uganda

1919 CE: First (Second) Pan-African Congress directed by W. E. B. DuBois

1920 CE: Mende script, in Sierra Leone, devised by Kisimi Kamala

1920 CE: Leo Wiener writes *Africa and the Discovery of America*

1921 CE: Second (Third) Pan-African Congress

1921 CE: Founding of the African National Congress in South America and the National Association for the Advancement of Colored People in the United States

1921 CE: Afro-Cubans begin Negrismo, celebrating African music, rhythms, art, folklore, and literature

1923 CE: Third (Fourth) Pan-African Congress

1925 CE: Raymond Dart, a South African, discovers the skull of a six-year-old creature in a limestone cave in Taung, South Africa; the creature walked on two legs with a forward stoop and was named *Australopithecus*

1927 CE: Fourth (Fifth) Pan-African Congress

1929 CE: Fifth Pan-African Congress called for but denied by the French government and the Great Depression

1930 CE: Bamana "Ma-sa-ba" syllabary devised by the Woyo Couloubayi in the Kaarta region of Mali

1930 CE: Somali script developed by Isman Yusuf, son of the Somali sultan Yusuf Ali

1931 CE: Admonishment from the League of Nations stops the practice of non-Americo-Liberian forced labor in Liberia

1931 CE: French depose Njoya, an original intellect and brilliant scholar of the nineteenth and twentieth centuries, king of the Bamun kingdom

1931 CE: Women become affiliated members of the African National Congress

1935 CE: Italians invade Ethiopia to teach a lesson to the only nation that has defeated its army

1939 CE: Isaiah Anozie discovers several bronze objects while digging a cistern to hold water in southeastern Nigeria

1939 CE: Aimé Césaire publishes *Cahier d'un retour au pays natal* and coins the term "Négritude"

1943 CE: Women become full members of the African National Congress

1944 CE: African National Congress Youth League created, with Nelson Mandela as a founding member

1944 CE: Félix Houphouët-Boigny, son of a Baule king, forms the first agricultural union with the aim of securing better working conditions for Africans in Côte d'Ivoire

1945 CE: Fifth Pan-African Congress is held in Manchester, England; Pan-African Federation organized by Kwame Nkrumah

1945 CE: Léopold Sédar Senghor publishes *Chants d'ombre*

1945 CE: Senghor elected to represent Senegal in the French Constituent Assemblies

1945–1951 CE: Libya under a United Nations Trusteeship

1947 CE: African National Congress allies with the Natal Indian Congress and the Transvaal Indian Congress to oppose the white government

1947 CE: Alioune Diop, a Senegalese intellectual living in Paris, creates *Présence Africaine*, a cultural journal

1947 CE: General Council of the Kikuyu Central Association decides to campaign against white usage of Kenyan land

1948 CE: Afrikaner political group votes for the National Party and creates the apartheid policy and Africans are restricted by their color for the first time on the continent of Africa

1948 CE: British force Kikuyu off their land in Kenya

1948 CE: Egypt fights war in Israel

1948 CE: Léopold Sédar Senghor publishes *Hosties noires*

1949 CE: White minority National Party comes to power in South Africa and Eduardo Chivambo Mondlane, the father of Mozambican independence, and other black students are expelled from Witwatersrand University

1950 CE: UN argues that Eritrea should become a part of federated Ethiopia

1950 CE: Kwame Nkrumah arrested and imprisoned but wins a seat on the Legislative Assembly under the colonial administration

1950s and 1960s CE: Cheikh Anta Diop proposes that Africa is the cradle of civilization

1951 CE: Malinke receive the right to vote in Liberia

1952 CE: Dr. Alain Bombard sails from Casablanca to Barbados in an African raft, testing the theory of African discovery of the Americas

1952 CE: King Jacob Egharevba writes about the majesty of Nigerian Benin king Oba Ewuare

1952 CE: African National Congress joins with other groups in a defiance campaign against apartheid

1952 CE: Ben Bella pushed out of Algeria

1952 CE: Egyptian officers in the British Free Officers Movement overthrow King Farouk I of Egypt

1952–1960 CE: Mau Mau revolt in Kenya to throw British settlers off land

1953 CE: Central Committee in Kenya renames itself the Council of Freedom

1953 CE: British-led African Christians become the Kikuyu Home Guard in Kenya

1953 CE: (March 26) Mau Mau viewed as bloodthirsty after they kill 70 people in the village of Lari, home to British supporters; British retaliate and kill 125 in the sweep of Aberdare Forest

1954 CE: (November 1) Algerian Front de Libération Nationale (FLN) guerrilas launch a series of attacks against the French colonial administration

1954 CE: (February 25) Gamal Abdel Nasser becomes president of Egypt and appeals to the masses with public works projects such as the Aswan High Dam

1954 CE: (October 26) Nasser shot at by Mahmoud Abd al-Latif, a member of the Muslim Brotherhood

1955 CE: Dr. Hannes Lindermann sails for 52 days to South America from the Cape Verde Islands, demonstrating the possibility of Africans sailing to South America

1955 CE: Congress of the People, African National Congress leads people to accept the Freedom Charter, the fundamental document of the anti-apartheid struggle

1955 CE: A military unit composed of Sudanese southerners mutinies at Torit

1956 CE: 156 members of the African National Congress arrested by whites in South Africa

1956 CE: Nasser vows to liberate Palestine

1956 CE: Freedom Charter adopted at a Congress of the People in Kliptown, South Africa

1957 CE: Gold Coast becomes independent and chooses the name Ghana

1957 CE: General Raoul Salan, the French commander in Algeria, challenges the FLN with quadrillage dividing the country into sectors to be policed by permanently garrisoned troops in each sector

1957 CE: Kwame Nkrumah promotes the idea of an independent West African Federation and becomes the leader of Ghana

1957–1960 CE: More than two million Algerians removed from their villages

1958 CE: Conference of Independent States led by Kwame Nkrumah

1958 CE: Mangaliso Robert Sobukwe creates the Pan-Africanist Congress

1958 CE: Nasser seeks a merger between Syria and Egypt to be called the United Arab Republic, which is dissolved in 1961

1959 CE: Excavation of Isaiah Anozie's site in southeastern Nigeria reveals it was a storehouse for ritual objects

1960 CE: Democratic Republic of the Congo establishes independence and names Patrice Lumumba prime minister, one of Africa's most ardent nationalist leaders

1960 CE: D. T. Niane tells story of Sundiata Keita in *Epic of Old Mali*

1960 CE: Côte d'Ivoire gains independence

1960 CE: Dahomey regains its independence

1960 CE: Senghor elected first president of Senegal

1960 CE: Virtually all of Africa is free of European control

1960 CE: Pan-African Congress peaceful protest against the Pass Laws, 69 people killed and 180 injured in the Sharpeville massacre, Sobukwe is arrested

1960 CE: First African National Congress campaign against the Pass Laws

1960 CE: African National Congress banned for trying to carry out the Freedom Charter, Nelson Mandela suggests setting up a military wing in the ANC

1960 CE: Kwame Nkrumah becomes the first president of Ghana

1960 CE: Albert Luthuli, leader of the African National Congress, wins the Nobel Peace Prize

1960 CE: Parliamentary conference agrees Kenyans should have a government based on "one person, one vote" majority rule

1960 CE: Nigeria gains independence

1961 CE: ANC agrees to allow the use of violence and creates the Umkhonto we Sizwe (Spear of the Nation)

1961 CE: Patrice Lumumba is murdered and Africans in the Congo lose their rights

1961–1974 CE: Angola struggles for liberation and freedom from Portugal until Portuguese sue for peace

1961 CE: 40,000 Angolans uprooted during the rebellion in Angola

1961 CE: Tanganyika achieves independence and Julius Nyerere becomes prime minister, Tanganyika later merges with Zanzibar to become Tanzania and Nyerere is elected president

1962 CE: Nelson Mandela arrested

1962 CE: Harold G. Lawrence writes *African Explorers of the New World*

1962 CE: Eritrea decides to end federation and unifies with Ethiopia

1962 CE: (July 1) Algeria gains independence

1962 CE: Frente de Libertação de Moçambique (Frelimo) forms to challenge the Portuguese control of Mozambique and select Mondlane as its first president

1963 CE: Julius Nyerere is a founding member of the Organization of African Unity

1964 CE: Mandela and eight other ANC members sentenced to life imprisonment, Mandela incarcerated at Robben Island Prison until 1982, when he is transferred to Pollsmoor Prison

1964 CE: (October 24) Kenneth David Kaunda becomes president and founding father of the new republic of Zambia

1964 CE: Nkrumah declares Ghana a one-party state and himself president-for-life

1965 CE: Sir Abubakar Tafawa Balewa, of the Nigerian National Alliance, wins election in Nigeria but the United Progressive Grand Alliance believes it was rigged

1966 CE: (February 24) Ghana government overthrown by United States-sponsored military coup d'état

1966 CE: Hausa and Igbo create a conservative political alliance which rules Nigeria

1967 CE: (May 30) Southeastern region of Nigeria secedes as the independent republic of Biafra under the leadership of Colonel Oumegwo Ojukwu

1967 CE: Six-Day War in Egypt, then called the United Arab Republic

1967–1970 CE: Nigerian Civil War

1968 CE: Creolized Mauritius becomes an independent country

1969 CE: Bantu Stephen Biko founds the South African Students' Organization, which provides legal and medical aid for disadvantaged black communities

1969 CE: Thor Heyerdahl sails from Africa to America in a simple boat, the *Ra II*

1969 CE: Sobukwe is released from prison but banished to Kimberley for five years

1969 CE: Bomb is planted under Mondlane's desk at Frelimo and kills him

1969–1970 CE: Nasser leads Egypt in war

1970 CE: Anwar Sadat becomes president of Egypt and builds political relationships that allow Arabs to live in peace with the Jews but is assassinated after signing a peace treaty with Israel

1972 CE: Richard Leakey finds skull 1470 near East Turkana in Kenya

1972 CE: Biko founds the Black People's Convention to aid the social and economic development of black people around Durban and is dismissed from school when elected president of the BPC

1972 CE: Eritrean rebels form Eritrean Liberation Front (ELF) then the Eritrean People's Liberation Front (EPLF), led by Osman Salah Sabbe, former head of the Muslim League

1972 CE: Sudanese peace agreement, the Addis Ababa Accords, between the southern Sudanese insurgents, the Anya Nya, and the Sudan government

1973 CE: Biko is banished to his hometown, King William's Town in the Eastern Cape

1974 CE: Dinqnesh, an *Australopithecus afarensis*, found by Maurice Taieb and Donald Johanson in the Hadar region of Ethiopia

1974 CE: Haile Selassie, the last remaining monarch in Africa, in Ethiopia, loses power

1974 CE: Sobukwe banned for five more years

1974 CE: Sixth (seventh) Pan-African Congress in Dar es Salaam, Tanzania

1974 CE: Portuguese forced to leave Mozambique

1975 CE: Dahomey changes name to Benin

1975 CE: Remains of an Australopithecine group of thirteen adults and children discovered near Hadar in Ethiopia

1975 CE: Portugal negotiates with Frelimo over the independence of Mozambique

1975 CE: Alexander von Wurthenau writes *Unexpected Faces in Ancient America*

1976 CE: Human footprints from 3¼ million years ago discovered near an extinct volcano near Olduvai

1976 CE: Hector Petersen, only 13 years old, leads an uprising by thousands of students to end the discriminatory educational practices in South Africa and is killed

1976 CE: United Eritrean forces push all government forces out of Eritrea but Osman breaks away from EPLF and forms the Eritrean Liberation Front–Popular Liberation Front (ELF–PLF)

1977, 1981, and 1994 CE: Roderick and Susan McIntosh excavate Jenne-Jeno

1977 CE: British government refuses to return the mask of Queen Idia during FESTA (2nd World Black-African Festival of Arts)

1977 CE: (August 21) Biko detained by the Eastern Cape security police and held in Port Elizabeth, and dies from brain damage

1977 CE: Festival of Black and African Countries in Lagos, Nigeria

1978 CE: Ethiopia defeats Eritrea with the help of the Soviet Union and Cuba

1979 CE: Côte d'Ivoire is the world's leading producer of cocoa

1980 CE: Michael Bradley writes *The Black Discovery of America*

1980 CE: Nigerians pay over $1,200,000 for four Benin pieces at an auction

1980 CE: Reformation and United People's Party calls for the resignation of Liberian president William R. Tolbert Jr., installs Master Sergeant Samuel Doe, executes Tolbert, and the economy plunges

1983 CE: Conflict resumes between the Anya Nya and the Sudan government when President Nimeiri imposes Shari'a law, an Islamic code, which causes the death of more than 1.5 million Sudanese by 1997

1983 CE: The Sudan People's Liberation Army (SPLA) forms

1989 CE: Opposition from the National Patriotic Front of Liberia flares

1990s CE: West African peacekeeping troops (ECOMOS) succeed in bringing competing factions in Liberia to negotiations

1990s CE: American revolutionaries cross the Limpopo River in South Africa to fight against apartheid

1990s CE: Fastest-growing religion in the Americas is, reportedly, Ogun, a derivative of Yoruba

1990 CE: (February 18) Nelson Mandela released from prison

1990 CE: F. W. de Klerk releases the ban on the African National Congress and the Pan-Africanist Congress

1991 CE: UN-controlled referendum allows Eritreans to declare for independence and pulls back Ethiopian army

1991 CE: Mandela elected president of the ANC, Oliver Tambo is made national chairman

1992 CE: Frelimo subdues the rebels and gets a peace treaty

1993 CE: (May 24) Eritreans declare independence and name Asmara the capital; Ethiopia is completely cut off from the Red Sea

1993 CE: (June 27) Melchi Ndadaye of the Front for Democracy wins the election in Burundi

1993 CE: (October 21) Ndadaye is murdered

1993 CE: Nelson Mandela wins the Nobel Peace Prize

1994 CE: Nelson Mandela becomes the first democratically elected president of South Africa

1994 CE: Organized slaughter of roughly one million ethnic Tutsis and their Hutu supporters in Rwanda within 100 days and Western countries refuse to intervene; the Tutsi-controlled Rwandan Patriotic Front takes over the country

1996 CE: Vice-governor of South Kivu Province issues an order that the Banyamulenge leave the country or face the death penalty and the anti-Mobutu forces combine to form the Alliance of Democratic Forces for the Liberation of Zaire (AFDL)

1996 CE: US government sends $20 million of military equipment through the "front-line" states of Ethiopia, Eritrea, and Uganda to help the Sudanese opposition overthrow the Khartoum regime

1996–1997 CE: First Congo Civil War leads to the overthrow of President Mobutu Sese Seko and changing the name of the nation back to Democratic Republic of Congo

1997 CE: (May 17) Mobutu leaves and Kabila takes power in Rwanda

1997 CE: (May 25) Armed Forces Revolutionary Council overthrows President Kabbah in Sierra Leone

1997 CE: Charles Taylor, of the National Patriotic Party, wins the election in Liberia but civil war breaks out

1998 CE: (March) President Kabbah is reinstated in a democratic election in Sierra Leone

1998 CE: (August 2) Kabila removes all ethnic Tutsis from government and orders all Rwandan and Ugandan officials out of the Democratic Republic of Congo, resulting in the Second Congo Civil War which last until 2002 and is referred to as Africa's World War

1999 CE: Attempt to overthrow the government in Freetown results in a massive loss of life and destruction of property

1999 CE: (July 7) President Kabbah and the Revolutionary United Front (RUF) leader, Foday Sankoh, sign the Lome Peace Agreement providing amnesty to members of the RUF and turn the RUF into a political party

1999 CE: Sierra Leone declares a state of emergency

2000 CE: (May 8) RUF kills twenty people protesting RUF's violation of Lome

2000 CE: (May 29) Nigerian Civil War receives closure when the *Guardian of Lagos* writes that President Olusegun Obasanjo commuted to retirement the dismissal of all military persons who fought for the breakaway state of Biafra

2001 CE: (July) The NEPAD strategic framework originates with a mandate given to the five initiating heads of state (Algeria, Egypt, Nigeria, Senegal, South Africa) by the Organization of African Unity (OAU) to develop an integrated socioeconomic development framework for Africa and is formally adopted by the OAU at its 37th summit

2001 CE: (September) Namibia files lawsuit to gain $2 billion in reparations from Germany

2002 CE: African Union replaces the Organization of African Unity

2002 CE: *Sahelanthropus tchadensis*, the oldest known fossil of a hominid, dated to 7 million years, found in Chad

2002 CE: Belgium admits to committing the murder of Patrice Lumumba

2002 CE: (July) African Union discussed in South Africa at the seminal assembly of African states

2003 CE: President Gbagbo and rebel leaders sign accords creating a government of national unity in Côte d'Ivoire

2003 and 2004 CE: Series of conferences, initiated by President Adboulaye Wade of Senegal, takes place to discuss the inclusion of Africans in the Americas and Europe in the African Union as a sixth region

2004 CE: (August) German government apologizes for the genocide during the Herero uprising

2004 CE: (October 6–9) First Conference of Intellectuals of Africa and of the Diaspora organized by the African Union in collaboration with the Republic of Senegal held in Dakar, Senegal

2004 CE: Thabo Mbeki wins the South African election, beating out the Inkatha Freedom Party and the Democratic Alliance

2005 CE: African Leaders Summit under the auspices of the African Union in Sirte, Libya

2005 CE: Agreement between the Southern People's Liberation Movement and the Sudanese government ends the conflict between the Anya Nya and the Sudan government

2005 CE: John Garang becomes president of the Republic of Sudan but dies in July 2005 in a helicopter crash

2006 CE: Former Liberian leader Charles Taylor, who had been given sanctuary in Nigeria in 2003, is arrested and handed over to the United Nations War Tribunal in Sierra Leone

2006 CE: Ellen Sirleaf Johnson is elected president of Liberia, becoming the first female leader in modern times to run an African nation

2006 CE: Ethiopian paleontologist Zeresenay Alemseged found the fossil remains of Selam, a hominid of the *A. Afarensis* in the Awash River Valley of Ethiopia, dating to 3.36 million years ago.

# Appendix 2
# Some African ethnic groups

| Ethnic group | Number | Language | Location |
|---|---|---|---|
| Afar | 3,000,000 | Afar | Ethiopia, areas of Eritrea, Djibouti, Somalia, the Horn of Africa, Awash Valley, and the forests located in northern Djibouti |
| Akan | 9,000,000 | Akan cluster of Twi languages, includes Akuapem, Asante, Aowin, Baule, Akyem, Fante | Ghana and southeastern Côte d'Ivoire |
| Anlo-Ewe | 2,000,000 to 3,000,000 | Ewe | Southeastern corner of the Republic of Ghana |
| Anyi | 100,000 | Anyi (Akan cluster of Twi) | Southeastern Côte d'Ivoire |
| Amhara | 7,800,000 | Amharic | Central plateau of Ethiopia |
| Babanki | 40,000 | Babanki (Macro-Bantu) | Northwestern Cameroon |
| Baga | 60,000 | Baga (Mel) | Coast of Guinea |
| Bakongo | 10,220,000 | Kikongo | Atlantic coast of Africa from Pointe-Noire, Congo (Brazzaville) to Luanda, Angola |
| Bali | 25,000 | Bali (Macro-Bantu) | Grasslands of central Cameroon |
| Bamana | 2,000,000 | Bamana (Mande) | Central Mali |
| Bambara | 3,315,000 | Bamana | Mali |
| Bamileke | 8,000,000 | Bamileke (Macro-Bantu) | Western Cameroon |
| Bamun | 100,000 | Bamum (Macro-Bantu) | Southeastern part of Cameroon |
| Bangubangu | 90,000 | KiBanguBangu (Bantu) | Southeastern Congo (Zaire) |
| Bangwa | 20,000 | Banga (Macro-Bantu) | Western Cameroon |
| Baule | 400,000 | Baule (Akan cluster of Twi) | Central Côte d'Ivoire |
| Beembe | 80,000 | KiBeembe (Bantu) | Southern Congo |
| Bemba | 70,000 | KiBemba/English | Northeastern Zambia and Southeastern Congo (Zaire) |

| Berber (Amazigh) | 3,000,000 | Tamazight, Rif, Kabyle, Shawia, Tuareg, Haratin, Shluh, Beraber | Morocco, Algeria, Tunisia, Libya, and Egypt |
|---|---|---|---|
| Bidyogo | 20,000 | Bidyogo | Coast of Guinea-Bissau |
| Bobo | 100,000 to 110,000 | Bobo or Mande | Western Burkina Faso and Mali |
| Bushoongo | 17,000 | Bushong (Bantu) | Southeastern Congo (Zaire) |
| Bwa | 300,000 | Bwamu (Voltaic) | Central Burkina Faso and Mali |
| Chewa | 2,486,070 | Chichewa, Chinyanja or Banti | Zambia, Zimbabwe, Malawi |
| Chokwe | 1,160,000 | Wuchokwe (Bantu) | Southwestern Congo (Zaire), Angola, and Zambia |
| Dan | 350,000 | Dan (Mande) | Liberia and Côte d'Ivoire |
| Diomande | 350,000 | Diomande (Mande) | Côte d'Ivoire |
| Dogon | 100,000 | Dogon (Voltaic) | Southeastern Mali and Burkina Faso |
| Eket | 1,000,000 | Eket (Bantu) | Southeastern Nigeria |
| Fang | 800,000 | Equatorial Bantu | Equatorial rainforests of Gabon and Cameroon |
| Fon | 2,000,000 | Fon | Southern Benin and Togo |
| Frafra | 30,000 | Frafra (Voltaic) | Northeastern Ghana |
| Fulani (Peul) | 5,118,000 | Fular and Fulfulde | Guinea-Conakry, BurkinaFaso, Mali, Nigeria, Niger, Cameroon, and Chad |
| Hausa | 53,000,000 | Hausa | Northern Nigeria and northwestern Niger |
| Hemba | 90,000 | Kihemba (central Bantu) | Southeastern Congo (Zaire) |
| Holoholo | 2,000 | Kiholoholo and KiSwahili | Southeastern Congo (Zaire) |
| Ibibio | 1,000,000 | Ibibio (Kwa) | Southeastern Nigeria |
| Idoma | 250,000 | Idoma (Idoma cluster of Kwa) | Central Nigeria |
| Igbo | 8,000,000 | Igbo (Kwa) | Southeastern Nigeria |
| Ijo | 200,000 | Ijo (Kwa) | Southern Nigeria |
| Kabre | 225,000 | Kabre (Voltaic) | Northeastern Togo |
| Karagwe | 40,000 | Kikaragwe, KiSwahili | Northwestern Tanzania between Rwanda and Lake Victoria |
| Kassena | 30,000 | Kassena | Northern Ghana |
| Katana | 10,000 | Chamba | Eastern Nigeria and western Cameroon |
| Kikuyu (Gikuyu) | 6,500,000 | Bantu | Kenya |
| Kom | 30,000 | Kom (Macro-Bantu) | Northwestern Cameroon |
| Kongo | 2,000,000 | KiKongo (central Bantu) | Southwestern Congo, Angola, and Congo |
| Kota | 75,000 | Kota (equatorial Bantu) | Eastern Gabon |

| | | | |
|---|---|---|---|
| Kuba | 250,000 | BaKuba (central Bantu) | Southeastern Congo |
| Kusu | 60,000 | KiKusu (central Bantu) | Southeastern Congo |
| Kwahu | 65,000 | Kwahu (Akan cluster of Twi) | Southern Ghana |
| Kwere | 50,000 | Kikwere (Eastern Bantu) | East central Tanzania near the coast |
| Laka | 100,000 | Laka/Mboum (Niger–Congo) | Southwestern Chad |
| Lega | 250,000 | KiLega (central Bantu) | Southeastern Congo |
| Lobi | 160,000 | Lobi (Voltaic) | Burkina Faso, Côte d'Ivoire, Ghana |
| Luba | 1,000,000 | Ciluba (Central Bantu) | Southeastern Congo |
| Luchazi | 15,000 | Luchazi (Bantu) | Eastern Angola and western Zambia |
| Luluwa | 300,000 | KiNalulua (Bantu) | Southeastern Congo |
| Lunda | 175,000 | Cilunda and Kiluba (Bantu) | Congo (Zaire), western Zambia, and northern Angola |
| Luvale | 20,000 | Luvale (Bantu) | Eastern Angola and western Zambia |
| Lwalwa | 20,000 | BuLwalwa (Bantu) | Southeastern Congo |
| Maasai | 350,000 | Ol Maa (Nilotic) | North central Tanzania and southern Kenya |
| Makonde | 1,374,000 | Makonde (Bantu) | Tanzania and Mozambique |
| Mambila | 25,000 | Mambila (Macro-Bantu) | Northwestern Cameroon and eastern Nigeria |
| Mandinka | 1,300,000 | Mandinka | West Africa: Senegal, Gambia, Guinea-Bissau, Burkina Faso, Mali, and Côte d'Ivoire |
| Mangbetu | 40,000 | Mangbetuti (central Sudanic) | Northern Congo |
| Manja | 24,000 | Manja (equatorial Bantu) | Northern Congo |
| Mbole | 150,000 | Mbole (central Bantu) | Southwestern Congo |
| Mende | 700,000 | Mende (Mande) | Southern Sierra Leone |
| Mossi | 3,500,000 | Moré (Voltaic) | Central Burkina Faso |
| Mumuye | 70,000 | Mumuya (Jukun) | Eastern Nigeria |
| Ngbaka | 400,000 | Gbaya (Ubangi) | Northern Congo |
| Nuna Oromo | 100,000 25,000,000 | Nuni Oromiffa | Southern Burkina Faso Ethiopia |
| Pende | 250,000 | KiPende (central Bantu) | Southwestern Congo |
| Pokot | 220,000 | Pokot (Nilo-Hamitic) | West central, northern, and southwestern Kenya |
| Punu | 80,000 | Punu (Bantu) | Southern Gabon and Congo |
| Samburu | 142,000 | Samburu, a Maa language | Foothills of Mount Kenya merging into the northern desert and slightly south of Lake Turkana in the Rift Valley province of Kenya |

| | | | |
|---|---|---|---|
| San | 100,000 | Khoisan languages | Botswana and northern Southern Africa |
| Senufo | 600,000 | Senufo (Voltaic) | Côte d'Ivoire and Mali |
| Shambaa | 200,000 | Kishambaa (Central Bantu) | Northeast Tanzania in the Usambara Mountains |
| Shona | 9,000,000 | Shona (Bantu) | Zimbabwe and southern Mozambique |
| Small People (Bambuti, Batwa, Bayaka, Bagyeli) | 140,000 | Languages differ, usually the language of their neighbors | Central and western Africa, in the Democratic Republic of Congo (DRC), Congo (Brazzaville), Cameroon, Gabon, Central African Republic, Rwanda, Burundi, and Uganda |
| Songo | 15,000 | Wasongo (Central Bantu) | Northern Angola |
| Songye | 150,000 | KiSongye (Bantu) | Southeastern Congo |
| Suku | 80,000 | Kiyaka (northwestern Bantu) | Southwestern Congo |
| Swahili | 200,000 to 400,000 | KiSwahili (Bantu) | Coastal Kenya and Tanzania |
| Tabwa | 200,000 | Kitabwa (Bantu) | Southeastern Congo |
| Tuareg (Tamaschek) | 1,500,000 | Tamaschek, Tamajeq, Tamahaq | Niger, Nigeria, Burkina Faso, Senegal, and Mali |
| Urhobo | 450,000 | Edo (Kwa) | Southern Nigeria |
| We | 100,000 | We (Kwa) | Côte d'Ivoire |
| Winiama | 25,000 | Winien | Central Burkina Faso |
| Wolof | 4,500,000 | Wolof | Senegal |
| Wum | 12,000 | Wum (Macro-Bantu) | Northwestern Cameroon |
| Yaka | 300,000 | Kiyaka (Northwestern Bantu) | Southwestern Congo and Angola |
| Yombe | 350,000 | Kiyombe and Kikongo | Northwest Congo |
| Yoruba | 25,000,000 | Yoruba (Kwa) | Nigeria and Benin |
| Zaramo | 200,000 | Kizaramo and KiSwahili | East central Tanzania |
| Zulu | 9,000,000 | Kwazulu (Nguni) | South Africa |

# Appendix 3
## Major linguistic complexes

| Language family | Subgroup(s) | Geographic location |
|---|---|---|
| Afro-Asiatic (this category has been challenged by African linguists, notably Obenga and Garba) | Amharic, Arabic, Tingrinya Amazigh Chadic (Hausa and Fulani) Oromo | Sudan, Ethiopia, Somalia, Egypt, Libya, Morocco, Algeria, Tunisia, Mauritania, Senegal, Mali |
| Niger-Congo (Over 900 languages in this group are spoken by 75 percent of Africans) | Kordofanian (often considered its own language group) Benue-Congo (Bantu, which includes Zulu, Shona, Xhosa, Makua, Nyanja, and Swahili) Mande Voltaic Kwa Adamawa–Eastern | Senegal to Cape of Good Hope eastern, central, and southern Africa Kenya, Tanzania, Uganda, Rwanda, Zimbabwe, Burundi, Democratic Republic of the Congo (eastern and northern), Malawi (northern), Mozambique (northern), Zambia (northern), and Somali Republic |
| Nilo-Saharan | Songhai Koman Chari-Nile Saharan | Sahel zone, The Nile to the Niger East Africa |
| Khoisan | | Namibia, South Africa, Botswana Northern Tanzania (by the San, Khoikhoi, Hadza, and Sandawe) |
| Malagasy (a Malayo-Polynesian language) | | Madagascar |

# Bibliography

## General references

The comprehensive treatments of Africa are:

*The Cambridge History of Africa*, 8 vols. (1976–86) Cambridge: Cambridge University Press.

UNESCO General History of Africa, 8 vols.

More specific works and references used in this book include the following:

Achebe, Chinua (1986). *Things Fall Apart*. London: Heinemann.

Agbodeka, F. (1969). *The Rise of the Nation States*. London: Nelson.

Ajayi, J. F. A. and M. Crowder (eds.) (1974). *History of West Africa*. vol. 2. London: Longman.

Ajayi, J. F. A. and Espie, I. (1966). *A Thousand Years of West African History*. London: Nelson.

Amin, Samir (1973). *Neo-colonialism in West Africa*. London: Zed Books.

Anderson, David (2005). *Histories of the Hanged: The Dirty War in Kenya and the End of Empire*. New York: Norton.

Anti, A. A. (1973). *Osei Tutu and Okomfo Anokye*. Accra: Ghana Publishing Corporation.

Appiah, Anthony Kwame (1993). *In My Father's House*. New York: Oxford University Press.

Asante, M. K. (1990). *Kemet, Afrocentricity, and Knowledge*. Trenton, NJ: Africa World Press.

Asante, M. K. (1993). *Classical Africa*. Saddle Brook, NJ: Peoples Publishing Group.

Asante, M. K. and Abu Abarry (1996). *African Intellectual Heritage*. Philadelphia: Temple University Press.

Assensoh, A. B. (1998). *African Political Leadership: Jomo Kenyatta, Kwame Nkrumah, and Julius Nyerere*. Malabar, FL: Krieger Publishing.

Assensoh, A. B. and Yvette M. Alex-Assensoh (2001). *African Military History and Politics, 1900–Present*. New York: Palgrave.

Awolowo, Obafemi (1981). *Selected Speeches of Chief Obafemi Awolowo*. Lagos, Fagbamigbe Publishers.

Azikiwe, Nnamdi (1934). *Liberia in World Politics*. London: Stockwell.

Azikiwe, Nnamdi (1970). *My Odyssey*. New York: Praeger.

Baines, John and Jaromir Málek (2000). *Cultural Atlas of Ancient Egypt*. York: Facts on File.

Barnes, Sandra T. (ed.) (1997). *Africa's Ogun: Old World and New*. Philadelphia: Oxford University Press.

Batutu, Ibn (1957). *Travels in Asia and Africa, 1325–54*, trans. H. A. R. Gibb. New York: Routledge.

Beach, D. N. (1980). *The Shona and Zimbabwe, 900–1850*.

Bekerie, Ayele (1997). *Ethiopic, an African Writing System: Its History and Principles*. Lawrenceville, NJ: The Red Sea Press.

Bernal, Martin (1987). *Black Athena*. New Brunswick: Rutgers University Press.

Bernal, Martin (1987). *Black Athena: The Afro Asiatic Roots of Classical Civilization, Vol. 1: The Fabrication of Ancient Greece, 1875–1985*. New Brunswick: Rutgers University Press.

Bernal, Martin (1991). *Black Athena: The Afro Asiatic Roots of Classical Civilization, Vol. 2: The Archaeological and Documentary Evidence*. New Brunswick: Rutgers University Press.

Birmingham, David (1999). *Portugal and Africa*. Athens, OH: University of Ohio Press.

378    *Bibliography*

Bissell, Richard E. and Michael Radu (1984). *Africa in the Post-decolonization Era.* New Brunswick: Transaction Books.

Blyden, E. W. (1967). *Christianity, Islam and the Negro Race.* Edinburgh: Edinburgh University Press.

Boahen, A. Adu (1964). *Britain, the Sahara, and Western Sudan.* Oxford: Clarendon Press.

Boahen, A. Adu (1966). *Topics in West African History.* London: Longman.

Boahen, A. Adu (1987). *African Perspectives on Colonialism.* Baltimore: Johns Hopkins University Press.

Botwe-Asamoah, Kwame (2005). *Kwame Nkrumah's Politico-cultural Thought and Policies: An African-Centered Paradigm for the Second Phase of the African Revolution.* New York: Routledge.

Bradley, Michael (1992). *Dawn Voyage: The Black African Discovery of America.* New York: A and B Distributors.

Butzer, K. W. (1976). *Early Hydraulic Civilization in Egypt.* Chicago: University of Chicago Press.

Casely Hayford, J. E. (1970). *Gold Coast Native Institutions.* London: Frank Cass.

Cavalli-Sforza, L. L. (1991). "Genes, peoples and languages," *Scientific American,* 265, 5 (November).

Chinweizu (1975). *The West and the Rest of Us.* New York: Vintage.

Chuku, Gloria (2005). *Igbo Women and Economic Transformation in Southeastern Nigeria, 1900–1960.* New York: Routledge.

Connah, Graham (2001). *African Civilizations: An Archaeological Perspective.* Cambridge: Cambridge University Press.

Crowder, M. (1977). *West Africa: An Introduction to Its History.* London: Longman.

Crowder, M. (ed.) (1984). *Cambridge History of Africa.* vol. 8. *1940–1975.* Cambridge: Cambridge University Press.

Dapper, O. (1668). *Description of Africa.* Amsterdam.

Davidson, Basil (1966). *The African Past.* New York: Penguin.

Davidson, Basil (1970). *Black Mother.* London: Longman.

Davidson, Basil (1971). *Old Africa Rediscovered.* London: Longman.

Davidson, Basil (1975). *Africa in History.* London: Paladin.

Davidson, Basil (1977). *The Growth of African Civilization: East and Central Africa to the Nineteenth Century.* London: Longman.

Davidson, Basil (1977). *The History of Africa, 1000–1800.* London: Longman.

Dei, George Sefa (2001). *Rethinking Schooling and Education in African Contexts.* Trenton, NJ: Africa World Press.

Diawara, Gaoussou (1992). *Abubakari II.* Bamako: Editions Lansman.

Diop, Cheikh Anta (1991). *Civilization or Barbarism: An Authentic Anthropology.* New York: Lawrence Hill.

Diop, Cheikh Anta (1993). *The African Origins of Civilization: Myth or Reality.* New York: Lawrence Hill, first edition 1974.

Dove, Nah (1998). *Afrikan Mothers: Bearers of Culture, Makers of Social Change.* Albany, NY: SUNY Press.

Dreyer, Günter (1999). *Das Prädynastische Königsgrab U-j und seine frü Schriftszeugnisse.* Mainz am Rhein: Verlag Philipp von Zabern.

Drioton, Etienne and Jacques Vandier (1962). *Les peuples de l'orient méditerranéen. Tome 2: L'Egypte.* Fourth edition, Paris: Editions PUF.

DuBois, W. E. B. (1990). *The World and Africa: An Inquiry into the Part which Africa Has Played in World History.* New York: International Publishers.

Dumont, René (1966). *False Start in Africa.* London: André Deutsch.

Dunn, Ross (2005). *The Adventures of Ibn Battuta: A Muslim Traveler of the 14th Century.* Berkeley, CA: University of California Press.

Edgerton, Robert (1995). *The Fall of the Asante Empire: The Hundred-Year War for Africa's Gold Coast.* New York: Free Press.

Egharevba, J. (1952). *A Short History of Benin.* Third edition, Ibadan. Aguebor Publishers.

Ehret, Christopher (2002). *The Civilizations of Africa: A History to 1800.* Charlottesville, VA: University Press of Virginia.

Ehret, Christopher and Mary Posnansky (eds.) (1982). *The Archaeological and Linguistic Reconstruction of African History*. Los Angeles and Berkeley, CA: University of California Press.

Elkins, Caroline (2005). *Imperial Reckoning: The Untold Story of Britain's Gulang in Kenya*. New York: Henry Holt.

Fage, J. D. (1978). *History of Africa*. New York: Knopf.

Falola, Toyin (ed.) (2002). *Tradition and Change in Africa: The Essays of J. F. Ade Ajayi*. Trenton, NJ: Africa World Press.

Falola, Toyin (2001). *Nationalism and African Intellectuals*. Rochester: University of Rochester Press.

Fanon, Franz (1983). *The Wretched of the Earth*. London: Penguin.

Finch, Charles (1991). *Echoes of the Old Dark Land*. Atlanta, CA: Khenti Inc.

Fyfe, C. (1962). *A Short History of Sierra Leone*. London: Longman.

Fyle, C. Magbaily (2001). *Introduction to the History of African Civilization*. Lanham, MD: University Press of America.

Fynn, John Kofi (1971). *Asante and Its Neighbours, 1700–1807*. London: Longman and Evanston, IL: Northwestern University Press.

Gadzekpo, Seth Kordzo (1999). *History of African Civilisations*. Accra: Royal Crown Press.

Gilbert, Erik and Jonathan Reynolds (2004). *Africa in World History: From Prehistory to the Present*. Upper Saddle River, NJ: Pearson.

Grimal, Nicolas Shaw (1992). *The History of Egypt*. Boston, MA: Blackwell.

Harbeson, J. W. and I. Kimambo (eds.) (1999). *East African Expressions of Christianity*. Athens, OH: Ohio University Press.

Hassan, F. A. (1993). "Town and village in ancient Egypt," in T. Shaw *et al.* (eds.) *The Archaeology of Africa*. London:

Hochschild, Adam (1998). *King Leopold's Ghost*. New York: Houghton Mifflin.

Jackson, John (2001). *Introduction to African Civilizations*. New York: Citadel Press.

Jackson, John G. (1990). *Ages of Gold and Silver and Other Short Sketches of Human History*. Foreword by Madalyn O'Hair. Austin, TX: American Atheist Press.

James, George G. M. (1954). *Stolen Legacy: The Greeks Were Not the Authors of Greek Philosophy, but the People of North Africa Commonly Called the Egyptians*. New York: Philosophical Library.

Karade, Baba Ifa (1999). *Imoye: A Definition of the Ifa Tradition*. Brooklyn, NY: Athelia Henrietta Press.

Karenga, Maulana (1999). *Odu Ifa: Ethical Teachings*. Los Angeles: University of Sankore Press.

Karenga, Maulana (2003). *Maat: The Moral Ideal in Ancient Egypt*. New York: Routledge.

Kenyatta, Jomo (1962). *Facing Mount Kenya*. New York: Vintage.

Khaldun, Ibn (1967). *The Muqaddimah: An Introduction to History*, trans. Franz Rosenthal, abridged and ed. N. J. Dawood, Bollingen Series. Princeton, NJ: Princeton University Press.

Ki-Zerbo, J. (1972). *Histoire de l'Afrique noire d'hier à demain*. Paris: Hatier.

Kropacek, L. (1997). "Nubia from the late twelfth century to the Funj conquest in the early sixteenth century," in J. Ki-Zerbo and D. T. Niane (eds.), *General History of Africa*. vol. 4. *Africa from the Twelfth to the Sixteenth Century*. New York: James Currey, UNESCO, University of California Press.

Krzyzaniak, L. (1991). "Early farming in the middle Nile basin: recent discoveries at Kadero," *Antiquity*, 65: 518.

Lam, Aboubacry Moussa (1992). *De l'Origine égyptienne des Peuls*. Paris and Dakar: Présence Africaine.

Lam, Aboubacry Moussa (2003–4). "L'origine des Peuls: les principales thèses confrontées aux traditions africaines et à l'égyptologie." *Ankh*, 12–13: 27–39.

Levtzion, N. (1973). *Ancient Ghana and Mali*. New York: Methuen.

Lichtheim, M. (1980). *Ancient Egyptian Literature*. Berkeley, CA: University of California Press.

Louw, Dirk J. (1998). "Ubuntu: an African assessment of the religious other". *Twentieth World Congress of Philosophy*.

Lucas, J. Olumide (2001). *The Religion of the Yorubas*. Lagos and Brooklyn, NY: Athelia Henrietta Press, first edition 1948.

Mazrui, Ali A. (ed.) (1982). *Africa since 1935: UNESCO General History of Africa*. Berkeley, CA: University of California Press.

Mafundikwa, Saki (2000). *African Alphabets*. New York: Mark Batty Publishers.

Mbiti, John (1991). *Introduction to African Philosophy and Religion*. London: Heinemann.

M'Bokolo, E. (1980). *La Continent convoité: l'Afrique au XXe siècle*. Paris and Montreal: Editions Etudes Vivantes, Coll. Axes Sciences Humaines.

McIntosh, Susan Keech (1995). *Excavations at Jenne-Jeno, Hambarketolo, and Kaniana: The 1981 Season*. Berkeley, CA: University of California Publications in Anthropology.

Monges, Miriam Maat Ka Re (1997). *Kush, the Jewel of Nubia: Reconnecting the Root System of African Civilization*. Trenton, NJ: Africa World Press.

Morris, W. O'Connor (1897). *Hannibal*. London: Putman.

Mote, Frederick (ed.) (1995). *The Cambridge History of China*, vol. 7. *1368–1644*. Cambridge: Cambridge University Press.

Niane, Djibril T. (1966). *Sundiata: An Epic of Old Mali*. London: Longman.

Niane, Djibril T. (1997). "Introduction," in J. Ki-Zerbo and D. T. Niane (eds.), *UNESCO General History of Africa*. vol. 4. *Africa from the Twelfth to the Sixteenth Century*. New York: James Currey, UNESCO, University of California Press.

Nkrumah, Kwame (1970). *Consciencism*. New York: Monthly Review.

Nkrumah, Kwame (1998). *Africa Must Unite*. New edition, London: Panaf.

Nyerere, Julius (1977). *Ujamaa: Essays on Socialism*. London: Oxford University Press.

Obenga, Theophile (1980). *Pour une nouvelle histoire*. Paris: Présence Africaine.

Obichere, Boniface I. (1971). *West African States and European Expansion: The Dahomey Niger Hinterland, 1898*. New Haven, CT: Yale University Press.

O'Connor, D. (1972). "A Regional Population in Egypt to *circa* 600 B.C.," in B. Spooner (ed.), *Population Growth*. Cambridge, MA: Harvard University Press.

Ogot, B. A. (1976). *History and Social Change in East Africa*. Nairobi: East Africa Publishing House.

Poe, Daryl Zizwe (2003). *Kwame Nkrumah's Contribution to Pan-Africanism*. New York: Routledge.

Ranger, Terry O. (1968). *Aspects of Central African History*. London: Heinemann.

Ranger, Terry O. (ed.) (1968). *Emerging Themes in African History*. Nairobi: East African Publishing House.

Rodney, Walter (1974). *How Europe Underdeveloped Africa*. Washington, DC: Howard University Press.

Sai, Akiga (1900). "The history of the Tiv," manuscript based on Lugard, *Report on the Munshi Campaign, 4 July, 1900*, C.O. 446/10/25250). Ibadan: MSS, Africana Collection, University of Ibadan Library.

Schoenbrun, D. L. (1991). "We are what we eat: ancient agriculture between the Great Lakes," *Journal of African History*, 34: 1–31.

Sertima, Ivan van (1976). *The African Presence in Ancient America: They Came before Columbus*. New York: Random House.

Shaw, T. (1977). "Hunters, gatherers, and first farmers in West Africa," in *Hunters, Gatherers and First Farmers beyond Europe*, (ed.), J. V. S. Megaw Leicester: Leicester University Press.

Shillington, Kevin (1989). *History of Africa*. New York: St. Martin's Press.

Vansina, Jan (1990). *Paths in the Rain Forest: Towards a History of Political Tradition in Equatorial Africa*. Madison, WI: University of Winconsin Press.

Vogel, Joseph O. (ed.) (1997). *Encyclopedia of Precolonial Africa: Archaeology, History, Languages*. Walnut Creek, CA: AltaMira Press.

Walker, E. A. (1957). *A History of Southern Africa*. London: Longman.

Wiener, Leo (1992). *Africa and the Discovery of America*. New York: A and B Distribution.

Wilks, Ivor G. (1975). *Asante in the Nineteenth Century*. Cambridge: Cambridge University Press.

Willis, A. J. (1964). *An Introduction to the History of Central Africa*. London: Oxford University Press.

# Index

# United Nations in the Contemporary World

*David J. Whittaker*

Fifty years after the creation of the United Nations, there exists a vigorous debate as to its limitations and possibilities. In *United Nations in the Contemporary World*, David J. Whittaker examines how the UN works and assesses its position as a world organisation.

The author explores the nature of the UN as a regime in contemporary international relations. He considers the changing terms of reference of the UN and includes discussion of:

- UN organisational procedures and principles
- recent historical case studies, including studies on peacekeeping
- the role of the UN in global urbanisation, arms control and in supplying aid for refugees
- past and future internal reform, goals, achievements.

With an annotated bibliography and a helpful glossary *United Nations in the Contemporary World* provides an interdisciplinary history of the UN and debates the key issues for its future.

ISBN10: 0-415-15317-4 (pbk)
ISBN13: 978-0-415-15317-1 (pbk)

Related titles from Routledge

# The Routledge Companion to Decolonization

*Deitmar Rothermund*

This is an essential companion to the process of decolonization – perhaps one of the most important historical processes of the twentieth century.

Examining decolonization in Africa, Asia, the Caribbean and the Pacific, the Companion includes:

- thematic chapters
- a detailed chronology and thorough glossary
- biographies of key figures
- maps.

Providing comprehensive coverage of a broad and complex subject area, the guide explores:

- the global context for decolonization
- nationalism and the rise of resistance movements
- resistance by white settlers and moves towards independence
- Hong Kong and Macau, and decolonization in the late twentieth century
- debates surrounding neo-colonialism, and the rise of 'development' projects and aid
- the legacy of colonialism in law, education, administration and the military.

With suggestions for further reading, and a guide to sources, this is an invaluable resource for students and scholars of the colonial and post-colonial eras, and is an indispensable guide to the reshaping of the world in the twentieth century.

ISBN10: 0-415-35632-6 (hbk)
ISBN10: 0-415-35633-4 (pbk)

ISBN13: 978-0-415-35632-9 (hbk)
ISBN13: 978-0-415-35633-6 (pbk)

Available at all good bookshops
For ordering and further information please visit:
www.routledge.com

Related titles from Routledge

# The Decolonization Reader

*Edited by James Le Sueur*

The process of decolonization transformed colonial and European metropolitan societies culturally, politically and economically. Its legacy continues to affect postcolonial politics as well as cultural and intellectual life in Europe and its former colonies and overseas territories.

Grouped around the most salient themes, this compilation includes discussions of metropolitan politics, gender, sexuality, race, culture, nationalism and economy, and thereby offers a comparative and interdisciplinary assessment of decolonization.

*The Decolonization Reader* will provide scholars and students with a thorough understanding of the impact of decolonization on world history and cross-cultural encounters worldwide.

ISBN10: 0-415-23116-7 (hbk)
ISBN10: 0-415-23117-5 (pbk)

ISBN13: 978-0-415-23116-9 (hbk)
ISBN13: 978-0-415-23117-6 (pbk)

Available at all good bookshops
For ordering and further information please visit:
www.routledge.com